GODPARENTS AND KINSHIP IN
EARLY MEDIEVAL EUROPE

JOSEPH H. LYNCH

GODPARENTS AND KINSHIP IN
EARLY MEDIEVAL EUROPE

PRINCETON, NEW JERSEY

PRINCETON UNIVERSITY PRESS

1986

Copyright © 1986 by Princeton University Press
Published by Princeton University Press, 41 William Street
Princeton, New Jersey 08540
In the United Kingdom
Princeton University Press, Guildford, Surrey

All Rights Reserved

Library of Congress Cataloging in Publication Data will be
found on the last page of this book

ISBN 0-691-05466-5

This book has been composed in Linotron Janson

Clothbound editions of Princeton University Press books
are printed on acid-free paper, and binding materials
are chosen for strength and durability

Printed in the United States of America
by Princeton University Press
Princeton, New Jersey

OVERLEAF: *The creation of spiritual kinship: The sponsor, on the right, takes an infant from the baptismal font. This miniature is an illumination of* Causa 30 *from a thirteenth-century manuscript of* Gratian's Decretals, *MS. 10.135, f. 276, reproduced by permission of the Walters Art Gallery, Baltimore.*

For
Charles and Anna,
Myron and Louise, and Beatrice,
with gratitude and love

CONTENTS

PART FOUR

THE CAROLINGIAN SYNTHESIS

ACKNOWLEDGMENTS

The author of a book ten years in the making contracts many debts of gratitude. I apologize in advance for any that I fail to repay. My research was begun during the tenure of a fellowship from the American Council of Learned Societies in 1975 and 1976. In addition, I am grateful to my university for its direct and indirect support over so many years. Both the Graduate School and the College of Humanities at the Ohio State University have granted me funds to conduct research abroad and time to write. Diether Haenicke, formerly dean of the College of Humanities and now provost of the university, gave me encouragement and practical help when I needed it very much, and Dean G. Micheal Riley of the College of Humanities has continued to encourage and support my work. Gary Reichard and Marvin Zahniser, chairmen of the Department of History, also understood the needs of a long-term project.

Libraries are crucial to the work of historians, and so it is only natural to thank the Ohio State University Library for its excellent collection and generous policy of acquisitions. I wish particularly to thank Mrs. Clara Goldslager, who cheerfully sought out obscure books from all over the world. I also acknowledge the generosity of the Bodleian Library, the Cambridge University Library, and the British Library for making their resources available to me.

The Bible translation in this book is that of *The Jerusalem Bible*, copyrighted in 1966, 1967 and 1968 by Darton, Longman and Todd Ltd. and Doubleday and Company. I wish to thank the following for permission to quote from their books:

Thomas L. Campbell, *Dionysius the Pseudo-Areopagite: The Ecclesiastical Hierarchy* (Lanham, Md., 1981).

Harvard University Press and the Loeb Classical Library, *The Anecdota or Secret History* by Procopius, edited and translated by H. B. Dewing (Cambridge, Mass., 1935).

The Catholic University of America Press, *Saint Caesarius of Arles: Sermons*, translated by Sister Mary M. Mueller, in the Fathers of the Church series, volumes 31, 47, and 66 (Washington, D.C., 1956–1973).

The Society for Promoting Christian Knowledge, *Egeria's Travels*, edited and translated by John Wilkinson (London, 1971).

Oxford University Press, *The History of the Franks* by Gregory of
Tours, translated by O. M. Dalton, 2 vols. (Oxford, 1927).

Unless otherwise indicated, all translations are by me.

I am also grateful to those friends and colleagues who read versions
of my work and gave me the benefit of their advice, especially Giles
Constable, John Contreni, Bernard Bachrach, Richard Sullivan, and
Thomas Noble. Anthony Melnikas of the Department of the History
of Art at the Ohio State University provided me with help and advice
on the iconography of sponsorship.

For their patient and efficient work in the preparation of the manuscript, I wish to thank Mrs. Jo White and Mrs. Nanci Alexander.
For their readiness to advise a novice in the arcane art of word proc-
essing, I thank the office staff of the Department of History. I am also
grateful to Jan S. Adams, director of the University Center for International Studies, for permitting me to use the center's facilities to print
my manuscript, and Christian Zacher, director of the Center for Medieval and Renaissance Studies, for aiding in the photocopying of the
manuscript. In addition, I am indebted to Martha Coolidge for her
help during the years that I directed the Center for Medieval and
Renaissance Studies. I thank Alida Becker as well for her thorough
and thoughtful copyediting of the text.

Finally, I would like to thank my own kin group for supporting me
in this project for so long: my wife, Ann, my children, Elizabeth,
Michael, and Matthew; my late mother; my father; my mother-in-law;
and my father-in-law.

Columbus, Ohio
April 1985

ABBREVIATIONS

AASS	Acta sanctorum, 60 vols., 3rd ed. (Paris and Rome, 1863–1870)
AB	*Analecta bollandiana*
ABR	*The American Benedictine Review*
AC	*Antike und Christentum*
ACW	Ancient Christian Writers
Admon	*Admonitio synodalis*, ed. R. Amiet, in "Une 'Admonitio Synodalis' de l'époque carolingienne. Etude critique et édition," *Mediaeval Studies* 26 (1964):12–82
AESC	*Annales. Economies, sociétés, civilisations*
AHR	*American Historical Review*
AKKR	*Archiv für katholisches Kirchenrecht*
ALMA	*Archivum latinitatis medii aevi (Bulletin Du Cange)*
Atto	Atto of Vercelli, *Capitulare, Patrologia latina*, vol. 134, cols. 27–52
BAC	Biblioteca de autores cristianos
BEC	*Bibliothèque de l'Ecole des Chartes*
BHF	Bonner historische Forschungen
BJRL	*Bulletin of the John Rylands Library*
BLE	*Bulletin de littérature ecclésiastique*
BZ	*Byzantinische Zeitschrift*
Cap ecc	*Capitula ecclesiastica*, in MGH Capitularia 1:178–179
Cap ex	*Capitula de examinandis ecclesiasticis*, in MGH Capitularia 1:109–111
Cap Fris	*Capitula episcopi cuiusdam Frisingensia*, in Emil Seckel, "Studien zur Benedictus Levita II," *NA* 29 (1904):287–294
Cap oc	*Capitula XV episcopi cuiusdam Franciae occidentalis*, in P. W. Finsterwalder, "Zwei Bischofskapitularien der Karolingerzeit. Ein Beitrag zur Kenntnis der bischöflichen Gesetzgebung des neunten Jahrhunderts," *ZSSRG*, Kanonistische Abteilung, 14 (1925):350–367
Cap ott	*Capitula* in Ms. Vaticanus Ottobonianus latinus 261, in A. Werminghoff, "Reise nach Italien im Jahre 1901," *NA* 27 (1902):580–587
Cap prim	*Capitula* that begin "Primitus" in P. Brommer, ed., "Die bischöfliche Gesetzgebung Theodulfs von Orléans," *ZSSRG*, Kanonistische Abteilung, 60 (1974):108–112

Cap sac   *Capitula a sacerdotibus proposita*, in MGH Capitularia
                 1:105–107
CCM   Corpus consuetudinum monasticarum
CCSL   Corpus christianorum, series latina
CF   Les classiques français du moyen âge
CHF   Classiques de l'histoire de France au moyen âge
CIC   *Corpus iuris civilis*
CSEL   Corpus scriptorum ecclesiasticorum latinorum
CT   Collection de textes pour servir à l'étude et à l'en-
                 seignement de l'histoire
CUA, SCA   Catholic University of America, Studies in Christian
                 Antiquity
CUA, SMH   Catholic University of America, Studies in Medieval
                 History
CUA, SST   Catholic University of America, Studies in Sacred
                 Theology
DACL   *Dictionnaire d'archéologie chrétienne et de liturgie*
DAEM   *Deutsches Archiv für Erforschung des Mittelalters*
DDC   *Dictionnaire de droit canonique*
DSAM   *Dictionnaire de spiritualité, d'ascétique et de mystique*
FC   Fathers of the Church
FS   *Frühmittelalterliche Studien*
Ghaer I   "Le premier statut diocésain de Gerbald, évêque de
                 Liége," ed. Carlo de Clercq, *La législation* (1936)
                 1:352–356
Ghaer II   "Le second statut diocésain de Gerbald, évêque de
                 Liége," ed. Carlo de Clercq, *La législation* (1936)
                 1:357–362
Haito   Haito of Basel, *Capitula ecclesiastica*, in MGH Capi-
                 tularia 1:362–366
Herard   Herard of Tours, *Capitula*, *Patrologia latina*, vol. 121,
                 cols. 763–774
Hildegar   Hildegar of Meaux, *Capitula*, ed. J. Mabillon, *Vetera
                 Analecta* 2nd ed. (Paris, 1723), p. 412
Hinc I   Hincmar of Rheims, *Capitula presbyteris data anno
                 852*, *Patrologia latina*, vol. 125, cols. 773–778
HJ   *Historisches Jahrbuch*
HRG   *Handwörterbuch zur deutschen Rechtsgeschichte*
HS   Historische Studien
Isaac   Isaac of Langres, *Canones*, *Patrologia latina*, vol. 124,
                 cols. 1075–1110
JRS   *Journal of Roman Studies*
JTS   *Journal of Theological Studies*
JW   *Regesta pontificum romanorum*, ed. P. Jaffé; 2nd ed.,

	G. Wattenbach, S. Löwenfeld, F. Kaltenbrunner, and P. Ewald (Leipzig, 1885–1888), 2 vols.
LCC	Library of the Christian Classics
LCP	Latinitas christianorum primaeva
Mansi	*Sacrorum conciliorum nova et amplissima collectio*, ed. J. D. Mansi, 31 vols. (Florence and Venice, 1759–1798)
MGH AA	Monumenta Germaniae historica, *Auctores Antiquissimi*, 15 vols. (Berlin, 1877–1919)
MGH Capitularia	Monumenta Germaniae historica, *Leges*, section 2: *Capitularia regum Francorum*, 2 vols., ed. A. Boretius and V. Krause (Hanover, 1883–1897)
MGH Concilia	Monumenta Germaniae historica, *Leges*, section 3: *Concilia*, 2 vols., ed. F. Maassen and A. Werminghoff (Hanover, 1893–1908)
MGH Epis	Monumenta Germaniae historica, *Epistolae*, 8 vols., ed. P. Ewald and L. Hartmann (Berlin, 1887–1939)
MGH SS	Monumenta Germaniae historica, *Scriptores*, 32 vols. (Hanover, 1826–1934)
MGH SSRG	Monumenta Germaniae historica, *Scriptores rerum Germanicarum* in usum scholarum, 61 vols. (1839–1935)
MGH SSRM	Monumenta Germaniae historica, *Scriptores rerum Merovingicarum*, 7 vols. (Hanover, 1884–1920)
MIOG	*Mitteilungen des Instituts für österreichische Geschichtsforschung*
MS	*Mediaeval Studies*
MSR	*Mélanges de science religieuse*
NA	*Neues Archiv der Gesellschaft für ältere deutsche Geschichtskunde*
PG	*Patrologia graeca*, 167 vols., ed. Jacques Paul Migne (Paris, 1857–1876)
PL	*Patrologia latina*, 221 vols., ed. Jacques Paul Migne (Paris, 1841–1864)
PO	*Patrologia Orientalis*, 42 vols. to date, ed. René Graffin and François Nau (Paris, 1907ff.)
Ps-Bon	Pseudo-Boniface, *Statuta, Patrologia latina*, vol. 89, cols. 821–824
Ps-Son	Pseudo-Sonnatius, *Statuta, Patrologia latina*, vol. 80, cols. 443–444
QLP	*Questions liturgiques et paroissiales*
RAC	*Reallexicon für Antike und Christentum*
RAM	*Revue d'ascétique et de mystique*
RB	*Revue bénédictine*
RBPH	*Revue belge de philologie et d'histoire*

REA	*Revue des études augustiniennes*
RH	*Revue historique*
RHDFE	*Revue historique de droit français et étranger*
RHE	*Revue d'histoire ecclésiastique*
RHEF	*Revue d'histoire de l'Eglise de France*
Riculf	Riculf of Soissons, *Statuta, Patrologia latina*, vol. 131, cols. 15–24
Rodulph	Rodulph of Bourges, *Capitula, Patrologia latina*, vol. 119, cols. 703–726
RQCAKG	*Römische Quartalschrift für christliche Altertumskunde und Kirchengeschichte*
RSR	*Revue de science religieuse*
RTAM	*Recherches de théologie ancienne et médiévale*
Ruotger	Ruotger of Trier, ed. M. Blasen, in "Die Canonessammlung des Erzbischofs Ruotger von Trier vom Jahre 927. Ein Beitrag zur Rechtsgeschichte der Diözese Trier," *Pastor Bonus* 52 (1941):61–72
SC	Sources chrétiennes
SJA	*Southwestern Journal of Anthropology*
SLH	Scriptores latini Hiberniae
SM	*Studi medievali*
SSAM	Settimane di studio del Centro italiano di studi sull'alto medioevo (Spoleto)
ST	Studi e testi
TAPS	Transactions of the American Philosophical Society
Theod I	Theodulph of Orléans, *Capitula ad presbyteros, Patrologia latina*, vol. 105, cols. 191–208
Theod II	"Le second statut diocésain de Théodulphe, évêque d'Orléans," ed. Carlo de Clercq, *La législation* (1936) 1:320–351
TQ	*Theologische Quartalschrift*
TRHS	*Transactions of the Royal Historical Society*
VC	*Vigiliae christianae*
Vesoul	"Statut diocésain du manuscrit de Vesoul," ed. Carlo de Clercq, *La législation* (1936) 1:367–374
Walter	Walter of Orléans, *Capitula, Patrologia latina*, vol. 119, cols. 725–746
ZKG	*Zeitschrift für Kirchengeschichte*
ZSSRG	*Zeitschrift der Savigny-Stiftung für Rechtsgeschichte*

GODPARENTS AND KINSHIP IN
EARLY MEDIEVAL EUROPE

In 1973, while reading the late eighth-century *Vita* of Saint Richarius, I came across Latin terms of relationship that I had not noticed before. In chapter five, for example, Richarius is reported to have visited his *cummater* (comother) Rictrudis, and at the end of the encounter he kissed his "genuine son by the law of the bath" (*filio meo germano et lege lavacri*).[1] My curiosity was piqued by this incident because Merovingian saints are not usually depicted visiting women or kissing babies. To decipher the passage, I searched for guidance in the standard dictionaries and encyclopedias, where I readily discovered that what I had read about was a manifestation of the spiritual kinship that is created by baptismal sponsorship. However, this formal explanation was unsatisfying because it did not account for the easy familiarity of the adults or the obvious affection of the spiritual father for the spiritual child. And so I decided to investigate further the social significance of baptismal sponsorship and spiritual kinship in Frankish society, with the naïve expectation that it would be a relatively simple task, resulting in a conference paper or a modest article.

I was soon cured of that belief, for even a cursory glance at the sources made it clear that spiritual kinship was a vital part of early medieval western society. And wider reading in secondary works also made me aware that forms of spiritual kinship based on baptismal sponsorship could be found in all premodern Christian societies, as well as in many contemporary societies, particularly in Latin America. Thus sponsorship and spiritual kinship turned out to be complex phenomena, evolving across time, differing somewhat from one society to another, shaping and being shaped by the liturgy, by the canon law of marriage, and by the life of society, and open to a wide range of imitations and expansions.

I found many scholarly studies that touched upon aspects of sponsorship and spiritual kinship, but I was puzzled by the fact that such an important and ubiquitous socioreligious phenomenon had received so little synthetic attention. And although some anthropologists had generalized about spiritual kinship in Latin America, no one had attempted a thorough study of such relationships in medieval Europe.

[1] *Vita Richarii sacerdotis Centulensis primigenia*, ch. 5, MGH SSRM 7 (Hanover and Leipzig, 1920), pp. 446–447.

One reason for this piecemeal approach to spiritual kinship lies in the nature of the medieval sources themselves. Since the authors of these sources took sponsorship and its consequences for granted, accepting it as part of the warp and woof of life, there are no medieval treatises on the subject. And while, from the twelfth century on, canonists and theologians wrote a great deal about the consequences of spiritual kinship for marriage, they studiously avoided comment on its other social manifestations. Because of this, an attempt to discover the fundamental structures and myriad details of medieval spiritual kinship would be much like the creation of a mosaic, assembling hundreds of references in laws, saints' lives, sermons, penitentials, chronicles, letters, literary texts, and the like. No one had undertaken this daunting task, with the result that specialized studies multiplied without any attempt at synthesis.

Another more fundamental reason why the study of sponsorship and spiritual kinship concentrated on the parts rather than the whole can be found in the historiography of the problem. Four distinct scholarly traditions—which I have designated as ecclesiastical, literary and folkloric, anthropological, and historical—have all taken a sustained interest in baptismal sponsorship and/or spiritual kinship, but each has been concerned primarily with its own self-defined view of what is significant. Of course, it would be an exaggeration to say that the four traditions have been utterly isolated from one another, for scholars in one do occasionally draw on the findings of the others. Nevertheless, the sociology of the learned professions in the twentieth century is such that each scholarly tradition defines its own problems for investigation, has its own set of working assumptions and relevant questions, and proceeds according to its own momentum. For scholars in each tradition, the other traditions provide only raw materials or peripheral insights that have generally had little impact on the way they go about their business.

Before we begin to analyze more precisely these traditions of studying sponsorship and spiritual kinship, we must first explain briefly the basic forms and essential vocabulary of spiritual kinship itself. When a child is baptized in many of the contemporary Christian traditions—including the Roman Catholic, Anglican, Lutheran, and Orthodox—that child has liturgical sponsors who are designated with correlated male-female terms: *patrinus/matrina* in Latin, *parraine/marraine* in French, *padrino/madrina* in Spanish, *padrino/madrina* in Italian, *Pate/Patin* in German, and godfather/godmother in English. In many contemporary and past societies, the sponsorship of a child has social consequences, initiating a relationship of the sponsor with the child and with its parents that can be both intimate and enduring. This relationship has traditionally been understood by the participants as a sacred bond, rooted in Christian images of spiritual rebirth.

In the New Testament, the image of baptism as a rebirth is present but not dominant, sharing the stage with such other images as washing, enlightening, anointing, and sealing.[2] Its development occurred in the patristic period; after that, at least in the Latin West, it came to predominate, although it did not entirely replace the other rival images. Thus, since the sixth century, the canon law and the Christian popular imagination have reinforced and elaborated the idea that in baptism a special kind of spiritual birth takes place, an event that is comparable to a natural birth, though of a higher nature. And, just as a natural birth results in ties of natural kinship, so a spiritual birth creates at baptism a spiritual kinship that embraces at least the baptizer, the natural parents, the sponsors, and the baptizee.

Our interpretations of sponsorship have been shaped by the fact that since late antiquity the baptizee has customarily been an infant or a young child. As a result of baptism, the youngster became the focus of a spiritual family, in addition to but overlapping with his natural family. Such a spiritual family was constituted out of two basic relationships, each of which was open to elaboration.

First, the bond uniting sponsor and sponsored, which we may visualize as a vertical relationship, was traditionally described in parent/child terminology. The sponsor (and also the baptizer) participated in the child's new birth and became his parent in a spiritual sense. Thus we may describe this relationship as spiritual parenthood. By the eighth century in the West, certain words had been coined to describe such a bond: the godfather and godmother were *patrinus/matrina* respectively, while the godchild was *filiolus* or *filiola*.

Second, as a consequence of inviting a sponsor, the child's mother and father were thought to share their parenthood both with the baptizer and with the sponsor. The natural parents, the sponsor(s), and the baptizer therefore became coparents to one another, a relationship that we may visualize as horizontal, uniting adults in the nurture of their common child. Coparenthood had become an important social relationship by the sixth century, and a Latin vocabulary based on neologisms began to be used to describe it as well. The relationship itself was designated by the abstract Latin term *compaternitas* (cofa-

---

[2] Joseph Ysebaert, *Greek Baptismal Terminology: Its Origin and Early Development*, Graecitas Christianorum primaeva, vol. 1 (Nijmegen, 1962), passim.

therhood), and the participants were, according to their sex, *compatres* (cofathers) and *commatres* (comothers) to one another.

In most modern European vernacular languages, there is an appropriate terminology for coparenthood that is generally based on these medieval Latin terms. For instance, *compère/commère/comparrainage* in French, *compadre/comadre/compadrazgo* in Spanish, and *compare/comare/comparaggio* in Italian clearly echo their Latin antecedents. Even in German, the terms *Gevatter/Gevatterin/Gevatterschaft* are built directly on the medieval Latin terminology. However, scholars writing about coparenthood in English have been handicapped by developments in their own language since the eighteenth century.

Old and Middle English had precise terms for all the baptismal kin, both parental and coparental, that were derived from Latin, either directly or through Norman French. In English-speaking areas the godparental bond, uniting sponsor and sponsored, has survived to the present and its vocabulary (godfather/godmother, godson/goddaughter) poses no serious problem for scholars. Unfortunately, it is quite different with the language of coparenthood. Since the sixteenth century, the coparental bond that linked sponsors to natural parents has withered in Western Europe and particularly in England. As a consequence, English speakers have little awareness that a serious coparenthood relationship ever existed or that it bound the participants to marital taboos as well as to a code of mutually altruistic behavior.

This is not the place to examine the reasons for such a major social change. It is enough merely to note that it paralleled the upheavals of the eighteenth and nineteenth centuries that were loosely associated with the Industrial Revolution and that there may be a causal link. Spiritual kinship in general does not remain vigorous in "modern" industrialized societies, and the English situation was probably intensified by the proliferation of religious groups (for example, the Baptists) that rejected infant baptism on theological grounds. In any case, as the coparental relationship faded in English society, its medieval vocabulary became archaic; nowadays it requires a stout dictionary indeed to learn the true etymology of *gossip* or *cummer*.

This cultural development and its linguistic reflex has meant that a modern scholar writing in English has no ready translation for either the medieval Latin or the vernacular terms for coparenthood that are encountered in the sources. But the temptation to render everything as "godfather"—an expedient occasionally adopted by those who are hazy about the distinction between sponsor as parent and sponsor as coparent—must be avoided, since it masks the reality and complexity of spiritual kinship. Thus, in order to be precise, I have either retained the medieval Latin terms for coparenthood (*compater*, *commater*, *compaternitas*) in the original language or translated them literally as "cofather," "comother," "coparent," or "coparenthood." The terms "spiritual parenthood" and "coparenthood" are based directly on medieval Latin terms. When medieval intellectuals wished to encompass both relationships at once they used the term *cognatio spiritualis*, which designated spiritual kinship of any kind. This is a handy term, but one that has not gained acceptance in modern scholarship, except in canon law and theology, where medieval Latin still influences terminology.

The most vigorous focus of the modern anthropological investigation of sponsorship has been in Latin American studies. But in searching for a term to encompass both spiritual parenthood and spiritual coparenthood, even the Latin American anthropologists have not been entirely successful. The inclusive term adopted in many of their studies has been the Spanish *compadrazgo*,[3] which etymologically embraces only the coparental bond; the parental bond, when it is specifically mentioned, is called *padrinazgo*. Such an emphasis fits Latin American conditions, where the coparental bond is dominant, but in other places the situation is different and so the word is misleading. Recently, a Spanish neologism, *compadrinazgo*, which contains both *compadre* and *padrino*, has appeared in scholarly literature.[4] The word serves its purpose, but is of little use outside a Spanish-speaking context.

Some anthropologists writing in English have referred to the entire phenomenon as "the godparent(hood) complex."[5] However, this term emphasizes the vertical bond of sponsor and sponsored and can obscure the vigor and even the existence of the coparental relationship. Thus, in order to separate the institution of sponsorship from an exclusively Latin American focus and to avoid giving verbal prominence to either the vertical or the horizontal bonds when such prominence is not intended, I shall use the term "spiritual kinship" or, if the context demands it, "baptismal kinship" to embrace both spiritual parenthood and spiritual coparenthood.

Such spiritual kinship has been an important element of social organization and interpersonal relationships in Christian societies for at least fourteen hundred years. Indeed, prior to the sixteenth century it

[3] See, for example, George M. Foster, "Cofradia and Compadrazgo in Spain and Spanish America," *SJA* 9 (1953):1–28; and Stephen Gudeman, "The *Compadrazgo* as a Reflection of the Natural and Spiritual Person: The Curl Prize Essay, 1971," *Proceedings of the Royal Anthropological Institute* (1972):45–71.

[4] Donn V. Hart, *Compadrinazgo: Ritual Kinship in the Philippines* (Dekalb, Ill., 1977).

[5] Gallatin Anderson, "Il Comparaggio: The Italian Godparenthood Complex," *SJA* 13 (1957):32–53.

was to be found, with many variations, wherever Christianity had taken root. But in the sixteenth century the Protestant reformers severely curtailed the social consequences of spiritual kinship, particularly by jettisoning its traditional sexual taboos. Hence in Protestant Europe the institution of sponsorship slowly declined in significance between the sixteenth and twentieth centuries. By way of contrast, in those areas that remained Roman Catholic or adhered to Eastern Orthodoxy, the traditional roles of sponsors and the institution of spiritual kinship continued to function, although they were not immune to the processes of change over time. In addition, the outward thrust of the Iberian peoples since the sixteenth century disseminated baptismal kinship in their colonial empires, where it has survived and flourished, often taking on forms quite unlike those existing in the European matrix.

Spiritual kinship, with its adaptations, extensions, and variations, is a huge field of study, encompassing large components of time and geography. For that reason, there has not been, and probably never will be, a comprehensive study of the phenomenon. However, more modest investigations that are still rather grand in scope are both desirable and feasible. In my opinion, there are three chief *desiderata*.

First, there is the need for a detailed study of the institution in fifteenth- and sixteenth-century Iberia, whence Latin American, Philippine, and some other modern forms took their origin. For until we have a clearer picture of the exact heritage the missionaries and lay Christians brought to the Spanish and Portuguese colonies, it will not be possible to assess properly the balance of tradition and innovation in the sponsoring practices that modern anthropological research has revealed. This task is complicated by the fact that the Council of Trent changed important features of sponsorship and that these revisions spread slowly in the sixteenth and seventeenth centuries, not entirely obliterating earlier patterns.

Second, the study of baptismal kinship in the Byzantine world and the Byzantine cultural sphere in Slavic lands is still in its infancy. Enough is known to be able to assert that baptismal sponsorship impinged on marriage law, social life, and political alliances,[6] but the precise contours of spiritual kinship in Byzantine Orthodox society have yet to be determined. There is thus a need for a systematic study of sponsorship in the Byzantine world.

Third, the medieval Latin West knew vigorous, deep-rooted forms

[6] Evelyne Patlagean, "Christianisation et parentés rituelles: le domaine de Byzance," *AESC* 33 (1978):625–636.

of spiritual kinship, whose origins and unfolding are poorly understood. In this book, I intend to trace the origins and development of these forms from the late Roman Empire to the late Carolingian period, when the main features of the western variety of spiritual kinship were fixed. This study could be extended into the high and late Middle Ages, where a process of variation on and extension of the basic baptismal paradigm was carried through. However, such an investigation must be left for later; here the emphasis will be on the origins and basic development of spiritual kinship in the medieval West.

PART ONE

THE HISTORIOGRAPHY OF
SPIRITUAL KINSHIP

ONE

HISTORIOGRAPHY TO THE 1880s

The search for *the* origin of institutions, customs, and inventions has been a characteristic activity of scholars in the ancient, medieval, and modern periods. By means of speculation, mythmaking, or investigation, intellectuals have made it their task to find the beginnings of those things that have interested them and their contemporaries. In this endeavor, controversy has often been the stimulus to search out the presumably pristine moment of creation. However, baptismal sponsorship was not a matter of controversy in ancient Christianity, and the institution was ordinarily taken for granted. In fact, Augustine's Letter 98, written early in the fifth century, was the sole attempt to justify the sponsor's role in infant baptism and its arguments were entirely theological; Augustine did not speculate about the institution's historical origins.

It was not until the ninth century that scholars occasionally took an interest in the origins of sponsorship. But in the period between the fifth and the ninth centuries sponsorship itself had evolved in important ways. In particular, the sponsorship of adults had withered and the sponsorship of infants had flourished. Speculation on the origins of the institution was conditioned, therefore, by the fact that from the ninth to the nineteenth centuries scholars assumed, on the basis of their own experience, that sponsorship had always been intimately connected with infant baptism.

The renaissance of ecclesiastical learning promoted by Charlemagne and his advisers bore its mature results during the second and third quarters of the ninth century when a generation of clergy that had been formed in the climate of wider educational opportunity succeeded to positions of authority. The best of them were marked by a didactic urge, a desire to teach their society the basics of Christian belief and behavior. To them, baptism and the religious instruction that traditionally preceded or followed it seemed an ideal occasion to reach the minds of parents, sponsors, and baptizees. In other words, sponsorship was perceived as closely bound up with the opportunity to instruct laymen in small groups.

In this intellectual climate, some Carolingian scholars speculated on

the circumstances in which sponsorship had arisen and on the purposes it fulfilled. Acting on such an impulse, Jonas, bishop of Orléans
(818–843), wrote a book of advice for a layman, Count Matfrid, entitled *De institutione laicali*, in which he elaborated upon a major duty of
lay people in Carolingian society, the proper rudimentary religious
instruction of their natural and spiritual children. In the context of
this discussion, Bishop Jonas explained the circumstances in which he
believed sponsorship had arisen:

> In the early period [*in primordio*] of the holy Church of God, no
> one was baptized before they were instructed both in belief in
> the Holy Trinity and the mystery of most holy baptism. Now,
> however, because the name of Christ flourishes everywhere, even
> children born of Christian parents and not yet able to speak are
> brought immediately to receive the grace of baptism (and this is
> not inappropriate, since those who are liable to punishment for
> others' sins are, by the carrying and response of others, freed
> from the treachery of original sin, such that, snatched from the
> power of darkness, they are transferred into the kingdom of their
> Lord). It is most important that when they reach the age of un-
> derstanding, they be instructed in belief and in the mystery of
> baptism, either by their parents or by those who received them
> from the holy bath of the font.[1]

Jonas made no attempt to fix an exact date when the sponsorship of
infants had begun. He did, however, tie the origins of sponsorship
both to a historical process (the spread of Christianity) and to a theological truth (original sin). In Jonas' view, when Christian converts
began to produce children, those children needed baptism to escape
from Adam's sin. Furthermore, he assumed on the basis of his own
experience that such children needed sponsors for "carrying and response" during baptism. Older children also needed instruction in the
basics of religion, a constant theme of the Carolingian reformers, and
Jonas asserted that sponsors should participate in that teaching along
with the natural parents with whom they shared parenthood.

The Carolingian poet, historian, theologian, and liturgist Walafrid
Strabo (ca. 808–849), abbot of Reichenau, possessed an awareness of
the historical development of ecclesiastical institutions that was quite
unusual. In about 840/42, he wrote a treatise on the development of
ecclesiastical institutions that, as Joseph de Ghellinck has remarked,

---

[1] Jonas of Orléans, *De institutione laicali*, book 1, ch. 8, in *PL* 106:135.

was composed *"avec esprit et discernement."*[2] In it, Walafrid argued that the doctrine of original sin necessitated the baptism of every human being, including infants:

> Therefore, since all whom grace does not liberate perish in original sin, even those who do not add their own sin, it is necessary that little children be baptized. Saint Augustine shows this in the book concerning the baptism of infants, and African councils and many texts of other fathers attest to it. Thus, from this fact it has come about that godfathers and godmothers are provided to receive little ones from the bath and to respond on their behalf all the things which because of the weakness of age they are not able to confess.[3]

Walafrid knew that the baptism of infants was at least as old as Augustine and was rooted in the growing realization of the meaning of original sin, which was believed to doom even those who had committed no "personal" transgression. However, since he lacked knowledge of crucial texts from Tertullian, Origen, and Cyprian, Walafrid could not be more precise about the time in which the new awareness of original sin had been translated into the institution of sponsorship. He simply assumed that such sponsorship had been a practical concession to the inability of infants to participate in their own indispensable baptism.

The Carolingian assessment of the historical origins and contemporary significance of baptismal sponsorship may be summarized as follows. (1) The sponsor was associated with infant baptism and with the theology of original sin, which implied that every human being, including helpless infants, needed to receive baptism. (2) The sponsor's role was liturgical and educational; that is, he or she was to act for infants during the liturgy and subsequently to instruct them in the rudiments of Christian faith and morals when they reached a suitable age. (3) The actual date assigned to the origin of the institution was vague and depended ultimately on the approximate date one assigned to the origin of infant baptism. There was no insistence that the sponsor was to be found in the New Testament or the early apostolic age. (4) Most social consequences of sponsorship were not discussed by the intellectuals. In particular, they ignored the secular alliance-building functions of spiritual kinship, which a modern scholar must seek

[2] Joseph de Ghellinck, "Le développement du dogme d'après Walafrid Strabon à propos du baptême des enfants," *RSR* 29 (1939):482.

[3] Walafrid Strabo, *Libellus de exordiis et incrementis quarundam in observationibus ecclesiasticis rerum*, ch. 27, in MGH Capitularia 2:512.

painstakingly in sources concerned with other things. However, there was one social consequence of sponsorship that did interest, indeed fascinate, Carolingian churchmen—the creation of marital taboos that prevented spiritual kinsmen from marrying one another. In fact, a superficial reading of the sources has led some scholars to conclude that the sole social consequence of sponsorship was the creation of sexual taboos, but in this they have merely been misled by the priorities of Carolingian intellectuals, who emphasized one feature to the neglect of others.

This Carolingian set of assumptions, attitudes, and emphases was not seriously challenged by intellectuals in the high and late Middle Ages, although it was considerably elaborated upon by the numerous theologians and canon lawyers of later centuries. It would, however, be a mistake to assume that medieval scholars gave a great deal of attention to the strictly historical origins of the godparent. For when theologians thought of origins, they most often considered the theological reasons that justified something. In this perspective, sponsors had their "origin" in the need for infant baptism that was, in turn, grounded in the doctrine of original sin. And since the institution of sponsorship was thus justified by the very structure of Christianity, its exact date of origin was a secondary matter. Consequently, medieval speculation on the historical origins of sponsorship is dwarfed by the mass of sources composed by canonists, theologians, and pastoral writers who dealt with the theological justification of sponsorship and its impact on marriage law in their society. The latter preoccupation had important consequences for all subsequent study of sponsorship.

A godparent was, as the very name implied, a parent of some sort. Between the sixth and eighth centuries this parenthood came to be understood in a very literal way, and one result was that sexual contact between persons related by spiritual parenthood or coparenthood was banned as incestuous. Thus the medieval approach to sponsorship was deeply marked from its Carolingian origins by the fact that canon lawyers and theologians, prolific writers in general, saw the primary significance of spiritual kinship in its effect on marriage law. In the face of the bulk of material emanating from these canonists and theologians, modern scholars have had difficulty remembering that spiritual kinship was a much broader phenomenon than the narrow professional interest of canonists and theologians might suggest.

Latin Europe experienced an intellectual revival of major proportions in the twelfth century, one characteristic of which was the attempt to assimilate and harmonize that society's complex intellectual heritage. The church's law, which had long been in confusing disarray, was one focus of this effort at restructuring and reordering.[4] As part of such a process, between 1139 and 1150, Gratian, a Camaldulese monk teaching at Bologna, compiled a massive compendium of legal texts arranged around topics and questions, and partially harmonized them by his own comments. He called his work *The Concordance of Discordant Canons*, but almost since his own day it has been known as the *Decretum*.[5]

Gratian's *Decretum* was an eminently useful work, ordering a mass of material in an intelligent way. In addition, it appeared at an opportune moment, at the beginnings of the professionalization of the study of canon law. It became a standard textbook of the medieval law schools, was studied by every canon lawyer, and was copied and commented upon innumerable times from the twelfth to the fifteenth centuries. And with the advent of printing, it was reproduced in many editions. Thus the *Decretum* served as an indispensable mine of proof texts not only for canon lawyers but also for other scholars who wished to discuss many aspects of the Christian church. In short, it was an intellectual achievement of the first order.

Gratian had access to many texts on spiritual kinship, and his choices about which to include in the *Decretum* influenced all later treatment of the topic. He touches on the matter in two places. First, in the third division of his *Decretum*, called *On Consecration*, he approaches the sacrament of baptism in *distinctio* 4, which includes 156 texts. In chapters 100 to 104 he cites brief texts that regulate certain aspects of the godparental institution: two texts specifying the proper number of sponsors; two texts forbidding monks to enter into a relationship of coparenthood; and one text requiring that potential sponsors themselves be baptized and confirmed. However, chapter 105 was the only one to refer to the godparents' duties to educate and guide their godchildren. This selection of six very brief texts is a meager representation of the available material, but it corresponds well to the minor significance accorded by the legal tradition to the qualifications for and educational role of godparents.

The second place where Gratian treats godparents is in *causa* 30, where he includes twenty-four texts—six attributed to councils and eighteen to popes—that served for centuries as the fountainhead of the canonists' treatment of godparents. The focus of *causa* 30 is exclusively on the consequences of spiritual parenthood and coparenthood for

[4] Stephan G. Kuttner, *Harmony from Dissonance: An Interpretation of Medieval Canon Law*, Wimmer Lecture no. 10 (Latrobe, Pa., 1960).

[5] Gratian, *Decretum*, ed. Emil Friedberg, *Corpus iuris canonici*, vol. 1 (Leipzig, 1879).

marriage law, an emphasis not lost until the revised code of canon law in 1917, which abolished many of the marital consequences of sponsorship.

The process of rationalizing the church's law and centralizing its government under papal leadership proceeded rapidly in the late twelfth and thirteenth centuries. The pace of this development left Gratian's *Decretum* insufficient or outdated on many topics, and so it was supplemented by collections of papal decretal letters that embodied the newer practice. The two thirteenth-century collections of decretals that entered the official canon law reinforced the canonists' preoccupation with the marital implications of spiritual kinship. When, for example, Gregory IX issued *Five Books of Decretals* in 1234, book 4, title 11, contained eight papal decretals clarifying disputed aspects of the marriage prohibition arising out of spiritual kinship.[6] In 1298, Pope Boniface VIII issued a sixth book of decretals, in which book 4, title 3, included three of his decisions on spiritual kinship and marriage.[7]

In view of the contents of the major legal collections and textbooks, it is no accident that generations of canon lawyers approached sponsorship as a major component of marriage law, a minor facet of sacramental law and religious education, and a social institution whose nonmarital consequences lay outside their ken.

Similar preoccupations reigned in medieval theology. Just as Gratian created the primary textbook of canon law, his contemporary, Peter Lombard, composed the most influential textbook of theology, the *Four Books of the Sentences*. The Lombard's work was similar in aim and form to that of Gratian: authoritative texts were arranged around problems and interspersed with comments from the compiler. In book 4, *distinctio* 42, Peter Lombard treats baptismal and other forms of spiritual kinship within the context of his discussion of marriage, using Gratian's *Decretum*, *causa* 30, as a source book. In the process, he cites fifteen of Gratian's twenty-four texts and quotes Gratian himself three times. Not surprisingly, his treatment follows that of Gratian on almost every point.[8] In effect, then, the theological tradition, with many nuances and variations to be sure, adopted the canonists' emphasis on marriage law as a proper context for the discussion of spiritual kinship.

[6] Gregory IX, *Decretales*, lib. 4, tit. 11, in *Corpus iuris canonici*, vol. 2, ed. Emil Friedberg (Leipzig, 1879), pp. 693–696.

[7] Boniface VIII, *Liber Sextus*, lib. 4, tit. 3, in *Corpus iuris canonici*, vol. 2, pp. 1067–1068.

[8] Petrus Lombardus, *Libri iv sententiarum*, lib. 4, dist. 42, ed. Patres Collegii S. Bonaventurae (Quarrachi, 1916), pp. 987–994.

In the high and late Middle Ages, speculation on the historical origins of sponsorship was unusual but not unknown. There were two particular source texts that supplied a basis for such speculation. First, an eighth-century Anglo-Saxon penitential, attributed either to Archbishop Theodore of Canterbury or to his anonymous Northumbrian disciple, put into circulation an apocryphal text that was subsequently attributed to Pope Higinus (ca. 136): "If necessity demands it, there can be one father in the catechumenate, in baptism and in confirmation. But that is not the custom; instead separate fathers receive in the separate ceremonies."[9] This apocryphal text received wide dissemination because of its inclusion in Gratian's *Decretum, De consecratione, distinctio* 4, chapter 100. And on the basis of this brief text some scholars concluded that sponsorship had existed in elaborate form (that is, for the catechumenate, baptism, and confirmation) by the early second century and might even have been instituted by Pope Higinus himself.

The second source text, which linked the historical origins of sponsorship to apostolic times, was the tract entitled *On the Ecclesiastical Hierarchy*, which passed under the name of Dionysius the Areopagite. Until the seventeenth century, it was believed that Dionysius was the convert of Paul mentioned in Acts 17:34. During the Carolingian period, this Dionysius was also identified with the first bishop of Paris, Saint Denis, whose tomb lay north of the city. The Greek corpus of Dionysian writings reached the West in the eighth century and was rendered into Latin by Hilduin, abbot of St. Denis, in about 835, and again by John Scotus Erigena before 862. In the tract *On the Ecclesiastical Hierarchy*, Dionysius, who was probably a late fifth-century Syrian Monophysite, discusses the sponsorship of both infants and adults.[10] And since Dionysius was considered a disciple of Paul, his tract could be used to argue for apostolic or immediate postapostolic credentials for the practice. Thus, on the basis of two apocryphal texts, sponsorship came to be traced historically to the later first or early second century.

It was rare that medieval authors sought for a direct biblical origin of sponsorship. Indeed, the fifteenth-century Carthusian spiritual

[9] *Discipulus Umbrensium*, bk. 2, ch. 4.8, ed. Paul W. Finsterwalder, *Die Canones Theodori Cantuariensis und ihre Überlieferungsformen. Untersuchungen zu den Bussbüchern des 7., 8. und 9. Jahrhunderts*, vol. 1 (Weimar, 1929), p. 317: "In catecumino et baptismate et confirmatione unus potest esse pater si necesse est non est tamen consuetudo sed per singula singuli suscipiunt."

[10] Dionysius the Areopagite, *De Hierarchia ecclesiastica*, ch. 2.2.1–8 and ch. 2.3.4 (on the sponsorship of adults); ch. 7.3.11 (on the sponsorship of infants), in *Dionysiaca*, vol. 2, ed. P. Chevallier (Bruges, 1950), pp. 1111–1128, 1140–1145, 1465–1476.

writer Ludolph of Saxony was one of the few who suggested that the sponsor had such an origin. In the Gospel of John, 1:35–42, it is recorded that Andrew joined Jesus' band of followers and subsequently sought out his brother Simon to encourage him to join, "and he led him to Jesus" (*Et adduxit eum ad Iesum*). Thus Ludolph argued that the origins of sponsorship lay in this act of "leading" someone to the Lord.[11] However, few scholars followed Ludolph in this unusual interpretation. On the contrary, although they expressed their views in diverse ways, most medieval scholars agreed that sponsorship had begun in the apostolic or immediate postapostolic period.

The search for the origin of sponsorship intensified in the sixteenth century, when the history of the early church became the focus of intense polemic among the contending religious parties. In the midst of this controversy, the nature and development of the two central Christian sacraments, baptism and the Lord's Supper, were probed on all sides. Although baptismal sponsorship was not initially a significant point of disagreement among the major groups, all of which had retained infant baptism, it did hold a place of interest among both Catholics and Protestants because, insofar as baptism was scrutinized, sponsors quite naturally emerged as a topic of discussion. There was general agreement among scholars from the Catholic, Lutheran, and Calvinist camps that the contemporary sixteenth-century practice of sponsorship needed reform because it had compromised its religious and pedagogical functions. The problems plaguing sponsorship were generally attributed to an overemphasis on gift-giving by godparents and to the complex web of marital impediments that sponsorship spun around its participants. But the contending parties disagreed about the nature and extent of the changes that were needed.

The Protestant reformers, with their ardent conviction that salvation was dependent on faith, might have been expected to abandon infant baptism as inconsistent with such a theological position. Indeed, the issue of infant baptism, on which sponsorship hung as a corollary, was hotly disputed in the sixteenth century. Some groups, always small and often persecuted, adopted "believers' baptism," which demanded that any baptizee be capable of consenting personally to the baptismal articles of faith. Thus, in their view, sponsors for the baptizee were superfluous. However, after varying degrees of hesitation, the major reformers repudiated such "anabaptists" and retained infant baptism.[12] Furthermore, in spite of objections to the way in which

---

[11] Ludolph of Saxony, *Vita Jesu Christi*, bk. 1, ch. 24 (Paris, 1865), p. 118.
[12] George H. Williams, *The Radical Reformation* (Philadelphia, 1962), pp. 193–195, 201–203.

late medieval Catholic sponsorship functioned, they preserved the institution.

Luther himself set this pattern of purification rather than abolition. In his view, sponsorship was a manmade addition to the sacrament of baptism, not essential but quite permissible as an ancient, pious, and still useful practice. And in his *Taufbüchlein* of 1523, which translates the traditional baptismal ceremonies into the vernacular, his treatment of sponsors is quite in line with late medieval Catholic conceptions of their liturgical and educational functions.[13] Similarly, the Brandenburg/Nuremberg Church Order of 1533, composed in large part by Luther's early supporter Andreas Osiander, clearly expresses the Lutheran view:

> In all ecclesiastical usages we must diligently mark what God has commanded and instituted, and what men have added thereto, in order that we may hold the divine as the essential part, and diligently practise it, and on the other hand judge the human additions, whether or not they are things indifferent, and if indifferent, whether they are also useful or not, in order that what is contrary to God's word, or otherwise unprofitable, may be done away.
>
> Now God himself has instituted and ordained baptism, that we should baptize with water in the name of the Father and of the Son and of the Holy Ghost. But men have added of their own accord prayer, [recitation of the] gospel, sponsors, chrisom-cloth, blessing of the font, oil, salt, and spittle, etc. Now, whatever of these things tends to profit and improvement should for the present be suffered to remain; but whatever is unprofitable and causes offense should be suffered to fall into disuse.
>
> Now the saying of prayer thereat, and the reading of the holy gospel, is not only allowable but also useful and good; therefore it should be suffered to remain. In like manner also sponsors, especially on account of the Anabaptists, who nowadays pretend that they do not know whether they be baptized or not; in order that the sponsors principally, together with other persons, may give testimony, and in the mouth of two or three witnesses, every matter may be established (Deut. 19). Also in order that some one may answer for the child, and if he should be prematurely deprived of his parents by death, they may remind the children what they have engaged on their behalf at their baptism, and keep

[13] J.D.C. Fisher, *Christian Initiation: The Reformation Period*, Alcuin Club Collections, vol. 51 (London, 1970), pp. 6–16.

a strict watch over them that they may fulfill it, and learn God's commandments, creed and prayer.[14]

Luther and his disciples were not content merely to preserve sponsorship in its contemporary form. Indeed, the Wittenberg professor disapproved vigorously and eloquently of the entire panoply of marital impediments that Catholic canon law and theology derived from sponsorship. Hence in his *Babylonian Captivity of the Church* (1520), Luther declared that:

> the nonsense about compaternity, commaternity, confraternity, consorority, and confiliety, ought to be completely blotted out, and the marriage contracted. These spiritual affinities are due purely to superstition. If neither the one who administers the baptism, nor the godparent at the baptism, is permitted to marry the one who has been baptized, then why is any Christian man permitted to marry any Christian woman? Does a fuller relationship arise from the rite or the sign of the sacrament, than from the sacrament itself? Is not a Christian man the brother of a Christian sister? Is not a baptized man spiritual brother to a baptized woman? What silly stuff they talk! If any husband teaches the gospel to his wife, and instructs her in faith in Christ, whereby in very truth he becomes her spiritual father—then ought she to no longer remain his wife? Would Paul not have been allowed to marry one of the Corinthian girls, all of whom he claims to have begotten in Christ [I Cor. 4:15]? See how Christian liberty has been oppressed by the blindness of human superstition![15]

The classic Lutheran position on sponsorship was well summarized in the early seventeenth century by the theologian Johannes Gerhard (1582–1637), who argued that the practice of sponsorship was neither scriptural nor apostolic in origin, although it was pious and useful. He was adamant that its functions were liturgical and educational, and that it had no impact on marriage. Gerhard was tangentially interested in the historical origins of the practice, although he did not cite the writings of Dionysius the Areopagite, about whose authenticity there was considerable skepticism in the seventeenth century. He did, however, give credence to the apocryphal text of Pope Higinus, which he

[14] Ibid., pp. 26–27. The translation is by Fisher.
[15] Martin Luther, *The Babylonian Captivity of the Church*, tr. A.T.W. Steinhauser and rev. F. C. Ahrens and A. R. Wentz, *Luther's Works*, vol. 36 (Philadelphia, 1956), pp. 99–100.

dated to about A.D. 154, and suggested that Higinus might have introduced the practice.[16] The Lutherans thus retained sponsorship, shorn of its marital consequences, as a pious, useful ecclesiastical tradition that did not conflict with the gospel.

It is almost a cliché of historiography that the Swiss Reformer John Calvin tended to be more thorough and systematic than Luther in breaking with the Catholic past. Whereas Luther had been tolerant of ecclesiastical ceremonies that were manmade but religiously useful, Calvin's strict biblicism led him to reject virtually all features of church life for which he could find no scriptural warrant. However, with a certain amount of exegetical ingenuity Calvin managed to retain infant baptism, for which some people in his own day and many since have seen no clear biblical mandate.[17]

Calvin and the Reformed tradition also retained sponsorship, but in a very attenuated form. They shared Luther's contempt for the marital impediments rooted in baptismal sponsorship and rejected entirely the notion of spiritual kinship as an impediment to marriage. The sponsoring figure was unimportant in the Calvinist theology of baptism, and Calvin never mentioned sponsorship in his defence of infant baptism in the *Institutes*. Instead, Calvin and the Reformed tradition placed natural parents on a par with sponsors for the future religious formation of the child; they even countenanced parents sponsoring their own children, a practice that had been forbidden in Byzantine and western Christianity since the eighth century. Thus the sponsor's role was emptied of content as the stress was placed on the parents' responsibility for their own children.

When Calvin composed and published a baptismal service in 1542, it was a more radical break with the Catholic liturgy than Luther's *Taufbüchlein* of 1523 had been. Calvin's service did retain sponsors, but their role was unclear, since the natural parents and the congregation shared with them the responsibility of presenting the child for baptism.[18] In other words, the sponsor survived in the Calvinist tradition only because infant baptism itself survived. But the role was vestigial, stripped of its kinship functions and tending to be eclipsed by or absorbed into the parental role.

[16] Johannes Gerhard, *Loci theologici*, ed. Johannes Cotta (Tübingen, 1768), vol. 9, locus 21, ch. 8.234, pp. 278–279, and vol. 9, locus 21, ch. 9.269, pp. 313–316.

[17] John Calvin, *Institutes of the Christian Religion*, bk. 4, ch. 16, tr. F. L. Battles, LCC, vol. 21 (Philadelphia, 1960), pp. 1324–1359. François Wendel, *Calvin: The Origins and Development of his Religious Thought*, tr. P. Mairet (London, 1963), pp. 322–329, described Calvin's "adventurous exegesis" of scripture in his efforts to refute the Anabaptists.

[18] Fisher, *Christian Initiation: The Reformation*, pp. 112–117.

In sixteenth-century England, disputes over the proper role of sponsors were common, but the institution emerged with its godparental dimension intact. The Reformed party within the Anglican church, the Puritans, took the lead from Calvin and John Knox in arguing that parents might—indeed should—sponsor their own children, but their efforts did not dislodge the traditional godparent figure, which survived in a Protestant form, shorn of significant spiritual kinship and of a serious coparental bond.[19]

Many Catholic reformers shared the Protestant uneasiness with sponsorship as it was practiced in late medieval society, particularly its marital complications. Indeed, a provincial council at Prague in about 1346 had listed an astounding twenty combinations of people who could not marry because of sponsorship at baptism or confirmation.[20] This complex web of marital impediments arising out of spiritual kinship invited litigation, fraud, and transgression of the rules. But in the classic pattern of Catholic reform in the sixteenth century, the perceived abuses were attacked without jettisoning the institution itself.

Usually, Catholic partisans in the sixteenth century defended the legitimacy of sponsorship within its medieval contours while attempting to eliminate the widely acknowledged abuses, particularly by restricting the marital impediments to a smaller number of participants. Thus, in November 1563, a canon of the Council of Trent ratified the institution, but limited the number of sponsors to one or at most two persons. In addition, the Council restricted the spiritual kinship contracted in baptism to (1) that binding the sponsor to the baptizee and to the baptizee's natural parents and (2) that binding the baptizing priest to the baptizee and the latter's natural parents.[21] In the official decree, the Council avoided any mention of the historical origins of sponsorship or its evolution across time.

In 1566 Pope Pius V issued the *Roman Catechism* in order to provide the parish clergy with a systematic explanation of the vast work of doctrinal clarification and institutional reform carried out by the Council. In part 2, chapter 1, sections 26–30, the *Roman Catechism* treated the institution of baptismal sponsors, whose historical origins were discussed tangentially. Thus the *Catechism* referred briefly to the

[19] Geoffrey W. Bromiley, *Baptism and the Anglican Reformers* (London, 1953), pp. 126–133.

[20] Mansi 26:95–96.

[21] Council of Trent, session 24, *Canones super reformatione circa matrimonium*, canon 2, in *Conciliorum oecumenicorum decreta*, ed. Joseph Alberigo, 3rd ed. (Bologna, 1973), p. 757.

apocryphal letter of Pope Higinus, and it cited the comments of the pseudo-Dionysius in order to describe the pedagogical duties sponsors had to fulfill as their spiritual child matured. The *Catechism* therefore implied that the practice had originated in postapostolic times, and made no effort to trace it directly to the New Testament or the apostles. It asserted explicitly that sponsorship was justified "from the most ancient custom of the Catholic Church," and that the marital impediments "had been instituted most wisely by the Holy Church."[22]

Neither the Council of Trent nor the *Roman Catechism* declared that the presence of a sponsor was essential to the administration of baptism. If it was not possible to have a sponsor, the ritual could nevertheless be performed. Thus the Catholic position in the later sixteenth century rested the legitimacy of a purified sponsorship on the church's "ancient custom" and suggested a date of origin in the late first or second century. But the retention of even a restricted range of marital impediments arising out of sponsorship meant that post-Tridentine Roman Catholic canon law and theology continued to have a pronounced interest in the consequences of sponsorship for marriage.

In spite of the religious turmoil of the sixteenth century, the institution of sponsorship, revised in varying degrees, remained part of the shared heritage of the major churches, the chief dividing line between Protestant and Catholic versions being the marital consequences. On the issue of the historical origins of the institution, the Catholic and Protestant positions involved no significant difference, for each believed that at some time between the end of the apostolic age and A.D. 150 the church introduced the sponsor to compensate for the infant's inability to cooperate actively in baptism. Some commentators, with an eye to contemporary Anabaptists, also suggested that the sponsor could serve as a witness to the fact of baptism. Thus the continuing need for such a person in connection with infant baptism justified the survival of sponsorship in the major religious traditions of sixteenth-century Europe.

In the seventeenth and eighteenth centuries, sponsorship continued to be an important social event in both Catholic and Protestant Europe, although by the late eighteenth century it was in obvious decline in most Protestant societies.[23] Sponsorship still entailed expenditures

[22] *Catechismus romanus*, pt. 2, ch. 1.26–30, in *Catecismo romano*, ed. Pedro Martin Hernandez, BAC, vol. 158 (Madrid, 1956), pp. 370–375.

[23] Early modern baptismal sponsorship and its social significance are largely *terra incognita*, but see Abbé Berthet, "Un réactif social: le parrainage. Du xvie siècle à la Révolution: Nobles, bourgeois et paysans dans un bourg perché du Jura," *AESC* 1 (1946):43–50; Karel Fojtik, "Die Inhalts- und Funktionswandlungen der Gevatterschaft

for gifts and feasts and served to create enduring bonds of formal friendship among the participants—and, at least in Catholic Europe, marital impediments as well. But baptismal sponsorship and its social consequences continued to have critics in both religious camps, in part because neither the Protestant Reformation nor the Catholic Reform had succeeded fully in reshaping the late medieval pattern of sponsorship that both had inherited.

According to John Bossy, the Catholic counterreformers attempted to make the parish the primary focus of religious life, a policy that demanded that competing religious institutions (confraternities, guilds, and family practices) be curtailed or abolished. As a result, baptismal kinship, particularly coparenthood, was perceived by Catholic critics as a potentially divisive force in parish life and efforts were made to curb its influence. However, the Catholic counterreformers had only limited success in the face of entrenched lay desire to use sponsorship for social purposes.[24]

In the other camp, the continuing stream of Protestant criticism took a rather different direction. Spiritual kinship was not a major problem after its vigorous rejection by Luther, but the expense, revelry, and breaches of decorum associated with popular baptismal celebrations drew the ire of ecclesiastical and political authorities. Because of this, sumptuary laws that limited the number of sponsors, the number of guests at feasts, and the cost of sponsors' gifts were common in Germany, but according to contemporary critics the laws were laxly enforced and exceptions were commonplace.[25]

In post-Reformation Europe, sponsorship attracted the scholarly at-

---

in Böhmen, Mähren und Schlesien vom XIV. bis zum XX. Jahrhundert," *Kontakte und Grenzen. Festschrift für Gerhard Heilfurth zum 60. Geburtstag* (Göttingen, 1969), pp. 337–343; David Sabean, "Aspects of Kinship Behaviour and Property in Rural Western Europe Before 1800," in *Family and Inheritance: Rural Society in Western Europe 1200–1800*, ed. J. Goody, J. Thirsk, and E. P. Thompson (Cambridge, 1976), pp. 96–111; Hans Boesch, *Kinderleben in der deutschen Vergangenheit*, Monographien zur deutschen Kulturgeschichte, vol. 5 (Leipzig, 1900), pp. 23–33.

[24] John Bossy, "The Counter-Reformation and the People of Catholic Europe," *Past and Present* 47 (1970):51–70, esp. 57–58; and "Blood and Baptism: Kinship, Community and Christianity in Western Europe from the Fourteenth to the Seventeenth Centuries," in *Sanctity and Secularity: The Church and the World*, ed. D. Baker (Oxford, 1973), pp. 129–143.

[25] Boesch, *Kinderleben*, pp. 27–31. Johannes F. Joachim, *Commentatio historico-iuridica de donis baptismalibus sive pecunia lustrica, vulgo von Pathen-gelde* (Halle, 1736), pp. 20–28, reviewed sumptuary laws curbing baptismal feasts and gifts. He concluded that they were ignored by ordinary people. Samuel Zuellich, *Jura conviviorum. . . .* (Iena, 1673), ch. 5, cited some sixteenth-century sumptuary legislation against excessive baptismal feasts.

tention of lawyers, theologians, and ecclesiastical historians, who issued pamphlets and larger works in which they aired their views about the origins and purposes of the institution. As a consequence of humanist philological skills put to the service of religious controversy in the sixteenth and seventeenth centuries, these scholars benefited from better editions of patristic texts, the detection of apocryphal items, a wider familiarity with early church history and, within limits, a sharper critical sense in dealing with historical matters.

Many of the published commentaries from this period are unoriginal and concerned primarily with contemporary legal matters. A favorite problem was the determination of who possessed the best legal title to the *Pathengeld*, the monetary gifts from godparents. In a pamphlet published at Strasbourg in 1715, J. H. Faber treated this issue in an ahistorical lawyer's brief, defending the position that the gifts belonged to the child under the rules of the Roman legal institution of *peculium adventitium irregulare*.[26] Faber had no original contribution to offer about the origins of sponsorship, but simply repeated the already outdated commonplace that Pope Higinus had created it in the second century to guarantee a Christian upbringing to children whose parents had died in persecution.[27]

Alongside the narrow discussion of contemporary legal issues that arose out of sponsorship, there were also, however, some seventeenth- and eighteenth-century attempts to treat the origins, essential nature, and contemporary problems of sponsorship in more comprehensive form. One of the most intriguing was published at Duisburg in 1670 by Gerhard von Mastricht, a Calvinist jurisconsult and professor whose interest in the topic had been stimulated by his own experiences as a sponsor (which he had found annoying) and as a parent seeking sponsors for his daughter.[28] He was highly critical of contemporary practices, particularly feasting and gift-giving, and he recommended that if the situation could not be remedied sponsorship should be abolished since "that rite is not necessary nor of divine institution."[29] However, he still saw it as potentially useful and had hopes for its reform. Von Mastricht was an intelligent critic of his written sources, familiar with the work of historians and philologists since

---

[26] Johannes Henricus Faber, *Dissertatio inauguralis juridica exhibens quaestiones aliquot de muneribus patrinorum, Germanice Vom Paten- oder Göttel-geld* (Strasbourg, n.d. [1715]), p. 12.

[27] Ibid., p. 8.

[28] Gerhard von Mastricht, *Susceptor; seu de susceptoribus infantium ex baptismo, eorum origine, usu et abusu schediasma* (Duisburg, 1670), pp. 1–3.

[29] Ibid., p. 89.

Erasmus. He knew that there were no extant sources prior to Tertullian's *De baptismo*, and this realization led him to surmise that the practice had been created in the second or third century for infants and only in the fourth century extended to adults.[30]

Another attempt at a comprehensive survey of sponsorship, this time from a Lutheran perspective, was published at Jena in 1678 by Johann Jacob Goetz. The eighty-eight-page pamphlet was a pedantic exercise organized according to "efficient causes, final causes, forms, and ends." In it, the author relied on von Mastricht for many points and listed the opinions of earlier scholars without any expression of preference. His aim, it seems, was a complete, if superficial, survey of sponsorship (vocabulary, historical origins, rules, and legal minutiae) leading up to contemporary Lutheran practice. His reluctance to choose among the many positions he described obscured his own view on the origins and purpose of the institution, but he did not seriously challenge the priority of infant sponsorship and its origin some time in the early postapostolic period.[31]

Yet another Lutheran view, published by Andreas Schuler at Wittenberg in 1688, was a sober, careful, critically alert approach to the issue. What distinguished Schuler's work from other contemporary treatments is his clear awareness that in antiquity *both* infants *and* adult converts had had sponsors; thus he refrains from attributing temporal priority to either, insisting that each was an early, separate office with a common purpose of providing someone to instruct and guide the new Christian.[32]

The discussion of the historical origins of sponsorship became more complex as a result of the revival of interest in the study of Hebrew in Christian circles during the sixteenth century.[33] In the process, some scholars became aware that in the rabbinic Judaism of the first and second centuries converts from paganism had been baptized in the presence of witnesses. In response to the disastrous Jewish defeat at Roman hands in A.D. 70, the rabbis became more circumspect in accepting converts. Henceforth, a committee of three (*beth dîn*) probed the proselyte's motives before permitting admission to Judaism. If a

[30] Ibid., pp. 29–30.

[31] Johann Jacob Goetz, *De iuribus patrinorum, vom Rechte der Gevattern* (Jena, 1678).

[32] Andreas Schuler, *De susceptoribus ex historia ecclesiastica* (Wittenberg, n.d. [1688]), reprinted in *Thesaurus commentationum selectarum et antiquiorum et recentiorum illustrandis antiquitatibus christianis inservientium*, vol. 2, ed. J. E. Volbeding (Leipzig, 1849), pp. 106–113; see esp. p. 109.

[33] Mitchell J. Dahood, "Hebrew Studies in the Christian Church," *New Catholic Encyclopedia*, vol. 6 (New York, 1967), pp. 976–978.

convert was accepted, he was circumcised, baptized, and offered a sacrifice (women, of course, were subject only to the second and third steps). At the baptism, in the presence of two or three witnesses, the convert was reminded of the commandments. The witnesses viewed the immersion itself and the candidate's submission to the yoke of the Law.[34]

This new information suggested to some early modern scholars, particularly from the Catholic side, that baptismal sponsorship might be rooted in Jewish practice. While von Mastricht (1670) ignored the issue of Jewish origins and Schuler (1688) explicitly denied it,[35] Goetz (1671), Joachim (1736), and Jundt (1755) were favorable, in varying degrees, to the assumption that the witnesses at Jewish proselyte baptism might have influenced early Christian sponsorship practices.[36] Indeed, Joachim argued that the practice of giving gifts (*Pathengeld*) at baptism was also derived from Jewish proselyte baptism. He believed that early Jewish converts to Christianity had brought with them these traditions of witnesses and gift-giving and he erroneously interpreted the coincidence of three witnesses in each tradition as proof of this view.[37] In fact, the presence of three sponsors at a Christian baptism was a rather late development and had not been a trait of the original institution.

In 1755 Isaac Jundt published a pamphlet at Strasbourg that synthesized the results of all these early modern reflections on the institution of sponsorship. Jundt wrote from the Catholic perspective, but was influenced by the age of *philosophes* in which he lived. He was widely acquainted with previous arguments on the subject of the origins and purpose of sponsorship, but he dismissed those scholars who defended a biblical or apostolic origin because they had been misled by apocryphal texts. Instead, on the basis of evidence from Tertullian, he leaned toward a second- or third-century date of origin.

Jundt's view of church history was organic and developmental. He believed that things had been simple in their early forms and had gradually become more complex. In his estimation, one of the early

---

[34] Michel Dujarier, *Le parrainage des adultes aux trois premiers siècles de l'Eglise. Recherche historique sur l'évolution des garanties et des étapes catéchuménales avant 313* (Paris, 1962), pp. 73–97. See also G. Lohfink, "Der Ursprung der christliche Taufe," *TQ* 157 (1976):35–54; S. Legasse, "Baptême juif des prosélytes et baptême chrétien," *BLE* 77 (1976):3–40; A. Manrique, "El bautesimo en el judaismo contemporaneo de Jesus," *El Ciudad de Dios* 89 (1976):207–220.

[35] Schuler, *De susceptoribus*, p. 107.

[36] Goetz, *De iuribus*, pp. 15–16; Joachim, *Commentatio*, pp. 8–10; Isaac Jundt, *De susceptorum baptismalium origine commentatio* (Strasbourg, 1755), pp. 35–44.

[37] Joachim, *Commentatio*, p. 13.

additions was sponsorship, which itself had been simpler in its beginnings; its contemporary complexity was the product of centuries of
development. Jundt also argued that sponsorship for adults and for
infants had begun more or less contemporaneously; he believed that
each practice was necessary and independent.[38]

Jundt's conviction that the two types of sponsorship had originated
independently and more or less simultaneously was not the conventional view in his era. Indeed, the most pervasive conceptual problem
of pre-twentieth-century scholars in dealing with sponsorship was the
failure to distinguish between sponsors for adults and those for infants. In this, the scholars' own experience of sponsorship, which ordinarily involved infants, conditioned them to read the sources with
the expectation that early Christian sponsorship would be similar in
structure and motives to what they themselves knew. Thus most
scholars either did not or could not distinguish between the two forms
of sponsorship, but rather treated them in pell-mell fashion. Furthermore, even those scholars who were aware that in the ancient church
adults had also been sponsored tended to assign primacy in origin and
importance to infant sponsorship, generally viewing the adult form as
a late imitation.

With Jundt's pamphlet of 1755, the search for the historical origins
of sponsorship and spiritual kinship had reached a plateau. The limited repertory of ancient texts, not much larger than what had been
available to Gratian in the twelfth century, had yielded all the information it could and had reinforced the conceptual framework that had
held sway since the Carolingian period. Accordingly, sponsorship was
seen as a concession to infant baptism, with adult sponsorship viewed
as an anomaly. Tertullian's *De baptismo* was recognized as the earliest
source, one that tended to set the historical parameters: that sponsorship of infants had begun in the second century and had later been
imitated for the baptism of adults. The few scholars who disagreed,
suggesting that infant and adult sponsorship were independent in origin, could not convincingly defend this view on the basis of the
sources available to them.

Finally, there are two other characteristics of the pre-nineteenth-
century study of sponsorship and spiritual kinship that must be noted.
First, all these scholars were concerned only with the situation in the
early church (certainly not beyond Augustine) and with the church in
their own day. They had no more than a sporadic interest in the
intervening centuries during which spiritual kinship had developed

[38] Jundt, *De susceptorum baptismalium.*

considerably. Second, it was also typical that these scholars had no sympathy for the social side of spiritual kinship, for its alliance-building functions. In fact, they were generally hostile to such functions in their own society and disapproved of feasting, friendships, marital impediments, and other expressions of solidarity as incompatible with the purely spiritual and pedagogical sponsoring institution they wished to encourage. Thus it was only in the later nineteenth and twentieth centuries that new evidence and new attitudes would open the way for a reexamination of sponsorship and spiritual kinship.

TWO

HISTORIOGRAPHY SINCE THE 1880s:
THE FOUR TRADITIONS

Between 1755 and about 1880 no significant advances were made in
the understanding of baptismal sponsorship and spiritual kinship as
historical phenomena.[1] The churches in Europe were on the defensive.
The Enlightenment, followed by anticlerical revolutions and confis-
cations of ecclesiastical property in the late eighteenth and the nineteenth centuries, had disrupted the traditional intellectual life in most
Christian traditions. Certain kinds of historical investigations were one
casualty. Of course, there continued to be academic treatments of
sponsorship, but the legal and canonical handbooks, liturgical studies,
histories, and encyclopedias generally copied in a perfunctory way
from one another and from their seventeenth- and eighteenth-century
predecessors. Sponsorship was perceived by many to be a moribund
institution, a part of the *ancien régime*, and was given only a brief notice
in the learned literature of the day. Because of this, no major article
or monograph of the period broke new ground through a rigorous use
of old or new sources or through a reconceptualization of the problem.

However, in the 1880s a new concern with sponsorship emerged,
fueled in part by the growing secularization of society and by the hope
on the part of churchmen that the ancient church could provide
models for dealing with an increasingly hostile or indifferent environment. Other factors also fed this stream of interest, including the rise
of folklore studies, the first stirrings of anthropology, the intense investigation of church history, and the discovery of new sources.

A striking feature of modern intellectual life has been its diversity
and luxuriance. The study of sponsorship in the last century has been
marked by this diversity, as well as by a differentiation into approaches so self-contained as to be called traditions in themselves. I
have detected four such modern scholarly traditions, each of which
approaches spiritual kinship from a distinct angle of vision and often
proceeds in relative ignorance of the other three. The oldest of these

[1] Michel Dujarier, *Le parrainage des adultes aux trois premiers siècles de l'Eglise. Recherche
historique sur l'évolution des garanties et des étapes catéchuménales avant 313* (Paris, 1962), pp.
27–28.

traditions is the ecclesiastical one, pursued by liturgists, canon law-yers, ecclesiastical historians, and pastoral theologians. Its scholars have stressed the strictly religious and legal aspects of sponsorship. The second tradition has been created by folklorists and literary schol-ars who have encountered traces of baptismal kinship in their work. The third tradition, which took its characteristic shape in the 1930s, is the anthropological study of contemporary manifestations of spon-sorship and spiritual kinship, primarily in Latin America and to a lesser extent elsewhere. And finally, the most recent innovation in the approaches to spiritual kinship has been that developed by historians since about 1950. In this discipline, a growing interest in social his-tory, and particularly in family history, has drawn attention to reli-gious practices that for almost fourteen hundred years have created kinlike behavior among Christian populations.

These four traditions of scholarship have rarely paid more than cur-sory attention to one another. Thus each must be sketched separately if we are to determine the current situation in the study of baptismal sponsorship and spiritual kinship.

The Ecclesiastical Tradition

The oldest tradition of study, with roots in the Middle Ages, is the one I have called ecclesiastical. Its practitioners have stressed the for-mally religious and legal aspects of sponsorship, with a heavy empha-sis on the historical traits of the practice before the fifth century. As a result, there has been a failure within the ecclesiastical tradition to perceive any social or secular significance in sponsorship beyond that associated with marriage impediments. For liturgists, the sponsor has been a minor detail of the baptismal ritual; for canonists, spiritual kinship has been a complicating factor in the treatment of marriage law; for ecclesiastical historians, the study of sponsorship has been primarily concerned with tracing the development of ecclesiastical rules, with only a rare glance at folk practice or elaboration; and, finally, for pastoral theologians the entire institution of infant spon-sorship has been a lamentable failure from a functional perspective, giving rise to debate over whether to abolish or revive it. In view of all this, one can read widely in this tradition of scholarship, both in detailed studies and in comprehensive treatments, without gaining anything more than frustrating hints of the wider social significance of spiritual kinship.

The stirrings of renewed ecclesiastical interest in sponsorship are first discernible in the last decades of the nineteenth century. In 1880 an Englishman, Henry Browne, published an article on "Sponsors" in the *Dictionary of Christian Antiquities.*[2] In many ways, Browne's work was part of the earlier nineteenth-century compiler tradition, breaking no new ground conceptually. In particular, the author accepted the notion that sponsorship had always been focused on infants, and thus he had difficulty making sense out of those few ancient texts that referred to adult sponsorship. Likewise, he uncritically compiled texts from the second to the ninth centuries, some genuine and some apocryphal, without regard to distinctions of time or place. However, in spite of its flaws, Browne's article foreshadowed certain developments in ecclesiastical scholarship, for he returned to the practice of relying on ancient sources, however imperfectly sifted, and he treated sponsorship both seriously and sympathetically.

An even more significant development took place in France at about the same time. There, in 1881, Jules Corblet published an article in two parts entitled "Parrains et marraines. Etude liturgico-historique."[3] Corblet's work was an enthusiastic compendium of ancient, medieval, and modern source materials, often inadequately annotated. From the perspective of a historian, it had serious deficiencies: first, Corblet was uncritical about his sources; second, he had a decidedly antiquarian bent, heaping up examples from widely different times and places, with little attempt to assess them in a context; third, he failed to document his assertions adequately. However, the article's merits clearly outweigh its deficiencies, for it succeeded in breaking out of the narrow confines of contemporary nineteenth-century ecclesiastical scholarship.

Corblet avoided the preoccupation with the origins of sponsorship. Instead, he demonstrated that godparents had a continuous history from antiquity to his own day, thus implying a dynamic view of the institution—that is, that it had not emerged fully developed but had changed across time. In addition, he abandoned the pattern of using a limited range of patristic and legal texts as sources. Rather, he threw his net wide, investigating such matters as the language of sponsorship and citing examples from folklore as well as from memoirs and diaries. He was interested in and open to the social significance of sponsorship and its abiding presence in French custom and folklore. In this, Corblet's approach was similar to that of subsequent folklorists and broke

[2] Henry Browne, "Sponsors," *Dictionary of Christian Antiquities*, vol. 2 (Hartford, 1880), pp. 1923–1925.

[3] Jules Corblet, "Parrains et marraines. Etude liturgico-historique," *Revue de l'art chrétien*, 2nd series, 14 (1881):336–353; 15 (1881):26–54. Reprinted in his *Histoire dogmatique, liturgique et archéologique du sacrement de Baptême*, 2 vols. (Paris, 1881–1882).

with that of the canonists, theologians, and liturgists of the ecclesiastical tradition.

In another development, also in 1880, Peter Göbl, a Roman Catholic priest, published a history of religious instruction in the Middle Ages, with special emphasis on Germany.[4] Göbl had contemporary quarrels in mind as he wrote, since he wished to rebut Protestant accusations that the medieval church was purposely obscurantist, having no serious interest in the religious education of the laity. In reaction to attacks on church schools during Bismarck's *Kulturkampf*, he also defended the right and duty of parents to direct the religious education of their children. These polemic purposes are quite visible in the book, but they do not obscure the fact the Göbl had read widely in the sources. In particular, he drew upon the abundant late medieval literature of moral and religious instruction for laymen, such as the various expositions of the Lord's Prayer, the Creed, and the Decalogue. Furthermore, by getting outside the circle of familiar legal texts that had been enshrined in Gratian's *Decretum*, Göbl's investigations uncovered a previously overlooked phenomenon, the godparent as religious teacher and guide. This aspect of the godparent's role had lain hidden behind canonical regulations on numbers, obligations, and marriage legislation. Thus Göbl revealed a deep-rooted social and religious tradition, only cursorily touched upon in earlier scholarly work, concerning the sponsor who cooperated with parents to foster a child's moral and religious growth.

These new approaches that became evident in late nineteenth-century studies of sponsorship were not without consequences. And since that time, the centuries-old trunk of the ecclesiastical tradition has continued to produce leafy young branches. Although liturgical and canonical studies have proliferated within well-worn boundaries, without widening their perspective, a historical concern with the origins and early development of sponsorship has been more fruitful and has necessitated changes in well-established patterns of analysis. As a result, a new approach akin to that of Göbl, which I have designated as pastoral-historical, has made significant advances in the understanding of godparents in their role as religious educators.

Although the ecclesiastical tradition has not generally taken an interest in the social significance of sponsorship, its achievements in the last century in elucidating the religious, liturgical, and legal aspects of sponsorship have been remarkable. Here the location of new sources

---

[4] Peter Göbl, *Geschichte der Katechese im Abendlande vom Verfalle des Katechumenats bis zum Ende des Mittelalters* (Kempten, 1880).

has made possible a precision unattainable by earlier generations, leading to the formulation of new working hypotheses about the relation
of adult and infant sponsorship to one another. The recognition—one
might almost say the "discovery"—of the significance of the ancient
catechumenate, within which the sponsorship of adults functioned,
was a turning point as well. Indeed, much of the innovative work in
the twentieth-century ecclesiastical tradition has been rooted in these
two major developments—that is, in a considerable increase in the
number and quality of available sources on the early history of sponsorship, and in the elaboration of a new framework within which to
understand such sources.

The improvement in the number and quality of sources was incre-
mental, for since the sixteenth century there has been a prodigious
effort to edit and authenticate the records of ancient church history.
In addition, the publication of sources in difficult languages (Arabic,
Syriac, Coptic, and so on) contributed important bits of information.
Thus by the early twentieth century the dossier of texts relating to
sponsorship was fuller and more reliable than that available to earlier
researchers. And there were not merely better editions of known
sources. There were also new sources, generally made available by
identifying and/or dating known but hitherto mysterious texts.

The most crucial addition to the historical record, announced by
Eduard Schwartz in 1910 and independently confirmed by Richard
Connolly in 1916, was the recovery of the *Apostolic Tradition* by Hippolytus, composed at Rome in about A.D. 215. To accomplish this
find, both Schwartz and Connolly solved a major intellectual puzzle,
linking a series of church orders that survived in Greek, Latin, Arabic,
Coptic, and Ethiopian versions.[5] Scholars had long known that these
orders were related to one another, but no one had been able to sort
out the tangled relationships among the texts until Schwartz and Connolly demonstrated that Hippolytus' *Apostolic Tradition* was the basic
document that had been reworked and adapted in each of them. Once
this had been realized, much of the *Apostolic Tradition* could be re-
covered by a critical comparison of the texts.

The *Apostolic Tradition* illuminated many aspects of early Christian

---

[5] Jean Michel Hanssens, *La liturgie d'Hippolyte: Documents et études* (Rome, 1970), published all the church orders derived from Hippolytus' *Apostolic Tradition*, translated into
Latin and arranged in parallel columns to facilitate comparison. On the recovery of the
Apostolic Tradition, see E. Schwartz, *Über die pseudoapostolischen Kirchenordnung*, Schriften
der wissenschaftliche Gesellschaft in Strassburg, vol. 6 (Strasbourg, 1910), esp. pp. 38–
40; and Richard H. Connolly, *The So-Called Egyptian Church Order and Derived Documents*,
Texts and Studies 8/4 (Cambridge, 1916).

liturgy. In particular, it contained a comparatively full section on the sponsorship of adults and a single brief reference to the sponsorship of infants.[6] The relative weight of these references in so early a text challenged the traditional assumption that sponsorship had always been primarily a practice for infants. Thus the secure identification of the *Apostolic Tradition* and its various adaptations in fourth- and fifth-century church orders helped to rejuvenate the study of ancient sponsorship.

The recovery of Hippolytus' text was revolutionary, but three other textual finds were also important. The discovery in 1884 of a first-person account by the nun Egeria, who traveled in the Near East in the late fourth century and who had an intense interest in liturgical matters, threw light on the sponsorship of adults at Jerusalem.[7] Later, in 1932 and 1933, Alphonse Mingana published some previously un-known Syriac catechetical homilies by Theodore of Mopsuestia, a fourth-century theologian and bishop, which also illuminated adult sponsorship.[8] And finally in 1957 Antoine Wenger published eight Greek catechetical homilies by John Chrysostom, who had delivered them at Antioch late in the fourth century.[9] These homilies further swelled the dossier on adult sponsorship in the ancient church.

Of course, the discovery of new sources does not by itself necessar-ily lead to major conceptual changes, for a new source can serve merely to confirm existing patterns of interpretation. However, in this instance the new sources were important because the *Apostolic Tradi-tion* and its derivatives undermined the belief, unchallenged since the Carolingian period, that sponsorship had always centered on infants. Instead, the sponsorship of adults was most prominent in these newly discovered texts and infant sponsorship was a secondary and distinct matter. Scholars had long known that the ancient church tested and trained its converts in a catechumenate, a probationary period that

[6] Hippolytus, *The Apostolic Tradition*, chs. 15–20, ed. Bernard Botte, SC, vol. 11[bis] (Paris, 1968), pp. 68–81. The sponsorship of infants was mentioned only briefly in ch. 21, p. 80.

[7] Egeria, *Itinerarium*, ed. A. Franceschini and R. Weber, CCSL, vol. 175 (Turnhout, 1965), pp. 29–103.

[8] *Commentary of Theodore of Mopsuestia on the Lord's Prayer and on the Sacraments of Baptism and the Eucharist*, tr. Alphonse Mingana, Woodbrooke Studies, vol. 6 (Cambridge, 1933), pp. 24–69; the Syriac manuscript of Theodore's catechetical sermons was reproduced photographically with a French translation in *Les homélies catéchétiques de Théodore de Mop-sueste*, ed. and tr. Raymond Tonneau and Robert Devreesse, ST, vol. 145 (Vatican City, 1949).

[9] John Chrysostom, "Second catechetical sermon," in *Huit catéchèses baptismales inédites*, ed. Antoine Wenger, SC, vol. 50 (Paris, 1957), pp. 141–143.

could last as long as three years. But what the *Apostolic Tradition* indicated was that sponsors of adult converts were active during this
catechumenate and that their role was quite different from that of the
sponsors of infants. The centrality of the catechumenate, and of adult
sponsorship within it, was therefore an idea that led to a fundamental
rethinking of the whole matter of sponsorship in the ancient church.

The implications of adult sponsorship within the context of the catechumenate were not immediately worked out, although the catechumenate itself received a good deal of attention from many perspectives.
For example, the pioneering article of Ernst Dick, "Das Pateninstitut
im altchristlichen Katechumenat," published in 1939,[10] attempted to
integrate information about ancient sponsorship into an explanation of
the roots from which the later godparent (*Pate*) had emerged after the
fifth century. In this article, Dick noted that after centuries of controversy there was no likelihood of discovering a specific "origin" for the
institution of sponsorship, of pinpointing a particular creator or creative moment. Instead, he was satisfied that the institution originated
in custom during the second century, citing the earliest secure reference to it in the sources, Tertullian's *De Baptismo*, chapter 18, written
about A.D. 206, which referred to an already existing practice of sponsoring infants.

Dick argued that the "godparent," as distinct from the sponsor,
emerged only after A.D. 450, and he attempted to sort out three
strands within early baptismal and sponsoring practice that he believed had contributed to the godparent of later times. First, relying
on the *Apostolic Tradition* and its allied texts, Dick described a figure
he called the *Katechumenatzeuge* (the catechumenate witness), a Christian in good standing with the church who testified that an adult pagan
seeking entry was fit, morally and otherwise, for admission to the first
stage of Christian initiation, the catechumenate. In order for the pagan
adult to advance to the next stage, the competentate, a period of intense preparation immediately before baptism, a witness was also required to testify to his satisfactory behavior during the catechumenate.
The *Katechumenatzeuge* had no role at the actual baptism, but there is
fourth- and fifth-century evidence that he or she was present at the
ceremony.[11] Second, in baptism itself, a helper (*Taufhelfer*), often a
deacon or deaconess, accompanied the baptizee to guide him or her
through the ritual acts and responses. The helper may also have given
some postbaptismal instruction to adults who for any reason had not

[10] *Zeitschrift für katholische Theologie* 63 (1939):1–49.
[11] Ibid., pp. 3–40.

been properly instructed during the catechumenate and competentate. Dick saw in this person a second root of the later godparent.[12] Third, from a very early period children were baptized in a rite designed for adults. But because of their youth they needed someone to act and respond for them, a *Sprecher* in Dick's terms, who was usually but not always one of the parents of the child.[13]

Dick's conclusion was important for the conceptualization of the problem: "In the course of this presentation, three roots of our contemporary institution of baptismal sponsorship have come into view, which are carefully to be kept separate because originally they had nothing to do with one another."[14] Thus Dick concluded that in the ancient church there were two separate forms of sponsorship, one for adults and another for infants, and that neither was identical to the familiar godparenthood of medieval and modern Christianity.

Dick's article was by no means perfect. In the first place, it failed to give serious attention to the possibility that the use of sponsors was influenced by Jewish precedents and attitudes. Furthermore, Dick paid little attention to the stages of development in the catechumenate itself, and retrojected later formalized stages into the second and third centuries, when the preparation of an adult for baptism was more fluid than it had become by the fourth and fifth centuries. Finally, the influence of the article was blunted by its appearance at the outbreak of World War II. Yet in spite of all this, Dick's work set the discussion of sponsorship on new, fruitful paths and has had considerable influence on German scholarship on the topic.

In 1951 Derrick Sherwin Bailey published *Sponsors at Baptism and Confirmation: An Historical Introduction to Anglican Practice.* This broad historical survey was motivated by an opinion, expressed at the Anglican Church's Lambeth Conference of 1948, that "it would be a valuable guide for future practice if research were made into the history of godparents and the functions assigned to them in the Church, particularly in early times."[15]

As a practical matter, Bailey's pastoral interests did not detract from his book. Although apparently unaware of Dick's article, he came to some of the same conclusions, including the necessity of treating adult sponsorship separately from infant sponsorship. He traced in systematic fashion the origins and liturgical functions of sponsors, sketched

---

[12] Ibid., pp. 40–45.
[13] Ibid., pp. 45–48.
[14] Ibid., p. 48.
[15] Derrick S. Bailey, *Sponsors at Baptism and Confirmation: An Historical Introduction to Anglican Practice* (New York, 1951), p. vii.

out the development of godparents down to the Reformation, described the accumulation of formal regulations governing the institution, and summarized the theology of sponsorship as it had been formulated by Augustine of Hippo.

Bailey's book is a solid, competent work in the ecclesiastical tradition, heavily influenced by canonical approaches to sponsorship. His sources for the medieval phase of development are primarily legal and normative, and the questions he poses are of the same sort, as the titles of some of his book's subdivisions indicate: "Qualifications and Disqualifications for Sponsorship," "The Number of Sponsors Permitted to each Candidate," and so on. One such subdivision has the promising title "Relations between Sponsor and Candidate," but in its nineteen pages no relationship aside from that favorite one of the canonists, spiritual kinship and its influence on marriage, is treated. Nevertheless, Bailey is unusual in his attitude toward spiritual kinship, for, unlike Roman Catholic scholars, he is not predisposed to accept it. Indeed, he actually dismisses it as the "artificial and unreasonable doctrine of *cognatio spiritualis*."[16] He does, however, share the ecclesiastical tradition's lack of interest in the social significance of sponsorship—that is, in its creation of a form of kinship and in the social values and personal emotions underlying its marital prohibitions.

In sum, Bailey's book is a good expression of the strengths of the ecclesiastical tradition's treatment of sponsorship and is rather more wide-ranging and historical in its approach than many others. But it shares the weaknesses of this tradition as well: a tendency to adopt a strictly legal focus; an indifference to the social impact of sponsorship, aside from its marital prohibitions; and an inability to transmit to the reader any sense of the force and life that must have characterized so ancient and widespread a practice.

The most recent expansion of the ecclesiastical tradition in the study of sponsorship has been the pastoral-historical approach. This recognizes that from its origins in the ancient church sponsorship has been associated with the religious education and moral formation of new Christians, though in fact those functions have tended in many historical circumstances to atrophy, to become, as Stenzel noted, a "liturgical lie."[17] Such was the case in the nineteenth century. Thus Paul Drews spoke for many when he wrote in 1907 that "some among those

---

[16] Ibid., p. 94.

[17] Alois Stenzel, *Die Taufe. Eine genetische Erklärung der Taufliturgie*, Forschungen zur Geschichte der Theologie und des innerkirchlichen Lebens, vols. 7 and 8 (Innsbruck, 1957), p. 297.

who recognize that it is practically an empty form are in favor of abolishing it altogether, while others would have it reformed and made once again a living reality."[18] In a similar vein, the Roman Catholic liturgical scholar Bernard Botte, commenting in 1963 on the sponsorship of adult baptizees, remarked that "clearly sponsorship in the baptism of adults has become a formality which does not amount to very much, rather like the sponsorship at confirmation, which no longer has any sense as it is practiced by us."[19]

Calls for the rejuvenation of the sponsor's religious and educational role have been a periodic phenomenon, often without much practical issue. Inertia has usually been sufficient to preserve a practice that does little good, but no obvious harm either. However, the postwar liturgical movement within Roman Catholicism fostered an impatience with rites having no evident purpose or clear meaning. Thus, as part of a general effort to rethink and recast the baptismal ceremonies, a serious attempt began during the late 1950s to revitalize the sponsor's role, an effort that had some success at the Second Vatican Council. Since it was a conviction generally shared by the liturgists that their task would be more successful if grounded in careful historical investigation, a by-product of the ferment of liturgical reform was a series of scholarly studies on the origins and early development of sponsorship, particularly by Roman Catholic scholars in France and Belgium.

The impulse behind these studies was essentially practical and pastoral, a conviction that in the increasingly dechristianized societies of industrial western Europe, a mature and convinced Christian godparent could once again fulfill a significant role. In the view of Marie-Magdeleine van Molle, for example, a renewed practice of sponsorship could provide support for converts and for young Christians in societies whose institutions are indifferent or even hostile to Christian beliefs and values.[20] The works inspired by such views were often as much pastoral as historical, but they were generally buttressed with adequate, and in some cases, outstanding historical research. As a consequence, in the last twenty years the historical role of the sponsor as a factor in religious education and moral formation has been clearly delineated.

[18] Paul Drews, "Taufpaten," in *Realencyklopaedie für protestantische Theologie und Kirche*, vol. 19 (1907), p. 450.

[19] Bernard Botte, review of Michel Dujarier's *Le parrainage des adultes aux trois premiers siècles de l'Eglise*, in *Bulletin de théologie ancienne et médiévale* 9 (1962–65):319.

[20] Marie-Magdeleine van Molle, "Les fonctions du parrainage des enfants en occident. Leur apogée et leur dégradation (du vie au xe siècle)," *Paroisse et liturgie* 46 (1964):121–146.

The research in this area has been characterized by thoroughness, by a systematic approach, and by a careful distinction between adult and infant sponsorship. The two most substantial studies both appeared in 1962. In the first, Michel Dujarier investigated the sponsorship of adults prior to A.D. 313, gathering a dossier of all relevant source texts for that period, classifying them geographically and chronologically, and subjecting them to a careful analysis. Another researcher, Thierry Maertens, analyzed the development of the catechumenate and the baptismal rituals from a pastoral viewpoint—seeking to determine what they were originally intended to accomplish and which historical factors governed and conditioned their evolution. Although he stressed the Jewish background and the earliest period, he also sketched out the major developments until the ninth century.[21]

In addition to these two books, research carried out under the inspiration of Dujarier and Maertens probed other aspects of sponsorship, with a conscious effort to be systematic. On adult sponsorship, Bernard de Guchteneëre wrote a dissertation in 1962 (*"Le parrainage des adultes aux ive et ve siècles de l'église"*) that continued Dujarier's investigations into the period after A.D. 313. L. Roques wrote an unpublished essay in 1961 on *"Le parrainage des adultes d'après les Homélies catéchétiques de Théodore de Mopsueste."* Infant sponsorship was treated in parallel fashion by Christiane Brusselmans (*"Les fonctions de parrainage des enfants aux premières siècles de l'Eglise"*), Marie-Magdeleine van Molle (*"Les fonctions de parrainage des enfants, en Occident, de 550 à 900"*), and Louise Bonnet (*"Les fonctions de parrainage d'après les homélies de St. Césaire d'Arles"*). Unfortunately, much of this research has remained unpublished and there may be other works that I have not located.

The results gained by the pastoral-historical approach have been significant for the understanding of the role of the godparent as a religious educator. Because of this research, certain crucial distinctions, hitherto neglected, have been carefully drawn. For example, contrary to the tendency to lump them together, the sponsorship of adults was investigated separately by Dujarier, de Guchteneëre, and Roques, while the very different practice of infant sponsorship was treated by Brusselmans and van Molle. And the background of the institution—more precisely, its prehistory—was sought in Jewish and New Testament sources, with interesting, if not entirely convincing results, by Maertens and Dujarier. Finally, Maertens also put forth

---

[21] Dujarier, *Le parrainage*; Thierry Maertens, *Histoire et pastorale du rituel du catéchuménat et du baptême*, Paroisse et liturgie, Collection de pastorale liturgique, vol. 56 (Bruges, 1962).

the view that sponsorship was not a static and insignificant detail of the baptismal liturgy. On the contrary, he argued that in the early Middle Ages a conscious restructuring of the baptismal liturgy gave the godparent a central role: "The ritual of entry of an infant into the Church became a ritual of presentation of an infant by the god-parents."[22]

Nevertheless, in spite of the real merit of the works written from this pastoral-historical perspective, certain shortcomings and lacunae must be noted. First, all these works share the relative isolation of the ecclesiastical tradition in examining sponsorship. The authors did not set as their task any aspect of sponsorship beyond the liturgical and pedagogical. They took no account of folkloric or anthropological work. And, in a mirror image of that insularity, I have never found these solid, careful works cited by folklorists or anthropologists, some of whom could have benefited from a firmer grasp of the ecclesiastical background to their own researches on sponsorship. Indeed, I have not found these works cited by any scholar outside the ecclesiastical tradition. Second, the pastoral-historical research has not had wide diffusion because much of it has never been published. Third, the scholars who have cultivated this approach have proceeded on the working assumption that after the fifth century sponsorship went into a profound decay, which modern efforts are intended to remedy. This guiding image of a golden age sliding into decline is expressed in the very title of an article by van Molle, "*Les fonctions du parrainage des enfants en Occident. Leur apogée et leur dégradation (du vi^e au xe siècle).*" This unwillingness to take seriously the development of sponsorship in the Middle Ages and beyond is readily comprehensible from these scholars' perspective, but it does limit the usefulness of their research for others working outside the ecclesiastical tradition, scholars who are often interested in modern manifestations of spiritual kinship, as well as in its wider social ramifications.

The Literary and Folkloric Tradition

The ecclesiastical tradition has sought its sources within well-defined limits, primarily liturgical and legal texts. For the ancient and early medieval periods, the same narrow selection of sources recurs in arti-cles and books as the basis of scholarly research. However, spiritual kinship in the medieval West was not reflected exclusively in the lit-urgy and the law, important as these areas were. In addition, from

[22] Maertens, *Histoire*, p. 232.

the early Middle Ages until modern times, baptismal kinship has also figured both in literature and in folklore.

Before the twelfth century, nonlegal and nonliturgical sources alluding to spiritual kinship are modest in number but certainly not negligible: saints' lives, sermons, chronicles, popular tales, even charters and financial accounts yield their harvest. Indeed, I have discovered more than three hundred references to baptismal kinship in Latin sources before A.D. 900, and new additions to the dossier are not unusual. Furthermore, during the twelfth century the body of relevant source material broadens and deepens significantly, so much so that it can be said with truth that almost every type of written source, from epic poetry and scholastic *quaestio* to personal correspondence and joke collections, touches occasionally on the role of spiritual kinsmen. In addition, artistic representations of the act of sponsorship, notably in manuscript illuminations,[23] add a new dimension to our knowledge of the practice.

Such literary materials—including both those emanating from "high" culture and those of a more popular stamp—have a unique contribution to make to the understanding of spiritual kinship. This is because the liturgy and canon law were normative: they expressed in formal terms how certain things should or should not be done, but their relation to actual practice could be fluid and their scope of interest was narrow. In contrast, literary and folkloric texts reveal aspects of spiritual kinship that were not even adumbrated in the normative texts, for the church's rituals and legal prescriptions were greatly elaborated in lay society and the impact of spiritual kinship was more diverse and pervasive than a familiarity with the normative texts would indicate.

Literary texts have the potential to complement the normative texts, especially by indicating the ways in which the Christian populace shaped, adapted, elaborated, and extended the consequences of a liturgical ritual. Indeed, it is not going too far to say that in some contexts spiritual kinship escaped from ecclesiastical control and took on an existence of its own, an existence we can know not so much through official channels as through a myriad of references in other genres. In addition, literary texts can also inform us, however imperfectly, about the emotions, expectations, and frictions that spiritual kinship aroused among nobles, townsmen, and villagers.

[23] For a selection of miniatures illustrating sponsorship at baptism in manuscripts of Gratian's *Decretum*, causa 30, see vol. 3 of Anthony Melnikas, *The Corpus of the Miniatures in the Manuscripts of Decretum Gratiani*, 3 vols., Studia Gratiana, vol. 16 (Rome, 1975), pp. 941–969.

Spiritual kinship in medieval literature has drawn the attention of three kinds of scholars in the literary and folkloric tradition. Thus, students of medieval literature (editors, translators, and critics) have commented on the matter as it appeared in the texts they were studying; folklorists, who have given considerable attention to sponsorship in the period from the sixteenth to the twentieth century, have also occasionally ventured into the Middle Ages to provide background to their work; and philologists have exercised their curiosity on the terminology of spiritual kinship in both Latin and the vernaculars. These three kinds of scholars have had to deal with a large, amorphous body of medieval literary materials that touches on spiritual kinship from various perspectives.

Almost always, spiritual kinship in a literary text is a secondary matter, a detail woven into the work, or a part of its sociocultural background. There is, to my knowledge, no freestanding medieval written work entitled "On Sponsors," no medieval author who set out to describe systematically the spiritual kinship of his day. Hence, the study of spiritual kinship as a religious and social phenomenon in the literature of the medieval West may be compared to a large jigsaw puzzle whose pieces lie scattered in a multitude of places. And the difficulty of assembling the puzzle has been such that no one has ventured to attempt it. There is no monograph or major article that takes a synthetic view of spiritual kinship as it is reflected in medieval literature, folklore, or language. But there *are* many books and articles that devote a few pages, paragraphs, or footnotes to aspects of the matter.

In the absence of specific broad-gauged treatments of spiritual kinship, one must turn to studies of baptism in medieval literature to find somewhat extended analyses of godparents. A typical study appeared in 1891 when Eugen Henninger published his *Sitte und Gebräuche bei der Taufe und Namengebung in der altfranzösischen Dichtung*, which was based on an examination of fifty-one Old French poems. Spiritual kinsmen were depicted quite often in Old French poetry and so, not surprisingly, Henninger devotes thirty-two pages specifically to "*die Paten*," the godparents, alluding to them at other points in the monograph as well.[24] Unfortunately, although the monograph gathers interesting and still useful material, it contains a number of serious flaws.

First, it must be recognized that Old French literature, dating from

---

[24] Eugen Henninger, *Sitte und Gebräuche bei der Taufe und Namengebung in der altfranzösischen Dichtung* (Halle, 1891), pp. 31–63.

the twelfth to the fifteenth centuries, was composed when sponsorship and the formal regulations governing it were already centuries old. And because Henninger was uncertain in his grasp of the liturgical and canonical norms governing sponsorship, his book is vague or inaccurate with regard to aspects of the background to the poems. Second, Henninger had unearthed more material in his fifty-one poems than he was willing or able to analyze; thus there is much unassimilated data in the book. Third, the author proceeds on the expressed premise that the poets were careful, accurate observers; consequently he makes no serious attempt to test their evidence against that provided by other contemporary sources. Because of this, there is a pervasive uncertainty about which statements in the poetry faithfully reflect the normative practices of the church, which are folk elaborations, and which are simply poetic license. Fourth, and most damaging, is a problem that mars many studies of spiritual kinship. The author apparently did not realize that baptismal sponsorship created *two* bonds, one between the sponsor and the sponsored (the godparental bond) and the other between the sponsor and the sponsored's parents (the coparental bond). In fact, he virtually ignores the coparental bond, an oversight probably rooted in his own experience. By the nineteenth century, the bond of godparent to godchild had virtually eclipsed the coparental bond in Europe, and Henninger retrojects this pattern into the high Middle Ages, where it was not in fact appropriate.

Another discussion of baptism in medieval literature appeared in 1936, when Antonie Tuschen published her dissertation, "*Die Taufe in der altfranzösischen Literatur*," a work that was well conceived and built on a broad data base. In it, Tuschen examines all the surviving Old French literature to the fifteenth century, which she subjects to a thorough and intelligent treatment. She has a firmer grasp of the baptismal liturgy than Henninger, although she treats "*die Paten*" more briefly, devoting about five pages to the topic, with scattered references elsewhere in the book.[25] Significantly, Tuschen notes that sponsors received different treatment according to literary genre; for example, spiritual kinsmen were prominent in folk epic and courtly epic, but ignored in strictly religious vernacular literature, such as translations of saints' lives. Yet in spite of Tuschen's comprehensiveness and her systematic treatment of baptism, the monograph remains flawed in several ways.

[25] Antonie Tuschen, *Die Taufe in der altfranzösischen Literatur* (Ph.D. diss., Rheinische Friedrich Wilhelms Universität zu Bonn, 1936), pp. 61–66.

Like Henninger, Tuschen does not make clear the distinction between godparent and coparent, and she treats the earlier history of the institution of sponsorship, which had shaped the practices reflected in the Old French literature, in a vague and cursory way. Thus, in traditional fashion, neither Henninger nor Tuschen see much significance in the *social* importance of spiritual kinship. The former detects only gift-giving as a social consequence of sponsorship,[26] while the latter devotes just a few lines to the marriage taboos that impeded the sexual union of spiritual kin.[27]

Aside from works like those of Henninger and Tuschen, the attention accorded to medieval spiritual kinship by scholars of literature and folklore has been piecemeal, incidental to some other scholarly project. The consequences of this situation are important, for in the present state of research on medieval spiritual kinship arising out of baptism, despite the fact that one can find adequate synthetic treatments of the normative aspects of the institution, it is all but impossible for a modern scholar to respond easily or with confidence to the questions "How did the participants feel about spiritual kinship?" and "How was behavior shaped by spiritual kinship?"

Three further observations about the present state of literary scholarship on spiritual kinship are in order. First, although most people know what a godparent is, the coparent is a more mysterious figure to Western Europeans and North Americans. Editors and translators of medieval texts often feel obliged to explain the term in some way (when they don't misunderstand it as a mere synonym for godparent). However, such explanations seldom pass beyond mere identification in terse, dictionarylike fashion. Second, sometimes the medieval popular understanding of sponsorship is sufficiently puzzling to moderns to demand brief, isolated comments as well. For instance, in the thirteenth-century German epic *Meier Helmbrecht*, lines 480–486, a peasant boy claims to be "of noble kin" because a knight had sponsored him at baptism. Clair Hayden Bell, the translator of *Meier Helmbrecht*, glosses the boy's assertion as follows:

> The relationship of godfather to godchild was highly esteemed in the middle ages, and was placed on a level with blood relationship. The popular belief still lingers in portions of Germany that qualities—particularly moral characteristics—pass from the godfather to his godchild. Cf. Sprenger, "Zum Meier Helmbrecht,"

[26] Henninger, *Sitte*, pp. 60–63.
[27] Tuschen, *Die Taufe*, pp. 61–62.

Germ XXXVII (1892), 414. This idea of heritage from the god-parent is expressed again below, vss. 1374ff.[28]

This notion that a spiritual father can transmit moral and spiritual qualities to his child is widespread, but has rarely been treated in any depth or explained within the full context of spiritual kinship.[29] Third, scholars often find only what they are seeking and miss what they are not predisposed to notice. Since the social significance of baptismal sponsorship has not traditionally been a topic of research in the ecclesiastical or the literary and folkloric traditions, scholars in these traditions are thus ill-prepared to recognize it when they encounter its manifestations. For instance, in several of the beast epics, including the *Ysengrimus*,[30] the *Ecbasis captivi*,[31] and the *Roman de Renart*,[32] certain characters address one another in the language of spiritual kinship, calling one another *patrinus/matrina*, *compater/commater*, *compère/commère*, or *gossip/gossip*, depending on the language of the text. Why the characters do this is not evident.

In their edition of the Middle English poem, *The Fox and the Wolf*, J.A.W. Bennett and G. V. Smithers encountered such a mode of address and were aware of similar behavior in other medieval literary texts. Yet the editors did not know what to make of the usage and decided that since the characters were not literally godkin to one another, the terminology was probably meaningless: "Presumably, no specific form of kinship was in the minds of the French and English poet."[33] However, the poet's use of spiritual kinship language was probably not so otiose as the editors thought, for spiritual kinship terminology can have social implications even when it is not used strictly for actual godkin. For instance, in areas of the modern world where baptismal sponsorship is still a living institution, addressing as "cofather" one who is not in fact related by spiritual kinship can be a form of respectful, honorific language that carries with it an invitation

[28] Clair Hayden Bell, *Peasant Life in Old German Epics* (New York, 1931), p. 139.

[29] See the brief comments in A. Bastow, "Peasant Customs and Superstitions in Thirteenth Century Germany," *Folklore* 47 (1936):320 and 327.

[30] *Ysengrimus*, ed. Ernst Voigt (Halle, 1884), bk. 3, l. 649; bk. 4, l. 463; bk. 6, l. 204 (*patrinus*); bk. 4, ll. 164 and 929 (*compater*); bk. 7, l. 13 and passim (*matrina*).

[31] *Ecbasis cuiusdam captivi per Tropologiam*, l. 496, ed. and tr. Edwin H. Zeydel, University of North Carolina Studies in the Germanic Languages and Literatures, vol. 46 (Chapel Hill, 1964), p. 50. Zeydel translates *patrinus* as "uncle," p. 16.

[32] See, for instance, branches 2–6 of *Le Roman de Renart*, ed. Mario Roques, CF, vol. 79 (Paris, 1951), ll. 3474, 4464, 4499 (*comère*); ll. 3493, 3507, 3512, 3516, 3521, 3570, and so on (*conpere*); l. 4545 (*filloil*); l. 4477 (*fillaus*).

[33] *The Fox and the Wolf*, ll. 115–116, ed. J.A.W. Bennett and G. V. Smithers, *Early Middle English Verse and Prose* (Oxford, 1974), p. 301.

to nonaggression and serves to integrate an outsider into the group.[34] Investigation along those lines might further illuminate the significance of the practice in the medieval beast epics and other literature.

From this brief illustration, it can be seen that the study of spiritual kinship in medieval imaginative literature holds out the promise of precious insight into the feelings, motives, and behavior of the spiritual kinsmen themselves. Clearly, the author of such a study would have to possess a firm grasp of the liturgical and canonical norms governing sponsorship in the high and late Middle Ages. He or she would also need to be sensitive to the folk elaborations that occasionally took the practice far beyond the ecclesiastical norms. And finally, such a scholar would have to be familiar with the basic contours of spiritual kinship in modern anthropological literature, which would provide suggestions about what to seek and how to interpret data, while at the same time remembering that medieval spiritual kinship should not be forced into the mold of contemporary Latin American variations. Since medieval society was not monolithic, it would be best (and also more manageable) to investigate spiritual kinship within specific geographical areas (England, the Rhineland, the Langue d'oc, the Langue d'oil, and so on), for which both Latin and vernacular texts could be mined for information. When such studies have been carried out, we shall be in a better position to assess spiritual kinship as a basic social reality in medieval society. Until then, this entire subject, particularly in its high and late medieval forms, will be known only in piecemeal fashion.

Although the fairy godmother is a relatively late literary invention, first appearing in a seventeenth-century retelling of the Cinderella story,[35] spiritual kinsmen have played a role in folk tales and folk practices since at least the late Carolingian period. And in spite of the wave of secularization that has washed over modern European societies, spiritual kinsmen (godparents and godchildren, in particular) are still familiar figures, although their social role is sometimes quite attenuated and the folk practices associated with them appear more and more quaint. However, in southern Europe and in Latin America, the spiritual kin continue to have a prominent place in both folklore and

[34] Julian Pitt-Rivers, *The Fate of Shechem or the Politics of Sex: Essays in the Anthropology of the Mediterranean* (Cambridge, 1977), p. 52, saw the use of terms of spiritual kinship for mere friends as a "frivolous derivative form." For other instances where spiritual kinship terms apparently mean "friend," see Wilhelm Grimm, "Altdeutsche Gespräche. Nachtrag," *Kleinere Schriften*, vol. 3 (Berlin, 1883), pp. 514–515.

[35] Roger L. Green, "Shakespeare and the Fairies," *Folklore* 73 (1962):99–100.

folk custom, particularly in association with life crises such as birth
and its companion, baptism.

Since at least the time of the brothers Grimm, folklorists have been
attentive to the significance of sponsorship.[36] In fact, they have collected many instances of local practices and beliefs that are rooted in
sponsorship and spiritual kinship. Without by any means exhausting
the list, one can cite as examples the recording of local traditions on
the choice of sponsors, the tendering of the invitation to sponsors, the
procession to and from church, the gift-giving, the long-term duties,
and the behavior expected of spiritual kinsmen toward one another.[37]
The accumulation of discrete facts about sponsorship is bewildering
in its variety, and its apparent arbitrariness and confusion is compounded by the scarcity of attempts to account for the facts in some
interpretive pattern.

In addition to the accumulation of information, there have been
some attempts by folklorists to treat aspects of sponsorship syntheti-
cally. For instance, in 1958 Reinhold Staudt completed an interesting
and rather comprehensive dissertation on *Patenbrauch* in Hesse, which
was traditionally a Lutheran region.[38] The *Atlas der deutschen Volkskunde*
had gathered responses to questions in about eight hundred villages in
Hesse on folk practices, including sponsorship, and in 1955 Staudt
had circulated a second questionnaire in selected villages to get some
perspective on the changes in sponsoring customs that had taken place
during the twentieth century. He also used archival material, notably

[36] See Jacob Grimm, "Über Schenken und Geben," *Kleinere Schriften*, vol. 2: *Abhandlungen zur Mythologie und Sittenkunde* (Berlin, 1865), pp. 191–195, on gifts from
godparents.

[37] See, for example, O. Schulte, "Taufsitten und Bräuche in einem oberhessischen
Orte vor 250 Jahren und heute," *Hessische Blätter für Volkskunde* 7 (1908): 65ff; Heinrich
Schauerte, "Volkskundliche zur Taufe," in *Europäische Kulturverflechtungen im Bereich der
volkstümlichen Überlieferung. Festschrift zum 65. Geburtstag Bruno Schiers* (Göttingen, 1967),
pp. 46–48 and passim; François Lebrun, "Le *Traité des superstitions* de Jean-Baptiste
Thiers. Contributions à l'ethnographie de la France du xviiᵉ siècle," *Annales de Bretagne
et des Pays de l'Ouest (Anjou, Maine, Touraine)* 83 (1976):448–449; George E. P. How,
English and Scottish Silver Spoons, 3 vols. (London, 1953), 2:76–77; Karel Fojtik, "Die
Inhalts- und Funktionswandlungen der Gevatterschaft in Böhmen, Mähren und Schlesien vom XIV. bis zum XX. Jahrhundert," in *Kontakte und Grenzen. Festschrift für Gerhard
Heilfurth zum 60. Geburtstag* (Göttingen, 1969), pp. 337–343; Marcelle Bouteiller, "Tradition folklorique et 'parentés parallèles.' Le couple parrain-marraine et ses implications
dans les lignées familiales," in *Echanges et communications. Mélanges offerts à Claude Levi-
Strauss à l'occasion de son 60ᵉᵐᵉ anniversaire*, 2 vols. (Paris and The Hague, 1970), 1:153–
161.

[38] Reinhold Staudt, *Studien zum Patenbrauch in Hessen* (Ph.D. diss., Johann Wolfgang
Goethe-Universität, Frankfurt am Main, 1958).

official regulations and correspondence between the pastors and the consistory, to carry his research back into the early modern period. Staudt's monograph is a model for studying baptismal kinship in a recent context and in a specific geographic area. However, it is certainly not a comprehensive study of baptismal sponsorship, particularly because he has very little to say about pre-sixteenth-century developments and because, in a Lutheran territory, he found almost no information on the sexual taboos that are so prominent in the Catholic and Orthodox versions.

A different approach was taken by Helga Schwarz in her 1950 dissertation.[39] In most versions of the godparent complex, the sponsor gives some sort of gift to the child on the occasion of baptism. Schwarz studied this *Taufgeld*, as she called it, concentrating on sources from the Austrian Steiermark, which were supplemented by German and Austrian historical sources from the later Middle Ages to the nineteenth century. To these she added numismatic material (there were actual medals and coins created to be used as baptismal gifts) from late antiquity to early modern times. The product of her investigations is a detailed study of monetary gifts and the folk explanations of these gifts, both of which varied considerably across time. The monograph is thorough in mustering material, but too often substitutes gathering for analysis. In addition, Schwarz made a decision about her topic which, from a historical point of view, was restrictive to the point of distortion. In modern times in the Austrian Steiermark, the *Taufgeld* is just that, money. And Schwarz defined her topic so as to investigate only monetary gifts, a choice that made sense in a money-oriented society, but that blinded her to earlier economic realities when the gift might be a cow, a piece of jewelry, or a pretty dress, and when coined money was a rather unusual gift. As a consequence, Schwarz virtually guaranteed that she would find little evidence of gifts before early modern times, even though baptismal gifts were a constant feature of sponsorship from very early on. Thus, in spite of its merits, Schwarz's study exhibits the danger of allowing modern sponsoring practices to predetermine what the scholar seeks in the past.

A third example of a folklorist's study of aspects of sponsorship focuses on eighteenth- and nineteenth-century Germany, where the invitation from the child's father to the sponsors was an occasion for the creation of folk art. The letter of invitation (*Patenbrief*), which was elaborately decorated and was intended to be kept as a memorial of

[39] Helga Schwarz, *Das Taufgeld. Ein Beitrag zur historischen Entwicklung der Taufbräuche* (Graz, 1950).

the occasion, was the subject of Christa Pieske's extensive article of 1958.[40] In such regional and/or topical studies, folklorists have illuminated important aspects of modern sponsorship, with more or less successful forays into pre-nineteenth-century practice.

Nevertheless, valuable as the contributions of folklorists have been in recording modern practices associated with spiritual kinship, they are of limited usefulness from the perspective of a scholar interested in the origins or development of the institution. The sixteenth century was tumultuous in religious matters, and baptism, in both its theological and its practical aspects, shared in the great changes associated with the Reformation and the Counterreformation. For it was not only Protestantism that rejected important aspects of late medieval life. Catholicism also scrutinized its fifteenth-century self, found much it didn't like, and "reformed"—that is, rejected—many institutions and practices that offended contemporary sensibilities. As a result, fifteenth-century baptismal sponsorship and spiritual kinship were altered in the sixteenth century by both Protestants and Catholics. The former rejected spiritual kinship altogether and attempted to make sponsorship a more sober, serious business. In contrast, the latter curbed spiritual kinship without abolishing it, attempting to shape it for new ends. In both religious camps, there was resistance from ordinary people to whom sponsorship was an important feature of social life. However, the point to be seen here is that all modern versions of spiritual kinship were "tampered with" by the religious enthusiasms of the sixteenth century. Therefore, the findings of modern researchers, including folklorists, can not simply be retrojected into an indefinite past because the sixteenth-century "reform" of sponsorship in western Europe substantially altered medieval customs.

It is also true that the very nature of folklorists' sources limits the historical "depth" they can reach. Like cultural anthropologists, from whom they are sometimes indistinguishable, folklorists generally proceed by recording beliefs and practices that still exist or that existed in a recent past. Their data are gathered from observation and from the oral statements of informants, procedures that effectively limit research to the nineteenth and twentieth centuries. Some folklorists supplement their research by resorting to printed and archival materials, which can carry a study further into the past, but usually not beyond the sixteenth century.

The very oldest sources are folktales and proverbs that are normally

[40] Christa Pieske, "Über den Patenbrief," *Beiträge zur deutschen Volks- und Altertumskunde* 2/3 (1958):85–121.

undated and undatable until they are recorded, which may be long
after their origin. The overwhelming majority of folktales and proverbs dealing with spiritual kin were recorded between the sixteenth
and the twentieth centuries, leaving the modest number of such tales
and proverbs from medieval sources submerged in the flood of more
modern texts. Thus a study of medieval tales about spiritual kinsmen—those, for instance, in medieval collections of *exempla*—would
be a valuable contribution to our knowledge of premodern practice.
In any case, however, it must be acknowledged that the folklorists'
sources are generally not suitable for research prior to the early modern period, when sponsorship was already very old, highly elaborated,
and undergoing significant change prompted by the currents of religious reform.

In many ways, the very complexity of sponsorship and spiritual
kinship in modern times has proved a problem for folklorists, who
have had more success in gathering material than in organizing it. The
immense number of discrete facts—who is chosen, what is expected,
what is said and believed about the unrolling of events—seems at
times to imply that every region, perhaps every village, has its own
version of baptism, sponsorship, and subsequent behavior among spiritual kinsmen. In strictly folkloric study, I have found no scholar who
deals consciously and successfully with this situation of bewildering
diversity within a shared framework rooted in Christian theology and
liturgy. Instead, the major contribution of folklorists to the understanding of sponsorship and spiritual kinship in Western European
society has been the gathering of a rich body of modern sources on
folk practice and belief.

Philology is another field of study that is related to literature and
folklore in which medieval spiritual kinship regularly receives attention. In this discipline, the language of sponsorship and spiritual kinship is seen as an artifact from the past and, as such, has been made
to yield information about the institutions that gave rise to it. Philologists, or students of language, have traditionally approached the terminology of spiritual kinship from three perspectives: first, as an example of the impact of Christianity on Latin and Greek and
subsequently on the vernaculars; second, as a subset of the vocabulary
of kinship; and third, as entries in etymological dictionaries, where
the study of word origins and of semantic evolution often results in
far more than a simple definition.

Christianity had a profound cultural and religious impact upon
Greco-Roman society between the second and the sixth centuries. In
addition, Christine Mohrmann and her collaborators have demon-

strated that Christianity's penetration of classical culture was a major linguistic phenomenon as well, bringing in its wake innovations in vocabulary, style, and syntax.[41] Thus there came to be a distinctive Christian form of Latin and Greek, influenced deeply by the liturgy and the Bible as well as by the linguistic demands of new institutions and beliefs, including baptismal sponsorship for adults and for infants. Neither the classical languages nor the various vernaculars in their pre-Christian phase possessed a suitable technical terminology to describe these institutions. Hence such a terminology had to be adapted from earlier forms or created *de novo*.

Christian Latin had its most creative period between the eras of Tertullian (d. 220) and Augustine (d. 429), when a theological, sacramental, and administrative language was elaborated. Sponsors are attested from the third century, but the emergence of a *socially significant* sponsor figure and of a vocabulary suited to it occurred later than Augustine, for reasons that will be noted in a subsequent chapter. Thus, even though there is a considerable body of scholarship on early Christian Latin, the vocabulary of sponsorship and spiritual kinship has fallen outside the investigators' purview because of its relatively late emergence. Occasionally, peculiar usages have attracted attention, as when the pilgrim Egeria referred to late fourth-century sponsors at Jerusalem simply as mothers and fathers (*matres*, *patres*).[42] However, such exceptions do not alter the fact that the Latin Christian vocabulary of baptismal sponsorship and spiritual kinship has escaped systematic investigation.

The relative neglect of sponsorship vocabulary is also seen in the study of early Christian Greek. Hence Ysebaert's thorough treatment in *Greek Baptismal Terminology*, which concentrates on writers of the second and third centuries with an occasional reference to fourth-century writers, does not once mention sponsors in more than four hundred pages.[43] The reason is not difficult to surmise: the earliest clear Greek references to sponsors as spiritual fathers (*pateres pneumatikoi*) and to the sponsored as spiritual sons (*tekna pneumatika*) are in a

[41] Christine Mohrmann's more important articles on Christian Latin have been reprinted in *Etudes sur le Latin des chrétiens*, in *Storia e Letteratura*, vol. 65 (1958), vol. 87 (1961), vol. 103 (1965), and vol. 143 (1977). In spite of the breadth of topics covered in these volumes, there is no mention of the language of sponsorship or spiritual kinship.

[42] Egeria, *Itinerarium*, ch. 45.2, ch. 46.1, and ch. 46.5; see A.A.R. Bastiaensen, *Observations sur le vocabulaire liturgique dans l'Itinéraire d'Egérie*, LCP, vol. 17 (Nijmegen-Utrecht, 1962), pp. 17–19.

[43] Joseph Ysebaert, *Greek Baptismal Terminology: Its Origin and Early Development*, Graecitas Christianorum primaeva, vol. 1 (Nijmegen, 1962).

baptismal sermon of John Chrysostom from about A.D. 390, considerably after the rest of the baptismal terminology analyzed by Ysebaert had taken form.

Philologists and linguists have also been interested in the vocabulary of ancient and medieval forms of kinship, a subject that, along with its underlying institutions, is complex and thus subject to dispute for at least two reasons. First, the cultural diversity of medieval Europe, rooted in successive waves of invaders who became settlers, was considerable and yielded no uniform kinship system. Second, until rather late in the Middle Ages, most source texts refer to kinship in a learned Latin vocabulary that originated in ancient Rome and that fit medieval realities only imperfectly. Thus considerable care must be taken in determining the contemporary meaning hidden under a venerable inherited Latin kinship word that might be a mere approximation of the actual relationship in a Celtic, Germanic, or Slavic society. Fortunately, the terminology of spiritual kinship has been relatively immune to these problems, for there were no ancient pagan Latin terms to confuse matters. Rather, the primary terms of spiritual kinship were Latin neologisms created between the sixth and eighth centuries, and these words, in turn, were the direct sources for vernacular usage, with the result that there was a close fit between the learned Latin and the popular vernacular words.

Any student of medieval social life will be aware that throughout the medieval West people thought of themselves as kinsmen through the mediation of baptismal sponsorship and certain other ecclesiastical ceremonies (notably confirmation). It is therefore quite normal for studies of medieval kinship to allude in passing to sponsorship. In her treatment of Anglo-Saxon kinship Lorraine Lancaster devotes less than a page to what she calls "ritual kinsmen."[44] Joseph Depoin also gives less than a page to spiritual kin in his terminological study of "*les relations de famille au moyen âge.*"[45] Pierre Maranda's *French Kinship*, although marred by excessive jargon, is a sophisticated and ambitious attempt to provide "a tentative synthetic treatment" of French kinship as it has evolved since the ninth century. To achieve this, he uses an interesting mix of linguistic analysis and historical explanation in accounting for the evolution of kinship terms and devotes two pages to

[44] Lorraine Lancaster, "Kinship in Anglo-Saxon Society," *British Journal of Sociology* 9 (1958):239.

[45] Joseph Depoin, "Les relations de famille au moyen âge," *Société historique et archéologique de l'arrondissement de Pontoise et du Vexin* 32 (1914):54.

compère/commère and *parrain/marraine*, on which his comments are perceptive but necessarily incomplete.[46]

Not all efforts to analyze the vocabulary of spiritual kinship within the general context of kinship vocabulary have been so successful as that of Maranda. The classic study by Ernst Tappolet, *Die Romanischen Verwandtschaftsnamen* (1895), describes briefly the existence of two terms (*compater* and *patrinus*) and the "victory" of *patrinus* over its rival in the modern Romance languages, but Tappolet never explains to his readers that the two terms were not, in fact, competing synonyms but referred to very distinct aspects of spiritual kinship.[47] Indeed, the chief pitfall of linguistic studies of spiritual kinship terms has been its practitioners' failure to understand the religio-social institution that gave rise to the words, especially in relation to the important difference between the godparental and the coparental bond.[48]

The many etymological dictionaries of the modern European languages provide a mine of information and specific examples of usage for the various terms of spiritual kinship. Thus, judicious use of a source like von Wartburg's *Französisches etymologisches Wörterbuch*, which traces the influence of Latin terms on the French language, can provide information about such varied matters as the principles upon which spiritual kinship terms were formed from Latin roots, their earliest appearance in the surviving written record, and their semantic evolution.[49] But these *are* dictionaries, and from the perspective of the social historian they provide only the raw material for analysis rather than the finished product.

It can be seen, then, that the literary and folkloric tradition works with source materials that have the potential to expand our comprehension of the place that spiritual kinship held in the sentiments and values of medieval society, and to a degree that normative legal and liturgical texts can not. Unfortunately, this potential has not been realized because of the nature of the separate scholarly traditions and their own definition of what is important. The practitioners of the literary tradition in particular have not generally included questions

[46] Pierre Maranda, *French Kinship: Structure and History*, Janua Linguarum, Series practica, vol. 169 (The Hague and Paris, 1974), pp. 57–58.

[47] Ernst Tappolet, *Die Romanischen Verwandtschaftsnamen* (Strasbourg, 1895), pp. 141–145.

[48] Ann Tukey, "Kinship Terminology in the Romance Languages" (Ph.D. diss., University of Michigan, 1962), pp. 63–66.

[49] See, for example, the treatment of *"commater,"* in *Französisches etymologisches Wörterbuch*, vol. 2 (Basel, 1946), pp. 945–946; *"compater,"* ibid., pp. 973–974; *"filiolus,"* ibid., vol. 3 (Leipzig, 1934), pp. 519–521; *"patrinus,"* ibid., vol. 8 (Basel, 1958), pp. 22–23.

of kinship and social structures within their bailiwick, although they might touch on them tangentially. Furthermore, the scattered evidence on the subject, even if abundant, requires a conceptual framework before it can be made sense of, and such a framework has clearly been lacking in the literary and folkloric tradition.

The Anthropological Tradition

The anthropological tradition of studying sponsorship and spiritual kinship, by far the most active and significant in the recent twentieth century, had its roots in the middle and late nineteenth century, when the same impulses that led to the recording of European folklore also spawned an interest in the customs of "primitive" non-European peoples. In fact, the fields of folklore and cultural anthropology have retained so many points of contact that it is often difficult to assign a scholar exclusively to one tradition or the other. The study of sponsorship in the recent past or in existing societies is one of the topics shared by both traditions.

The practice of creating godparents in baptism did not, of course, cease with the end of the Middle Ages. Although the Reformation, in eliminating spiritual kinship, had initiated the slow decline of the sponsor as a figure of importance in Protestant societies, sponsorship in southern and eastern Europe and in areas of the world colonized from Iberia continued to function as an important religious and social institution into modern times. This growing difference between northern, primarily Protestant Europe, where spiritual kinship withered, and southern and eastern Europe (and their respective cultural spheres), where it flourished, had an important impact upon the anthropological tradition.

The ecclesiastical tradition of study, in its many phases, has been almost exclusively the domain of insiders—that is, of people who themselves have participated in spiritual kinship and understand it as a living thing, a set of practices that seem so normal and natural as to need little justification or to evoke much wonder. In contrast, the representatives of the anthropological tradition, particularly those writing in English, have been products of the northern European milieu, either by their culture or their training, or both. Thus the anthropological tradition of godparent study has been deeply influenced by the fact that since its beginnings in the nineteenth century its practitioners have been outsiders who do not instinctively empathize with the institution or understand its power to motivate or control its participants' behavior. Such an outsider stance is an advantage in stimulating

analysis, but it can also lead to a failure to assess properly the religious
and emotional aspects of the institution.

In the spring and summer of 1856, the pioneering English ethnol-
ogist Edward B. Tylor traveled in Mexico, later publishing an account
of his journey in *Anahuac* (London, 1861). His brief comments on the
godparent complex are among the earliest in the anthropological tradition; they provide information on the *compadrazgo* in Mexico, but
they also betray the situation in nineteenth-century England, where
the godparental institution had lost most of its social importance, in
particular its capacity to bind godparent and natural parent together
as coparents.

> I mentioned the word "compadrazgo" a little way back. The
> thing itself is curious, and quite novel to an Englishman of the
> present day. The godfathers and godmothers of a child become,
> by their participation in the ceremony, relations to one another
> and to the priest who baptizes the child, and call one another ever
> afterwards *compadre* and *comadre*. Just such a relationship was once
> expressed by the word "gossip," "God-sib," that is "akin in God."
> Gossip has quite degenerated from its old meaning, and even
> "*sib*," though good English in Chaucer's time, is now only to be
> found in provincial dialects; but in German "sipp" still means
> "kin."
> In Mexico this connexion obliges the compadres and comadres
> to hospitality and honesty and all sorts of good offices towards
> one another; and it is wonderful how conscientiously this obli-
> gation is kept to, even by people who have no conscience at all
> for the rest of the world. A man who will cheat his own father
> or his own son will keep faith with his *compadre*. To such an
> extent does this influence become mixed up with all sorts of af-
> fairs, and so important is it, that it is necessary to count it among
> the things that tend to alter the course of justice in the country.[50]

In this passage, Tylor foreshadowed several of the anthropological
tradition's primary preoccupations in its approach to the sponsorship
complex, for it has been variously treated as the creator of a moral
code, as a system of respect, as a facilitator of social alliances, and as
an influence on such matters as economic life, political life, and justice. (Tylor had noted a few pages earlier that along with bribery,
intimidation, political influence, and private friendship, the *compadrazgo* was a factor in the administration of justice in nineteenth-cen-

50 Edward B. Tylor, *Anahuac* (London, 1861), p. 250.

tury Mexico.)[51] Tylor's stress on the *compadrazgo*, which is the horizontal coparental element in the sponsorship complex, has also been characteristic of much analysis by subsequent anthropologists, who have formulated their views in the context of Latin American societies where the role of the *compadre* (cofather) was more important than that of the *padrino* (godfather), a situation that was not true of the traditional European spiritual kinship.

An institution with such an obvious impact on important aspects of life has quite naturally attracted the attention of anthropologists. Indeed, ever since the 1930s it has been routine procedure for anthropologists reporting on field work in Latin America to include some comments on the *compadrazgo* in the society under study. And since the 1960s a modest number of studies have been devoted to the *compadrazgo* itself. Thus in 1971 Stephen Gudeman reviewed the findings of fifty-one works, published between 1936 and 1970, touching on *compadrazgo*, about 80 percent of which dealt with Latin America.[52] And in 1980 Hugo Nutini and his collaborator Betty Bell published a veritable *summa* on *compadrazgo* in Tlaxcala, a Mexican state. In this work, the authors note the existence of two hundred fifty anthropological studies that deal with Latin American variants of the godparent complex, though not necessarily with great depth or sophistication.[53] In a bibliographical essay appended to their book, Nutini and Bell argue persuasively that in spite of the number of studies, "compadrazgo is known only superficially" and the studies "on compadrazgo in Latin America are inadequate." Among the faults that they attribute to the anthropological literature are a failure to be systematic and thorough, as well as a lack of "amplitude and precision."[54]

The Latin American manifestations of spiritual kinship continue to dominate the anthropological literature, but since 1964 studies have been published on spiritual kinship in Greece, Hungary, Yugoslavia, the Philippines, and Ceylon (Sri Lanka).[55] Indeed, it is now clear that

---

[51] Ibid., p. 248.

[52] Stephen Gudeman, "The *Compadrazgo* as a Reflection of the Natural and Spiritual Person: The Curl Prize Essay, 1971," *Proceedings of the Royal Anthropological Institute* (1972), p. 68.

[53] Hugo G. Nutini and Betty Bell, *Ritual Kinship: The Structure and Historical Development of the Compadrazgo System in Rural Tlaxcala*, 2 vols. (Princeton, 1980 and 1984), 1:12.

[54] Ibid., pp. 405–428. The quotations are from pp. 426, 419, and 416.

[55] John K. Campbell, *Honour, Family and Patronage: A Study of Institutions and Moral Values in a Greek Mountain Community* (Oxford, 1964), pp. 217–224; Stanley Aschenbrenner, "Folk Model vs. Actual Practice: The Distribution of Spiritual Kin in a Greek Village," *Anthropological Quarterly* 48 (1975):65–86; Edit Fel and Tamas Hofer, *Proper*

sponsorship and spiritual kinship are pan-Christian institutions, with many variants to be sure, that must be investigated and ultimately explained.

The experience of the anthropologists has been parallel to that of the folklorists, with forty years of field studies uncovering a large number of variations in the sponsorship complex, revealing evidence that the institution has been extremely malleable, adapting itself to many cultures while retaining some general features. Anthropological field studies, by their very nature, concentrate upon a relatively small area, and so, like the folklorists, few anthropologists have investigated the historical development either of the complex itself or of those of its features that have persisted across many cultures and/or centuries. However, folklorists and anthropologists have had rather different experiences with respect to their attempts to generalize from the disparate data on baptismal sponsorship and its consequences. Whereas the literary and folkloric tradition has produced no useful synthesis, there have, in contrast, been four influential attempts by anthropologists to structure the wealth of empirical data about the godparent complex: those of Benjamin D. Paul in 1942, Sidney Mintz and Eric Wolf in 1950, Stephen Gudeman in 1971, and Hugo Nutini and Betty Bell in 1980.

By 1942, anthropologists working in Latin America were well aware that baptism created a kind of kinship with social consequences. In that year, Benjamin D. Paul wrote an influential, though unpublished, doctoral dissertation at the University of Chicago entitled "Ritual Kinship: With Special Reference to Godparenthood in Middle America," in which he developed a theoretical framework for a comparative study of the godparent complex. In constructing this framework, Paul argued that there were three forms of kinship—consanguineal, affinal, and ritual—and that the third had too often been neglected. "The present paper," he continued, "seeks to establish ritual kinship as a branch of comparative sociology ranking alongside associations and kinship proper."[56] He noted that the *compadrazgo* was only one variety of ritual kinship and that there were other forms, including ritual brotherhood and parenthood: "the term 'ritual kinship' comprehends

---

Peasants: Traditional Life in a Hungarian Village (Chicago, 1969), pp. 163–167; Eugene A. Hammel, *Alternative Social Structures and Ritual Relations in the Balkans* (Englewood Cliffs, N.J., 1968); Donn V. Hart, *Compadrinazgo: Ritual Kinship in the Philippines* (DeKalb, Ill., 1977); R. L. Stirrat, "Compadrazgo in Catholic Sri Lanka," *Man*, new series, 10 (1975):598–606.

[56] Benjamin D. Paul, "Ritual Kinship: With Special Reference to Godparenthood in Middle America" (Ph.D. diss., University of Chicago, 1942), p. 1.

all those instances of artificial relationship growing out of a ritual compact and obligating the contracting parties to behave as kinsmen to each other and to the members of each other's families."[57]

Paul had at his disposal a modest body of published anthropological data on the *compadrazgo* in Mexico and Guatemala, which he reviewed in detail in order to present specific cases upon which to formulate his theory. He was aware of the diversity of local practice, which has always impeded attempts at synthetic treatment, but from his analysis of the data he drew important conclusions concerning the religious, moral, and mundane ends served by spiritual kinship. Some of his insights had been anticipated by others, but his was the first sustained attempt to describe the matter in a coordinated whole. Paul's conclusion was that godparenthood must be understood as a subset of ritual parenthood, which is in its turn a variety of ritual kinship: "Ritual parenthood may be defined as (1) a ritually-established (2) long-lasting relationship (3) of a parent-child order (4) between individuals not otherwise related."[58]

Paul's observations about the social ends fulfilled by godparenthood have had a considerable impact upon the conceptualization of the problem in subsequent treatments. For example, he noted that in Latin American practice, the choice of godparents could serve either to create new relationships among persons not previously related or to intensify existing relationships. This intensification-extension *topos* has been a useful category of investigation in many subsequent studies of the *compadrazgo*.

Paul's dissertation was an important step in a much-needed process of abstracting generalizations from the myriad local variants of the godparent complex. In particular, the clarification of the concept of ritual kinship, modeled on blood kinship but voluntary and more sacred than the latter, has helped to place the godparent complex in a wider context and to distinguish it from other forms of relationship.

It is often true that the maps drawn by pioneers in new territory do not satisfy their successors, who have the opportunity to pay attention to details. Paul was such a pioneer, and while the general contours of his map were a valuable advance, the details have required revision. First, the data he drew from published works were all contemporary and virtually all from Mexico and Guatemala. Thus his rare nods in the direction of a historical view of the godparent complex were necessarily brief. Because of this, he gave no attention whatso-

[57] Ibid., p. 2.
[58] Ibid., p. 120.

ever to the European background of the complex and his comments on its development in Latin America during the four centuries since the Spanish conquest were merely surmises, although intelligent ones. He asserted that the godparent complex had been introduced along with baptism at the time of the conquest, and he suggested that it had evolved in response to native practices: "There is abundant evidence that elements of European origin have experienced differential success in becoming established in the emergent amalgam of Spanish-Indian culture. . . . Catholic godparenthood in general is congruent with pre-Columbian institutions—that [is,] it constitutes a change in form but a continuity of function."[59] Paul's dissertation did not, however, claim to be a historical work; rather, its author set out to examine the institution of spiritual kinship synchronically in a restricted area, and thus its development in other areas or in the medieval West was never at issue.

Another point to bear in mind when considering Paul's work is the fact that the godparent complex has two dimensions, though they may be given different stress from one society to another: a vertical one joining godparent to godchild and a horizontal one joining godparent to natural parent. Students of the godparent complex have often had difficulty in maintaining a clear terminology to describe the horizontal, vertical, and total relationships, and in this Paul was no exception. He distinguished in explicit fashion two varieties of ritual kinship: ritual parenthood and ritual brotherhood. The former was a term that could describe the vertical dimension of baptismal kinship and the latter was a term with no direct relevance to sponsorship. But while using these two terms he actually described three varieties of relationship, the third being ritual coparenthood, which is the horizontal relationship within the sponsorship complex. Sometimes he referred to coparenthood as godparenthood, but at other times he used the latter term to describe the entire complex. And this linguistic confusion detracted from his important conclusions.

For almost forty years, Paul's analysis of godparenthood as a subset of ritual kinship with social uses has served as the guiding hypothesis of the anthropological tradition in dealing with the godparent complex. However, subsequent research has increased the data available to scholars both in amount and in temporal and geographical extent, and in the light of this research it has become evident that Paul's work omitted some important dimensions of the institution. Nevertheless, as Gudeman noted in 1971 with respect to Paul's view that *compadrazgo*

[59] Ibid., p. 99.

can extend or intensify relationships, "although today most analyses go beyond these generalizations, they have yet to be refuted."[60] Similarly, Nutini and Bell have also conceded that Paul's work was "a good beginning" in identifying "some of the most important structural and functional attributes of compadrazgo."[61]

Unfortunately, despite Paul's contribution to the understanding of spiritual kinship from an analytical perspective, he added little of substance to another topic of interest to anthropologists—that is, the historical origin and development of the complex. Not every anthropologist who is describing spiritual kinship in a Latin American village does extensive personal research into its historico-religious background. Instead, such field researchers customarily draw upon some dependable account of what is, to them, a secondary aspect of their work. For more than twenty-five years, anthropologists have relied heavily for their knowledge of the European medieval background of the godparent complex on an article by Sidney W. Mintz and Eric R. Wolf, which appeared in 1950.[62] In it, the authors review five important Latin American studies that treat the *compadrazgo* in various contexts, and they attempt to formulate some generalizations—for the most part refinements of Paul's extension-intensification suggestion—about its function in different societies.

Mintz and Wolf preface their remarks with nine pages that trace the historical antecedents of what they call "ritual co-parenthood," that is, the aspect of spiritual kinship that binds natural parents and sponsors together. Although it is brief, this article has had a remarkable impact, particularly among anthropologists writing in English. Indeed, until Gudeman's article of 1971, there was no alternative to the Mintz and Wolf treatment. It has been reprinted and has been praised by the successive anthropologists who referred to it to provide background for their more restricted studies.

Nutini and Bell, who are generally critical of their fellow anthropologists, give praise to the Mintz and Wolf article, which as late as 1980 retained its influence among students of the *compadrazgo*. As Nutini and Bell see it, the article

> is probably the best-known source on compadrazgo in the published literature, and in many ways deservedly so. . . . this is still the only comprehensive historical treatment and is the article's

[60] Gudeman, "The *Compadrazgo*," p. 45.
[61] Nutini and Bell, *Ritual* 1:407.
[62] Sidney W. Mintz and Eric R. Wolf, "An Analysis of Ritual Co-Parenthood (Compadrazgo)," *SJA* 6 (1950):341–368.

most important contribution. . . . In an elegant analysis they trace the changes in compadrazgo throughout the latter part of the Roman Empire, the Dark Ages, the Middle Ages, the Renaissance, and into modern times. In their historical analysis Mintz and Wolf go into much detail about the functions of compadrazgo and its place in the wider European society, as that society developed from empire, to feudalism, to nationalism, and on to the peasant setting of modern Europe.[63]

In brief, the Mintz and Wolf article has taken its place in the anthropological tradition as the classic account of the historical development that lay behind the Latin American *compadrazgo*. It represents that tradition's working knowledge of the history of sponsorship in its pre-sixteenth-century forms.

The article is a serious and useful pioneering attempt, but it has significant shortcomings in its historical introduction because the authors draw only upon secondary sources. They obtained much of their information from a published canon law dissertation by Richard J. Kearney, *Sponsors at Baptism According to the Code of Canon Law* (Washington, D.C., 1925), a particularly mediocre representative of the ecclesiastical tradition of scholarship. Kearney's *Sponsors* treated legal texts without providing their context, was inaccurate both in detail and in large matters of historical development, was poorly documented at important points, and was quite uncritical in its use of sources. Yet it was the only extended English language account of its kind available to Mintz and Wolf in 1950. In addition to Kearney's book, the authors had at their disposal a modest group of secondary works, dictionaries and encyclopedias, almost exclusively in English and German, which dealt with religion, folklore, and medieval history. However, there were several important studies of sponsorship and spiritual kinship in the ancient church, including Henri Leclercq's brief article in the *Dictionnaire d'archéologie chrétienne et de liturgie*[64] and Ernst Dick's article of 1939, that were not cited in the article. A second, less serious, problem is that there are errors and imprecisions in the dating and identification of some of the medieval texts, errors that may derive from the secondary works used by the authors.

Mintz and Wolf built on an insecure base of data concerning the medieval godparent, and their catch-as-catch-can method of gathering material meant that in nine pages they cite examples from Bosnia to England and from the sixth to the fifteenth centuries. The article's

---

[63] Nutini and Bell, *Ritual* 1:407.

[64] Henri Leclercq, "Parrain et marraine," *DACL* vol. 13, pt. 2 (1938), pp. 2236–2240.

problems with data are also compounded by conceptual flaws. These derive from the fact that the early Middle Ages, during which the sponsorship complex originated, differ significantly in myriad ways from the later Middle Ages, when the complex had acquired great elaboration in church law and folk culture. Any treatment that slights the recognition that during its millennium of existence medieval society experienced immense development and regional differentiation will naturally be inadequate. Unfortunately, Mintz and Wolf succumbed, perhaps unconsciously, to the temptation to see the "Middle Ages" as an undifferentiated whole, and thus their article lacks a sense of historical development. Legislation and anecdotal material from very different times and places are telescoped into one another, and the character of an important institution in a complex society across a thousand years is treated in a mechanical, external fashion that would immediately be perceived as unacceptable if applied by an anthropologist to a contemporary society.

The article by Mintz and Wolf served the function of providing anthropologists with some of the factual information contained in the ecclesiastical tradition of scholarship. But the authors were not content merely to trace the external steps in the evolution of coparental custom and legislation in medieval Europe. They also sought to do what an anthropologist would ordinarily do with data about a contemporary society: to explain why the *compadrazgo* functioned as it did, and to explain what it meant in societal terms. But when the authors turn to these personal views—or "guesses,"[65] as they modestly call them—about the social functions and significance of the *compadrazgo* in medieval society, both the limitations of the sources available to them and the problems encountered by a nonmedievalist in dealing with medieval society stand out in stark relief.

Here the authors become enmeshed in the coils of that marvelously flexible and ambiguous term "feudal,"[66] setting themselves the task of explaining how the *compadrazgo* functioned "under feudal conditions" without explaining what such conditions might be or when and where they existed. They also employ a Marxist vocabulary of class struggle that, at the least, demands careful documentation and chronological precision, neither of which is provided.

The inspiration for some of their "guesses" is not hard to determine. In the second section of the article, the authors review the findings of

[65] Mintz and Wolf, p. 345.

[66] Elizabeth A. R. Brown, "The Tyranny of a Construct: Feudalism and Historians of Medieval Europe," *AHR* 79 (1974):1063–1088, demonstrated the pitfalls of objectifying the term "feudalism."

anthropologists who had described functions fulfilled by the *compadrazgo* in contemporary Latin American societies, functions that are very similar to those Mintz and Wolf had postulated in the previous section for the Middle Ages. It appears that their efforts at analysis were frustrated by the special preoccupations of the ecclesiastical tradition. And since the authors could find in the scholarly works of this tradition little information directly relevant to their purposes (not surprisingly, as it was not interested in such matters), they retrojected findings about modern Latin American conditions into the "feudal" Middle Ages. Thus the Latin American model influenced what Mintz and Wolf sought and found in the Middle Ages.

One aspect of the article may serve to illustrate this process of preselection. Mintz and Wolf treat only the *compadrazgo*—that is, the horizontal relationship of parent and godparent to one another. In other words, they conspicuously neglect the vertical relationship of godparent and godchild. Such an approach is well suited to the Latin American experience, where the *compadrazgo* bond has become far more important than the *padrinazgo*. But such an approach does not do justice to the medieval situation, where the tie of godparent to godchild was often as important or even more important than the coparental bond.

In spite of the caution demanded in using the generalizations and "guesses" of Mintz and Wolf, their familiarity with the Latin American *compadrazgo* does provide a useful base from which to make suggestions and hypotheses about the medieval variety or varieties of godparenthood. This is because, despite significant changes that have occurred during four centuries of divergent development, the Latin American and Western European godparent complexes share a common ancestor in the medieval complex and thus are, in a manner of speaking, cousins. Hence we may anticipate similarities of ideology, function, and form, and a knowledge of one undoubtedly aids in understanding either of the others, even though each variety is distinct. However, only research in the original sources can establish which of the possible similarities and differences actually occurred and can give some chronological precision to the course of development of spiritual kinship.

A final, serious reservation about the account by Mintz and Wolf is its slight attention to the godparent complex as a *religious* phenomenon. In its origins and in the basic presuppositions that governed its medieval development, a religious conception of rebirth and spiritual life was crucial; only gradually did that core of religious ritual and meaning attract to itself other, more secular elements. It may be suggested that the authors underestimated the religious significance of the *compadrazgo* in medieval Europe because of their familiarity with Latin America, where the overtly and formally religious elements have often been overwhelmed by more secular folk additions or have vanished entirely. In contrast, in the late medieval period, although tendencies toward the secularization of the godparent complex are discernible, the religious element still remained important. Thus the assessment of the medieval sponsorship complex through the prism of its Latin American descendant has led to a stress on certain of its aspects and to a relative neglect of others, notably the religious core and the godparent-godchild tie.

The Mintz and Wolf article has not been replaced in the anthropological tradition as the standard treatment of the historical development and functioning of the *compadrazgo* in the Middle Ages. However, in 1971 an attempt to account for important aspects of the medieval godparent complex was published by Stephen Gudeman in "The *Compadrazgo* as a Reflection of the Natural and Spiritual Person."[67] Like so many of his predecessors and successors, Gudeman praised the Mintz and Wolf article, noting that it had provided "a superb contextual account of the history of 'ritual kinship.' "[68] He announced that his intention was not to duplicate or replace this work but to complement it.

Gudeman's essay does not rectify all the misunderstandings that have marred attempts to grasp the origin and development of the godparent complex, but it is still an extremely important contribution on several grounds. Significantly, Gudeman turned attention away from the "uses" to which the godparent complex was put, which had been a preoccupation of Paul, Mintz and Wolf, and the majority of those conducting empirical field studies. Instead, he attempted to understand the theology that undergirded spiritual kinship and to assess the meaning of the institution for those who participated in it, with emphasis on the medieval period. He was aided in this effort by the fact that by 1971 the progress of research had made it clear that spiritual kinship was not a phenomenon restricted to Latin America. Rather, it was, in various forms, pan-Christian. Gudeman's familiarity with research in Europe made him more aware that both the horizontal (coparental) and vertical (godparental) dimensions of the complex demanded attention, and thus his essay is the first synthetic treatment

[67] Stephen Gudeman, "The *Compadrazgo*," pp. 45–71.
[68] Ibid., p. 50.

in the anthropological tradition to deal successfully with both dimensions of spiritual kinship.

Gudeman also perceived that the range of sources used by the ecclesiastical tradition, upon which he drew for data, had been narrow. Because of this, he took the important step of examining the views of a medieval theologian, Thomas Aquinas, for insight into the way in which a medieval person understood the meaning of the institution. Most important, Gudeman grappled with the heretofore intractable problem of generalizing about the empirical data on the distribution and variation of the godparent complex on a worldwide scale.

As ethnographic investigations have multiplied, a bewildering number of variants or subspecies of spiritual kinship have been described in the literature. Mintz and Wolf had commented on the "flexibility" and adaptability of the institution, and the accumulation of evidence in the last quarter century only reinforced the validity of that observation. Gudeman argued that these variations were neither random nor unlimited. He designated the historic pattern, which was elaborated in medieval Europe, as the "great tradition" and argued that the variations of the great tradition can be described by five rules and three subrules that account for the ways in which the institution adapts to new circumstances while retaining its basic structure.[69]

Gudeman's primary insight was that the godparent complex is not merely a system for intensifying or extending relationships, or for dealing with practical problems like land tenure or bureaucracy or social harmony, despite the fact that it has been all these things and more in various contexts. Rather, Gudeman uses his essay to argue that the basic structure of the institution, the appeal that makes such practical uses possible, lies in a matter of theology, a dichotomy that was felt by ancient and medieval Christians and is widespread in modern societies as well. Thus he believes that "it is possible to see the historical reworking of the concepts of spiritual paternity and spiritual relationship as a series of attempts to resolve and to trace out the implications of the fundamental antinomy of man as a natural and spiritual being."[70]

In Gudeman's view, deeply held attitudes toward human nature lie at the root of baptismal kinship. In traditional Christian theology, every child is born in corruption, in original sin, which is his natural existence. But by baptism the child enters a new spiritual existence

[69] Ibid., pp. 61–64.
[70] Ibid., p. 54.

that is pure and angelic. Accordingly, the natural life has its natural parents and the spiritual life its spiritual parents, the godparents.

Gudeman is not certain when these views emerged—he notes twice that godparenthood is "2000 years old"—but he finds in the thirteenth-century *Summa Theologiae*, III, questions 65–69 and question 56, article 3, composed by Thomas Aquinas, the following analogies that draw in explicit fashion the contrasts between the natural and the spiritual life:

> natural : spiritual :: birth : rebirth ::
> death : life :: natural parents : spiritual parents.[71]

In the most extreme formulations, as among medieval dualist heretics, the realms of nature and spirit are sundered and the former is seen as evil. But Gudeman is dealing with an orthodox theologian in Aquinas, one for whom the realms of nature and supernature are distinct but complementary. According to this view, every Christian partakes of both realms and possesses two sets of parents, with whom and among whom significantly different relationships are necessary.

Gudeman's analysis of the proper relations of an individual to his spiritual and natural kin is complex and difficult to summarize briefly.[72] It is sufficient here to note that when dealing with one's spiritual kin—godparent or godchild or coparent—one must act with respect, act "spiritually" in a classic Christian sense of the word. That is, between spiritual kin there must be no sexual acts or talk, no cheating, no strife, and no harmful behavior of any kind. The relations of spiritual kin should be a mirror image of natural kin relations, the former sacred and the latter profane.

To buttress his argument that spiritual kinship is rooted primarily in an insight about natural and spiritual birth, Gudeman exploits the traditional collection of legal texts so often used in the ecclesiastical tradition. But in doing so, his citation of Aquinas' *Summa Theologiae* is an important innovation, for his serious and sympathetic attention to a medieval theologian's assessment of spiritual kinship expands the range and quality of evidence available to an anthropologist studying the godparent complex and invites more exploration of this type. Indeed, Gudeman points to a path that more scholars in the ecclesiastical tradition could pursue with profit, that of moving beyond legal and liturgical texts to investigate the vast amount of material on spiritual kinship to be found in theological and pastoral writings.

[71] Ibid., pp. 49–50, 69.
[72] Ibid., pp. 59–61.

Gudeman was aware that spiritual kinship in medieval Europe had not been a static phenomenon, that it had undergone change across time as certain elements were elaborated while others atrophied or were suppressed by church authorities. Thus, in thirteen diagrams containing "notations not normally used by anthropologists,"[73] he represented graphically both the permanent and the changing aspects of the godparent complex from the period of the early church to modern Los Boquerones in Verguas province, Panama, where his own field work was done.[74] For the Middle Ages, the diagrams rely on data from the ecclesiastical tradition's legal and normative sources.

Gudeman's concentration on the inner meaning of spiritual kinship rather than on its practical uses was an important departure, one that provided a sympathetic and well-conceived view of certain of the presuppositions upon which spiritual kinship is built. Field studies have shown repeatedly that spiritual kin do in fact act more positively toward one another (with lapses from the ideal, to be sure) and Gudeman's essay helps to explain why this is so. However, there are three aspects of the essay that require cautious consideration. First, in spite of his profitable use of Aquinas, Gudeman continued to draw primarily upon the well-worked ecclesiastical tradition—errors, myopia, and all—for his source materials on the medieval complex. There is no evidence that he was aware of or able to draw upon the large body of medieval sources in Latin and the vernaculars. In addition, he made no use of the more important studies in the ecclesiastical tradition— for example, those of Dick and Bailey, to name only two. Further, it must be recognized that Thomas Aquinas was a highly educated university intellectual who was writing about an institution that was in his day already seven centuries old. It cannot be assumed that his views accurately reflect the far-off historical origins of the complex, and even for his own century Aquinas' views must be employed with critical sense. Both his education and his occupation made Aquinas more articulate and sophisticated—perhaps radically so—than the contemporary parish priest who baptized or the ordinary lay Christians who chose godparents, served as godparents, and interacted daily with spiritual kinsmen. Hence Aquinas' views must be tested against other sources to separate what may be his own unique, intellectualized contribution from those elements that reflect common belief.

Latin American varieties of the *compadrazgo* loom very large in the

[73] Ibid., pp. 47–54.

[74] See Stephen Gudeman, *Relationships, Residence and the Individual: A Rural Panamanian Community* (Minneapolis, 1976), pp. 190–231, in which Gudeman reports in detail his findings about *compadrazgo* in Los Boquerones.

modern anthropological literature, and Gudeman attempted to show briefly that Aquinas' views were directly relevant for Latin America by way of the Council of Trent. Thus Gudeman asserts that on the issues of baptism and godparents the Council "was influenced strongly by his ideas"[75] and that it was the Tridentine formulation of godparenthood that was transmitted from Spain to Latin America in the sixteenth century. This is a murky area and more research is required before such positive assertions can be accepted with assurance. Aquinas' predominance in Roman Catholic philosophy and theology is a development of the nineteenth century and his exact influence on the Tridentine debates about sponsorship and spiritual kinship cannot simply be assumed. In addition, the Council of Trent's impact upon Catholic belief and practice was slow and uneven in making itself felt. It is not clear what, in fact, was transmitted to the New World by the missionaries whose evangelization efforts had begun even before the Council took place.

In conclusion, I wish to make a comment rather than a criticism, for Gudeman's insight is a convincing one. Medieval society *did* feel a dichotomy between a profane natural world and a sacred spiritual one, each with its own values and proper behavior. But Gudeman's exposition of that insight has been partially frustrated by the tendency of the four scholarly traditions to ignore one another. The ecclesiastical tradition did not provide an accessible, historically oriented, and wide-ranging treatment of the medieval sources. Since Gudeman apparently had access to these sources only through secondary works and translations, he was thus dependent on the source-poor ecclesiastical tradition. He had the productive idea to examine a theological work of Aquinas, but he had no access to the sermons, saints' lives, and other materials that might have corroborated or enriched his views.

In recent years, anthropologists have become interested in giving greater time depth to their field studies of the sponsorship complex. In particular, the Spanish church and bureaucracy generated and often preserved extensive records in their great colonial empire, and it is possible to use these records for information on *compadrazgo*. For instance, Donn V. Hart's book on *Compadrinazgo: Ritual Kinship in the Philippines* (1977) is a fairly traditional account of field study among the Bisayan peoples of Mindanao. However, the author places his study within a larger context, drawing upon Mintz and Wolf, Gudeman, and some sixteenth- and seventeenth-century Spanish legal and administrative records. This effort is certainly promising, but the book

[75] Gudeman, "The *Compadrazgo*," p. 49.

remains primarily a contemporary field study with some historical prolegomena.

The most recent and by far the most substantial attempt to combine field study with time depth has been published by Hugo G. Nutini and Betty Bell in *Ritual Kinship: The Structure and Historical Development of the Compadrazgo System in Rural Tlaxcala*, (2 vols., 1980 and 1984). Since 1959 Nutini and his collaborators have done extended periods of field work in Santa Maria Belen Azitzimititlan, a village of about nine hundred people in the Mexican state of Tlaxcala. In their massive study, Nutini and Bell minutely describe the elaborate *compadrazgo* system in the village, identifying thirty-one occasions for creating the coparental bond.

Nutini and Bell's careful description of *compadrazgo* in the present (defined as circa 1970) has been complemented by a concerted effort to trace its development from the arrival of the Spanish missionaries in 1519. Anthropologists have long recognized that late medieval Spanish *compadrazgo* did not take root in New Spain in pristine purity, for pre-existing Amerindian sponsoring practices certainly shaped and conditioned the development of the Spanish Catholic model. Nutini and Bell have investigated closely this process of syncretism, which occurred when Spanish Catholicism was transplanted to the Tlaxcalan milieu.

Nutini and Bell's *Ritual Kinship* is a remarkable study for its content, although its wordy and jargon-ridden literary style detracts from its impact. Nevertheless, the degree of detail on a specific system of sponsorship and spiritual kinship is unmatched in any earlier work and the understanding of the situation in Belen is enhanced by the author's wide knowledge of *compadrazgo* in other Latin American contexts.

Tlaxcala was one of the earliest areas of Mesoamerica to feel the Spanish impact. Franciscan friars were active there by 1519 and there are written records, with gaps and deficiencies, from the sixteenth century to the present. The unusual features of Nutini and Bell's book, which make it ground-breaking within the anthropological tradition of studying *compadrazgo*, are their recognition that sponsorship developed across time and their concerted effort to study this development in Tlaxcala on the basis of documents, oral history, and educated guesses. The resulting analysis of the development and proliferation of sponsoring practices is extensive (forty-six pages), quite original and, in the view of its authors, tentative, since they are still continuing historical research on the matter.[76]

[76] Nutini and Bell, *Ritual* 1:332–378.

Although *Ritual Kinship* is innovative in its thorough, systematic, and historically oriented investigation of *compadrazgo* in a relatively small area, it is quite conventional in its approach to the late medieval Spanish sponsoring practices that were brought to Mexico and adapted to the new environment. Hence, as so many other anthropologists have done, Nutini and Bell recommend that the interested reader consult the Mintz and Wolf article for information on the medieval background:

> Mintz and Wolf (1950) have ably discussed the historical antecedents of the Spanish compadrazgo system, and some of the symbolic and theological implications of the concept of ritual sponsorship within the context of Catholicism. The reader can find the historical background of ritual kinship sponsorship in their work.[77]

Literary qualities aside, Nutini and Bell's book is a model of ethnohistorical research and will probably have a great impact on future studies of Latin American *compadrazgo*, particularly now that volume 2 has appeared. This second volume deals with "the structural analysis of compadrazgo and its multidimensional levels of meaning; its functional analysis and different levels of local and regional integration; the theoretical foundations of the entire study; and a limited-range theory of acculturation, modernization, and secularization."[78] However, the book has nothing direct to say about sponsorship prior to the arrival of the Franciscans in Tlaxcala. The previous medieval development of the sponsorship complex remains virtually *terra incognita*, mapped out only sketchily by Mintz and Wolf and by Gudeman.

The anthropological tradition has been prolific on the subject of sponsorship, primarily in a Latin American context, but elsewhere as well, including along the Mediterranean littoral. In addition to the sheer bulk of comment on sponsorship practices, there have been notable attempts to make some sense out of the whirl of details. Mintz and Wolf, Gudeman, and Nutini and Bell all saw in the history of sponsorship in medieval Europe one component of a suitable explanation of the nature and significance of modern sponsorship, but all were frustrated in their attempts to explore a rather remote past, prior to the sixteenth century. Nutini and Bell simply relied on Mintz and Wolf. Gudeman also accepted Mintz and Wolf and described his own

[77] Ibid., 1:335.
[78] Ibid., 1:4.

work as a complement to theirs: they had sketched the history and he would investigate the inner meaning of baptismal sponsorship.

Mintz and Wolf made a pioneering attempt, but they were hindered by the difficulties inherent in formulating sweeping generalizations about a culture that lasted a millennium and embraced a multitude of peoples, languages, and cultural levels. They were also stymied by the nature of the ecclesiastical tradition itself, which has never been interested in the social implications of sponsorship and which has generally filtered out or ignored evidence on that score. Mintz and Wolf overlooked important studies, but even if they had surveyed the writings of the ecclesiastical tradition more thoroughly they would not have harvested much source material suitable to their task. Only a fresh look at the abundant medieval sources, bearing historical and anthropological questions in mind, will yield what Mintz and Wolf needed but could not find.

Historians and Spiritual Kinship

Medieval historians regularly encounter spiritual kinsmen in their sources and, like the scholars in the literary and folkloric tradition, often comment on them. Thus there is no shortage of relatively brief references by historians to aspects of spiritual kinship or to specific instances of sponsorship. Since 1950, some historians have also investigated aspects of medieval spiritual kinship in greater depth, although the studies are few in number when compared with the production of the ecclesiastical, literary and folkloric, or anthropological traditions.

As in these traditions, however, a major recurring conceptual problem among historians has been the failure to distinguish clearly between the godparental and the coparental bond in spiritual kinship. Just as anthropologists have been led, with some notable exceptions, to emphasize the coparental bond as a result of Latin American realities, so medieval historians have tended to stress the godparent/godchild bond because it has been most prominent in their experience in modern times. The coparental bond is sometimes ignored by historians, sometimes blithely assimilated to the godparental bond, and sometimes recognized without any apparent comprehension of its implications.

One notable exception has been seen in the work of Arnold Angenendt, who distinguished clearly between *Patenschaft* (godparent/godchild) and *Kompaternität* (coparenthood) in his 1980 article on the spiritual bond between eighth-century popes and Carolingian rulers,[79] although in his 1973 article on *"Taufe und Politik"* he paid almost exclusive attention to *Patenschaft*.[80] The general failure to distinguish between and to see the significance of both bonds arising out of baptismal sponsorship severely limits the usefulness of much historical scholarship on the medieval varieties of spiritual kinship.

It has generally been true that historians have been most attracted by the intersection of sponsorship and politics in the period before 1100.[81] During this era, kings and great princes sponsored one another or one another's children with the obvious aim of creating a politically useful bond. The most famous such case was the coparenthood that bound Charlemagne and Pope Hadrian I, created in 781 by the baptism of a royal child for whom the pope stood as sponsor. The emergence of the Papal-Frankish alliance in the mid-eighth century has fascinated medieval historians, particularly Germans, and almost every study of its creation has taken account of the coparenthood that was used on several occasions to bind a pope to a Carolingian prince. The most comprehensive treatment of the topic is Arnold Angenendt's article, which reviewed earlier scholarship and placed the coparenthood between Hadrian and Charlemagne in a religio-historical context.[82]

This inclination to see spiritual kinship as a political tool has meant that most historical treatments place it within the context of alliance-building and kin-extending mechanisms like adoption, formal treaties, blood brotherhoods, and *Schwurfreundschaft*. An example of this approach is the 1959 dissertation by Margret Wielers, *Zwischenstaatliche Beziehungsformen im frühen Mittelalter (Pax, Foedus, Amicitia, Fraternitas)*, which devotes a few pages to sponsorship in a chapter concerning adoption as a political tool. Here Wielers emphasizes the godpa-

---

[79] Arnold Angenendt, "Das geistliche Bündnis der Päpste mit den Karolingern (754–796)," *HJ* 100 (1980):1–94.

[80] Arnold Angenendt, "Taufe und Politik im frühen Mittelalter," *FS* 7 (1973):143–168.

[81] For example, see Isrun Engelhardt, *Mission und Politik in Byzanz. Ein Beitrag zur Strukturanalyse byzantinischer Mission zur Zeit Justins und Justinians*, Miscellanea byzantina monacensia, vol. 19 (Munich, 1974), pp. 80–90; Richard Weyl, *Die Beziehungen des Papstthums zum fränkischen Staats- und Kirchenrecht unter den Karolingern*, Untersuchungen zur deutschen Staats- und Rechtsgeschichte, vol. 40 (Breslau, 1892), pp. 216–230; Karl A. Eckhardt, "Adoption," *Studia merovingica*, Bibliotheca rerum historicarum, vol. 11 (Aalen, 1975), pp. 240–261; Reinhard Schneider, *Brüdergemeine und Schwurfreundschaft*, HS, vol. 388 (Lübeck and Hamburg, 1964), p. 150.

[82] Angenendt, "Das geistliche," pp. 32–40.

rental tie, with little overt attention to coparenthood.[83] Similarly, Ludwig Buisson pursued the theme of alliance-building in the political development of Normandy from the ninth to the eleventh centuries. The Vikings who settled at the mouth of the Seine placed great emphasis on loyalty to kin, whether that kinship arose in blood bonds, marriage, or in a myriad other ways (for example, in fosterage and oath brotherhood) including *Patenschaft*, which is treated by Buisson in about three pages. In Buisson's view, Christian sponsorship fitted well with pre-Christian Viking patterns of fictive kinship and was heartily adopted by the superficially Christianized invaders. Buisson also perceived primarily godparent/godchild bonds in his sources and slighted the coparental bond.[84]

Thus it can be seen that medieval historians have approached the issues bound up in sponsorship relatively recently and with a restricted set of questions. And except for Angenendt, who acknowledged the possibility of wider social significance for spiritual kinship, few have ventured beyond documenting the role of baptismal sponsorship and godparenthood in early medieval politics.

It is no accident that sponsorship has received greater attention in a period of rising historiographical interest in questions of social and family history. To a student of such varieties of history, spiritual kinship in its medieval forms can be both fascinating and puzzling, partly because it is so alien to modern North Atlantic sensibilities. This puzzlement is only heightened by the fact that medieval historians have not generally been familiar with the findings of the anthropological tradition, which might have suggested to them both questions and approaches.

Nevertheless, even familiarity with the anthropological tradition is no guarantee of success in dealing with medieval spiritual kinship, for the Latin American data and theories do not fit well with medieval realities. The anthropological data are almost always derived from peasant societies, whereas the bulk of medieval data originate in and concern the upper strata of society. It is a truism that the sponsorship complex is highly adaptable to its milieu and one would expect that medieval kings, princes, and urban bourgeois would practice a form of the complex different from that of impoverished contemporary Guatemalan peasants. Thus, while medievalists who are familiar with

[83] Margret Wielers, *Zwischenstaatliche Beziehungsformen im frühen Mittelalter (Pax, Foedus, Amicitia, Fraternitas)* (Ph.D. diss., Münster, Westphalia, 1959), pp. 55–59.

[84] Ludwig Buisson, "Formen normannischer Staatsbildung (9. bis 11. Jahrhundert)," *Studien zum mittelalterlichen Lehenswesen*, Vorträge und Forschungen, vol. 5 (Lindau and Konstanz, 1960), pp. 109–111.

the anthropological tradition have an advantage, they must also correct for the unique features of Latin American spiritual kinship, which is not the same as the medieval European variety.

The only serious and sustained attempt to place the medieval political uses of sponsorship in a social and religious context is the doctoral dissertation of Ursula Perkow, *Wasserweihe, Taufe und Patenschaft bei den Nordgermanen* (Hamburg, 1972), in which she attempts to explain why sponsorship for political ends became so prominent among the Anglo-Saxons and Scandinavians, as well as why the Christian institution of baptismal sponsorship was such a successful transplant into the Germanic north. Latin American anthropologists generally believe that pre-Columbian sponsoring practices eased the transition to Christian forms of sponsorship,[85] and while Perkow was not familiar with the Latin American data, she argued for an analogous situation in the north: that pre-Christian Germanic customs disposed their practitioners to welcome Christian sponsorship, a fact that was seized upon by the Christian missionaries.

Specifically, Perkow defends the view that pre-Christian north Germanic peoples practiced a *Wasserweihe*, a ceremony for accepting a newborn child into protected human status within its kin group. The ceremony, originally performed by the father, consisted of sprinkling the child with water and giving it a name.[86] At some point in the development of the practice (Perkow suggests the tenth century),[87] it became customary for the pre-Christian *Wasserweihe* to be performed by an invitee, a sponsor who created a kinlike bond with the child. The *Wasserweihe* is a controversial topic among historians and ethnologists of the early Germanic period, since all the written sources on the ceremony were recorded by Christians several centuries after the conversion of the north Germanic peoples. Skeptics argue that whatever lies behind the saga accounts of the *Wasserweihe* has been contaminated by the retrojection of Christian baptismal patterns into the pre-Christian past.[88]

[85] Nutini and Bell, *Ritual* 1:333–334.

[86] Ursula Perkow, *Wasserweihe, Taufe und Patenschaft bei den Nordgermanen* (Ph.D. diss., Hamburg, 1972), pp. 7–13.

[87] Ibid., pp. 28–29.

[88] See ibid., pp. 7–13, where Perkow reviews the historiography of the *Wasserweihe*. On the problem of using documents written by Christians as sources for pre-Christian Scandinavian religious customs, see Walter Baetke, "Christliche Lehngut in der Saga-religion," *Berichte über die Verhandlungen der Sächsischen Akademie der Wissenschaften*, Phil.-hist. Klasse, vol. 98, pt. 6 (1952), pp. 24–30; or Walter Baetke, "Die Aufnahme des Christentums durch die Germanen. Ein Beitrag zur Frage der Germanisierung des Christentums," *Die Welt als Geschichte* 9 (1943):143–166.

Perkow saw in the *Wasserweihe* a precursor of baptismal sponsorship and she marshaled the evidence in favor of its existence. She then argued that when Christianity, with its well-developed sponsoring practices, was introduced into Scandinavia by Anglo-Saxon missionaries in the tenth and eleventh centuries, baptismal sponsorship was consciously assimilated to the preexisting *Wasserweihe* patterns.[89] Whether such a firm conclusion is warranted is open to question, but once Perkow had settled the matter to her own satisfaction, she turned to the analysis of baptismal sponsorship in the north, a matter well attested in the sources.

Her observations, based strictly on northern Germanic sources, with an occasional reference to Frankish practice, are very interesting. Thus she describes the way in which baptismal sponsorship led to important social and economic bonds between sponsor and sponsored. The sources clearly indicate the existence of coparenthood, which she describes in relation to the rise of elaborate marital prohibitions, but in which she detects little social or economic importance.[90]

When Perkow had established that baptismal sponsorship (she refers only in passing to other forms of sponsorship) had taken root in the Christianized north, where it had far more than mere liturgical or religious impact, she then turned to its political functions among kings and great aristocrats, arguing convincingly that the political uses of sponsorship made sense as specialized forms of a society-wide phenomenon.[91]

Perkow achieved what no historian, to my knowledge, previously had: she placed sponsorship in a context that makes cultural and historical sense out of the widely noted practice of using sponsorship for political or, as she calls them, "worldly" ends.[92] In view of the intrinsic merit of her dissertation, it is unfortunate that it has had no perceptible influence on any tradition of studying sponsorship. As is common with German dissertations, *Wasserweihe, Taufe und Patenschaft* was published by the author in a simple format and in a limited number of copies. It has not been reviewed in appropriate journals, and although it has occasionally been cited it has not been used to any extent by subsequent scholars. In addition, its concentration on Scandinavia and Anglo-Saxon England, which makes good sense in many ways, narrowed the author's perspective and, in my opinion, led her to an erroneous conclusion about the significance of what she found.

[89] Perkow, *Wasserweihe*, pp. 46–53, 55.
[90] Ibid., pp. 61–70.
[91] Ibid., pp. 77–91.
[92] Ibid., p. 56.

In the study of the early medieval period among the Germanic peoples, scholarly arguments often turn on whether or not something is
authentically "Germanic" or whether it is influenced by outside (often
Mediterranean Christian) forces (as is seen in the *Wasserweihe* debate).
In Perkow's case, she described several features of sponsorship and
spiritual kinship on the basis of the sagas, Germanic law codes, and
related sources. She knew that sponsorship had not been invented in
the north, but she assumed that the particular "worldly" form of it
that she encountered was somehow unique to the north Germans. If
indeed the *Wasserweihe* existed, then it could well have influenced the
reception of baptismal sponsorship and given it a Germanic patina.
But in fact the features that Perkow discovered (kinlike bonds, sexual
taboos, mutual aid, alliance-building) are widely associated with baptismal sponsorship and there is nothing particularly "Germanic" about
them. In the early sixth century, the Byzantine Emperor Justinian
used baptismal sponsorship to create alliances with Turkic peoples and
incorporated into Roman law sexual taboos arising out of sponsorship.[93] Similar behavior patterns were found elsewhere in the Mediterranean world, where Germanic influence was negligible. In short,
Perkow described in a Germanic context a set of practices that had,
since the sixth century, been pan-Christian. Perkow's study is a good
one as far as it goes, but a knowledge of sponsorship as it was brought
from the Christian Mediterranean to the north would have made it
even better by clarifying the relation of the imported practices to their
Germanic variations.

In closing, one can note that it is remarkable that four scholarly
traditions have accorded so much attention to sponsorship and spiritual kinship with such relatively modest synthetic results. As previously indicated, one major part of the problem has been the gulf separating the traditions from one another. Their respective practitioners
accord little or no attention to the work of the others and indeed are
generally not even aware of their existence. Such insularity has created
a kind of tunnel vision within the research of each tradition. Furthermore, the ecclesiastical tradition, which has had almost a monopoly
on the study of the sponsoring phenomenon in its premodern forms,
has been so preoccupied with the liturgical, canonical, and marital
aspects of baptismal sponsorship and spiritual kinship that it has had
almost nothing to say about the social, economic, and even popular
religious aspects. Thus a conscientious scholar from the literary and
folkloric tradition or the anthropological tradition who sought out in-

[93] Engelhardt, *Mission*, pp. 84–86.

formation on medieval sponsorship from ecclesiastical sources would probably draw the conclusion that nothing could be known beyond the normative liturgical and canonical material. This book is intended to dispel that impression.

No medieval historian can aspire to the wealth of detail achieved in the work of anthropologists, who have the advantage of being able to ask their native informants for more information. Nevertheless, as we shall see in the chapters that follow, the historical sources *do* permit the description and analysis of the fundamental features of sponsorship and spiritual kinship as they developed in the early medieval West.

PART TWO

BAPTISMAL SPONSORSHIP IN THE ANCIENT CHURCH, CA. 170 TO CA. 500

THREE

THE SPONSORSHIP OF ADULTS

The ecclesiastical tradition of studying baptismal sponsorship has devoted the bulk of its effort during the last twenty-five years to the examination of sponsoring practices before the sixth century. Sources for this period have been painstakingly gathered and analyzed, particularly by Dujarier.[1] The resulting view of early Christian sponsorship, while not widely disseminated, is complete and sophisticated, although it devotes little attention to the nonliturgical and nonformal aspects of the practice. This chapter is not intended to reinspect ground that has been so thoroughly explored. Rather, I will use it to provide a more wide-ranging sketch of sponsorship prior to the sixth century, drawing heavily and gratefully on the ecclesiastical scholarship mentioned above.

The emergence of baptismal sponsorship was a response to two distinct developments that the Christian church experienced from the mid-second century onward. One was the influx of adult converts from Greco-Roman paganism, which challenged the informal reception practices of the earliest days and led to the demand by Christian communities for concrete assurances as to the converts' sincerity and suitability. The second was the increase in the number of baptizees who were children born to Christian parents, a development that prompted a provision for participation by an infant or young child in the liturgy and for the subsequent religious formation of the child. These two developments have often been confused, but they were so different in their origin and impact that they must be treated separately for clarity's sake. I shall begin with the sponsorship of adults.

Between the third and fifth centuries, the major Christian communities in the Roman Empire developed elaborate procedures for testing, training, and initiating converts. Modern scholars have designated

---

[1] Michel Dujarier, *Le parrainage des adultes aux trois premiers siècles de l'Eglise. Recherche historique sur l'évolution des garanties et des étapes catéchuménales avant 313* (Paris, 1962), pp. 37–67; see also Christiane Brusselmans, "Les fonctions de parrainage des enfants aux premiers siècles de l'Eglise (100–550)" (Ph.D. diss., Catholic University of America, 1964); and Bernard de Guchteneëre, *Le parrainage des adultes aux ive et ve siècles de l'Eglise*, Excerpta ex dissertatione ad Lauream in facultate theologica Pontificiae Universitatis Gregorianae (Louvain, 1964).

this institution, which was one of the earliest formal structures of the Christian church, as the catechumenate. In this catechumenate, lay Christians recommended or "sponsored" adult converts to the church authorities, testifying that the converts were properly disposed to be admitted to the process of initiation. The practice of sponsoring adults for baptism has frequently been misinterpreted because our understanding of it has, in a sense, been contaminated by the very different institution of infant baptism and its own form of sponsorship. In late antiquity the supply of adult converts slowly dried up in the formally Christianized Mediterranean societies; thus, infants became the ordinary candidates for baptism. In this new environment, adult sponsorship was assimilated into that of infants and lost its originally distinct features, which have been rediscovered only in modern times.

In describing the sponsorship of adult converts in the ancient church, it is crucial to avoid easy identification with later practices. In particular, sponsors must not be called "godparents" in the later sense of that term. For, in contrast to the godparent of later times, the ancient sponsor of an adult (1) had prebaptismal duties and probably did not incur lifelong obligations; (2) incurred neither marital taboos nor onerous bonds to the baptizee's family; (3) was not conceived as the parent of a newborn "spiritual" child, but rather as a guarantor to a contract; and (4) was not necessarily one and the same person throughout the initiation process. The practice of sponsoring adults must, therefore, be understood on its own terms.

The missionary methods of the first-century Christian movement, as reflected primarily in New Testament texts, were those of a group convinced that the world's end was near, a group eager to make converts before the last day dawned.[2] A superficial reading of the relevant New Testament texts might lead one to conclude that in such circumstances baptism was conceded easily to all who were seeking it. However, Dujarier has argued convincingly that early Christian communities, like their contemporary Jewish counterparts, had criteria by which to decide whom they would admit to membership. Thus, even in scriptural texts where baptism follows quickly upon preaching, Dujarier detected a pattern in which converts had exhibited clear signs of faith and sincerity, or had been recommended by Christians in good standing with the community before they were baptized. In presenting his findings, Dujarier was careful not to read the later catechu-

[2] John Gager, *Kingdom and Community: The Social World of Early Christianity* (Englewood Cliffs, N.J., 1975), pp. 37–49, argues that the failure of the Second Coming of Jesus spurred missionary activity as a means for the group to cope with the doubts that failure aroused.

menate back into first- or early second-century Christianity. However, he did attempt to trace back into Jewish and Christian practices of that period the presuppositions that lay behind and made sense of the later institution of sponsorship. In doing so, he demonstrated that even though neither first-century Judaism nor incipient Christianity had sponsors as such, both were keenly concerned with scrutinizing the sincerity of converts, a preoccupation that could, in the right circumstances, lead to formal sponsorship.[3] Hence Dujarier's approach has rejuvenated the study of the origins of the catechumenate and of sponsorship by directing attention away from the search for explicit texts and toward the clarification of the presuppositions, fears, and values out of which the institutions emerged in the later second and the third centuries.

In the Acts of the Apostles, there is no indication that Paul and other itinerant preachers imposed a waiting period in which converts were tested before baptism. Nevertheless, in virtually every case in which Acts is explicit, the converts received instruction, professed belief, and only then were baptized.[4] For example, in Acts 2, Peter addresses a crowd of Jews at Jerusalem, arguing within a framework familiar to them that "God has made this Jesus whom you crucified both Lord and Christ" (Acts 2:36). Luke describes the result of Peter's preaching in this way: "He spoke to them for a long time using many arguments, and he urged them, 'Save yourselves from this perverse generation.' They were convinced by his arguments, and they accepted what he said and were baptized" (Acts 2:40–41).

This pattern of instruction/profession of belief/baptism is also discernible in Acts 8:26–40, in which Philip's conversion of the Ethiopian eunuch is described. The Ethiopian was apparently a "godfearer," one of those gentiles who was interested in Judaism, sometimes attended synagogue services, and observed some features of Judaic practice, but had not formally adopted Judaism and the full burden of the Law. He was returning from a pilgrimage to Jerusalem and was reading the prophet Isaiah when Philip approached him, as a result of a command from an angel. Philip used the occasion of Isaiah 53:7–8 to explain the "Good News of Jesus" to the man, who believed and whose worthiness was attested implicitly by the angel's command. The Ethiopian requested baptism: "Look, there is some water here; is there anything to stop me being baptized?" Philip obliged him and the Ethiopian

---

[3] Dujarier, *Le parrainage*, pp. 69–171; Joachim Jeremias, *Infant Baptism in the First Four Centuries*, tr. D. Cairns (Philadelphia, 1962), pp. 33–42, argues that Jewish proselyte baptism, including its use of witnesses, was a "parent" of Christian baptism.

[4] Dujarier, *Le parrainage*, pp. 121–148.

went on his way. But some early Christian reader apparently thought this was not sufficiently explicit and added in the "Western" text of the Acts a clearer profession of faith immediately after the Ethiopian's request: "And Philip said, 'If you believe with all your heart, you may [be baptized].' And he replied, 'I believe that Jesus Christ is the Son of God.' " Thus, from the first century, acceptance of new members had been conducted within a framework that demanded circumspection and some assurance that the convert had been instructed and that he believed before receiving baptism.

The thought and behavior of early Christians was colored by the expectation that Jesus would soon return. Quite naturally, the recession of that hope from a vivid immediacy to a vague future time had profound implications for the development of structures to organize life in the interim before the Second Coming. Thus, by the second century, serious problems had apparently been perceived, problems that cast doubt on the wisdom of baptizing converts soon after their profession of faith. The earliest converts had been Jews or gentiles with ties to Judaism, like the Ethiopian or the Roman centurion Cornelius, who was also a godfearer (Acts 10). Such people were familiar with and largely adhered to the ethical norms and beliefs of Judaism, which early Christianity simply adopted. For such converts, it was not a large step to accept the belief that the man Jesus had been the fulfillment of Judaism, the Messiah. For them, a brief instruction followed by a profession of faith and an expeditious baptism was the simplest and most sensible course.

However, the growing alienation of Christianity from Judaism after the Jewish War (A.D. 66–70) and the growing success of Christianity in the urban, hellenized eastern Mediterranean led to an increasing proportion of converts directly from Greco-Roman paganism. These converts did not share the Jewish heritage in ethics, scripture, and world view; indeed, their values, morals, and beliefs were often quite incompatible with those of Judaism or Christianity.

Early missionaries like Paul had asked their converts to assent to a brief credal statement, along the lines of "Jesus is Lord."[5] This was sufficient because the missionary could generally assume that the convert already shared the complex of ideas that were at the heart of the loose Jewish doctrinal consensus (monotheism, God's sovereignty, the Chosen People, and the coming Messiah). But when increasing numbers of Christian converts were unfamiliar with Judaism, local

[5] Vernon H. Neufeld, The Earliest Christian Confessions, New Testament Tools and Studies, vol. 5 (Grand Rapids, Mich., 1963).

churches demanded a more searching examination and systematic instruction of the newcomers.

Theological disputes within the Christian movement also promoted a more circumspect attitude toward converts. From its beginnings, Christianity was prone to internal disagreements, but in the course of the second century fundamental and bitter disputes over the meaning of Jesus' life and teaching erupted.[6] Adherents of various positions regarded their opponents as heretics and attempted to guard their followers against conflicting views. Statistics concerning these schisms are, of course, impossible to gather, but it may have been true that during much of the second century none of the competing Christian sects commanded a majority of the adherents to the wider Christian movement.

One of these competing traditions ultimately bested its rivals, in part with the aid of the Roman state in the fourth and fifth centuries. This victorious tradition, which may be called the Catholic (or, in the second century, the proto-Catholic) consensus, is described by Joseph B. Tyson as follows:

> In particular, the writing of Irenaeus exemplifies an attempt to create a single form for the Christian faith with definite and clear limits. To him, the church must rest upon the authority of the apostles and bishops, a definite creed, and a limited canon of sacred writings. These three formal elements became the building blocks for catholic Christianity, giving it a controlling organization and a means for distinguishing true and false faith.[7]

This Catholic tradition, which was shared by a loose confederation of local churches around the Mediterranean, moved gradually in the later second century and throughout the third century to structure a formal pattern of initiation into Christianity, a pattern modern scholars have called the catechumenate.

The catechumenate was a paradigm of unity in diversity, a microcosm of pre-Constantinian Catholic Christianity's federal character. It grew out of the fact that the independent churches in Rome, Alexandria, North Africa, and Syria-Palestine all experienced similar pressures to deal more carefully with converts. In response, they devel-

---

[6] For a survey of pre-third-century varieties of Christianity, see Joseph B. Tyson, *A Study of Early Christianity* (New York, 1973), pp. 273–335, which divides the Christian movement into primitive, Pauline, Johannine, Jewish, Gnostic, and proto-Catholic strands.

[7] Ibid., p. 325.

oped roughly similar structures, partly generated out of shared
attitudes and assumptions and partly through imitation of one another.

The local, concrete expressions of the catechumenate varied in liturgical symbolism and actions, as well as in the sequence of events.[8]
However, when stripped to its essentials, the catechumenate was a
process by which an adult who had expressed a desire to join the
church and was thus already a believer in some sense was tested,
purified by exorcism, and instructed over an extended period of time
before he or she was admitted to full initiation in baptism. But while
the intellectual formation of the convert had a significant role, the
catechumenate was not primarily a short course in theology. Rather,
the convert was expected to behave during this time as a Christian,
thus making the catechumenate a time to manifest sincere conviction
in actual deeds. The catechumenate was also a period during which
the convert was being ritually purified for baptism. Many scholars
have found it difficult to assess at its true weight the early Christian
conviction that the unbaptized, including catechumens, were in the
grip of demonic forces that had to be expelled gradually by the repeated exorcisms, prayers, and fasts that punctuated the preparation
for baptism. Capelle even argued that the catechumenate in the *Apostolic Tradition* of Hippolytus was "dominated by the idea of
exorcism."[9]

Prior to the fourth century, the only source that treats the adult
catechumenate in an extended manner is the one just cited, Hippolytus' *Apostolic Tradition*. (There are other texts that refer to the catechumenate incidentally or briefly and there are also sources for the very
different matter of the initiation of infants.) From 313 to 450, western
sources referring at length or unambiguously to the catechumenate
and sponsorship of adults are scarce. But during the same period there
are numerous sources from the area of Syria and Palestine, which was
the *"place privilégiée"*[10] of baptismal preparation.

One series of church orders, which depends to a greater or lesser
degree on Hippolytus' *Apostolic Tradition*, is difficult to assess properly

[8] Dujarier, *Le parrainage*, pp. 37–67. For studies of the major versions of the catechumenate, see B. Capelle, "L'introduction du catéchuménat à Rome," *RTAM* 5
(1933):129–154; Robert de Latte, "Saint Augustin et le baptême. Etude liturgico-historique du rituel baptismal des adultes chez Saint Augustin," *QLP* 56 (1975):177–223; de
Guchteneëre, *Le parrainage des adultes*; Thomas M. Finn, *The Liturgy of Baptism in the
Baptismal Instructions of St. John Chrysostom*, CUA, SCA, vol. 15 (Washington, D.C.,
1967), pp. 25–85.

[9] Capelle, "L'introduction," p. 148.

[10] Dujarier, *Le parrainage*, p. 291.

on the issue of sponsorship and the catechumenate because its constit-
uents are "a mixture of apostolic fiction, of ideal reform and of reality."[11] These fourth- and fifth-century church documents include (a)
the *Canons of Hippolytus* (mid-fourth century, perhaps Egyptian),
which survive in an Arabic translation;[12] (b) the *Testament of Our Lord
Jesus Christ* (450–500, Monophysite Syria), which survives in Syriac,
Coptic, Ethiopian, and Arabic recensions;[13] (c) book 7 of the *Apostolic
Constitutions* (about 380, Syria or Constantinople);[14] and (d) the so-
called *Egyptian Church Order*, which survives in Latin, Sahidic, Bo-
hairic, Arabic, and Ethiopian versions.[15] It was on the basis of these
texts that Bernard Botte carried out his meticulous and critically ac-
claimed reconstruction of the source on which each depended, Hippolytus' *Apostolic Tradition*.[16]

Other eastern sources, which are important because they are independent of Hippolytus and record actual usages, include the sermons
of John Chrysostom[17] and Theodore of Mopsuestia,[18] which reflect
Syrian practices of the late fourth century, and the travel account of
the pilgrim Egeria, which describes the customs she observed at Jerusalem about 390.[19]

It would be quite incorrect to treat these sources, scattered as they
are across three centuries and across the eastern Mediterranean and its
hinterlands, as reflections of a tightly knit system. Indeed, it can be
seen that the more extensive accounts differ in large and small details,
as might be expected in view of the uncentralized, federal character of
the early church. This can clearly be shown in Jean Michel Hanssens'
publication in parallel columns of the Latin translations of the church

---

[11] Ibid., p. 44.

[12] *Les Canons d'Hippolyte*, ed. R. G. Coquin, *PO*, vol. 31, pt. 2 (Paris, 1966), with a
French translation.

[13] *Testamentum domini nostri Jesu Christi*, ed. I. E. Rahmani (Mainz, 1899), in a Syriac
version with a Latin translation.

[14] *Didascalia et Constitutiones Apostolorum*, vol. 1, ed. F. X. Funk (Paderborn, 1905),
pp. 461–595.

[15] For the editions of the Egyptian Church Order in its various recensions, see Berthold Altaner and Alfred Stuiber, *Patrologie*, 8th ed. (Freiburg, 1978), pp. 83, 557.

[16] Bernard Botte, *La tradition apostolique de saint Hippolyte. Essai de reconstitution* (Münster, 1963). Botte presented the results of his work in *La tradition apostolique d'après les
anciennes versions*, 2nd ed., SC, vol. 11bis (Paris, 1968).

[17] John Chrysostom, *Huit catéchèses baptismales inédites*, ed. Antoine Wenger, SC, vol.
50 (Paris, 1957).

[18] Theodore of Mopsuestia, *Les homélies catéchétiques de Théodore de Mopsueste*, ed. and
tr. Raymond Tonneau and Robert Devreesse, ST, vol. 145 (Vatican City, 1949).

[19] Egeria, *Itinerarium*, ed. A. Franceschini and R. Weber, CCSL, vol. 175 (Turnhout,
1965), pp. 27–90.

orders and related documents that depended on Hippolytus' *Apostolic Tradition*.[20] For even within this family of documents the variations are significant enough to warn against hasty homogenization. And in sources not derived from Hippolytus, the differences are even more striking, reflecting a situation in which the practices of testing and instruction became more elaborate and more particularized over the course of time.

Nevertheless, in spite of the rich variety of detail, the central purpose and main structural features of the catechumenate remain discernible. From the third to the mid-fourth century, initiation into Catholic Christianity was a structured experience that extended over as many as three years and included elements of testing, religious and moral formation, and purification through exorcism, prayer, and fasting. It culminated in a brief, intense burst of activity immediately preceding full initiation, which included baptism as well as what were later regarded as the sacraments of confirmation and first communion. It was in conjunction with the moral testing demanded of each adult catechumen that the practice of sponsoring arose and, to keep some perspective on the matter, became a minor aspect of the elaborate initiation processes of the ancient church.

The earliest surviving description of the catechumenate is found in the *Apostolic Tradition* of Hippolytus. In spite of Hanssens' argument for an Alexandrian origin,[21] the present consensus is that the *Apostolic Tradition* probably represents a somewhat idealized description of the liturgy at Rome in the early third century.[22] In sections 15 to 22, the *Apostolic Tradition* describes as traditional for converts a three-year period of initiation, the practices of which were quite well developed and may represent the usages of an earlier generation, perhaps those of A.D. 180. The guiding principle that is discernible in this catechumenate was the reluctance of the Christian community to accept converts without assurances as to their sincerity and their comprehension of the beliefs and behavior patterns they were accepting.

In the course of Hippolytus' catechumenate, there were two decisive examinations. At each one, Christians in good standing had to

---

[20] Jean Michel Hanssens, *La liturgie d'Hippolyte: Documents et études* (Rome, 1970), pp. 30–157.

[21] Jean Michel Hanssens, *La liturgie d'Hippolyte. Ses documents, son titulaire, ses origines et son caractère*, Orientalia christiana analecta, vol. 155 (Rome, 1959), pp. 506–511, and passim.

[22] *The Study of Liturgy*, ed. Cheslyn Jones, Geoffrey Wainwright, and Edward Yarnold (New York, 1978), pp. 57–59.

testify for the candidate; such testimony was the main function of sponsors. The first examination is described by Hippolytus as follows:

Those who are brought forward for the first time to hear the word should first be brought to the teachers before the people enter; and let them be questioned about the reason on account of which they are coming to the faith. Let those who brought them give testimony as to whether they are fit to hear the word. Let them be questioned concerning the manner of their life.[23]

The text continues with a listing of the things that might lead to the immediate rejection of the candidate, including objectionable sexual practices, demonic possession, and an occupation that was immoral, idolatrous, or involved the shedding of blood.[24] At this moment of first formal contact between the interested non-Christian and the Christian community, intermediaries, whom we may presume to be members of the church, are described as "those who brought them"; their function is to "give testimony as to whether they are fit to hear the word." Thus the community clearly wished to have assurances from a reliable person that the candidate was properly disposed and motivated. The text does not explicitly say that "those who brought them" participated in the detailed examination of the candidate's "manner of life," but that is certainly a reasonable assumption. These intermediaries (or witnesses), called *Katechumenatszeuge* by Dick,[25] may also be designated as sponsors, although that technical term is not in Hippolytus' work.

If the candidate was found to be acceptable, both on the testimony of those who brought him and on the investigation of his life, he was admitted as a *katechumenos* ("one who is being instructed"). The *Apostolic Tradition* notes that "catechumens should hear the word for three years. However, if anyone is zealous and attends to the matter well, the length of time will not be judged but the conduct alone is what will be judged."[26] This concern with the conduct of the catechumen highlights the probationary character of the process.

During the period of probation, the catechumen was expected to demonstrate in a visible way sincerity and firmness of intentions. A relapse into unacceptable behavior could delay baptism and even lead to expulsion. The catechumen was a member of the church, but was distinguished from and regarded as inferior to those members who

[23] Botte, *La tradition*, ch. 15, p. 68.
[24] Ibid., chs. 15–16, pp. 68–74.
[25] Dick, "Das Pateninstitut," pp. 3–36.
[26] Botte, *La tradition*, ch. 17, p. 74.

were fully initiated, who constituted the "faithful." The *Apostolic Tradition* refers briefly to meetings at which teachers instructed the catechumens, who prayed together and received a laying on of hands from the teacher, who might be a layman or a cleric. The catechumens were kept separate from the faithful and did not participate in the eucharistic meal, which was a mystery reserved for the initiated.[27]

During the probationary period, the catechumens no doubt learned a considerable amount about the beliefs and rituals of their new religion. However, the instructional aspects of the catechumenate must not be exaggerated, for some of the major beliefs of the group were purposely kept from the catechumen, to be explained after initiation.[28] Instead, the emphasis of the catechumenate was on moral testing and on the behavior of the candidate.

At any time within the three years of probation, the catechumen could be examined again and, if the examination was favorable, be "set apart" to receive baptism. Sponsors were needed by the candidate during this second examination as well. The *Apostolic Tradition* describes the procedure as follows:

> When those who are going to receive baptism are chosen, let their life be examined as to whether they lived piously while they were catechumens, whether they honored the widows, whether they visited the sick, whether they did every sort of good thing. *And when those who brought them forward give testimony over each: 'he acted in this way,' let them hear the gospel.* From the time when they are set apart, let hands be laid on them daily while they are exorcised. When the day approaches on which they will be baptized, let the bishop exorcise each of them, that he may know whether he is pure.[29]

There is no precise indication of the length of this intense period of exorcism, liturgical action, and instruction, except that it culminated on a Sunday at cockcrow.[30] In the third and fourth centuries, this period after the candidates had been "set apart" for baptism came to be more sharply distinguished from the preceding part of the catechumenate. It was called the competentate, after those who were seeking baptism (*competentes*), and filled three or four weeks preceding Easter

---

[27] Ibid., chs. 18–19, p. 76.

[28] On the *disciplina arcani*, a policy of veiling in secrecy the precise nature of baptism, the Eucharist, the Creed, and the Lord's Prayer, see Jones, et al., *The Study of Liturgy*, pp. 109–110. The *disciplina* was most evident in the fourth and fifth centuries.

[29] Botte, *La tradition*, ch. 20, p. 78. Italics added.

[30] Ibid., chs. 20–21, pp. 78–80.

or Pentecost, which became the preferred dates for baptism in the ancient church. This period of intensive preparation for baptism was the core around which the Christian season of Lent developed.[31]

The *Apostolic Tradition* did not specify whether the sponsors for the first examination were the same as those for the second. However, we may surmise that in order to be qualified to testify to a candidate's behavior over as many as three years, the sponsor should have been acquainted with the candidate and might even have taken some responsibility for him during the probationary period. But any such continuity of sponsors must remain hypothetical.

In Hippolytus' work, the role of sponsors ceased at the successful completion of the second examination and the beginning of the immediate preparation for baptism. Henceforth, the ceremonies unfolded with the adult candidates, the clergy, and the Christian community as the only identified actors. Thus we may conclude that the sponsor for an adult had a role that was restricted and entirely prebaptismal. In other words, the sponsor acted solely as a witness that the candidate was both willing and able to be initiated, that he or she was properly disposed to hear the word and was conforming to the behavior expected of a sincere convert.

Hippolytus' catechumenate was not normative for the whole of third-century Christianity: it was merely the way such things were done at Rome (or perhaps the way the author wished they were done). In the third century, Tertullian and Origen alluded to catechumenal practices, but we do not know in detail how their respective churches conducted the matter; nor do we know about sponsorship within their respective catechumenates.[32]

When informative sources reappear in the fourth century, there are notable differences from the pattern described in the *Apostolic Tradition*, differences that may be rooted in the legalization of Christianity and its growing social prominence, which had turned Hippolytus' trickle of converts into a flood. Not everyone was pleased with these developments and a series of fourth- and fifth-century church orders

[31] S. G. Hall, "Paschal Baptism," *Studia evangelica* 6 (1973):239–251, notes that Tertullian, *De baptismo*, ch. 19, was the earliest clear reference to baptizing on the vigil of Easter. According to Thierry Maertens, *Histoire et pastorale du rituel du catéchuménat et du baptême*, Paroisse et liturgie, Collection de pastorale liturgique, vol. 56 (Bruges, 1962), p. 126, the Lenten preparation for Easter in the fourth and fifth centuries lasted three weeks at Rome, four weeks at Jerusalem, and four weeks in Gaul.

[32] On the history of catechumenal practices in Egypt and North Africa during the third century, see the brief survey by Michel Dujarier, *A History of the Catechumenate: The First Six Centuries* (New York, 1979), pp. 41–63. For a fuller treatment, see Dujarier's *Le parrainage*, pp. 217–290.

based on the *Apostolic Tradition* were written as if Hippolytus' three-year catechumenate were still the standard. However, these texts were archaizing, idealizing a perfect "apostolic" time, and probably did not accurately describe contemporary fourth- and fifth-century practices.

But other texts do reflect the customs surrounding the initiation of adult converts in some fourth- and fifth-century churches. In the simplest terms, the pattern described by Hippolytus, consisting of a long period of moral testing and instruction in the catechumenate and a shorter period of intense liturgical and intellectual preparation in the competentate, had been replaced during the fourth century by a situation in which the major part of a church's attention to converts was concentrated on the latter period, which became quite formalized and structured. The long catechumenate survived, but it was mostly ritual, with no substantive concern for moral testing or instruction.

In early fifth-century North Africa, Augustine of Hippo described a somewhat idealized process for becoming a catechumen. According to this method, when a person presented himself at the bishop's house he was interrogated as to his motives and his understanding of what it meant to become a Christian. Christian relatives or friends might testify to the applicant's sincerity, but such sponsors were not very important in Augustine's practice, since he was generous in conceding entry to the catechumenate in the hope that even dubious applicants would improve once they were within the church. The session continued with a rapid telling of the history of salvation but without explicit comments on the deeper mysteries of the Creed, the Eucharist, or baptism. The meeting ended with a brief ritual consisting of the symbolic rites of making a sign of the cross on the candidate, giving him salt or salted bread, laying on hands, and performing a brief exorcism.[33] At the end of this meeting, which might last anywhere from half an hour to two hours, the individual was a catechumen, that is to say, a second-class variety of Christian, sharply distinguished from the baptized faithful.

Catechumens were eligible, as were any pagans or Jews, to attend Christian services in order to hear the scripture readings and the sermon. However, all unbaptized persons, including the catechumens, were ushered out of the church before the eucharistic mysteries began. And while Hippolytus had described regular meetings among catechumens and their teachers outside the eucharistic reunions, in Au-

[33] Robert de Latte, "Saint Augustin et le baptême," *QLP* 56 (1975):178–191. Frederik Van der Meer, *Augustine the Bishop: Church and Society at the Dawn of the Middle Ages*, tr. B. Battershaw and G. R. Lamb (London, 1961), pp. 353–357.

gustine's church, which was typical in this regard, there were no services directed expressly to the catechumens, who were expected to learn about Christianity in the context of the community's regular round of sermons and liturgical readings. In his sermons, Augustine occasionally alluded to the presence of catechumens, and in deference to the *disciplina arcani* he avoided public sermons on the Eucharist, baptism, or the Creed, exact knowledge of which was reserved for the baptized.[34]

By the middle of the fourth century, the catechumenate had become a sort of holding pattern and it was the competentate that demanded a decision to convert. It became customary for many adult catechumens, even those born to Christian families, to delay baptism indefinitely, perhaps to old age or final illness, in order to avoid postbaptismal sin and the serious business of penance.[35] Many of the most eminent theologians and bishops of the fourth and fifth centuries, including Ambrose, Jerome, and Augustine, postponed baptism until their twenties or thirties.[36]

Augustine's comments in his *Confessions* help us to enter into the ethos of the rather vestigial fourth-century catechumenate:

> While still a boy I had been told of the eternal life promised to us by Our Lord, who humbled himself and came down amongst us proud sinners. As a catechumen, I was blessed regularly from birth with the sign of the Cross and was seasoned with God's salt, for, O Lord, my mother placed great hope in you. Once as a child I was taken suddenly ill with a disorder of the stomach and was on the point of death. You, my God, were my guardian even then, and you saw the fervour and strength of my faith as I appealed to the piety of my own mother and to the mother of us all, your Church, to give me the baptism of Christ your Son, who is my God and my Master. . . . Had I not quickly recovered, she [his mother, Monica] would have hastened to see that I was admitted to the sacraments of salvation and washed clean by acknowledging you, Lord Jesus, for the pardon of my sins. So my washing in the waters of baptism was postponed, in the surmise that, if I continued to live, I should defile myself

---

[34] Van der Meer, *Augustine*, p. 354.

[35] On the delay of baptism in the fourth century, see Brusselmans, "Les fonctions," pp. 57–67. See also Van der Meer, *Augustine*, pp. 148–151, and Jeremias, *Infant Baptism*, pp. 87–97.

[36] Jean Danielou and Henri Marrou, *The Christian Centuries*, vol. 1: *The First Six Hundred Years* (London, 1964), p. 306.

again with sin and, after baptism, the guilt of pollution would be greater and more dangerous.[37]

In spite of complaints from bishops who saw in procrastinating catechumens a tendency to excuse sins because they would later be washed away in baptism,[38] the fourth-century catechumenate was far different from the rigorous probationary period recommended by Hippolytus and his latter-day imitators. It was open-ended and many adults were catechumens for decades until illness, religious conversion in the Pauline sense, or some other motive led them to seek baptism.

When fourth- or fifth-century catechumens finally did take the step to seek baptism, they entered into an intense and serious phase of the initiation process, quite in contrast to the loosely regulated catechumenate. Catechumens who had been accepted for baptism received a new title. At Rome they were called the "elect" from *electus* ("one who has been chosen") and elsewhere in the Latin-speaking world they were called *competentes* ("those who seek");[39] in Greek they were designated as *photisomenoi* ("those who are to be enlightened"). In order to designate this second phase of the catechumenate, which took on greater importance as the earlier phase withered, modern scholars have coined the terms "competentate" or "photismate."

If the competentate was to be tightly structured and managed efficiently by the bishop or his delegates, then baptisms had to be performed at the same time, preceded by the liturgical, moral, and intellectual preparation of the candidates in groups. If an emergency, particularly a serious illness, demanded it, baptism could be performed at any time. However, for healthy candidates the tendency since the third century had been to restrict baptism to the Christian festivals of rebirth and new life, Easter and Pentecost.[40] In the fourth and fifth centuries, the competentate coincided with a period preceding Easter, extending over three to seven weeks, depending on local practice.

A precious source for the competentate at Jerusalem about 390 is the travel account written by a nun from Aquitania or Galicia for the

[37] Augustine, *Confessions*, bk. 1, ch. 11, tr. R. S. Pine-Coffin (Baltimore, 1969), pp. 31-32.

[38] Van der Meer, *Augustine*, p. 150; Brusselmans, "Les fonctions," pp. 77-142.

[39] On the technical term *competens*, see A.A.R. Bastiaensen, *Observations sur le vocabulaire liturgique dans l'Itinéraire d'Egérie*, LCP, vol. 17 (Nijmegen and Utrecht, 1962), pp. 15-16.

[40] Hall, "Paschal Baptism," pp. 239-251, argues that the connection between baptism and Easter cannot be securely documented before Tertullian, *De baptismo*, ch. 19. It was only in the later third and fourth centuries that the linkage became customary.

edification of her stay-at-home sisters.[41] Egeria (which was probably her name)[42] was an energetic tourist and a tireless observer of liturgical services. She was particularly impressed by the liturgies conducted at Jerusalem, where her visit may have coincided with the last years of the great bishop Cyril (348–386), who was especially interested in liturgical matters.[43] She described with relish the busy, indeed exhausting, Lenten services and observances that she saw at Jerusalem, and it was in this context that she told her sisters about the competentate:

> I feel I should add something about the way they instruct those who are to be baptized at Easter. Names must be given in before the first day of Lent, which means that a presbyter takes down all the names before the start of the eight weeks for which Lent lasts here, as I have told you.[44]

Those who "gave in their names" were usually, but not always, long-time catechumens who had decided to be baptized. Elsewhere in Syria and Palestine, the names of sponsors were entered on the written list along with the names of the *competentes*.[45] Egeria continued:

> Once the priest has all the names, on the second day of Lent at the start of the eight weeks, the bishop's chair is placed in the middle of the Great Church, the Martyrium, the presbyters sit in chairs on either side of him, and all the clergy stand. Then one by one those seeking baptism are brought up, men coming with their fathers and women with their mothers. As they come in one

[41] Egeria, *Itinerarium*, pp. 27–90. The English translations in my text are from John Wilkinson, *Egeria's Travels* (London, 1971).

[42] On the controversy surrounding the pilgrim's name (Silvia, Aetheria, Egeria, and others), see Hélène Pétré, *Ethérie. Journal de voyage*, SC, vol. 21 (Paris, 1948), pp. 9–11. (Pétré chose Etheria, but subsequent scholarship has defended Egeria); and Wilkinson, *Egeria's Travels*, pp. 235–236.

[43] Cyril's literary legacy includes twenty-four catechetical sermons, eighteen of which were directed to *competentes* and five to the newly baptized in the week after Easter, on which see Altaner and Stuiber, *Patrologie*, pp. 312–313, 614. The sermons were translated by L. P. McCauley and A. A. Stephenson in *The Works of Saint Cyril of Jerusalem*, FC, vols. 61 and 64 (Washington, D.C., 1969–1970). On Cyril's initiation practices, see Hugh M. Riley, *Christian Initiation: A Comparative Study of the Interpretation of the Baptismal Liturgy in the Mystagogical Writings of Cyril of Jerusalem, John Chrysostom, Theodore of Mopsuestia and Ambrose of Milan.* CUA, SCA, vol. 17 (Washington, D.C., 1974).

[44] Egeria, *Itinerarium*, ch. 45.1, p. 87; Wilkinson, *Egeria's Travels*, p. 143.

[45] On listing the names of the *competentes* and their sponsors, see Theodore of Mopsuestia, Catechetical Sermon 12.16, in *Les homélies*, p. 347. On the practice of "giving in one's name" for baptism at the beginning of Lent, see Finn, *The Liturgy of Baptism*, pp. 43–58.

by one, the bishop asks their neighbors questions about them: 'Is this person leading a good life? Does he respect his parents? Is he a drunkard or a boaster?' He asks about all the serious human vices. And if his inquiries show him that someone has not committed any of these misdeeds, he himself puts down his name; but if someone is guilty he is told to go away, and the bishop tells him that he is to amend his ways before he may come to the font. He asks the men and women the same questions. But it is not too easy for a visitor to come to baptism if he has no witnesses who are acquainted with him.[46]

This public examination by the bishop of Jerusalem early in Lent was equivalent to Hippolytus' second examination for admission to preparation for baptism. Like its predecessor of almost two centuries, it stressed behavior and not knowledge about Christianity; the teaching during the competentate would provide the missing information.

The form of the questions reported by Egeria leads us to conclude that they were directed not to the candidate but to his Christian neighbors (*vicini*), who were asked to comment on his behavior. Each male catechumen was also accompanied by his "father" and each female catechumen by her "mother," terms that have puzzled most commentators. In view of what is known from other roughly contemporary sources, the normal impulse is to see these persons as sponsors; yet the Latin terms that were used (*pater* and *mater*, without any qualifying adjective or clause) do not necessarily demand such an interpretation. And so the explanation of this puzzling use of words must be sought in fourth-century sponsoring practice, and in the fourth-century Christian use of language.

Few commentators have seriously entertained the idea that Egeria was literally correct and that these "fathers" and "mothers" could actually have been the natural parents of the *competentes*. Yet when that possibility is examined, an affirmative reaction, qualified in certain ways, is probably correct. It is well attested by Hippolytus,[47] Augustine,[48] John the Deacon,[49] and the church orders based on Hippolytus'

[46] Egeria, *Itinerarium*, ch. 45.2–4, p. 87; Wilkinson, *Egeria's Travels*, pp. 143–144.

[47] Botte, *La tradition*, ch. 21, p. 80: "first baptize the little ones. All who are able to speak for themselves, let them speak. As for those who are not able to speak for themselves, let their parents or someone from their family speak for them."

[48] Augustine, Letter 98, ch. 6, ed. A. Goldbacher, *S. Aureli Augustini Hipponiensis episcopi epistulae*, CSEL, vol. 34 (Vienna, 1895), p. 527.

[49] John the Deacon, *Letter to Senarius*, ch. 7, in André Wilmart, "Un florilège carolingien sur le symbolisme des cérémonies du baptême, avec un Appendice sur la lettre de

Apostolic Tradition[50] that parents ordinarily sponsored their own infants.[51] However, I don't wish to draw from this fact too firm a conclusion about adult sponsorship, since I argued earlier that the two forms should be kept separate.

The tenor of Egeria's comments (for example, "Is he a drunkard or a boaster?") points to adults or adolescents as the object of the bishop's inquiry. (There must have been infants baptized at Jerusalem, but Egeria said nothing about them, perhaps because there were no serious divergences from the practices with which she was familiar at home.) Is there any reason to think that a Christian father could not sponsor his adult son or a Christian mother her adult daughter? By the eighth century, as we shall see, parent sponsors were officially excluded at Byzantium and in parts of the Latin West, but in the fourth century there is not a scrap of evidence to that effect.

Is there any evidence that parents did in fact sponsor their adult children? There is the text of Egeria, which can bear that interpretation, but I know of no other clear text.[52] Nevertheless, I believe that the weight of probabilities leans to the conclusion that some of the candidates whom Egeria saw around the bishop were accompanied by a natural parent. However, it defies common sense to believe that they all were. Obviously, those candidates born to pagan or Jewish families could not have had a parent sponsor; and in an era of high mortality, it is unlikely that every adult catechumen from a Christian family had the appropriate parent still living. In such cases, the "father" or "mother" was probably a Christian of good reputation who was acquainted with the candidate, so as to be able to testify along with neighbors about his or her conduct.[53]

Jean Diacre," *Analecta Reginensia*, ST, vol. 59 (Vatican City, 1933), p. 175, and tr. by E. C. Whitaker in *Documents of the Baptismal Liturgy* (London, 1960), pp. 144–148.

[50] Hanssens, *La Liturgie d'Hippolyte* (1970), arranged in Latin translation the parallel passages from church orders of the fourth and fifth centuries that were based on Hippolytus' *Apostolic Tradition*. On the sponsoring of infants, see ch. 39, pp. 110–119, where the appropriate passages from the Syriac, Arabic, and Ethiopian recensions of the *Egyptian Church Order*, the *Testament of Our Lord Jesus Christ*, and the *Canons of Hippolytus* are found. In each version, parents or kinsmen speak and act for their infant.

[51] Brusselmans, "Les fonctions," argues that parents were the normal sponsors of infants because of their primary role in providing for the moral and religious formation of their children.

[52] Brusselmans, "Les fonctions," pp. 112–113, concludes that the *matres* and *patres* in Egeria's text were actually natural parents.

[53] De Guchteneëre, *Le parrainage des adultes*, pp. 46–50, came to the conclusion that the terms *matres* and *patres* "designent tous ceux, parents charnels des candidats et chrétiens dévoués de leur entourage, qui acceptent de guider les catéchumènes vers la fontaine baptismale."

The second means of understanding who Egeria's "fathers" and "mothers" were lies in fourth-century Christian language, since early Christianity was accustomed to use kinship words to convey theological and spiritual tenets. For instance, the mysterious inner workings of the Godhead were expressed in terms of the Father and the Son, the Begetter and the Begotten; a bishop was father to his congregation; Christians were brothers and sisters to one another and children of God by adoption. Baptismal practices were also bathed in the atmosphere of kinship, a matter we will discuss more fully later.

The kinship vocabulary associated with baptism was initially quite ambiguous and evolved only slowly toward greater precision. Hence early usage took current kinship terms and usually, but not always, modified them with adjectives or clauses. By the sixth century, the commonest pattern was to call kinsmen created in baptism "spiritual" kinsmen. The earliest extant example of this pattern as applied to sponsors and baptizees comes from within a decade of Egeria's visit to Palestine. At Antioch about 390 John Chrysostom, who was then a priest apparently delegated to conduct the Lenten instructions, delivered a sermon to the *competentes* and their sponsors in which he referred to the former as spiritual children (*tekna pneumatika*) and the latter as spiritual fathers (*pateres pneumatikoi*).[54]

Egeria was writing before or while that linguistic convention took shape and she may not have known it. Thus her words may be better understood by comparing them with a text by Rufinus, initially Jerome's friend and later his bitter opponent. Here sponsors in baptism were not the only parents created, for the baptizer also became a "father" to the baptized, as did the person who instructed the *competens* in preparation for baptism. In 399/401 Rufinus referred in the following terms to his own baptism as a young man at Aquileia about 370:

> As he and all know, almost thirty years ago, when I was already settled in a monastery, I was reborn through the grace of baptism and received the sign of faith through those holy men, Chromatius, Jovinus and Eusebius, most famous and virtuous bishops of God's church, the first of whom was at that time a priest of [bishop] Valerian of blessed memory, the second was an archdeacon and the third was a deacon and at the same time a father to me and a teacher of creed and faith [*simulque pater mihi et doctor symboli ac fidei fuit*].[55]

[54] John Chrysostom, Second Catechetical Sermon, ch. 16, in *Huit catéchèses*, p. 143.
[55] Rufinus of Aquileia, *Apologia contra Hieronymum*, ch. 4, ed. M. Simonetti, CCSL, vol. 20 (Turnhout, 1961), p. 39.

Eusebius was not Rufinus' father in the natural sense of that term; rather, he was his spiritual father as a consequence of instructing him in the creed, a notion of paternity deriving from Paul's view that "you might have thousands of guardians in Christ, but not more than one father and it was I who begot you in Christ Jesus by preaching the Good News" (I Cor. 4:15–16).

It is significant that Rufinus could refer simply to Eusebius as *pater mihi et doctor* and assume that his readers would understand the term in the context of baptism. Kinship terms in Christian circles were multivalent and the context determined the actual meaning. Thus, while Egeria's "fathers" and "mothers" might or might not be actual blood relatives, this was a secondary matter in comparison to the fact that each was certainly a spiritual parent to the *competens*, a situation the pious audience in Aquitaine or Galicia would certainly understand.

Egeria observed, almost parenthetically, that "it is not too easy for a visitor to come to baptism" at Jerusalem unless he had witnesses who were acquainted with him (*testimonia qui eum nouerint*). In pursuing this aspect of the matter, Franz Joseph Dölger investigated fourth- and fifth-century accounts, some historical and some legendary, of individuals who wished baptism but could not get the required witnesses to attest to their good character.[56] The typical figure in these stories is a prostitute, for whom the fourth-century Egyptian *Canons of Hippolytus* demanded three witnesses.[57] Dölger also examined accounts of prominent pagan intellectuals and officeholders who demonstrated their fitness for baptism by their deeds rather than by character witnesses. For example, Arnobius may have written his seven books *Against the Pagans* as a demonstration of his sincere desire for baptism. Dölger also found a prefect of the city of Rome, Gracchus, who suppressed a Mithraic shrine in 377 as a guarantee of his sincerity and fitness for baptism.[58] This research gives clarity to the church's demand for some assurance that a convert was fit in behavior and motive to be received. But Dölger's rather exotic prostitutes, intellectuals, and aristocratic magistrates must not obscure the fact that for most converts the guarantors of fitness were their Christian relatives, friends, and neighbors, as in the situation Egeria described.

---

[56] Franz Joseph Dölger, "Die Garantiewerk der Bekehrung als Bedingung und Sicherung bei der Annahme zur Taufe. Die Zertrümmerung eines Mithras-Heiligtums durch den Stadtpräfeckten Gracchus und ähnliche Vorkommnisse in kultgeschichtlicher Beleuchtung," *AC* 3 (1932):260–277.

[57] *Canons of Hippolytus*, canon 78, in Hanssens, *La liturgie*, p. 102.

[58] Dölger, "Die Garantiewerk," pp. 262–266.

Egeria explained more fully to her sisters the character of the Lenten preparation of *competentes* at Jerusalem:

> Those who are preparing for baptism during the season of the Lenten fast go to be exorcised by the clergy first thing in the morning, directly after the morning dismissal in the Anastasis. As soon as that has taken place, the bishop's chair is placed in the Great Church, the Martyrium, and all those to be baptized, the men and the women, sit round him in a circle. There is a place where the fathers and mothers stand, and any of the [baptized] people who want to listen can come in and sit down, though not catechumens, who do not come in while the bishop is teaching. His subject is God's Law; during the forty days he goes through the whole Bible, beginning with Genesis, and first relating the literal meaning of each passage, then interpreting its spiritual meaning. He also teaches them at this time all about the resurrection and the faith. And this is called *catechesis*. After five weeks' teaching they receive the Creed, whose content he explains article by article in the same way as he explained the Scriptures, first literally and then spiritually.[59]

As this text indicates, the *competentes* were exorcised and instructed for three hours (six a.m. to nine a.m.) daily during the forty days; their "fathers" and "mothers" participated in this period of liturgy and preaching. While baptized Christians were welcome to attend as a way to improve their knowledge, the catechumens who had not "given in their names" were excluded.

Egeria is silent on the routine of the *competentes* when they were not in the Great Church at Jerusalem, but roughly contemporary sources from Hippo in North Africa indicate that the demands of preparation tended to engulf the entire Lenten season. In addition to the daily round of exorcisms and scriptural exegesis, the *competentes* in Augustine's church were bound by a strict asceticism that involved fasting, abstinence from meat and wine, sexual abstinence even for the married, and the avoidance of such creature comforts as the baths. Those candidates who did not live in the episcopal city of Hippo had to go there each day or take up temporary residence to fulfill the role expected of *competentes*.[60]

During the final week before Easter, which Egeria called the Great Week, the focus of preparation shifted from instruction to liturgy. It

[59] Egeria, *Itinerarium*, ch. 46.1–3, pp. 87–88; Wilkinson, *Egeria's Travels*, p. 144.
[60] Van der Meer, *Augustine*, pp. 357–359; de Latte, "Saint Augustin," pp. 191–192.

was a very full round of ceremonies, and she noted that "there is no time for them to have their teaching if they are to carry out all the services I have described."[61] At the beginning of the Great Week,

the bishop comes early into the Great Church, the Martyrium. His chair is placed at the back of the apse, behind the altar, and one by one the candidates go up to the bishop, men with their fathers and women with their mothers, and repeat the Creed to him. When they have done so, the bishop speaks to them all as follows: 'During these seven weeks you have received instruction in the whole biblical Law. You have heard about the faith, and the resurrection of the body. You have also learned all you can as catechumens of the content of the Creed. But the teaching about baptism itself is a deeper mystery, and you have not the right to hear it while you remain catechumens. Do not think it will never be explained; you will hear it all during the eight days after Easter after you have been baptized. But so long as you are catechumens you cannot be told God's deep mysteries.'[62]

The "fathers" and "mothers" accompanied the candidates when the latter stepped forward to recite the Creed to the bishop. This recitation, called the *redditio symboli*, took place late in the competentate, although the exact date varied from one region to another.[63] The catechetical instructions preceding baptism respected the discipline of secrecy and the bishop promised the *competentes* that during the week after Easter, when they were still in their white robes, they would learn much from the mystagogical sermons. Delivered behind closed doors, these sermons probed the deeper spiritual meaning of the initiation ceremonies the neophytes had recently experienced. Egeria was impressed by the demonstrativeness of the congregation at Jerusalem during the mystagogical sermons:

While the bishop is teaching, no catechumen comes in, and the doors are kept shut in case any try to enter. The bishop relates what has been done, and interprets it, and, as he does so, the applause is so loud that it can be heard outside the church. Indeed the way he expounds the mysteries and interprets them cannot fail to move his hearers.[64]

[61] Egeria, *Itinerarium*, ch. 46.4, p. 88; Wilkinson, *Egeria's Travels*, p. 145.
[62] Egeria, *Itinerarium*, ch. 46.5–6, ibid.
[63] On the *traditio symboli*, see Maertens, *Histoire*, pp. 134–137.
[64] Egeria, *Itinerarium*, ch. 47.2, p. 89; Wilkinson, *Egeria's Travels*, pp. 145–146.

Egeria did not describe the "awe-inspiring"[65] rites of baptism themselves, probably out of respect for the discipline of silence, which moved many Christian writers to omit or describe vaguely the central mysteries of their religion. Thus we do not know from her account whether the fathers and mothers were present at the baptism or had any role in it.

Egeria's account of the role of sponsors in the competentate at Jerusalem is precious but strangely external, for in her description the fathers and mothers simply accompanied their candidates. Even in the important examination for admission to the competentate, the sponsors were overshadowed by or probably absorbed into the larger group of "neighbors" who answered questions about the candidate. Indeed, the sponsors are not recorded as saying anything.

Egeria's intention was to report to her sisters the interesting things she saw in the course of her pious tourism, and liturgy ranked high in her universe of interests. She recorded what she saw of the formal aspects of the competentate. In her descriptions of the somewhat stereotyped public gatherings, the sponsors were not active participants, in comparison either to the bishop and the clergy or to the *competentes* themselves. However, it is fortunate that other sources, contemporary in time and not too distant in space, flesh out our understanding of the more private functions of sponsors, which were carried out when the candidate and the sponsor were not in church. Egeria did not allude to this period of time, perhaps because it was inaccessible to her on account of the language barrier (Greek and Syriac were in use)[66] or perhaps because it was not interesting to such a liturgically minded observer.

Jerusalem was venerable because of its associations with the life and death of Jesus and with the struggles of the nascent church. However, in the fourth and fifth centuries it was small and politically unimportant, a cultural backwater. By contrast, Antioch, three hundred miles to the north, was a bustling and populous center of commerce, political life, and culture. Two of its priests, John Chrysostom and Theodore of Mopsuestia, delivered extant sermons to *competentes* and neophytes (those newly baptized) that complement the description of sponsorship in Egeria's travel account.

John, later called Chrysostomos (the "golden-mouthed"), was born at Antioch about 344/54 to a Christian family and spent part of his

[65] See Edward Yarnold, *The Awe-Inspiring Rites of Initiation: Baptismal Homilies of the Fourth Century* (London, 1972).

[66] Egeria, *Itinerarium*, ch. 47.3–4, p. 146.

adolescence and early manhood as a monk. In 381 he became a deacon of the church of Antioch and five years later a priest. For the next eleven years, he was distinguished as a preacher at Antioch. Then, in 397, he was chosen patriarch of Constantinople, where strife with the Empress Eudoxia and the Alexandrian patriarch Theophilus marked his tenure. His career and his life ended tragically in Anatolian exile in 407.[67]

John was the premier preacher of the Greek church and a prolific writer whose sermons, tracts, and letters fill eighteen stout volumes of Migne's *Patrologia graeca*. These were further enriched in 1955 when Antoine Wenger discovered eight of John's baptismal catecheses in a manuscript of the Stavronika monastery on Mount Athos.[68] Combined with other known sermons, they made up a series of twelve that John delivered to *competentes* and neophytes around Easter 390.

In the second catechesis edited by Wenger, John directly addresses the sponsors, who were called in Greek *anadechomenoi*, which was basically a financial term that described a person who acted as surety for a loan, that is, who would be responsible for paying back the creditor if the debtor defaulted. *Anadechomenos* could also mean "one who receives," a term equivalent to the common Latin one for a sponsor, *susceptor*.

In his sermon John reminds the sponsors, who were present in the audience, of the seriousness of their task:

> Do you wish me to address a word to those who are sponsoring you, that they too may know what recompense they deserve if they have shown great care for you, and what condemnation follows if they are careless? Consider, beloved, how those who go surety for someone in a matter of money set up for themselves a greater risk than the one who borrows the money and is liable for it. If the borrower be well disposed, he lightens the burden for his surety; if the dispositions of his soul be ill, he makes the risk a steeper one. Wherefore, the wise man counsels us, saying: "If thou be surety, think as if thou wert to pay it." If, then, those who go surety for others in a matter of money make themselves liable for the whole sum, those who go surety for others in matters of the spirit and on an account which involves virtue should be much more alert. They ought to show their paternal love by encouraging, counseling, and correcting those for whom they go surety.

[67] On John's career see Altaner and Stuiber, *Patrologie*, pp. 322–323.
[68] Wenger described the discovery in *Huit catéchèses*, pp. 7–15.

16. Let them not think that what takes place is a trifling thing, but let them see clearly that they share in the credit if by their admonition they lead those entrusted to them to the path of virtue. Again, if those they sponsor become careless, the sponsors themselves will suffer great punishment. That is why it is customary to call the sponsors "spiritual fathers" [*pateras pneumatikous*], that they may learn by this very action how great an affection they must show to those they sponsor in the matter of spiritual instruction. If it is a noble thing to lead to a zeal for virtue those who are in no way related to us, much more should we fulfil this precept in the case of the one whom we receive as a spiritual son [*teknon pneumatikon*]. You, the sponsors, have learned that no slight danger hangs over your heads if you are remiss.[69]

John's comments are an informative complement to Egeria's observations. For while he says nothing about the sponsors' liturgical duties, he does lift the veil a bit on the spirit of their task. His fundamental image for the sponsor is that of what we would today call the cosigner of a loan, the guarantor. Incidentally, we are informed that the sponsor's official title was *anadechomenos*, a word from contract law. But the role of guarantor was expanding to involve leading, advising, encouraging, and befriending the *competens*. To express this obligation, John resorts to a parent/child image, like that apparently used by Egeria, and he intimates that popular linguistic practice at Antioch lay at its origin. Thus the sponsor in John Chrysostom's day was not yet a "godparent," but his stress on new, amity-building elements in sponsoring practice indicate one of the roots from which the godparent/godchild notion would ultimately arise.

The other great preacher and theologian who was John Chrysostom's contemporary and friend at Antioch was Theodore, who was bishop of Mopsuestia in Cilicia from 392 to 428.[70] Around 390, while he was still a priest at Antioch, Theodore delivered sixteen catechetical sermons that survive in a Syriac translation. In 1933, Alphonse Mingana edited these sermons and provided an English translation;[71]

[69] Second Catechetical Sermon, chs. 15–16, in *Huit catéchèses*, pp. 141–144. English translation from Paul W. Harkins, *John Chrysostom: Baptismal Instructions*, ACW, vol. 31 (Westminster, Md., 1963), pp. 48–49. On the baptismal practices described by John Chrysostom, see Finn, *The Liturgy of Baptism*.

[70] On Theodore's career, see Altaner and Stuiber, *Patrologie*, pp. 319–320, and Robert Devreesse, *Essai sur Théodore de Mopsueste*, ST, vol. 141 (Vatican City, 1948), pp. 1–52.

[71] Alphonse Mingana, *Commentary of Theodore of Mopsuestia on the Lord's Prayer and on*

in 1949, Raymond Tonneau and Robert Devreesse published a photographic copy of the manuscript accompanied by a French translation.[72]

In sermon 12 of the Tonneau/Devreesse series, Theodore speaks of the role of the sponsor, mixing liturgical details with recommended behavior. In the course of this, he compares baptism to the process of seeking and gaining citizenship in a heavenly city, for which the sponsor serves as a guarantor of worthiness, a thoroughly traditional role, as well as a guide to the customs and laws of the city. When Mingana translated Theodore's use of the Syriac word "*eràbha*," he rendered it as "godfather," which is an anachronism. In contrast, Tonneau and Devreesse were more literal and rendered it in French as "*garant*," meaning "surety" or "guarantor," which is undoubtedly the correct emphasis. The following translation is Mingana's, except for the substitution of "guarantor" where he used "godfather":

He, therefore, who is desirous of drawing nigh unto baptism comes to the Church of God through which he expects to reach that life of the heavenly abode. He ought to think that he is coming to be the citizen of a new and great city. . . . He comes to the Church of God where he is received by a duly appointed person—as there is a habit to register those who draw nigh unto baptism—who will question him about his mode of life in order to find out whether it possesses all the requisites of the citizenship of that great city. After he has abjured all the evil found in this world and cast it completely out of his mind, he has to show that he is worthy of the citizenship of the city and of his enrollment in it. This is the reason why, as if he were a stranger to the city and its citizenship, a specially appointed person [sponsor], who is from the city in which he is going to be enrolled and who is well versed in its mode of life, conducts him to the registrar and testifies for him to the effect that he is worthy of the city and of its citizenship and that, as he is not versed in the life of the city or in the knowledge of how to behave in it, he himself would be willing to act as a guide to his inexperience.

This rite is performed for those who are baptised by the person called guarantor, who, however, does not make himself responsible for them in connection with future sins, as each one of us

the Sacraments of Baptism and the Eucharist, Woodbrooke Studies, vol. 6 (Cambridge, 1933), contains six sermons.

[72] Les homélies catéchétiques de Théodore de Mopsueste, ed. and tr. Raymond Tonneau and Robert Devreesse, ST, vol. 145 (Vatican City, 1949).

answers for his own sins before God. He only bears witness to what the catechumen has done and to the fact that he has prepared himself in the past to be worthy of the city and of its citizenship. He is justly called a sponsor because by his words [the catechumen] is deemed worthy to receive baptism.

. . . It is therefore incumbent on us all, who are under the power of His Kingdom, to pray and desire that through faith we might draw nigh unto baptism and be worthy of being enrolled · in heaven.

It is for this reason that as regards you also who draw nigh unto the gift of baptism, a duly appointed person inscribes your name in the Church book, together with that of your guarantor, who answers for you and becomes your guide in the city and the leader of your citizenship therein. This is done in order that you may know that you are, long before the time and while still on the earth, enrolled in heaven, and that your guarantor who is in it is possessed of great diligence to teach you, who are a stranger and a newcomer to that great city, all the things that pertain to it and to its citizenship, so that you should be conversant with its life without any trouble and anxiety.[73]

Subsequently, Theodore indicates that the sponsor accompanied the catechumen during the baptismal ceremonies and at one point, after the bishop anointed the forehead of the kneeling candidate, the sponsor, "who is standing behind you, spreads an orarium of linen on the crown of your head, raises you and makes you stand erect."[74]

Theodore's elucidation of the role of the sponsor in fourth-century Antioch reinforces the comments of John Chrysostom and is congruent with those of Egeria. From these it can be seen that the long catechumenate described by Hippolytus a hundred and seventy-five years earlier still existed in a vestigial form. But the full effort of the church in Syria and Palestine was exercised on the *competentes* during the weeks prior to Easter.

When a catechumen gave in his or her name for baptism, both the candidate and the sponsor were recorded on a list by a church official. The sponsor's first task was the traditional one of providing testimony as to the candidate's behavior and sincerity on the occasion of the examination that followed the "giving in" of names. The sponsor also accompanied the candidate to the formal assemblies for instruction and liturgical action, including the baptismal services on the vigil of

[73] Mingana, *Commentary of Theodore*, sermon 2, ch. 2, pp. 24–26.
[74] Ibid., sermon 2, ch. 3, p. 47.

Easter. At these formal occasions, the sponsor had a modest role of support, involving ritual gestures and accompaniment of the *competens*, who, as an adult, spoke and acted for himself.

John and Theodore insisted that during the remainder of the Lenten preparation, in the interstices between sermon and ceremony, the sponsor was expected to be active in aiding, instructing, encouraging, and admonishing the *competens*. Theodore's image of a guide to a new city and John's of a spiritual parent and a spiritual child are suggestive of this personal role that was carried out by sponsors during the competetate. It is clear, then, that sponsors were guarantors of the worthiness of a specific person to receive baptism. In late fourth-century Syria, there is also evidence that the rather stark legal notion of guarantor was being modified in the direction of personal guidance by the sponsor during the competetate.

Scholars have often misunderstood the role of deacons and deaconesses in the sponsorship of adults. For as baptismal rituals became more elaborate and stylized, the *competentes* needed not only sponsoring but also certain kinds of assistance during the baptism itself. In the course of the complex ceremonies on the vigil of Easter and at Easter dawn, the baptizees had to undress, descend into the water, respond to the questions of the baptizer, ascend from the water, be anointed, dry off, and dress again, often in a special white baptismal garment. In Hippolytus' *Apostolic Tradition*, it is directed that "a deacon will descend [into the water] with him in this manner,"[75] and the fourth- and fifth-century church orders that derived from Hippolytus' work reiterate this stage direction, with only slight revisions.[76] Thus deacons took an active role in helping the candidates to pass from one stage of the ritual to another.

The adult *competentes* were naked during much of the baptismal ritual; indeed, there was an explicit ban on anyone, but especially women, taking any object of clothing or jewelry into the baptismal waters.[77] In the ancient church, with its puritanical strain, the nudity of female *competentes* presented a problem, since the clergy were male

---

[75] Botte, *La tradition*, ch. 21, p. 84.

[76] Hanssens, *La liturgie d'Hippolyte*, sec. 39, pp. 110–121, passim.

[77] Botte, *La tradition*, ch. 21, pp. 80–82: "Postea baptizate viros, tandem autem mulieres quae solverunt crines suos omnes et deposuerunt ornamenta auri et argenti quae habent super se, et nemo sumat rem alienam deorsum in aqua." W. C. van Unnik, "Les cheveux défaits des femmes baptisées. Un rite de baptême dans l'ordre ecclésiastique d'Hippolyte," *VC* 1 (1947):77–100, argues that the removal of jewelry and the loosening of hair derived from Jewish practices in proselyte baptism and Jewish rituals expressing a state of impurity in women.

and contemporary notions of propriety disapproved their seeing the women naked. In the East, from the middle of the third century, female functionaries called deaconesses were introduced to care for ill women who might need anointing with holy oil or bathing, and whose male relatives could be expected to frown on male clergy participating in such acts. These deaconesses also aided females during baptism.[78]

One of the earliest and clearest statements on the role of deaconesses in dealing with women is to be found in the *Didascalia Apostolorum*, which was probably composed by a Syrian bishop in the first half of the third century. The ideal bishop, to whom the *Didascalia* was addressed, was instructed to choose suitable assistants:

> Wherefore, O bishop, appoint thee workers of righteousness as helpers who may co-operate with thee unto salvation. Those that please thee out of all the people thou shalt choose and appoint as deacons: a man for the performance of the most things that are required, but a woman for the ministry of women. For there are houses whither thou canst not send a deacon to the women, on account of the heathen, but mayest send a deaconess. Also, because in many other matters the office of a woman deacon is required. In the first place, when women go down into the water, those who go down into the water ought to be anointed by a deaconess with the oil of anointing; and where there is no woman at hand, and especially no deaconess, he who baptizes must of necessity anoint her who is being baptized. But where there is a woman, and especially a deaconess, it is not fitting that women should be seen by men: but with the imposition of hand do thou anoint the head only. As of old the priests and kings were anointed in Israel, do thou in like manner, with the imposition of hand, anoint the head of those who receive baptism, whether thou thyself baptize, or thou command the deacons or presbyters to baptize—let a woman deacon, as we have already said, anoint the women. But let a man pronounce over them the invocation of the divine Names in the water.
>
> And when she who is being baptized has come up from the water, let the deaconess receive her, and teach and instruct her how the seal of baptism ought to be (kept) unbroken in purity and holiness. For this cause we say that the ministry of a woman deacon is especially needful and important.[79]

[78] On the origin and functions of deaconesses, see Roger Gryson, *The Ministry of Women in the Early Church* (Collegeville, Minn., 1976), esp. pp. 109–114.

[79] *Didascalia Apostolorum*, bk. 3, ch. 12, ed. F. X. Funk, *Didascalia et Constitutiones*

Thus the office of deaconess was a practical solution to the tension between a desire for a baptism in which the "old man or woman" was put off entirely, right down to clothes and ornaments, and a feeling that it was improper for male clergy to see or touch naked female candidates.

Roger Gryson has argued convincingly that from about 250 in the eastern Mediterranean, excluding Egypt, deaconesses were members of the clergy with the specific role of mediating between the male clergy and female Christians. But the institution of the deaconess never took hold in the West, in spite of sporadic attempts to introduce it there in the fourth and fifth centuries.[80] However, the *Statuta ecclesiae antiqua*, a canonical collection compiled in Gaul about 475, perhaps by Gennadius, a priest of Marseilles, recommended that widows and nuns assume the tasks of caring for and instructing uneducated female baptizees.[81] Thus, at least from the third century, prevailing notions of propriety gave deaconesses (or other quasi-official women) a role in the baptism of adult women.

Some texts, including those quoted above from the *Didascalia* and the *Statuta ecclesiae antiqua*, also attributed a teaching role to these women. This is frankly puzzling because in a well-ordered competentate there was no obvious place for it. After all, if a female candidate had participated in the competentate before baptism and in the week of mystagogical instruction after baptism, the role of a deacon or deaconess in her instruction was superfluous. However, even though the preferred procedure was public and solemn baptism for all adults at Easter or Pentecost, preceded by the full panoply of instruction, there were reasons why private, less elaborate baptisms might take place. The rites of menstruating women were delayed until a later time,[82]

Apostolorum, 2 vols. (Paderborn, 1905), 1:208–210; tr. R. H. Connolly, *Didascalia Apostolorum* (Oxford, 1929), pp. 146–147.

[80] See Gryson, *Ministry*, pp. 25–34, on the absence of deaconesses in Egypt, and pp. 92–108 on the failure of the church in the West to adopt the institution.

[81] *Statuta ecclesiae antiqua*, ch. 100, ed. Charles Munier, *Concilia Galliae A.314–A.506*, CCSL, vol. 148 (Turnhout, 1963), p. 184: "Viduae uel sanctimoniales, quae ad ministerium baptizandarum mulierum eliguntur, tam instructae sint ad id officium, ut possint aperto et sano sermone docere imperitas et rusticanas mulieres, tempore quo baptizandae sunt, qualiter baptizatoris ad interrogata respondeant et qualiter accepto baptismate uiuant." Munier suggests that Gennadius was the compiler of the *Statuta* (p. 163).

[82] Botte, *La tradition*, ch. 20, p. 78; on the corresponding sections of the fourth- and fifth-century church orders derived from the *Apostolic Tradition*, see Hanssens, *La Liturgie*, ch. 38, pp. 108–111. On the significance of menstruation in premodern Jewish and Christian theology and folk belief, see Peter Browe, *Beiträge zur Sexualethik des Mittelalters*, Breslauer Studien zur historischen Theologie, vol. 23 (Breslau, 1932), pp. 1–14.

the seriously ill could be baptized as needed,[83] and among the hundreds of bishops some were less diligent, or merely absent, at Easter. As a consequence of such special circumstances, a baptizee might have missed the Lenten preparation or the bishop's postbaptismal sermons, which were closed to all but the baptized. It is within such a context that the teaching role of deacons or deaconesses must be understood. They gave the neophyte a period of personal instruction (probably a week) that substituted in some measure for the structured competentate and mystagogy.

An important text to support such a view is the *Life of St. Pelagia*, written by a deacon named Jacobus in the second half of the fourth century.[84] The *Life* is a highly romanticized literary work, but it nevertheless sheds light on fifth-century Antiochene circumstances. Pelagia was a prostitute, and such people were received for baptism only after firm guarantees that they had given up their trade.[85] Thus she was rebuffed in her request for baptism until her public repentance and her fervent request convinced a bishop named Nonnus to relent and baptize her immediately, outside the traditional times.[86] After the baptism, Pelagia was entrusted to Romana, described as "first of the deaconesses," who took charge of her intellectual and moral formation. The two women lived together for a week in a part of the church reserved for catechumens. Romana was also described as Pelagia's spiritual mother (*mētēr pneumatikē*) or simply as her "mother."[87] At the end of the week, Pelagia fled secretly to adopt an ascetic life, masquerading as a male named Pelagius until her death.[88]

On the basis of such evidence, some scholars adopted the view that deacons and deaconesses were official sponsors in the ancient church.[89] Ernst Dick did not accept so extreme a statement of the matter, but

[83] On clinical baptism (named from the fact that the recipients were ill in their *kline*, their bed or bier), see Finn, *Liturgy*, pp. 27–30.

[84] Jacobus Diaconus, *Vita sanctae Pelagiae*, ed. Hermann Usener, *Die Legenden der heiligen Pelagia* (Bonn, 1879), pp. 3–16. There is a Latin translation by Eustochius in AASS, vol. 4, pp. 261–268 and in PL, vol. 73, pp. 663–672. Joseph-Marie Sauget, *Bibliotheca Sanctorum*, vol. 10 (Vatican City, 1968), col. 431, called the *Life* a "romanzo edificante," but concurred in its dating to the fifth century.

[85] Botte, *La tradition*, ch. 16, p. 72.

[86] Jacobus, *Vita sanctae Pelagiae*, chs. 7–8, pp. 7–11.

[87] Ibid., chs. 8–12, pp. 10–13. Romana was called "the first of the deaconesses" in ch. 8, p. 10, ll. 8–9.

[88] On the motif of the female ascetic transvestite, see John Anson, "The Female Transvestite in Early Monasticism: The Origin and Development of a Motif," *Viator* 5 (1974):1–32; and Evelyne Patlagean, "L'histoire de la femme déguisée en moine et l'évolution de la sainteté féminine à Byzance," *SM*, 3rd series, 17 (1976):597–623.

[89] Joseph Bingham (1668–1723), the English ecclesiastical historian, defended the idea that deacons and deaconesses were the ordinary sponsors in book 11.8.9 of *Origines*

he did argue that such assistants at baptism (*Taufhelfer*) were one of the roots out of which later godparentage arose.[90] In contrast, Derrick Bailey, who did not know Dick's article, rejected firmly the notion that deacons and deaconesses had any direct relationship to sponsorship, as it is properly understood. In Bailey's view, they "acted as Church officials and not as sponsors for the candidates" and they "might have undertaken the general oversight and education of the catechumens from the time of their enrolment. But there is nothing here to indicate that special responsibility and personal relationship which sponsorship at adult baptism properly implies."[91]

I believe that Bailey's stance is the correct one, and that Dick's error, like that of so many good scholars before him, was a confusion of adult and infant sponsorship. It is quite true that from the Carolingian period at least, the sponsor for an infant was charged with various helping duties to compensate for the child's weakness, duties that might include carrying, undressing, drying off, dressing, responding, and similar activities. Such tasks are analogous to the deacon's and deaconess' functions at baptism in the ancient church, and because of this Dick was led by his guiding image of "roots" (*Würzeln*) to see the deacons as a point of origin for later godparents. The similarities are, however, deceiving, for the duties of the infant sponsor are, as we shall see, explicable within the framework of that institution and have no direct link with deacons in adult baptism.

A further piece of evidence that has been cited in favor of the position that deacons and deaconesses were sponsors is the designation of Romana as Pelagia's spiritual mother,[92] a term that after the eighth century was definitely a technical term for "godmother." However, it is anachronistic to understand a fifth-century term in that way. In a Christian tradition going back to Paul and in a parallel classical pagan tradition,[93] the person who gave spiritual enlightenment to another

ecclesiasticae; or, the Antiquities of the Christian Church, in *The Works of the Learned Joseph Bingham, M.A.,* 2 vols. (London, 1726), 2:512–513. However, that view was not generally accepted. Johann Jacob Goetz, in *De iuribus patrinorum* (Jena, 1678), p. 35, argued briefly that deaconesses were not true sponsors, but aided female candidates for the sake of modesty (*pro pudore*); Isaac Jundt, in *De susceptorum baptismalium origine commentatio* (Strasbourg, 1755), pp. 63–65, also argued against Bingham, stating that deacons and deaconesses served at baptism primarily as liturgical helpers and for the sake of propriety.

[90] Dick, "Das Pateninstitut," p. 48.

[91] Bailey, *Sponsors,* pp. 13–14.

[92] Jacobus Diaconus, *Vita sanctae Pelagiae,* ch. 8 and ch. 12, p. 10, l. 28 and p. 13, l. 13.

[93] On Greco-Roman notions of spiritual parenthood, see Hendrik Wagenvoort, " 'Re-

was the latter's spiritual parent. For instance, in Apuleius' *Metamorphoses*, when Lucius has been initiated into the mysteries of Isis he calls the initiating priest his *parens*, his parent or father.[94] Thus Romana's epithet is comprehensible within this tradition of thought: she is a spiritual mother not because of sponsorship but because she has instructed her charge in the deeper meaning of Christianity.

It is clear, then, that deacons and deaconesses were not sponsors in adult baptism and emphatically not godparents. Rather, they were liturgical functionaries, like the priests and bishops who were also active in baptismal ceremonies. They assisted baptizees whom they might not even know personally. It was, of course, not impossible that a deacon might sponsor a convert, but such sponsoring had nothing to do with his official status as a deacon. For this reason, the attempt to link the diaconate in some official way to sponsorship is a fruitless one.

In the ancient church's varied provisions for the probation, instruction, and baptism of adults, there was no single person who, like the godparent of later centuries, presented the candidate at each stage, accompanied him during the liturgy, and received him from the baptismal waters. Instead, neighbors, relatives, and clergy shared the tasks involved in initiating new Christians. Sponsoring itself was conceptualized in the context of contract law, making baptism a *pactum* with God and the sponsor a testifier to the good faith and worthiness of the human participant.[95] Prior to the fifth century, the sponsor's role was entirely prebaptismal and there is no reliable evidence for an official postbaptismal function for the adult sponsor. It is likely that in some cases sponsor and sponsored remained close after the baptismal ceremonies were terminated, since on more than one occasion the participants were already natural kinsmen. But in the conception of the institution there was no official place for such a continuing relationship. Indeed, Theodore of Mopsuestia explicitly denied that the guarantor at baptism was responsible for any subsequent lapse of the candidate.[96]

---

birth' in Profane Antique Literature," in his *Studies in Roman Literature, Culture and Religion* (Leiden, 1956), pp. 132–149.

[94] Apuleius, *Metamorphoses*, bk. 11, ch. 25, ed. J. Gwyn Griffiths, in *The Isis-Book (Metamorphoses, Book XI)* (Leiden, 1975), pp. 102–103: "When I had prayed thus humbly to the supreme deity, I embraced Mithras the priest, who was now as my father [*parens*], and clinging to his neck with many kisses I begged him to pardon me because I was unable to recompense him justly for so great favours."

[95] Joseph Crehan, *Early Christian Baptism and the Creed: A Study in Ante-Nicene Theology* (London, 1950), pp. 96–110, traces the notion of baptism as a contract from Tertullian to the fourth century.

[96] Theodore, *Commentary*, sermon 2, ch. 2, tr. Mingana, p. 25.

Furthermore, one basis for the later enduring relationship between the godparent and godchild was that baptism came to be thought of as a birth in which the sponsor was a parent in a spiritual sense. Conversely, while in the ancient church baptism was explained occasionally by birth images, a competing and initially more important image was that of baptism as a dying and rising from the tomb, a view derived from Paul. In this tradition, the baptismal font was the tomb.[97]

Clement of Alexandria, writing in the early third century, was apparently the first to call the baptismal font a womb, a view that grew in popularity in the fourth and fifth centuries.[98] However, it is crucial to note that in the early use of the birth image for baptism it was rare that a human being was described as a parent in that birth. In the eastern Christian tradition the baptismal font was described as a virgin mother, giving birth to her children alone, and in the western Christian tradition the font was the womb of Mother Church.[99] Tertullian wrote that in baptism God is the father, the Church is the mother, and other Christians are the siblings of the baptized.[100] And in Sermon 57, Augustine of Hippo told the *competentes* that "we have a father and mother on earth, so that we may be born to toils and death. We get other parents, God the Father and Mother Church, from whom we are born to eternal life."[101] Thus, until a major shift in the conceptualization of baptismal rebirth occurred, the sponsor for an adult could not readily be regarded as a parent, a key element of later godparentage.

The fate of adult sponsorship was mirrored in its intellectual history, for there has survived from the ancient church no effort at theoretical or theological justification of the practice. The customs surrounding the initiation of adults were noncontroversial, self-explanatory, encapsulated very early in liturgical formulae and church orders, and never the focus of extended theological speculation.

[97] Walter M. Bedard, *The Symbolism of the Baptismal Font in Early Christian Thought.* CUA, SST, 2nd series, vol. 45 (Washington, D.C., 1951), pp. 4–16.

[98] Clement of Alexandria, *Stromata*, bk. 4, ch. 25, cited in Bedard, *Symbolism*, p. 18. For the font/womb motif, see Bedard, pp. 17–36.

[99] Bedard, *Symbolism*, pp. 24–36; on the notion of "Mother Church," see Joseph C. Plumpe, *Mater Ecclesia: An Inquiry into the Concept of the Church as Mother in Early Christianity*, CUA, SCA, vol. 5 (Washington, D.C., 1943).

[100] Tertullian, *De baptismo*, ch. 20, sec. 5, ed. R. F. Refoulé and French tr., M. Drouzy, SC, vol. 35 (Paris, 1952), p. 96.

[101] Augustine, Sermon 57, PL 38:387, "Habemus patrem et matrem in terra, ut nasceremur ad labores et mortem: invenimus alios parentes, Deum Patrem et Matrem Ecclesiam, a quibus nascamur ad vitam aeternam."

Augustine's *De catechizandis rudibus* (ca. 400)[102] was the first and only handbook for the reception of adult catechumens and it reflected a situation in which adult sponsorship was already in decline. The sponsor in Augustine's day had a minimal role because of the presence of a clerical catechist. To be sure, lay Christians often acted as the point of initial contact between interested pagans and the church, but there was in Augustine's view no necessity for such recommenders: a convert could be examined by the catechist without sponsors.[103] The initial interview of the convert with the catechist consisted not of an examination about intentions and lifestyle, as had been recommended by Hippolytus, but of a brief retelling of the Christian story of salvation, suitably vague at certain points to respect the *disciplina arcani*. Clearly, the role of lay sponsors was vestigial, since the catechist admitted virtually all adults to the catechumenate, putting off a strict examination until the catechumen sought entry to the competentate, a few weeks before baptism. And even in that final examination, clerics took the lead, with Augustine remaining vague about any role entrusted to lay sponsors.[104] In short, the admission of adults to the church underwent a gradual clericalization that left little place for a lay sponsor.

The sponsorship of adults was also profoundly transformed in the fifth and sixth centuries by cultural developments in the Christianized lands of the Mediterranean. Infant baptism grew more common in late antiquity, eventually becoming the norm, and thus adult baptismal practices began to conform in large measure to those originally created for infants. Gradually, the institution of adult sponsorship was obscured and distorted as it was assimilated into infant sponsorship, with its very different needs and presuppositions. As adults came to be baptized like infants, they too gained sponsors whose responsibilities were postbaptismal and lifelong. But for the sake of clarity it must be understood that pre-fifth-century Christianity knew no godparents for adults and the term "sponsor" must be kept free of the godparental associations that are so often and so easily attributed to it.

[102] Augustine, *De catechizandis rudibus*, ed. I. B. Bauer, CCSL, vol. 46 (Turnhout, 1969), pp. 115–178.

[103] Robert de Latte, "Saint Augustin et le baptême. Etude liturgico-historique du rituel baptismal des enfants chez Saint Augustin," *QLP* 57 (1976):54; Augustine, *De catechizandis*, ch. 5, sec. 5, pp. 129–130.

[104] Robert de Latte, "Saint Augustin et la baptême. Etude liturgico-historique du rituel baptismal des adultes chez Saint Augustin," *QLP* 56 (1975):178–191; or Van der Meer, *Augustine the Bishop*, pp. 353–361.

FOUR

THE SPONSORSHIP OF INFANTS

Since the sixteenth century, the practice of infant baptism has been the occasion for fierce theological controversy and for historical research to buttress one view or another. Roman Catholicism and the major sixteenth-century Protestant traditions (Lutheran, Calvinist, Zwinglian, and Anglican) retained the custom of baptizing infants in the face of demands by radical reformers, often collectively called Anabaptists, that the practice be abandoned in favor of baptizing only those who were sufficiently mature to accept baptismal obligations after personal conversion. For the most part, the Anabaptists were fiercely persecuted by the established churches, whether Catholic, Lutheran, or Reformed, and survived only as small, voluntarily withdrawn communities.[1] But in the British Isles during the Cromwellian period in the middle decades of the seventeenth century, such groups took firm root and in the nineteenth century they flourished in rural and frontier America as well.[2] Hence the survival of views opposed to infant baptism has continually renewed the arguments over the practice of the earliest Christian communities and the conclusion to be drawn from that practice for later Christian churches.

In 1938, and in a revised edition of 1958, Joachim Jeremias published a work challenging the scholarly consensus that held infant baptism to be unattested in the New Testament or in second-century Christian sources.[3] In other words, Jeremias defended the view that infant baptism could be found, generally by implication, in the New Testament itself. His chief argument turned on an analysis of New Testament texts describing group conversions. He noted that all New Testament baptisms were missionary baptisms—that is, those in which a gentile or Jew was baptized. Insisting on the significance of

[1] On the Anabaptists and their challenge to infant baptism, see George H. Williams, *The Radical Reformation* (Philadelphia, 1962), pp. 118–148, 417–452; Owen Chadwick, *The Reformation*, vol. 3 of the Pelican History of the Church (Harmondsworth, Eng., 1964), pp. 188–197.

[2] Sydney Ahlstrom, *A Religious History of the American People* (New Haven, 1972), pp. 170–176, 441–444.

[3] Joachim Jeremias, *Die Kindertaufe in den ersten vier Jahrhunderten*, 2nd ed. (Göttingen, 1958), tr. David Cairns, *Infant Baptism in the First Four Centuries* (Philadelphia, 1962).

so-called "*oikos*" texts in which someone was baptized "with his or her entire household (*oikos*)," Jeremias argued by analogy to Jewish proselyte baptism that such a phrase surely embraced infants as well.[4] He conceded that for children born to Christian parents, as distinct from children in the families of pagan or Jewish converts, it is more difficult to make a case that infant baptism was customary. But while there is no evidence for it in the first century, he nevertheless argued that by the late second century it was customary both in the East and the West to baptize even the children of Christian parents. According to his view, there was a brief reaction against infant baptism among wealthy Christian families between about 329 and about 365, after which the older custom, which had survived intact among humbler Christians, reasserted itself in the upper classes.[5]

Jeremias' bold revisionism generated a great deal of controversy. In 1961, Kurt Aland published an explicit, point-by-point reexamination of his arguments and evidence, coming to the very different conclusion that "infant baptism is certainly provable only from the third century and that its earliest literary traces belong to the outgoings of the second century".[6] Aland criticized Jeremias' practice of using assumptions made at one point in his argument as firm evidence later on. He also decried Jeremias' unprovable assumption that the *oikos* formula included infants (indeed, Aland doubted there even was an *oikos* formula), as well as Jeremias' explanation for the delay of baptism in the fourth century (Aland saw it as a last echo of what had been "the practice of the ancient Church; it is not something new and unheard of, as Jeremias would have us believe").[7] Aland hewed closely to the sources and avoided torturing them to support his conclusions; hence, he successfully defended the traditional view and proved in detail that Jeremias' revisionist thesis was not demonstrable. And so we may agree with Aland that, whatever is concluded about the "prehistory" of infant baptism, only in the early third century did it emerge in the sources, and even then it was not universally observed.

It is clear that baptism of at least some infants became a part of Christian custom without recorded debate or dissent during the second century and subsequently received a theological rationale in the

[4] Jeremias, *Infant Baptism*, pp. 19–42.

[5] Ibid., pp. 43–58, 87–97.

[6] Kurt Aland, *Die Säuglingstaufe im Neuen Testament und in der Alten Kirche. Eine Antwort an Joachim Jeremias*, Theologische Existenz Heute, Neue Folge, vol. 86 (Munich, 1961), tr. G. R. Beasley-Murray, *Did the Early Church Baptize Infants?* (London, 1961); quotation on p. 10.

[7] Aland, *Early Church*, p. 101.

third and fourth centuries, when it was correlated with the sharpening belief in the inherited consequences of Adam's sin, the original sin. Conversely, in the first and second centuries, Christian thinkers had taken an optimistic or at least neutral view of the moral state of pre-rational infants and children, particularly those born to Christian parents. They shared Paul's view, expressed in I Cor. 17:14–15, that "the unbelieving husband is made one with the saints through his [Christian] wife, and the unbelieving wife is made one with the saints through her [Christian] husband. If this were not so, your children would be unclean, whereas in fact they are holy." Such thinkers were inclined to regard infants born to Christian families as innocent and sinless. Tertullian, writing in North Africa in the early third century, was the last significant proponent of this optimistic view, which supported his well-known but qualified disapproval of the custom of baptizing infants.[8]

By the middle of the third century, a different assessment of the infant's status came to prominence and ultimately prevailed. Since Adam's transgression was thought to be both hereditary and unavoidable, because all human beings had been "in" Adam, anyone, including an infant, who died without baptismal remission of that sin would suffer serious consequences. One proponent of this view, Cyprian, bishop of Carthage from 248 to 258, defended the necessity of immediate infant baptism against Bishop Fidus, who had recommended, using an analogy to Jewish circumcision, that baptism be delayed until the eighth day. In a letter to Fidus, Cyprian explained the decision of sixty-six North African bishops on the matter:

> But, in turn, if, in the case of the greatest sinners and those sinning much against God, when afterward they believe, the remission of their sins is granted and no one is prevented from baptism and grace, how much more should an infant not be prohibited, who, recently born, has not sinned at all, except that, born carnally according to Adam, he has contracted the contagion of the first death from the first nativity. He approaches more easily from this very fact to receive the remission of sins because those which are remitted are not his own sins, but the sins of another.[9]

---

[8] Jaroslav Pelikan, *The Emergence of the Catholic Tradition (100–600)*; vol. 1 of *The Christian Tradition: A History of the Development of Doctrine* (Chicago, 1971), pp. 290–292; Julius Gross, *Geschichte des Erbsündendogmas. Ein Beitrag zur Geschichte des Problems vom Ursprung des Übels*, 4 vols. (Munich and Basel, 1960), 1:118–120; Aland, *Early Church*, pp. 80–86, 104–106.

[9] Cyprian of Carthage, *Epistulae*, Letter 64, ed. W. Hartel, CSEL, vol. 3, pt. 2 (Vi-

In view of such considerations, Cyprian and the bishops rejected any delay in the baptism of infants. Their opinion was not universally accepted, but by the third century the fact of infant baptism and its theological grounding in the doctrine of original sin were interacting with one another to give the practice currency and the aura of apostolic sanction.

The need to baptize at least seriously ill infants and adults (called clinical baptism, from *klinē*, the Greek word for bed) came to seem obvious. Even healthy infants were sometimes baptized, although that practice was only slowly becoming universal and mandatory. By the fourth century, the Arian preacher Asterius the Sophist recommended early baptism of all infants to protect them from demons, heresy, and the danger of dying without the baptismal seal. Thus the interaction of practice and theology strengthened the hold of infant baptism, until in the fifth century Augustine could, with justification, view it as the norm.[10]

The baptism of infants posed practical problems for the performance of the baptismal liturgy. The earliest converts to Christianity had been adults and until the fifth century the needs of adults had shaped the catechumenate, the competentate, and the baptismal ceremonies themselves. The increase in the number of infants had little immediate influence on this liturgy, for once they become fixed such patterns are quite conservative and resistant to change.

In the earliest texts on infant baptism, which are admittedly laconic, there was no more than a superficial adjustment of the adult ceremony to infant realities. And even when infants predominated as the baptizees, the baptismal liturgy remained recognizable as a ritual for adults, adapted lightly for the new clientele.[11] The chief adaptation was the interposition of one adult, ordinarily a parent, to speak and act on behalf of the infant. For example, adult *competentes* were asked to respond whether they renounced Satan, adhered to Christ, and believed certain propositions represented in the baptismal creeds. The Roman liturgy, which was very conservative, continued to put such questions to infants in the second person: "Do you believe . . . ?" The person

enna, 1871), pp. 720–721. Tr. Rose B. Donna, *Saint Cyprian: Letters*. FC, vol. 51 (Washington, D.C., 1964), p. 219.

[10] On Asterius' views, see J. C. Didier, "Le pédobaptisme au ivᵉ siècle. Documents nouveaux," *MSR* 6 (1949):233–246.

[11] J. C. Didier, "Une adaptation de la liturgie baptismale au baptême des enfants dans l'église ancienne," *MSR* 22 (1965):87; Burkhard Neunheuser, "Die Liturgie der Kindertaufe. Ihre Problematik in der Geschichte," *Zeichen des Glaubens. Studien zu Taufe und Firmung. Balthasar Fischer zum 70. Geburtstag* (Zurich, 1972), pp. 319–334.

carrying the infant answered in the first person: "I believe. . . ." In fourth century North Africa, Spain, and Gaul, there was a modest adaptation in which the adult was asked "Does he believe . . . ?" and responded "He believes . . ."[12] In either situation, someone was required to answer for the infant in order to make a liturgy designed for adults function for those who could not speak. This person was a parent who acted as *sponsor*, a word meaning "surety" or "guarantor of the good faith of another person."

When the person to be baptized was a retarded, deaf and dumb, or comatose adult, the church authorities were confronted with a situation analogous to that of infant baptism. Hesitations about baptizing adults who were incapable of responding on their own behalf persisted, but they waned in the face of the almost irresistible model of infant baptism. In such cases, the adult liturgy was maintained and a sponsor was used. In line with these practices, the North African, Fulgentius of Ruspe, defended the baptism of a comatose youth on the grounds that his behavior during the catechumenate was a sufficient expression of his intentions. And Gennadius of Marseilles further argued that those whose intellect was too weak to grasp religious instruction (whom I take to mean the retarded) could be represented by those who offered them for baptism.[13] Such cases involving adults would always have been rare, but they were handled by applying the traditional practice with regard to infants.

It was not only the baptismal liturgy itself for which infants required sponsors. The catechumenate, too, with its instruction and testing of adults, was long maintained for infants in increasingly ritualistic form, until it was replaced in the sixth century by the *scrutinia*, which stressed ceremony and exorcism to the virtual exclusion of formal instruction.[14] It was from this humdrum and purely practical re-

[12] *Didier*, "Une adaptation," pp. 83–87.

[13] Gennadius of Marseilles, writing in the late fifth century, assimilated a mentally impaired baptizand into the category of infants in chapter 21 of his *Liber sive Definitio ecclesiasticorum dogmatum*, ed. Charles Turner, *JTS* 7 (1906):93–94: "si uero paruuli sunt uel hebetes qui doctrinam non capiant, respondeant pro illis qui offerunt iuxta morem baptizandi." For the case of a catechumen who fell into a coma and was baptized, see the exchange of letters between Deacon Ferrandus and Bishop Fulgentius of Ruspe in North Africa, about 525, in *Fulgentii episcopi Ruspensis opera*, ed. J. Fraipont, CCSL, vol. 91 (Turnhout, 1968), pp. 357–381. Augustine of Hippo preferred to err on the side of lenience in cases of emergency baptism, as seen in Frederik Van der Meer, *Augustine the Bishop: Church and Society at the Dawn of the Middle Ages*, tr. B. Battershaw and G. R. Lamb (London, 1961), pp. 351–353.

[14] A. Dondeyne, "La discipline des scrutins dans l'église latine avant Charlemagne," *RHE* 28 (1932):5–32, 751–787.

quirement of an adult to speak and act for an infant that the sponsor for infants was launched on a long and important career in Christian societies. This was a very different point of departure from that which gave rise to the sponsor for adults, for the adult candidate acted for himself or herself in the liturgy, and the sponsor of an adult was asked to testify only to the candidate's behavior and attitude during the period of testing.

The sole notice of infants and children in Hippolytus' description of early third-century baptismal practice at Rome was as follows:

> First baptize the little ones. Let all who are able to speak for themselves speak. However, if they are not able to speak for themselves, let their parents or someone from their kin speak for them.[15]

Other evidence confirms Hippolytus' assertion that parents ordinarily assisted and responded for their infants or young children during baptism and perhaps also during the required period of instruction, exorcisms, and blessings that took place in the weeks preceding baptism.[16] The exact age at which children no longer needed assistance and could respond for themselves was never authoritatively stated. Gregory of Nazianzus suggested that at three children could participate actively in their own baptism,[17] while Augustine approved seven as a proper age.[18] It must often have been an individual judgment, shaped by local custom.

The baptism of infants thus added a new participant to the initiation process, the parent/sponsor who acted and responded for the child before and during baptism and, as Brusselmans demonstrated, took responsibility for the child's subsequent moral and religious development, a responsibility rooted primarily in the parental role and only secondarily in the sponsoring role. It is crucial to note that the parent/sponsor of the early church was not a socially significant figure because sponsorship added nothing fundamentally new to the moral, religious, and personal obligations of a parent. It was only in the early Middle Ages that parent/sponsors were replaced by outsider/sponsors.

[15] Bernard Botte, *La tradition apostolique d'après les anciennes versions*, ch. 21, 2nd ed., SC, vol. 11bis (Paris, 1968), p. 80.

[16] Brusselmans, "Les fonctions," passim.

[17] Gregory of Nazianzus, Sermon 40.28, tr. Charles Browne and James Swallow in *The Nicene and Post-Nicene Fathers*, 2nd series, vol. 7 (New York, 1893; reprint ed., Grand Rapids, Mich. 1955), p. 369.

[18] Augustine, *De natura et origine animae*, bk. 3, ch. 9, sec. 12, ed. C. F. Urba and J. Zycha, CSEL, vol. 60 (Vienna, 1913), p. 370.

Then sponsorship became socially important because it created new obligations and served to unite an outsider with the child and with the child's parents.

The scholarly debate about whether the sponsorship of adults developed out of the sponsorship of infants or *vice versa* has arisen from misconceptions about the nature of each practice. Both emerged virtually simultaneously in the written sources of the early third century and have quite properly been assumed to have taken shape in the second century. Each responded to its own set of stimuli: adult sponsorship met the Christian community's need to detect unworthy converts and to prepare promising ones carefully while infant sponsorship met the prosaic need to assist a helpless infant (or a seriously impaired adult) in the course of an initiation process structured to serve healthy adults. The two institutions remained quite distinct until late antiquity, when the decline of adult baptisms upset their equilibrium and the two fused into godparentage and spiritual kinship, with the greater weight of influence coming from infant sponsorship.

The earliest sources laid emphasis on the task of responding or speaking by the sponsor on behalf of the infant. Hippolytus noted simply that parents or relatives should speak for those children who could not do so themselves. But even earlier than Hippolytus' reference were comments by the fiery North African Christian controversialist, Tertullian, who composed his *De baptismo* about 200/206 to counter the views of the Cainites, a Gnostic sect.[19] In chapter 18, Tertullian argues for greater discretion in admitting candidates to baptism, particularly those who are hasty in taking on its responsibilities (*pondus baptismi*). He singles out for mention those who are unmarried, those who intend to lead a virginal life, and those too young to seek baptism for themselves. Within this context of emphasis on the seriousness of baptism and the need to avoid haste, he expresses disapproval of infant baptism. However, this disapproval was rooted in prudential rather than theological considerations, and his comments attest to the existence of the practice in his region.

One element of Tertullian's reserved stance toward infant baptism was his perception of the risk that those who acted as guarantors (*sponsores*) for the infant would run if the child turned out badly or if they themselves died before fulfilling their guaranty. This is how Tertullian expressed his view of sponsors:

[19] Tertullian, *De baptismo*, ch. 18, ed. R.F. Refoulé, French tr. M. Drouzy, SC, vol. 35 (Paris, 1952), pp. 91–93.

Any request can both disappoint and be disappointed. It follows that deferment of baptism is more profitable, in accordance with each person's character and attitude, and even age: and especially so as regards children. For what need is there, if there really is no need, for even their sponsors to be brought into peril, seeing they may possibly themselves fail of their promises by death, or be deceived by the subsequent development of an evil disposition? It is true our Lord says, *Forbid them not to come to me.* So let them come, when they are growing up, when they are learning, when they are being taught what they are coming to: let them be made Christians when they have become competent to know Christ. Why should innocent infancy come with haste to the remission of sins? Shall we take less cautious action in this than we take in worldly matters? Shall one who is not trusted with earthly property be entrusted with heavenly? Let them learn how to ask for salvation, so that you may be seen to have given to one that asketh.[20]

Tertullian's warning that the guarantors ran the risk of not being able to fulfill their promises, either because they died or because the infant turned out to have an evil disposition, pointed to the fact that there was an important perceived difference between the duties of an adult's sponsor and those of an infant. In the case of adults, the sponsors attested to prebaptismal worthiness, to sincerity of conversion and behavior—in short, to an actual situation of which they had knowledge. Their role during and after the baptism was minimal. In sharp contrast, the role of the sponsor for an infant was primarily *baptismal* and *postbaptismal*. The child had no "track record," and thus it made no sense to attest to its sincerity. Instead, the parent/sponsor spoke and acted for the child during the ceremonies and accepted the obligation to foster religious and moral development as the child matured. In Tertullian's view, this obligation carried with it a risk of failure that could be avoided simply by postponing baptism until children could answer for themselves.

Responding on behalf of the child was not the only service a sponsor would need to perform in a baptism. In the classic western version of the godparent complex, as it emerged in the Frankish realms, the godparent offered (*offerre*) the child for baptism, carried it (*gestare*) during the ceremonies, made promises on its behalf (*spondere*), and received it

---

[20] Ibid., ch. 18.3–4, p. 92. Tr. by Ernest Evans, *Tertullian's Homily on Baptism* (London, 1964), p. 39.

from the font after it had been baptized (*suscipere* or *recipere*).[21] In the ancient church, helpless infants certainly needed such aid, but the various actions had not yet been concentrated in a single nonparent, who may properly be called a godparent.

Aside from Hippolytus' direction that parents or relatives should respond for youngsters who could not do so for themselves and Tertullian's critique of such responses, the sources prior to the mid-fourth century are virtually silent about the particulars of infant sponsorship. But in the later fourth and the fifth centuries, information on the sponsor's duties becomes fuller. Here we learn that an infant had to be brought forward or offered for baptism. Augustine called the people who performed this duty "*offerentes*" and identified them as parents of the infants.[22] Furthermore, Brusselmans has shown conclusively that in the ancient church, whenever it was possible, a parent presented a child for baptism, although others could do so if the parents were dead or unknown.[23] Only in the ninth century was the role of presenter taken from the natural parent and committed to a godparent.

During the long, complex ceremonial of baptism, each child had to be carried, undressed and dressed, handed to the clergy at certain moments, and taken back from them. These were practical matters that had probably not yet taken on ritual significance. The *Canons of Hippolytus* (not to be confused with Hippolytus' *Apostolic Tradition*, although derived from it) is a mid-fourth-century Egyptian church order that includes a description of baptism. In it is the command that "those who respond for infants should remove the latter's clothes."[24] Although members of the clergy probably carried infants during specific rituals, the youngsters were generally borne by the parent/sponsor.[25]

---

[21] Marie-Magdelaine van Molle, "Les fonctions de parrainage des enfants, en Occident, de 550 à 900" (unpublished *mémoire*, Année de Pastorale Liturgique, Abbaye de Saint André, Bruges 1961), pp. 57–83, treated the vocabulary employed to describe the liturgical actions associated with the sponsorship of infants. She summarized her findings, including those on vocabulary, in "Les fonctions du parrainage des enfants en Occident. Leur apogée et leur dégradation (du vi^e au xe siècle)," *Paroisse et liturgie* 46 (1964):121–146. I wish to thank Sister van Molle for graciously providing me with a copy of her thorough and useful *mémoire*. Derrick S. Bailey, *Sponsors at Baptism and Confirmation: An Historical Introduction to Anglican Practice* (New York, 1951), pp. 139–145, has an appendix on sponsorship vocabulary.

[22] Augustine, Letter 98.2 and passim, in *S. Aureli Augustini hipponiensis episcopi epistulae*, ed. A. Goldbacher, CSEL, vol. 34 (Vienna, 1895), pp. 520–533.

[23] Brusselmans, "Les fonctions," pp. 24–26 and 39.

[24] Canon 19, in R. G. Coquin, ed. *Les Canons d'Hippolyte*, PO, vol. 31, p. 2 (Paris, 1966), p. 379.

[25] Augustine, Letter 98.5, *S. Aureli Augustini epistulae*, p. 526, refers to those who bear (*gestare*) the infants in their hands.

The act of taking a child dripping wet immediately after baptism ultimately came to be seen as the crucial moment in creating a godparental relationship. And Bailey, van Molle, and Brusselmans all agree that the Christianized version of this practice was rooted in pre-Christian mores and linguistic usage.[26] In archaic pagan Greek and Roman society, it had been customary for a father to lift (*suscipere* or *levare*) his newborn child from the ground to signify publicly his acknowledgment of its legitimacy, and an analogous practice had existed in some primitive Germanic societies.[27] By imperial Roman times, the custom of lifting a newborn may no longer have been practiced, but its memory survived in linguistic usage. Thus the locution "*suscipere infantem ex femina*," meaning literally "to take a child from a woman," had come to mean "to beget or have a child." This way of describing birth was taken over to indicate baptismal sponsorship, where there was an actual lifting, although it was from the font rather than from the ground.

When early medieval texts refer to one who *suscipit/excipit/levat* someone from the baptismal font, the phrase is to be understood in the common Latin usage of giving birth to or begetting that person from the font, which was frequently referred to as a womb. But no pre-fifth-century text explicitly says who that receiver was. It might have been the parent/sponsor, although van Molle entertained the idea that some third person might always have done so.[28] In any case, in the pre-fifth-century church, parents took the major role at baptism in offering, carrying, responding for, and perhaps receiving their infant fron the font, with some assistance from the clergy. Only the act of responding attracted much comment because of the theological questions that it raised. This dominance of the parent/sponsor is a key feature of ancient infant sponsorship, one that effectively prevented the emergence of a true godparent figure.

Just as adult sponsorship was not a focus of controversy or theological arguments, so the sponsorship of infants developed without elaborate intellectual justification. Indeed, it was only after two centuries of existence that infant sponsorship became the object of theological

[26] Bailey, *Sponsors*, pp. 4–5; van Molle, "Les fonctions" (1961), pp. 2–6; Brusselmans, "Les fonctions," pp. 159–163.

[27] G. Binder, "Geburt II (religionsgeschichtlich)," *RAC* 9 (1976):115–116; W. Ogris, "Aufnehmen des Kindes," *HRG*, vol. 1 (1971), pp. 253–254. On the Germanic custom of sprinkling a newborn with water to accept it into protected human status, see Ursula Perkow, *Wasserweihe, Taufe und Patenschaft bei den Nordgermanen* (Ph.D. diss., Hamburg, 1972), pp. 7–46.

[28] Van Molle, "Les fonctions," (1964), pp. 136–138.

speculation. As in the case of adult preparation for baptism, it was Augustine of Hippo who attempted for the first time to place a theological substructure under the already venerable custom of sponsoring infants. Augustine's voluminous writings, which exceed in quantity those of any other pagan or Christian author from antiquity, provide some information about the sponsors of infants.[29] It was particularly in the course of his polemic against the Pelagians that his views on infant baptism and sponsorship were worked out.

The British monk Pelagius arrived in North Africa from Rome in 411 and was soon embroiled in controversy with Augustine over the issue of God's grace and human will.[30] One point of contention between them was the state of an infant's soul before he or she had an opportunity to commit "personal" sins. Pelagius argued for the child's innocence, while Augustine countered with a sharpened defense of the proposition that every human, including infants, inherits Adam's sin and needs baptism for salvation.[31] Augustine pointed to the custom of baptizing infants and used this fact as an argument that the church would not have admitted such a practice if it were superfluous. He also defended the idea that in some way sponsors contributed to the efficacy of infant baptism.

In his *Seven Books Concerning Baptism*, written in 400/401 to refute Donatist views of baptism, Augustine had taken a rather external view of sponsorship, seeing in it chiefly a liturgical function. In his opinion, the sponsors compensated for an infant's weakness, which threatened to prevent the adult-oriented ceremonies from unfolding properly:

> Thus in baptized infants the sacrament of regeneration comes first and, if they hold Christian piety, conversion, whose sign preceded in the body, will follow in the heart. Just as in that thief [Luke 23:40–43] the benevolence of the Almighty added what was lacking from the sacrament of baptism, so in infants who die baptized it must be believed that the same grace of the Almighty adds [what is lacking], because it is not from a wicked will, but from a weakness of age that they are able neither to believe with the heart for justice nor to confess with the mouth for salvation. Therefore, when others respond for them, in order that the cel-

[29] Robert de Latte, "Saint Augustin et le baptême. Etude liturgico-historique du rituel baptismal des enfants chez Saint Augustin," *QLP* 57 (1976):51–55, surveys Augustine's views.

[30] On Augustine's dispute with Pelagius, see Gerald Bonner, *St. Augustine of Hippo: Life and Controversies* (London, 1963), pp. 312–393.

[31] Gross, *Geschichte*, 1:275–322.

ebration of the sacrament may be fulfilled with regard to them, it certainly suffices for their consecration, since they themselves are not able to respond. But if someone else should respond for him who is able to respond, it does not suffice then.[32]

This practical, nontheological view of sponsorship was insufficient to meet the issues raised in the Pelagian controversy, but even before that quarrel Augustine had treated at length the role of sponsors in infant baptism. Augustine was without doubt the most learned bishop of his generation in the West and was consulted frequently on all sorts of matters. Such consultations were the occasion for many of his letters and treatises, which were the equivalent of pamphlets in modern controversies. Thus, some time between 408 and 411, Augustine's friend and fellow bishop, Boniface of Cataquas, wrote a letter expressing the questions, hesitations, and problems that he felt about the sponsorship of infants. Boniface's letter and Augustine's response predated the outbreak of the Pelagian controversy[33] and hence reflect a situation before the heat of argument exaggerated the participants' positions. This exchange of letters also throws light on the pastoral concerns and theological unclarity that gave Pelagius an audience in North Africa. Boniface's letter does not survive, but Augustine's habit of quoting a question more or less verbatim before responding permits us to eavesdrop on the conversation.

Boniface was troubled by an apparent implication of infant sponsorship: that one person could act for another in something as serious as salvation. He asked Augustine why the opposite was not true, why a parent could not also work the damnation of his baptized child, for instance, by tainting it with demon worship. In view of Augustine's heavy reliance on an argument from church custom in his later controversy with Pelagius, there is a certain irony in Boniface's request that Augustine explain things to him on the basis of reason (*ratio*), not custom (*consuetudo*).[34] Boniface's first question, as repeated by Augustine, was:

You ask me whether parents do harm to their baptized babies when they try to cure them by means of sacrifices to demons,

---

[32] Augustine, *De baptismo libri vii*, bk. 4. ch. 24, sec. 31, ed. M. Petschenig, CSEL, vol. 51 (Vienna, 1908), pp. 259–260.

[33] J. C. Didier, "Observations sur la date de la lettre 98 de Saint Augustin," *MSR* 27 (1970):115–117, argues that the traditional date of 408 is too early and that the letter belongs to the period just prior to the arrival of Pelagius in North Africa (411).

[34] Augustine, Letter 98.7, *S. Aureli Augustini epistulae*, p. 529: "Ad istas ergo quaestiones peto breuiter respondere digneris, ita ut non mihi de consuetudine praescribas, sed rationem reddas."

and, if they do not harm them, how the faith of parents is bene-
ficial to their children when they are baptized, whereas their in-
fidelity cannot harm them.[35]

Augustine responded that an unbaptized infant was tainted by Adam's
sin because all humankind had been "in" Adam, indeed had been
Adam in some way when the latter sinned. As each potential human
being becomes an actual, individual person, he takes from Adam that
sin as an inheritance. In baptism, the Holy Spirit, which is present
both in the sponsor and in the infant, cleanses the child of Adam's
sin. But Augustine argued that the alternative proposed by Boniface
was quite different. After a child has been baptized, nothing the parents do can transmit guilt to the child, since the child is not "in" the
parents but is a separate individual (*homo in seipso*).[36] Furthermore,
when parents offer sacrifices to demons on behalf of their child, the
Holy Spirit is not shared by parent and child, as it is in baptism. The
sin in offering to demons is strictly that of the parents. In effect,
parents can participate in cleansing an infant from Adam's sin, but
thereafter only the child can forfeit the innocence so gained:

> It follows from this that a child born of his parents' flesh can be
> born again of the Spirit of God, so that the taint contracted from
> them is washed away, but one born again of the Spirit of God
> cannot be reborn of the flesh of his parents so as to contract again
> the taint that has been washed away. Therefore, the child does
> not lose the grace of Christ once conferred, except by his own
> sinful act[37]

Bishop Boniface's second difficulty lay in his knowledge of many
parents' motives in sponsoring their children at baptism. Christian
theology understood baptism in terms of cleansing, healing, and sanc-
tifying, but in a folk interpretation of that theology parents saw it as
a means to preserve or obtain good health for their infants. In short,
they believed that baptism would expel the demons to whose agency
sickness was attributed. Boniface wondered how such a misguided
sponsor could participate in the cleansing of the infant's soul.

On the basis of his general view of the working of the sacraments,
hammered out in long controversy with the Donatists, Augustine responded that the Holy Spirit worked even through imperfectly motivated human beings, provided that the sacramental actions and words

[35] Augustine, Letter 98.1, ibid., p. 520; tr. Sister Wilfrid Parsons, *Saint Augustine: Letters (83–180)*, FC, vol. 18 (New York, 1953), p. 129.
[36] Augustine, Letter 98.1, *S. Aureli Augustini epistulae*, p. 520.
[37] Augustine, Letter 98.2, ibid., pp. 522–523; tr. Parsons, *Saint Augustine*, p. 131.

were performed correctly: "The Holy Spirit . . . , does His work sometimes through the agency not only of the merely ignorant, but even of the utterly unworthy."[38] But he added a new note to his defense of sponsorship in stressing the activity of the church itself in the person of the sponsors:

> Surely, the little ones are offered for the reception of the spiritual grace, not so much by those in whose arms they are carried— although they are offered by them if they are good and faithful— as by the whole company of the saints and believers. We rightly understand that they are offered by all who consent to the offering, and by whose holy and indivisible charity they are helped to share in the outpouring of the Holy Spirit. Mother Church who is in the saints does this wholly, because she wholly brings forth all and each.[39]

Augustine's view of sponsors had clearly developed since 400; for he had come to believe that sponsors acted in the place of all believers, who constituted the church. This body of believers compensated for any inadequacy on the part of the actual parent/sponsor in some dusty North African town. It is quite probable that such a complex of ideas does not reflect what the sponsors themselves thought they were doing, but Augustine's theology shaped subsequent attempts in the Latin West to explain and defend the practice, even beyond the Reformation into modern times.

In Boniface's experience, parents customarily sponsored their own children and he was puzzled about the situation in which a parent could not or would not do so. He apparently believed, or at least entertained the notion in passing, that it was obligatory for the parent to be the sponsor. He reasoned that since parents stood in the immediate line of transmission of Adam's sin to their child, they should participate in the removal of that sin. Augustine quoted his correspondent's words on this important point, "For you write in these words: 'As their parents were responsible for their punishment, so let the faith of their parents bring them likewise to be justified.' "[40] In response, Augustine confirmed that it was normal for a parent to spon-

---

[38] Augustine, Letter 98.5, *S. Aureli Augustini epistulae*, p. 526; tr. Parsons, *Saint Augustine*, pp. 133–134.

[39] Augustine, Letter 98.5, *S. Aureli Augustini epistulae*, p. 526; tr. Parsons, *Saint Augustine*, p. 134.

[40] Augustine, Letter 98.6, *S. Aureli Augustini epistulae*, p. 527: "sic enim scribens dicis: 'Ut, sicut parentes fuerunt auctores ad eorum poenam, per fidem parentum identidem iustificentur' "; tr. Parsons, *Saint Augustine*, p. 134.

sor an infant, but he denied that it was obligatory. Augustine always
laid stress on what actually happened and he pointed out to Boniface
contemporary counterexamples: slave children were sometimes sponsored by their masters; orphans were occasionally brought to baptism
by people willing to do them that kindness; foundlings were sometimes sponsored by consecrated virgins who rescued them from death
and perhaps raised them as well.[41] In short, Augustine defended the
view that in unusual circumstances any believer could be sponsor to
an infant not his own.

Boniface's final problem with the sponsorship of infants was his
most theological. He was troubled by the very notion that one person
could make a commitment on behalf of another person who had not
agreed and could not at the time agree. In ordinary human affairs,
noted Boniface, it was impossible to know how a child would turn out
as an adult. No one could assert confidently that a particular baby,
held in his arms, would be a chaste or honest adult. Likewise, no one
could assert unequivocally that he knew what an infant was thinking
about or indeed whether the infant was thinking at all. Yet in the
course of the baptismal services the parent/sponsor asserted such
weighty things as the child's renunciation of Satan and adherence to
specific beliefs. Bishop Boniface wondered how anyone could make
such declarations with confidence or propriety.[42]

Augustine responded that the Christian sacraments are holy acts
quite unlike their secular counterparts. In some way, the sacrament *is*
the very thing it represents:

> As, then, in a certain manner the sacrament of the Body of Christ
> is the Body of Christ, and the sacrament of the Blood of Christ
> is the Blood of Christ, so the sacrament of faith [baptism] is faith.
> To believe is the same as to have faith. That is why the response
> is made [by the sponsor] that the child believes, although he has
> as yet no conscious knowledge of faith; the answer is made that
> he has faith because this is the sacrament of faith, that he turns
> to God because this is the sacrament of conversion.[43]

---

[41] Augustine, Letter 98.6, *S. Aureli Augustini epistulae*, pp. 527-528: "cum uideas mul-
tos non offerri a parentibus sed etiam a quibuslibet extraneis, sicut a dominis seruuli
aliquando offeruntur. et nonnumquam mortuis parentibus suis paruuli baptizantur ab
eis oblati, qui in illis huius modi misericordiam praebere potuerunt. aliquando etiam,
quos crudeliter parentes exposuerint nutriendi a quibuslibet, nonnumquam a sacris uir-
ginibus colliguntur et ab eis offeruntur ad baptismum."
[42] Augustini, Letter 98.7, ibid., pp. 528–529.
[43] Augustini, Letter 98.9, ibid., p. 531; tr. Parsons, *Saint Augustine*, p. 137.

Augustine thus assured Boniface that baptism itself gave the infant faith, although in a form that must subsequently develop into a consciously accepted thing. When a baptized infant grew older, he did not receive faith again, but rather he made it active and personally appropriated, with the aid of his parent/sponsor and the church. If a child died before attaining the state of active, understood faith and personal moral responsibility, the faith given in baptism was adequate to free the child "from that condemnation 'which by one man entered the world,' " that is, from Adam's sin.[44]

Augustine's letter to Boniface was a unique attempt to integrate infant sponsorship into the sacramental theology of the Christian church, and the importance of its author guaranteed it a continuing influence in the Latin West. It also offered some incidental testimony to the functioning of the institution in the Christian communities of early fifth-century North Africa. From it we learn that the sponsor was ordinarily a parent, although others could serve if necessary. Augustine's perspective in the letter was strictly theological and pastoral and he had nothing explicit to say about secular social consequences. However, certain inferences about these consequences can be drawn. The most obvious and crucial is that if a natural parent was the sponsor, then the social consequences were negligible. After all, a parent's obligation to care for and train a child was traditional and thus was only marginally increased, if at all, by sponsorship.[45] In particular, by sponsoring their own child the parents created no bond with outsiders, and neither did the infant.

But Augustine alluded to other situations that were more promising in their potential for postbaptismal consequences. He noted that orphans were brought to baptism by persons who were offering *misericordia* (mercy) to the unfortunates.[46] Were these persons kinsmen? Were they, for example, uncles or aunts? There is no way to tell, but such a situation offered the possibility for the creation of a lasting, nurturing relationship. Augustine also reminded Bishop Boniface that "sometimes, even children who have been exposed by their parents are rescued and fed by others, often enough by the consecrated virgins, and then they are brought to baptism by them, although these certainly have no children, since they have renounced the prospect of having any."[47] In the case of an abandoned child, the rescuer would

---

[44] Augustine, Letter 98.10, *S. Aureli Augustini epistulae*, p. 532, quoting *Romans* 5.12; tr. Parsons, *Saint Augustine*, p. 138.

[45] Brusselmans, "Les fonctions," pp. 39 and 52.

[46] Augustine, Letter 98.6, *S. Aureli Augustini epistulae*, p. 527; quoted above in note 41.

[47] Ibid., pp. 527–528; tr. Parsons, *Saint Augustine*, p. 135.

not ordinarily be a relative and thus baptismal sponsorship could have formed part of a decision to care for the child, indeed perhaps to "adopt" it in some sense of that term.

Here was a very promising place for a socially significant relationship to develop. However, I have found no evidence from Augustine's day that such a relationship did, in fact, emerge. On the other hand, in southern Gaul in the early sixth century Bishop Caesarius of Arles referred indirectly to the social consequences of sponsorship when he forbade the nuns in the strictly cloistered convent that he had founded to be sponsors:

> No one should presume to sponsor in baptism a child of anyone at all, either rich or poor; for she who for the love of God has disdained the freedom to have children of her own ought not wish for nor possess this freedom belonging to others, so that without any hindrance she may give her time unceasingly to God.[48]

Caesarius seems to be saying that sponsorship gave the nun "a child of her own" who would constitute a "hindrance" to her life of withdrawal from the world.[49] In Augustine's letter, such a negative view of sponsorship by nuns was not implied, perhaps because the bishop did not see negative consequences of such sponsorship in the rather loosely organized lifestyle of the North African *sacrae virgines*.

Augustine also noted that masters occasionally offered young slaves for baptism.[50] Was their relationship different in quality or in expected behavior from that of the master to other slaves? There is no ancient evidence on the basis of which to answer this question, but one may understand the potential of such a relationship by noting that in the eight-century Byzantine law code known as the *Ecloga* a slave was considered freed "if the master or the mistress, or their children with their parents' consent, become sponsors of the slave in Holy and Salvation-bringing Baptism."[51] It is a possibility that in Augustine's day the master *was* the child's father and in sponsoring it he was merely

---

[48] Caesarius of Arles, *Statuta sanctarum virginum*, ch. 11, ed. Germain Morin in *Florilegium patristicum* vol. 34 (Bonn, 1933), p. 7, tr. Maria Caritas McCarthy, *The Rule for Nuns of St. Caesarius of Arles: A Translation with a Critical Introduction*, CUA, SMH, new series, vol. 16 (Washington, D.C., 1960), p. 174.

[49] Caesarius originated a tradition of reluctance by monks and nuns to serve as sponsors because of the social obligations that were incompatible with a proper life of withdrawal from worldly things, on which see Joseph H. Lynch, "Baptismal Sponsorship and Monks and Nuns, 500–1000," *ABR* 31 (1980):108–129.

[50] Augustine, Letter 98, cited above in note 41.

[51] *Ecloga*, ch. 8.4, tr. Edwin H. Freshfield, *A Manual of Roman Law: The* Ecloga *Published by the Emperors Leo III and Constantine V of Isauria* (Cambridge, 1926), p. 89.

acting as a parent/sponsor, while out of concern for propriety he avoided direct acknowledgment of the fact of paternity. In any case, the variations of infant sponsorship that carried potential for social significance were, in Augustine's day, quite atypical and the firm norm was the parent/sponsor.

The fifth century was very important in the transformation of infant sponsorship from a liturgical detail to a social phenomenon. At the beginning of this century, Augustine adhered to the traditional view that natural parents were the ordinary sponsors for their own children, with the provision that in cases of necessity others could assume the task. However, by the end of the century there was evidence, particularly from the pseudo-Dionysius in the East and from Caesarius of Arles in the West, that even children whose parents were living were being sponsored by invited outsiders, although there was as yet no formal ban on parental sponsorship.

The practice of inviting outsiders to be sponsors grew, until by the eighth century both Latin and Byzantine Christianity forbade parents to sponsor their own children. But this development is a matter for a later chapter. The most important conclusion to be drawn from the present examination of infant sponsorship up to the fifth century is a negative one: the godparent complex and spiritual kinship did not exist, there was no clearly understood new relationship initiated between the infant and the sponsor or between the infant's parents and the sponsor, and there was no web of sexual taboos created among the participants. As long as parents ordinarily filled the role, infant sponsorship could never be more than a modest liturgical detail.

A fundamental change in the sociology of Christianity brought about an amalgamation of the two kinds of sponsorship. From the second to the fifth centuries, they had evolved in distinct ways out of different origins. But as the Greco-Roman world became Christian, adult baptism and its form of sponsorship were overwhelmed both numerically and conceptually by infant baptism and its form of sponsorship. The ancient pattern of adult sponsorship ceased to function and adults were increasingly sponsored as if they were infants. In particular, even though adults acted and responded for themselves, each of them had one sponsor with postbaptismal responsibilities. Nor was infant sponsorship itself static, for in it too parents were beginning to be replaced by invited sponsors. It was in the course of this amalgamation of earlier practices, with a preponderance of influence accorded to infant sponsorship, that the early medieval godparent complex and spiritual kinship emerged.

By the fifth century, a crucial phase in the history of Christianity was reaching its apogee. Aside from a flirtation with Arianism, the Roman state since Constantine's conversion had favored Catholic and Nicene Christianty at the expense of paganism, Judaism, and other varieties of Christianity. Thus the spiritual conquest of the Mediterranean and its hinterlands, notwithstanding truces on some issues, was nearing completion, with important vestiges of the earlier religious traditions surviving as folk practice or being incorporated into the triumphant Christian church. Religious dissent in organized form was in decline and a Christian version of Greco-Roman culture was taking shape. In this culture, the practice of delaying baptism had disappeared and infant baptism was vigorously promoted by the church, with the consequence that the overwhelming majority of persons born to Christian families entered the Christian community as infants.

The baptism of adults did not, of course, completely disappear, for occasional converts from paganism, Judaism, and certain Christian dissident groups still joined the Church through this means. It did, however, become unusual in the Christianized lands around the Mediterranean. Indeed, large numbers of adult baptizees were usually associated only with missionary situations, either beyond the imperial borders or within those borders when Germanic, Slavic, and Asiatic peoples entered as settlers.

In a legally and culturally Christian society, the traditional rationale and specific provisions of adult sponsorship ceased to be functional and there was no longer any serious effort to screen out unworthy candidates. In fact, the situation was quite the contrary, as social and legal pressure promoted early baptism for all. Thus the rejection of candidates became quite unusual. The catechumenate was adapted to this new situation, becoming shorter, more ritualized, and more oriented toward the infants who were its main clientele. However, the conservative character of the liturgy masked these changes somewhat, since many venerable prayers and ceremonies, framed originally for adults, continued to be directed toward infants, who were addressed by the old epithets of *competentes* and *electi*.[52]

One moment in the drift toward an amalgamated institution of sponsorship is captured in the treatise *On the Ecclesiastical Hierarchy*, composed by a writer who strove to make his readers believe that he was a first-century Christian. Sometime in the late fifth century in Syria, an anonymous author of Monophysite leanings set out boldly to promote his views by identifying himself with Dionysius the Ar-

---

[52] Thierry Maertens, *Histoire et pastorale du rituel du catéchuménat et du baptême*, Paroisse et liturgie. Collection de pastorale liturgique, vol. 56 (Bruges, 1962), pp. 181–207.

eopagite, Paul's convert at Athens (Acts 17:34). There survive from the pen of this pseudo-Dionysius four treatises (*On the Divine Names, On Mystical Theology, On the Celestial Hierarchy*, and *On the Ecclesiastical Hierarchy*) and eleven letters, all composed in an esoteric Greek style and thoroughly permeated by Neo-platonic philosophy.[53] Within a century, the author's pious deception had succeeded in the East, where Maximus the Confessor commented on him, and in the West, where Pope Gregory the Great cited him. And as time passed, the pseudo-Dionysius' works were an important conduit of neo-platonized Christianity into the Latin and Byzantine Middle Ages. In the West they were known initially through two ninth-century Latin translations, one by Abbot Hilduin of St. Denis, who identified the author with his monastery's patron saint,[54] and another by John Scotus Erigena.[55]

In *On the Ecclesiastical Hierarchy*, the pseudo-Dionysius treats the three kinds of clergy (deacons, priests, and bishops), the three sacraments (baptism, the Eucharist, and anointing) and the three kinds of laity (catechumens/penitents, baptized "initiates," and monks) within the context of a vast Neo-platonized scheme of redemption.[56] And when he discusses the baptism of adults, he unveils a new situation that had emerged within the familiar old liturgical forms. In it, the sponsor, called *anadochos* (guarantor) and *theios pater* (divine father), does not merely attest before the bishop to the candidate's fitness. The sponsor also undertakes to guide the adult candidate *after* the baptism.

Thomas Campbell's translation retains only a hint of the treatise's bombastic style:

> 2. Whoever desires sacred participation in these truly supramundane things goes to one of the initiated and persuades him to act as his guide on the way to the bishop. Then, he promises to follow completely all the prescriptions, and asks his sponsor to undertake the supervision of his introduction to all that concerns his future life. Though piously desiring the man's salvation, when

[53] The pseudo-Dionysius' works are printed in parallel with nine Latin translations, a Greek paraphrase, and a French translation in *Dionysiaca*, 2 vols., ed. P. Chevallier (Bruges, 1937 and 1950).

[54] On Abbot Hilduin and his translation see Gabriel Théry, *Etudes dionysiennes*, 2 vols., Etudes de philosophie médiévale, vols. 16 and 19 (Paris, 1932 and 1937).

[55] Max L. W. Laistner, *Thought and Letters in Western Europe, A.D. 500 to 900*, 2nd ed. (Ithaca, N.Y., 1957), pp. 245–247.

[56] For a paraphrase of *On the Ecclesiastical Hierarchy*, with pious commentary, see Denys Rutledge, *Cosmic Theology, The Ecclesiastical Hierarchy of Pseudo-Denys: An Introduction* (Staten Island, N.Y., 1965).

the sponsor measures human frailty against the sublimity of the undertaking, all at once he is seized with fear and anxiety. Nevertheless, with good grace, he finally promises to make the petition. He takes the man in charge and leads him to the chief of the hierarchy.

3. Joyfully, the bishop receives the two men as sheep upon his shoulders. . . .

4. Then he assembles the whole of the sacred order in the holy place to cooperate and rejoice together in the salvation of this man, and to give thanks to the divine goodness. . . . After this, when he has kissed the holy table, he advances to the candidate standing before him and asks him for what purpose he has come.

5. When, out of love for God, the candidate has confessed his impiety, his lack of the divine life, and his ignorance of the truly beautiful, in accordance with the instructions of his sponsor, he asks to attain to God and divine things through his holy mediation. . . . After he has explained to him the divine way of life, asked him if he would live in this manner, and received his consent, the bishop places his hand on the candidate's head. When he has sealed him, he orders that the priests register the candidate and his sponsor.[57]

The bishop immediately proceeded to the renunciations and professions of faith that precede immersion in the baptismal waters. Thus, if we are to believe the pseudo-Dionysius literally, the ancient catechumenate had been telescoped into a single session, during which a candidate was admitted, instructed, and baptized. His sponsor accompanied him during the entire session, presenting him and prompting him at important moments. The climactic moment was the immersion itself:

When one of the priests has read his name and that of his sponsor from the lists in a loud voice, he is led over to the water by the priests, conducted by their hands to the hand of the bishop. While the priests near the bishop call out three times the name of the initiate standing in the water, the bishop, standing on an elevation, plunges him into the water, invoking at each of the three immersions and emersions of the initiate the threefold Personality of the divine Beatitude. Then the priests take him in charge and

---

[57] *On the Ecclesiastical Hierarchy*, ch. 2.2.2–5, in *Dionysiaca* 2:1114–1120. The translation is by Thomas L. Campbell, *Dionysius the Pseudo-Areopagite: The Ecclesiastical Hierarchy* (Lanham, Md., 1981), pp. 24–25.

confide him to his sponsor, the one in charge of his introduction. With his help they put appropriate clothing around the one being initiated.[58]

Thus the adult candidate's sponsor was a guide entrusted with the responsibility to "introduce" his charge to the Christian way of life *after* the baptism. It is striking how close this pattern was to the task of an infant's sponsor.

The pseudo-Dionysius refers to infant baptism in the same treatise and attempts to defend the practice from the "ridicule of the profane." Such ridicule arose because baptizing infants with an adult-oriented ritual resulted in certain incongruities. Thus the bishop seemed to "teach divine things to those who cannot hear, and in vain hand down the sacred traditions to those who do not understand." In addition, the "profane" (who may in fact have included Christians in their ranks) also ridiculed the fact that "others pronounce the abjuration and sacred promises for them".[59]

The pseudo-Dionysius acknowledged that such an arrangement was difficult to understand ("not all divine things can be comprehended by our intelligence"), but he affirmed that his defense of it was "what our godlike instructors, initiated in ancient tradition, have transmitted to us."

> They assert . . . that infants brought up according to sacred law will contract a habit of holiness, be guarded from all error, and be inexperienced in an evil life. When our godly leaders arrived at this conclusion, they decided to receive infants in this holy manner: on condition that the physical parents of the child presented confide the child to someone of the initiated in divine things who is a good teacher. Henceforth, the child will be his care to perfect; he will be a god-father [*theios pater*] and the sponsor [*anadochos*] of his holy salvation. When this person has agreed to educate the child in a holy life, the bishop asks him to pronounce the abjurations and sacred promises, not, as those who laugh would say, that the sponsor is initiated in divine things instead of the child, because he himself does not say, "I abjure," and make the sacred promises in place of the child, but the child himself is the one who abjures and promises. In other words, he says, "I promise to persuade the child by my instructions in godly

[58] *On the Ecclesiastical Hierarchy*, ch. 2.2.7, in *Dionysiaca* 2:1125–1127; tr. Campbell, *Dionysius*, pp. 26–27.

[59] *On the Ecclesiastical Hierarchy*, ch. 7.3.11, in *Dionysiaca* 2:1465–1466; tr. Campbell, *Dionysius*, p. 89.

matters, when he is able to understand holy things, to renounce completely all that is contrary, and profess and realize the divine promises." I do not think there is anything absurd if the child is brought up according to a divine education, since he has a master and holy sponsor who implants in him a habit for divine things and keeps him safe from what is contrary. The bishop gives the child a share in the sacred symbols in order that he may be nourished by them and have no other life than that of always contemplating divine things, sharing in them by holy progressions, acquiring a holy disposition for them, being educated to holiness by his godlike sponsor.[60]

About a century earlier, Augustine had defended infant baptism and sponsorship on high theological grounds, having to do with the efficacy of the sacrament, the solidarity of all persons sharing the Holy Spirit, and the various meanings of "faith." In contrast, the pseudo-Dionysius was a veritable rationalist and naturalist, arguing that proper nurture would gradually lead a growing child to be a good Christian. In his view, the sponsor was simply a good teacher, invited by parents to take charge of the child's formation. Thus the sponsor made a contract, an agreement "to educate the child in a holy life."

Clearly, the pseudo-Dionysius' views represent a distinct break with the past. In them, the sponsor of an infant is explicitly stated to be a nonparent and to have a serious postbaptismal responsibility that would last for years, perhaps for a lifetime. Furthermore, once allowances have been made for the obvious advantage an adult baptisand had because he was able to speak and act for himself in the ceremonies, it is difficult to detect an essential difference between the sponsor for an adult and that for an infant in the pseudo-Dionysius' treatise. The two have merged, with the legacy of infant sponsorship most visible in its impact.

The liturgy that lay behind the pseudo-Dionysius' comments was a Syrian one, familiar in general outline from the works of Theodore of Mopsuestia and John Chrysostom. However, there has been a strong presumption among scholars that the pseudo-Dionysius was elaborating, extending, indeed inventing on the basis of that liturgy. If the author was describing something that actually existed, then spiritual kinship was emerging by A.D. 500 in Syria and Palestine, which had for generations been a pioneer in the development of sponsoring insti-

---

[60] On the Ecclesiastical Hierarchy, ch. 7.3.11, in Dionysiaca 2:1469–1474; tr. Campbell, Dionysius, pp. 90–91.

tutions.[61] But if, as is likely, the text contained a mixture of real practice, wishful thinking, and pious fiction, then it was prophetic of the actual direction in which sponsorship was to evolve in the early Middle Ages: the merging of adult and infant baptism, to the effacement of the former; the exclusion of the natural parents from sponsorship; and the creation of long-term bonds between the sponsor and the child as well as between the sponsor and the natural parents.

It was always possible for adults to be baptized in the adult manner, acting and speaking for themselves, but even in those circumstances the figure of the sponsor of an infant gradually imposed itself, for everywhere in the Christian Mediterranean the decline in the number of adult baptisms continued. Except in missionary lands or in extraordinary situations, such as the forced conversion of Jews,[62] the infant and the infant's sponsor held sway as the paradigm of baptismal rebirth. It was in such circumstances that sponsorship took on greater social significance and a true godparent complex emerged.

[61] Dujarier, *Le parrainage*, p. 291.

[62] Michel Rouche, "Les baptêmes forcés de juifs en Gaule mérovingienne et dans l'Empire d'Orient," in *De l'antijudaïsme antique à l'antisémitisme contemporain*, ed. V. Nikiprowetzky (Lille, 1979), pp. 105–124, which also discusses Byzantine efforts to force heretics to accept baptism.

PART THREE

THE EMERGENCE OF SPIRITUAL KINSHIP
IN THE WEST, CA. 500 TO CA. 750

FIVE

CAESARIUS OF ARLES

In 1950, Sidney Mintz and Eric Wolf stressed the adaptability of the modern godparent complexes with which they were familiar,[1] and subsequent research has confirmed the accuracy of their assertion. Within a common framework of ritual and religious ideas, sponsorship and spiritual kinship can vary significantly, both from society to society and from class to class within a society. Thus the anthropologists' findings are a caution against the easy assumption that in the early Middle Ages the sponsors of infants possessed the same religious and social significance everywhere or that spiritual kinship developed at the same pace in every area where it existed.

The sponsorship of infants was pan-Christian practice, known from the Atlantic fringes of Celtic Christianity to the Monophysite and Nestorian outlands in the East. If modern anthropological investigation is a guide, we should expect to find variations in the social and religious significance of sponsorship and in the aspects of it that received emphasis. If the early medieval sources permitted, such variations might be detectable from one linguistic or ethnic group to another and at national, regional, or even village levels. However, the written sources for early medieval history, both in the East and the West, are uneven and scanty. And while they do permit the examination of aspects of spiritual kinship in different places, they do not lend themsleves to the microscopic perspective of an anthropologist investigating a small village in Latin America.

For the early Middle Ages, research will necessarily create a rather generalized picture of spiritual kinship, with occasional opportunities to note differences and variations. This study will emphasize Gallo-Roman and Frankish society between the sixth and the tenth centuries, primarily because it was there that the distinctive western version of sponsorship and spiritual kinship emerged. Thus the Byzantine East, papal Italy, and other western societies will be examined only when they impinge on or illuminate the situation in Gaul.

The form of sponsorship and spiritual kinship that developed in late Roman and Frankish Gaul is fairly well documented in the literary

[1] "An Analysis of Ritual Co-Parenthood (Compadrazgo)," *SJA* 6 (1950):347.

evidence. Initially, there was one sponsor for each baptizee, of the same sex as the candidate, who might or might not be the child's parent. But in the eighth and ninth centuries, the number of sponsors grew, the same-sex requirement was relaxed, and parents were forbidden to sponsor their own children. The sponsor spoke and acted for the child in the liturgy and was expected to share in the subsequent religious and moral instruction of the godchild. These were traditional duties, with roots in early Christian practice.

The chief innovation in the late Gallo-Roman and Frankish form of sponsorship was that the sponsor had a moral obligation to observe a special code of behavior in dealing with the godchild and the child's parents, who in turn were seen as having a special relationship with the sponsor. There was one feature of this code that marked it as unusual. For despite the fact that virtually all known variants of baptismal kinship have demanded that the spiritual kin avoid sexual contact with one another, in Roman and Frankish Gaul there were no explicit indications before the eighth century that sexual taboos and marital impediments were consequences of sponsorship.[2]

Any investigation of Gallo-Roman sponsorship and spiritual kinship must rely heavily on the evidence provided by the works of Caesarius, bishop of Arles from 502 to 542. Caesarius was a remarkable ecclesiastical and political figure, certainly the most important bishop in the West in his generation.[3] His political activities during a tumultuous period of conflicting Frankish, Visigothic, and Ostrogothic ambitions in southern Gaul do not concern us here, but his writings, with their clear pastoral orientation, are a rich mine of information on religious, cultural, and intellectual phenomena in sixth-century Gaul.

Caesarius' writings were not composed in a vacuum. They reflected the concerns of a conscientious, busy bishop. He had been a monk at Lerins before his election to the see of Arles and as bishop he promoted the monastic life. He composed a *Rule for Nuns* and a *Rule for Monks*, as well as three letters of spiritual instruction for nuns. In his role as intellectual leader of the episcopate of southeastern Gaul, he took a leading part in important synods and composed a tract against

[2] Jean Fleury, *Recherches historiques sur les empêchements de parenté dans le mariage canonique des origines aux Fausses Décrétales* (Paris, 1933), pp. 84–113; Paul Mikat, "Die Inzestverbote des Konzils von Epaon—Ein Beitrag zur Geschichte des fränkischen Eherechts," *Rechtsbewahrung und Rechtsentwicklung. Festschrift für Heinrich Lange zum 70. Geburtstag* (Munich, 1970), pp. 63–84.

[3] Carl F. Arnold, *Caesarius von Arelate und die Gallische Kirche seiner Zeit* (Leipzig, 1894); A. Malnory, *Saint Césaire, évêque d'Arles, 503–543*, Bibliothèque de l'Ecole des hautes études, vol. 103 (Paris, 1894). As a consequence of ninety years of research on Caesarius' writings and career, a new synthetic study is badly needed.

semi-Pelagianism, a tract on the Trinity, a commentary on the book of the Apocalypse, and a tract against heresies.[4]

Caesarius' most lasting literary contribution is to be found in his sermons, for he was the greatest preacher of the Latin world since Augustine, who was his model. These sermons are also a unique source for the comprehension of important aspects of sixth-century Gallo-Roman society and religion. In addition to being informative historical documents in their own right, they had an immense and still inadequately assessed influence on subsequent medieval preaching, theology, spirituality, and religious practice.[5]

Caesarius consciously cultivated a simple, direct, and vivid style of preaching that recommended itself to other preachers dealing with popular audiences.[6] Indeed, during his own lifetime Caesarius distributed copies of his sermons to the priests of his diocese for use in rural churches, as well as to visiting clergy and to correspondents.[7] Succeeding generations copied, adapted and reworked these sermons, with the result that they became the common coin of early medieval preaching, although they were often attributed to others or circulated anonymously. It was only in 1937, after half a century of labor, that Dom Germain Morin succeeded in identifying some 238 sermons as belonging in whole or in part to Caesarius.[8] And the work of identification is not yet complete for other anonymous and misattributed sermons have been restored to Caesarius since the publication of Morin's work.[9]

Sixth-century Arles was a focal point for political and religious ac-

---

[4] Caesarius' monastic rules, letters, and tracts were edited by Germain Morin in vol. 2. of *Sancti Caesarii episcopi Arelatensis opera omnia* (Maredsous, 1942). The *Rule for Nuns* and three letters of spiritual direction were also edited by Morin in *Sancti Caesarii Arelatensis episcopi Regula sanctarum virginum aliaque opuscula ad sanctimoniales directa*, Florilegium patristicum, vol. 34 (Bonn, 1933).

[5] See, for instance, Dieter Harmening, *Superstitio. Überlieferungs- und theoriegeschichtliche Untersuchungen zur kirchlich-theologischen Aberglaubensliteratur des Mitterlalters* (Berlin, 1979), which amply demonstrates Caesarius' influence on western views of superstition; Franz Hautkappe, *Über die altdeutschen Beichten und ihre Beziehungen zu Cäsarius von Arles* (Münster, Westphalia, 1917); or H. Millemann, "Caesarius von Arles und die frühmittelalterliche Missionspredigt," *Zeitschrift für Missionswissenschaft* 23 (1933):12–27.

[6] On Caesarius' style, see I. Bonini, "Lo stile nei sermoni di Cesario di Arles," *Aevum* 36 (1962):240–257; Pierre Riché, *Education and Culture in the Barbarian West*, tr. John J. Contreni (Columbia, S.C. 1976), pp. 91–95.

[7] Cyprian of Toulon et al., *Vita Sancti Caesarii*, bk. 1, ch. 55, in *Sancti Caesarii episcopi Arelatensis opera omnia*, vol. 2, p. 319; Caesarius sent collections of his sermons into Francia, the Gauls, Italy, Spain, and diverse provinces; sermon 2, pp. 20–21.

[8] *Sancti Caesarii opera omnia*, vol. 1, reprinted in CCSL, vols. 103 and 104 (Turnhout, 1953).

[9] See, for example, A. Höfer, "Zwei unbekannte Sermones des Caesarius von Arles,"

tivity in southeastern Gaul. It was during Caesarius' lifetime that the region passed forever from Roman rule, first to the Visigoths in the 470s, then briefly to Burgundian and Ostrogothic control before the definitive Frankish conquest in 534. In the sixth century, the urban population was probably entirely Christian, with the exception of a small Jewish community.[10] Formal paganism, with its priesthoods and temples, was extinct, although important remnants of it survived as folk practice, against which Caesarius preached often and vigorously.[11] Particularly in the rural areas, which had not yet been organized into parishes, unbaptized adults who practised paganism were not uncommon.[12]

Infants and young children born to Christian parents were the usual baptizees, although adults and older children were occasional candidates as well. In his sermons Caesarius referred to catechumens, but the venerable institution of the catechumenate survived only as a name hallowed by tradition.[13] Easter was the preferred date for baptism and Caesarius encouraged candidates to give in their names at the beginning of Lent and to attend meetings for prayer, anointing, exorcism, and preaching. (Parents acted as surrogates for their infants in such matters as fasting.) There are comments in Caesarius' sermons that indicate that this Lenten preparation was breaking down, particularly because of the Augustinian emphasis on the need to baptize infants lest they die in original sin.

Caesarius wanted the many baptisms that took place on days other than Easter to be preceded by at least seven days of fasting and prayer.[14] He complained that some women brought their children for-

RB 74 (1964):44–53; R. Etaix, "Nouveau sermon pascal de Saint Césaire d'Arles," RB 75 (1965):201–211; Jean-Paul Buhot, "Le sermon Dominus et Salvator. Première forme dérivée d'un sermon perdu de saint Césaire," RB 80 (1970):201–212.

[10] On Caesarius and the Jews, see J. Courreau, "Saint Césaire d'Arles et les Juifs," BLE 71 (1970):92–112.

[11] On the folk paganism of Christians in southern Gaul, see Henry G. J. Beck, The Pastoral Care of Souls in South-East France During the Sixth Century, Analecta Gregoriana, vol. 51 (Rome, 1950), pp. 243–248, 281–283; Guillaume Konda, Le discernement et la malice des pratiques superstitieuses d'après les sermons de Saint Césaire d'Arles (Rome, 1970). Harmening, Superstitio, p. 328, lists ten of Caesarius' sermons that were directed against pagan practices.

[12] On the survival of rural paganism, see Beck, Pastoral Care, pp. 184–185.

[13] On the baptismal liturgy as it is reflected in Caesarius' sermons, see Karl Berg, Die Werke des hl. Caesarius von Arles als liturgiegeschichtliche Quelle, Excerpta ex Dissertatione ad Lauream in facultate theologica Pontificiae Universitatis Gregorianae Urbis (Munich, 1946), pp. 18–56.

[14] Sermon 225.6, Sancti Caesarii opera omnia, 1:846: "Sicut iam anno superiore conmonui caritatem vestram, iterum rogo, fratres carissimi, et ammoneo, ut quotiens sanc-

ward for baptism at the last minute, thus avoiding all liturgical and intellectual preparation. He warned such people that they were committing a sin by their negligence, but he permitted the infants to be baptized, since it would be a serious mistake on his part if they died without the sacrament.[15]

The practice of providing baptism on demand for the ill as well as the tendency to baptize infants on saints' days in rural churches hastened the decay of the ancient catechumenate in Gaul. A council of nine metropolitans and fifty-five bishops or their representatives, meeting at Mâcon in 585, attempted in vain to check this development:

> We have learned from the report of some of our fellow bishops that Christians do not respect the prescribed day for baptism but baptize their sons on almost any day or martyr's feast, with the result that scarcely two or three children who are to be reborn through water and the Holy Spirit can be found on Easter. Therefore, we command that henceforth no one be allowed to do that, except for those people whom a serious illness or impending death compels to seek baptism for their sons.[16]

The efforts to preserve the custom of Easter baptism were largely unsuccessful, and it was already true in the early sixth century that many infants were baptized in a ceremony that was less solemn and elaborate than that used in bishops' churches. We know little about such baptisms because the sources, including Caesarius' sermons, give most of their attention to solemn Easter baptism.

By Caesarius' day, the predominance of infants and children as baptizees had worked significant changes in the nature of sponsorship, analogous to those reflected in the work of Caesarius' eastern contemporary, the pseudo-Dionysius. Caesarius was a practical man, concerned with making effective the religious ceremonies and institutions that had been passed on in his tradition. In view of the dearth of other contemporary sources, we shall never know whether Caesarius' sermons on sponsorship represent an innovation or merely the common

---

torum specialius festa celebraturi sumus, quicumque de suis baptizari desiderant, vel ante decem dies, aut certe vel ante unam septimanam cum eis, qui baptizandi sunt, ad ecclesiam veniant, et ad oleum et ad manus inpositiones accedant. Ante omnia, secundum quod vires habent, etiam illi, qui filios suos baptizari desiderant, ieiunent, ad vigilas suas frequentius veniant: ut et filii eorum ordine legitimo accipiant baptismatis sacramentum, et parentes eorum adquirant indulgentiam peccatorum."

[15] Ibid., Sermon 84.6, p. 333; Sermon 229.6, p. 846.

[16] Council of Mâcon (585), canon 3, in *Concilia Galliae A. 511–A.695*, ed. Carlo de Clercq, CCSL, vol. 148A (Turnhout, 1963), p. 240.

practice of his region. In any case, he formulated in his sermons what became the western view of the religious and pedagogical duties of a sponsor.

It made little sense for a sponsor to attest to the prebaptismal fitness of infants, and so Caesarius abandoned this fiction, carrying to completion developments that had already undermined it. Thus the focus of his preaching to sponsors was on their postbaptismal duties. In this Caesarius continued to use language sanctioned by a tradition going back at least to Tertullian, but he infused it with new meaning and supplemented it with other language that he might have coined, but more likely drew from his surroundings.

To Caesarius, the sponsor remained a *fideiussor* for the baptizee, that is, a guarantor of the contract with God that baptism represented. The notion of *fideiussor*, borrowed from Roman law, carried in it the idea that if the baptizee failed to observe the terms of the contract, then the guarantor would intervene to see to its fulfillment or would be held responsible.[17] To this traditional role of *fideiussio*, Caesarius added the more recent view that the sponsor was a "parent" to the "child" who was reborn in baptism, a notion first stated explicitly by John Chrysostom about 390.[18] This tendency to view baptismal sponsorship as the moment when a parent/child relationship was created had great success, and in Caesarius' sermons it was a recurring, explicitly developed theme.

In sixth-century Gaul, it was still possible for parents to sponsor their own children, so that the parent/child imagery may occasionally have represented both literal and spiritual reality. A neglected piece of evidence on the matter is the *Vita sancti Desiderii episcopi Cadurcensis*, which was composed in the late eighth or ninth century and concerned Desiderius, bishop of Cahors from 630 to 655.[19] Although the anonymous author wrote the *Vita* in the Carolingian period, he appears to have had access to earlier materials, including letters from Desiderius' mother, Herchenfreda. In two of these letters, which refer to events of about 590, Herchenfreda apparently alludes to her own baptismal promises on behalf of her son.

In the first letter Herchenfreda writes: "Son, always remember

---

[17] On *fideiussio*, see Richard Leage, *Roman Private Law Founded on the Institutes of Gaius and Justinian*, 3rd ed. by A. M. Pritchard (London, 1961), pp. 343–345.

[18] John Chrysostom, *Second catechesis*, secs. 15–16, in *Huit catéchèses baptismales inédites*, ed. Antoine Wenger, SC, vol. 50 (Paris, 1957), pp. 141–143.

[19] *Vita sancti Desiderii episcopi Cadurcensis*, ed. Bruno Krusch, MGH SSRM, vol. 4 (Hanover, 1902), pp. 547–602; reprinted in CCSL, vol. 117 (Turnhout, 1957), pp. 343–401.

what I promised for you to God and therefore always walk with circumspection."[20] In the second she further encourages him: "Read
often and take to heart and hold with all the striving of your mind the
letter which I sent to you earlier, so that my promise to God concerning you, sweet son Desiderius, may be fulfilled by you."[21] Thus, in
her moral exhortations to her son, Herchenfreda reminded him that
she had made promises for him that he must now fulfill. In a similar
vein, Martin of Braga (556–572) encouraged his rustic Galician hearers
to be virtuous by recalling for them the "pact with God" that they, or
someone on their behalf, had made at baptism.[22]

Although parents could sponsor their own children, Caesarius was
familiar with a situation in which natural and spiritual parents were
often different persons. Hence he drew a distinction between "the
sons who are born from you" (*filii qui de vobis nati sunt*) and "the sons
whom you have received from the font" (*filii quos de fonte excepistis*).[23]
In early sixth-century Arles, the customary pattern for choosing sponsors was in transition from the strict preference for a parent, characteristic of the ancient period, to the strict preference for a nonparent,
characteristic of the Carolingian period. Because of this, some parents
elected to sponsor their own children, while others chose an outsider
for the task. Unfortunately, nowhere did Caesarius or other contemporary sources state why a parent would choose to follow either pattern. Caesarius was interested only in the sponsor's religious role and
consequently avoided commenting on what might have motivated a
parent's choice.

One may surmise, on the basis of later evidence, that parents chose
outsiders in order to bind them more closely to their child and to
themselves. And Caesarius provided some indirect evidence that tends
to confirm such an explanation.[24] In his *Rule for Nuns*, and in other
monastic rules of the sixth and seventh century that were influenced
by it, monks and nuns were forbidden to sponsor any infant. When

---

[20] *Vita Desiderii*, ch. 9, MGH SSRM 4:354: "Recordare, fili, semper, quid Deo pro
uobis spopondi, et ideo cum timore semper progredere."

[21] Ibid., ch. 10: "Epistolam uero quam ante tempore uobis direxi sepius legite et
animo commendate ac tota mentis ambitione tenete, ut promissio mea de uos aput
Deum per uos, dulcis filius Desideri, impleatur."

[22] Martin of Braga, *De correctione rusticorum*, ch. 15, in *Martini episcopi Bracarensis opera
omnia*, ed. Claude Barlow, Papers and Monographs of the American Academy in Rome,
vol. 12 (New Haven, 1950), p. 196.

[23] Sermon 13.2, *Sancti Caesarii opera omnia*, 1:64; see also Sermon 50.3, ibid., p. 217;
Sermon 71.2, ibid., p. 288; Sermon 130.4, ibid., p. 515.

[24] Joseph H. Lynch, "Baptismal Sponsorship and Monks and Nuns, 500–1000," *ABR*
31 (1980):108–121.

we understand why Caesarius and other monastic legislators forbade such sponsorship, we shall have a greater insight into the social, as distinct from the religious, implications of sponsorship in sixth- and seventh-century Gaul.

Prior to Caesarius, no eastern or western monastic regulation had concerned itself with baptismal sponsorship by monks or nuns. Ascetics did occasionally sponsor adults, but adult baptisms were decreasing in number as monasticism took form in fourth- and fifth-century Egypt and the obligations incurred by sponsoring an adult were prebaptismal and less enduring than those incurred by sponsoring an infant. Furthermore, the opportunity for an outsider to sponsor an infant rarely arose before the sixth century. For so long as parents were the ordinary sponsors for their children, there would be no occasion to invite a monk or nun to perform this duty. Given such reasons as these, sponsorship obviously posed no problem for monastic legislators.

Gradually, however, it became more common to ask an outsider to sponsor an infant. And in light of the prestige enjoyed by ascetics, it is not surprising that their admirers or kinsmen occasionally requested that they serve in this role. Indeed, Arnold Angenendt has demonstrated that some prominent seventh- and eighth-century Frankish aristocrats actually sought out a holy man, a *vir dei*, to sponsor their children because such a person's spiritual powers, gained through a lifetime of ascetic striving, were believed to benefit the child spiritually as well as with such material advantages as a successful life and career.[25] Peter Brown has also emphasized the importance of the holy man as a font of power and a conduit of divine favor in the late Roman world, although Brown does not identify a sponsoring role for the holy men whom he studied.[26]

Because of his personal interest and because of the changing nature of sponsorship in his lifetime, Caesarius was well placed to assess the compatibility of sponsorship with the monastic life. He himself had been an ascetic at the eminent island monastery of Lerins, and he never abandoned his deep interest in the promotion and welfare of monasticism. In fact, he was an innovator and pioneer in the religious life for women.

In sixth-century Gaul, male asceticism was widespread and organized in many monastic communities, but such was not the case for

[25] Arnold Angenendt, "Bonifatius und das Sacramentum initiationis. Zugleich ein Beitrag zur Geschichte der Firmung." *RQCAKG* 72 (1977):164–169.

[26] Peter Brown, "The Rise and Function of the Holy Man in Late Antiquity," *JRS* 61 (1971):80–101.

women.[27] There were, however, females in sixth-century Gaul who adopted an ascetic life according to the traditional norms. Such women were designated in the sources by various terms, including *sanctimoniales* and *devotae*. But in Gaul these women did not ordinarily dwell in cenobitic communities. Instead, female ascetics often lived in their own homes or in loosely organized small groups; they frequently retained their personal property, their freedom of movement, and many ties to the secular world. Such a situation led to some disorder and occasionally even to scandal, especially when an ascetic woman decided to marry.[28]

Caesarius labored to provide a stable, financially sound, and disciplined community setting for nuns. To this end in 512 he organized a community of women at Arles under the direction of his sister Caesaria, and for the subsequent thirty years of his episcopate he attempted to secure the material and spiritual well-being of this beloved nunnery. Thus he sought papal approval to exempt the house from the authority of his successors in the bishopric of Arles; he alienated diocesan property to support it; and in his testament he made the convent his principal heir.[29] As a reflection of his concern, he composed a *Rule* for the nuns, which he subsequently revised. He was also interested in the monastic life for men, compiling a *Rule for Monks* that was, as Adalbert de Vogüé has demonstrated, based squarely on the earlier *Rule for Nuns*.[30]

[27] On early monasticism in Gaul, see Friedrich Prinz, *Frühes Mönchtum im Frankenreich. Kultur und Gesellschaft in Gallien, den Rheinlanden und Bayern am Beispiel der monastischen Entwicklung (4. bis 8. Jahrhundert)* (Munich and Vienna, 1965), pp. 19–117; Jean-Martial Besse, *Les moines de l'ancienne France. Période gallo-romaine et mérovingienne*, Archives de la France monastique, vol. 2 (Paris, 1906).

[28] On ecclesiastical attempts to regulate the status of ascetic women through the use of vows and liturgical ceremonies of dedication, see René Metz, *La consécration des vierges dans l'Eglise romaine. Etude d'histoire et de la liturgie*, Bibliothèque de l'Institut de droit canonique de l'Université de Strasbourg, vol. 4 (Paris, 1954), pp. 77–124 and passim.

[29] On Caesarius' foundation of the nunnery dedicated to Saint John and his efforts to provide it with spiritual and material security, see Maria Caritas McCarthy, *The Rule for Nuns of St. Caesarius of Arles: A Translation with a Critical Introduction*, CUA, SMH, new series, vol. 16 (Washington, D.C., 1960), pp. 1–30; see also Prinz, *Frühes Mönchtum*, pp. 76–77.

[30] The *Rule for Nuns (Statuta sanctarum virginum)* was edited by Germain Morin in *Florilegium Patristicum*, vol. 34 (Bonn, 1933), pp. 4–27, and again in *Sancti Caesarii episcopi Arelatensis opera omnia*, vol. 2 (Maredsous, 1942), pp. 101–129. There is an English translation in McCarthy, *Rule*, pp. 170–204. The *Rule for Monks (Regula monachorum)* was edited by Morin in *Sancti Caesarii opera omnia* 2:149–155, on which see Adalbert de Vogüé, "La Règle de Césaire d'Arles pour les moines: un résumé de sa Règle pour les moniales," *RAM* 47 (1947):369–406.

Caesarius' *Rule for Nuns* is not only the oldest surviving monastic rule designed for women; it also embodies an innovation that was to have an enduring influence on western views of female spiritual life. For to the traditional ideal of virgins and widows dedicated to prayer, fasting, and renunciation, Caesarius added the requirement of cloistering, that is, a strict physical and moral separation from the world. In his view, the ascetic life lived in the world had too many distractions and dangers. Hence, insofar as was possible, his nuns were to avoid contact with outsiders, including their own relatives.[31]

To understand Caesarius' concern with separating nuns from worldly human relationships, one must analyze his use of the term *familiaritas*. In ordinary usage, it implied close friendship and intimacy, although Caesarius generally employed it in a negative sense. In his sermons, which were addressed to lay people rather than to nuns or monks, the word was regularly joined to pejorative adjectives such as *inhonesta, suspecta, perversa*, and *incauta*, and referred to sexual intimacy outside of marriage.[32] But when he wrote to the nuns, Caesarius used the word *familiaritas* to designate the bonds of kinship and secular friendship that he wished them to avoid. In a letter of spiritual advice, he expressed himself this way:

> A soul chaste and devoted to God ought not to have frequent friendly contact [*assidua familiaritate*] either with outsiders or with her own relatives, either by having them come to her or by going herself to them: lest she hear what is not fitting or see anything that can be detrimental to chastity. . . . just as holy vessels cannot serve for human uses and must not be taken back from the Church, so it is neither proper, nor fitting, nor right that any religious whatever be involved in any obligations toward her relatives, or bound by dangerous friendship [*perniciosa familiaritas*] with any externs whatever.[33]

[31] On Caesarius' role in the development of cloistered convents for women, see Emile Jombart and Marcel Viller, "Clôture," *DSAM* (Paris, 1953), 2:987–988; Cyrille Lambot, "Le prototype des monastères cloîtrés des femmes, l'Abbaye Saint-Jean d'Arles au viᵉ siècle," *Revue liturgique et monastique* 23 (1937/38):169–174.

[32] Sermon 41.1, *Sancti Caesarii opera omnia*, 1:172: all Christians, and especially clerics and monks, are warned to flee *indigna et inhonesta familiaritas* if they wish to guard their chasity; Sermon 92.6, ibid., p. 366: "cum dei adiutorio familiaritatem inh[on]estam atque suspectam effugere festinemus, ut castitatis nitorem servare possimus"; sermon 41.2, ibid., p. 173: "perversa familiaritas"; Sermon 134.3, ibid., p. 529: "incauta familiaritas mulierum." The *Regula Macarii*, written between 450 and 506 in Provence, shared Caesarius' view of *familiaritas*. See ch. 6 of the text edited by Helga Styblo, *Wiener Studien* 76 (1963):152.

[33] *Letter* 2 "*Vereor*," ch. 5, *Florilegium*, pp. 41–42.

The same concern with preventing close contact with outsiders is expressed in chapter 51 of Caesarius' *Recapitulatio* of his *Rule for Nuns*:

No one shall have a secret intimacy or companionship [*familiaritatem aut quamlibet societatem . . . secretam*] of any kind with religious or lay persons, either men or women, nor should a woman and a man be allowed to speak together alone for more than a moment. Neither should anyone receive clothing from them to wash or to dye or to repair or to sew; as we have established in the rule, no one shall dare to send out secretly anything from within, nor to receive within from the outside.[34]

In order to achieve such strict cloistering, Caesarius systematically eliminated occasions and excuses whereby nuns might leave the convent or outsiders might enter the cloistered parts of it. It is within this context of concern over worldly ties that the bishop's prohibition of sponsorship must be understood:

No one should presume to sponsor in baptism a child [daughter] of anyone at all, either rich or poor; for she who for the love of God has disdained the freedom to have children of her own ought not wish for nor possess this freedom belonging to others, so that without any hindrance she may give her time unceasingly to God.[35]

The implication of Caesarius' prohibition is clear: to be a baptismal sponsor in sixth-century Arles involved gaining a "child" with attendant obligations that could distract the nun from her calling. These obligations were specified more precisely in later monastic rules, which reflect the fact that Caesarius' concern about sponsorship by monks and nuns was shared by other monastic legislators in southeastern Gaul during the sixth and seventh centuries, who quite consciously modeled their rules on those that he had set down.

Aurelian (546–551), Caesarius' second successor in the see of Arles, issued a rule for the monks of the Holy Cross and a rule for the nuns of Saint Mary, and in each he forbade sponsorship, without explaining

---

[34] Caesarius, *Statuta*, ch. 51, *Florilegium*, p. 19; tr. McCarthy, *Rule*, p. 188.

[35] Caesarius, *Statuta*, ch. 11, *Florilegium*, p. 7: "Nulla cuiuslibet filiam in baptismo, neque divitis neque pauperis, praesumat excipere: quia quae suorum libertatem pro dei amore contempsit, aliorum expetere vel habere non debet; ut sine aliquo impedimento deo vacare iugiter possit"; tr. McCarthy, *Rule*, p. 174. Caesarius also forbade monks to be sponsors, *Regula monachorum*, ch. 10, *Sancti Caesarii opera omnia*, 2:150, but he offered no reason for the ban.

his reasons.[36] Similarly, between 551 and 573 the unknown author of the *Regula Tarnantensis* also drew on Caesarius for a prohibition on monks becoming *patres spirituales*, which scholars have taken to refer to sponsorship, although the text might refer to the unauthorized spiritual direction of adults.[37] Between 573 and 581, Ferreolus, Bishop of Uzès, also composed a rule for monks that drew upon the Caesarian tradition, invoking as a reason for his prohibition of sponsorship the bond between the sponsor and the child's parents. Thus in chapter 15 he declares:

> We have regarded it as unnecessary for little children to be baptized in the monastery, just as it is observed in other monasteries; nor should a monk anywhere receive the children of anyone from the holy bath: lest, as usually happens, he be gradually united to the parents of the child by an improper or shameful bond of closeness [*illicita . . . vel turpi familiaritate*]. If anyone presumes to do this, he should be punished as a transgressor of the rule.[38]

Finally, Bishop Donatus of Besançon (627–658) issued a rule for the nunnery of Saint Mary, which combined provisions from the rules of Columban, Benedict, and Caesarius, and in which he repeated *verbatim* Caesarius' prohibition on sponsoring the daughter of anyone, rich or poor.[39]

In the monastic tradition of Gaul, bishops were influential as founders of houses and as legislators for these houses. Many extant rules are attributed to bishops, and each of the rules that forbade sponsorship to monks and nuns was apparently issued by a bishop. In addition, two extant episcopal councils from the sixth and seventh

[36] Aurelian, *Regula ad monachos*, ch. 20, PL 68:390; *Regula ad Virgines*, ch. 16, PL 68:402. On Aurelian's borrowing from Caesarius' monastic legislation, see Albert Schmidt, "Zur Komposition der Mönchsregel des heiligen Aurelian von Arles," *Studia Monastica* 18 (1976):17–54.

[37] *Regula Tarnantensis*, ch. 3, in Fernando Villegas, "La 'Regula Monasterii Tarnantensis.' Texte, sources et datation," *RB* 84 (1974):19–20: "[None of the brethren] should agree to be made a spiritual father without the command of the abbot; but if a reason of significant necessity is present or if he is moved by the prayers of some faithful person and cannot avoid these forbidden things, that which is recognized as imposed on a reluctant person should be overlooked entirely for the sake of charity." In the seventh-century *vita* of Saint Segolena, the young woman welcomed a traveling holy man, who was to be her *pater spiritualis*, certainly her spiritual adviser rather than her godfather, *Vita sanctae Segolenae viduae*, ch. 8, AASS July, vol. 5, p. 632.

[38] Ferreolus of Uzès, *Regula*, ch. 15, PL 66:965. On the authorship and dating of this rule, see Georg Holzherr, *Regula Ferioli. Ein Beitrag zur Entstehungsgeschichte und zur Sinndeutung der Benediktinerregel* (Zurich and Cologne, 1961), pp. 15–23, 190–201.

[39] Donatus of Besançon, *Regula ad virgines*, ch. 54, PL 87:290.

centuries turned their attention to sponsorship by monks. Thus a diocesan synod held at Auxerre between 561 and 605 and attended by Bishop Aunacherius, thirty-four priests, three deacons, and seven abbots decreed that "it is not permitted for an abbot to have sons from baptism or for a monk to have comothers."[40] Between 663 and 675, Bishop Leudgar of Autun also issued a series of monastic regulations, including one that declared that "none of them should dare to have cofathers."[41]

Each of these bits of evidence is modest and laconic. But together they reveal that, from the time of Caesarius, south Gallic monastic legislators showed a marked reluctance for nuns and monks to contract the social bonds arising out of sponsorship. Indeed, such bonds were perceived by the bishops as inappropriate for ascetics, since they might involve ties to the baptizee and his family so close as to undermine the proper behavior of a monk or nun. Hence the social consequences of sponsorship were "worldly" from the perspective of a monasticism that disapproved of *familiaritas* and yearned for separation from secular distractions.

If we extrapolate from a monastic to a lay setting, then these prohibitions of sponsorship by a monk or nun can tell us something about the motives that might move a parent to seek a sponsor. For the same sort of intimate relationship, binding sponsor to child and to parents, that was inappropriate for ascetics was unobjectionable for lay people and even for secular clergy. Here the bishop saw nothing to criticize because lay people were not bound by the same special lifestyle and elaborate set of taboos that defined an ascetic. The lay person who chose a kinsmen, a neighbor, or a social superior to sponsor a child was creating a holy bond that had important social consequences. In other words, the sort of intimate friendship that was distracting to a cloistered person might be a valuable asset to an ordinary Christian.

In his sermons to the laity, Caesarius never alluded approvingly or disapprovingly to the purely social obligations arising out of sponsorship. Presumably, he did not see it as his concern. He emphasized instead the religious bond between sponsor and child, and it is probably significant that he passed over entirely the bond between the sponsor and the natural parents. Coparenthood lagged behind godparenthood in ecclesiastical approval. It was not acknowledged in liturgical words or gestures; indeed, it was not created by the church at

---

[40] Diocesan Synod of Auxerre, canon 25, in *Concilia Galliae A. 511–A.695*, ed. Carlo de Clercq, CCSL, vol. 148A (Turnhout, 1963), p. 268.

[41] *Canones Agustudunenses*, canon 5, ibid., p. 319.

all but by popular practice. Only with difficulty over a fairly long period of time was coparenthood accepted and domesticated by the official church, and this relative freedom from ecclesiastical control probably enhanced its appeal. However, within a half century of Caesarius' death contemporary sources begin to inform us more specifically about the nature of coparenthood as a social phenomenon.

Caesarius' sermons illuminate only one consequence of sponsorship: the moral and religious obligation of sponsor to child, but they illuminate it rather well. Consider, for example, Caesarius' sermon 204, which he delivered at Easter to a congregation that had witnessed the baptism of that year's *competentes*. On this occasion, in comments borrowed from a sermon by Maximus of Turin,[42] Caesarius reminded his hearers of their own baptism and of the promise of future resurrection that baptism contained. Then, toward the end of the sermon, he turned to an original theme, that of the responsibility of sponsors, a matter not mentioned by Maximus. In this, Caesarius directly addressed the sponsors in the congregation, both those who had served at the most recent Easter and those of longer standing. The text is worth quoting at length because it expresses his most important ideas about a sponsor's obligation to give his or her godchild moral guidance.

> As often as the Paschal feast comes, if any men or women spiritually receive sons from the sacred fount, they should realize that they are bondsmen [*fideiussores*] for them in the sight of God, and therefore should bestow on them the solicitude of true love. They should admonish, reprove, and rebuke them, in order that they may cling to justice, guard chastity, preserve virginity until marriage, refrain from curses or false oaths, and not utter evil or wanton songs with their lips. They should further not be proud or envious, not consult fortune tellers, never hang amulets or devilish signs on themselves or their household. Let them avoid magicians as ministers of the devil, hold to the Catholic faith, eagerly and often attend church services, condemn verbosity, and listen to the divine lessons with attentive ears. Let them receive strangers and, in accord with what was done for themselves in baptism, wash the feet of their guests; they should also both keep peace themselves and strive to recall the discordant to harmony, and they should pay to priests and to their parents the honor and

---

[42] Sermon 204, *Sancti Caesarii opera omnia*, 1:776–778, based on Maximus' Sermon 53, in *Maximi episcopi Tauriensis sermones*, ed. Almut Mutzenbecher, CCSL, vol. 23 (Turnhout, 1962), pp. 214–216.

love of true charity. If, then, you endeavor to admonish your sons and daughters about all these truths and similar things, then you will happily come to eternal bliss along with them.[43]

This catalogue of duties, prohibitions, and exhortations was composed of traditional elements of Christian moral teaching; it was also one that Caesarius recommended often to his hearers.[44] Every Christian had a duty to provide good advice and good example to his neighbor, and parents in particular had for centuries been reminded of their serious obligation to foster the moral and religious formation of their children.[45] However, Caesarius adapted this traditional material to a new situation.

In sixth-century Arles, many children had a third parent, a baptismal parent, who had strong secular bonds to the child and to the child's parents. Caesarius attempted to build on this social reality for pastoral ends, encouraging sponsors to share with natural parents in the religious nurture of their common child. Thus, although he continued to exhort parents to fulfill their role, he also innovated in formulating a clear, feasible participation in that role for sponsors. Ideally, each adult would behave with the same concern toward both his natural and spiritual children; each child would be encouraged, instructed, watched and, if necessary, punished by both natural and spiritual parents. In other words, sponsorship would broaden the circle of people upon whom fell the task of socializing the young into their religious and secular roles.

To the role of moral educator Caesarius added that of teacher of the central tenets of Christianity, in the form of the Creed and the Lord's Prayer. Accordingly, in sermon 13—a powerful and in later generations much repeated plea for his flock to live up to the name "Christian"—Caesarius addressed himself directly to sponsors:

Remember the Creed and the Lord's Prayer yourself, and teach it to your children. I do not know with what boldness a man says he is a Christian, if he refuses to learn the few lines of the Creed and the Lord's Prayer. Remember that you stood as surety before God for the sons you received in baptism, so always reprove and rebuke those whom you adopted at the font just as you do those who were born of you, so that they may live chastely, justly, and

[43] Sermon 204.3 *Sancti Caesarii opera omnia*, 1:777–778; tr. Mary M. Mueller, *The Sermons of Saint Caesarius of Arles*, FC, vol. 66 (Washington, D.C., 1973), pp. 73–74.

[44] Beck, *Pastoral Care*, pp. 274–280.

[45] Christiane Brusselmans, "Les fonctions de parrainage des enfants aux premiers siècles de l'Eglise (100–550)" (Ph.D. diss., Catholic University of America, 1964).

soberly. Do you yourself live in such a way that, if your children want to imitate you, they will not burn with you in the fire but together with you obtain eternal rewards.[46]

Caesarius' succinct description of the obligations of a sponsor became the classic formulation in the Latin West of the strictly *religious* duties of a godparent: to encourage the child in word and deed to live chastely, soberly, and justly; and to teach the child the Creed and the Lord's Prayer, each of which had been an integral part of the preparation of adult catechumens since the third century. To fulfill these duties, the godparent had to maintain ties with the child at least through adolescence, thus encouraging a long-term religious and social bond.

Caesarius was a pioneer in the attempt to formulate and propagate a clear religious role for the godparent, and his vocabulary reflected the primitive tools that many pioneers must use. Language development generally lags behind social change and only gradually does an adequate vocabulary emerge to describe a new social reality. Such was the case with spiritual kinship in late Gallo-Roman society. But the difficulties inherent in assesssing Caesarius' vocabulary are not so serious as they would be for a writer after 800, when literate persons used a learned Latin quite different from the vernaculars that were in daily use. In contrast, Caesarius' simple Latin was close to that actually spoken in sixth-century Arles.[47]

Caesarius had inherited a traditional Christian vocabulary to deal with baptismal sponsorship. Even since Tertullian's *De baptismo*, Latin terms for the sponsor had been marked by a legal flavor—*fideiussor* and *sponsor*—that laid emphasis on the contract with God to which the sponsor was a party. Other inherited terms were purely descriptive, derived from some visible act performed by the sponsor—for instance, *suscipere/susceptor* (to "receive" from the font) and *offerre/offerentes* (to "offer" for baptism).

Caesarius used some of this traditional vocabulary. Thus, each time he alluded to sponsors he called them *fideiussores*, and he commonly employed the verb *suscipere* to describe the act of sponsoring.[48] But Caesarius also wished to express notions that had arisen as the ancient parent/sponsor evolved into the early medieval nonparent/godparent.

[46] Sermon 13.2, *Sancti Caesarii opera omnia*, 1:63–64; tr. Mueller, FC, vol. 31, pp. 75–76.
[47] Dag Norberg, "A quelle époque a-t-on cessé de parler Latin en Gaule?" *AESC* 21 (1966):348–349.
[48] Sermon 50.3, *Sancti Caesarii opera omnia*, 1:217: "Filios, quos in baptismo suscipitis"; sermon 71.2, ibid., p. 288: "Recordamini, quaeso, fratres carissimi, quid fideiussor vester, id est, ille qui de sacris fontibus vos suscepit, promisit vos esse facturos."

In particular, there were no traditional technical terms to express the notion that baptism was a birth in which the sponsor was granted a share in the life of the child and the child was provided with a third parent.

Already in the early fifth century, the North African bishop Boniface had drawn Augustine's attention to the parallel between a parent's transmitting Adam's sin to his child and that same parent's transmitting spiritual life by means of baptismal sponsorship. In the subsequent century, such images of birth and parenthood had grown more important, although, as is often the case in linguistic change, they had by no means ousted the earlier contractual view of sponsorship and its special terminology.

To express the notion that sponsor and baptizee stood in relation to one another as spiritual parent and spiritual child, Caesarius and his society had to create appropriate terminology. The results of their efforts reflect the difficulty of adapting language to a recent social change. Thus Caesarius uses ambiguous terms borrowed from ordinary kinship language, as well as clumsy circumlocutions that reduce ambiguity at the expense of brevity. His problem was analogous to that of someone attempting to explain "the hitter" in baseball to a person unfamiliar with the game. In this connection, the technical term "hitter" would be of little use; indeed, it carries in it ordinary connotations of violence that are misleading. Because of this, the explainer must certainly resort to a wordy circumlocution—"a hitter is a player who holds a wooden stick and attempts to strike a ball thrown toward him by an opposing player called a pitcher"—in order to clarify what is to the hearer an unfamiliar use of a word in everyday parlance. In a similar manner, when preaching to his flock about baptismal sponsorship, Caesarius could not use unadorned, conventional kinship terms because they could mislead. Furthermore, in dealing with a relatively recent development, he possessed no well-recognized technical vocabulary that would distinguish readily between natural and spiritual kinship.

Sometimes, Caesarius qualified his use of ordinary terms of kinship. For example, in sermon 200 he refers to sponsors and baptizees as "both the fathers and the sons" (*tam patres quam filii*). However, these terms were ordinary kinship terms and as such could have been misunderstood by his auditors; hence, he glosses them by placing in parallel the statement "both those who receive and those who are received" (*tam illi qui excipiunt quam qui excipiuntur*).[49]

At other times, Caesarius resorts to circumlocutions that are pri-

---

[49] Sermon 200.6, ibid., p. 769.

marily descriptive. Thus sponsors are identified as those "who desire
to beget sons and daughters by a religious love" (*qui filios aut filias
excipere relegioso amore desiderant*),[50] in an implied contrast to natural
parents, who beget their children by means of carnal love. The spiritual children are distinguished from natural children by circumlocutions as well; the former are "those whom you took from the font"
(*illos quos de fonte excepistis*), while the latter are those "who are born
from you" (*qui de vobis nascuntur*).[51] Such unwieldy terminology with
respect to spiritual kinship supports the view that baptismal sponsors
at Arles had taken on the attributes of spiritual parents recently
enough that language had not caught up with reality. However, the
notion of the sponsor as a spiritual parent quickly became rooted in
Gallo-Frankish mores, and within fifty years of Caesarius' death the
sources reveal the emergence of a more precise vocabulary of spiritual
kinship, distinct from that of ordinary kinship.

On an important aspect of spiritual kinship, Caesarius' sermons provide significant negative evidence. Virtually every known variant of
baptismal kinship, ancient or modern, has imposed some sort of prohibition on sexual contact among spiritual kin. In Caesarius' lifetime,
the Byzantine Emperor Justinian had incorporated such a ban—on
sexual contact between godfather and goddaughter—into the civil law,
a taboo that widened over several centuries to envelop all spiritual
kinsmen.[52] As a pastor and popular preacher, Caesarius was concerned
about marriage and sexual behavior.[53] but he gave no hint that the
spiritual kinship with which he was familiar created marital impediments. The explanation for this puzzling silence in a preacher who
was not otherwise reticent on issues of sexual morality may lie in a
significant difference between Byzantine and Gallo-Frankish customs
for choosing sponsors.

Caesarius was quite explicit that both men and women served as
sponsors at Arles,[54] but he did not make clear whether the sponsored
were customarily of the same sex as the sponsor. It appears, however,
that such was the practice. For instance, in his *Rule for Nuns* Caesarius
forbade a nun to sponsor the *filia*, literally the "daughter," of anyone;[55]

[50] Ibid., p. 768.

[51] Sermon 13.2, ibid., p. 64.

[52] Justinian, *Codex*, bk. 5, title 4, law 26 in *CIC*, ed. Paul Kruger (Berlin, 1895), 2:197.

[53] Beck, *Pastoral Care*, pp. 223–257.

[54] Sermon 204.3, *Sancti Caesarii opera omnia*, 1:777–778: "Et ideo rogo et admoneo, ut
quotiens paschalis sollemnitas venit, quicumque viri vel mulieres de sacro fonte filios
spiritualiter exceperunt, cognoscant se pro ipsis fideiussores aput deum extitisse."

[55] *Statuta sanctarum virginum*, ch. 11, *Florilegium*, p. 7: "Nulla cuiuslibet filiam in
baptismo . . . praesumat excipere."

similarly, in his *Rule for Monks* he forbade a monk to sponsor the *filius*, literally the "son," of anyone.[56] In this, his choice of words was deliberate, for each child had one sponsor of the same sex.

In the sixth-, seventh- and early eighth-century Frankish sources, I have never found an instance in which a boy was sponsored by a woman or a girl by a man. Hence, if it is correct to conclude that same-sex sponsorship was the custom in the earliest form of the Gallo-Frankish godparent complex, then marriage between the spiritual parent and child would not occur and there would be no occasion to make explicit the sexual taboo that is probably implicit in all variants of the baptismal kinship. In contrast, in the middle and later eighth century, when instances of cross-sex sponsorship did occur, the Frankish church made explicit the prohibition on sexual contact between spiritual kin.

The custom of choosing sponsors in Byzantine regions was demonstrably different, and this accounts for Justinian's concern with the matter. In other words, his law against marriage between sponsor and sponsored is explicitly based on the assumption that a girl could have a male sponsor who might subsequently wish to marry her. Similarly, Pope Gregory I attested to the existence of cross-sex sponsorship in late sixth-century Byzantine Italy when he recounted the punishment of a man who had raped his goddaughter.[57] Thus the Byzantine custom of cross-sex sponsorship created the possibility of marriage between spiritual kin and prompted the early prohibition. But in the West, outside of Italy, the possibility of marriage between godparent and godchild had not yet emerged in Caesarius' day.

Caesarius was also silent about the case of sexual contact between natural and spiritual parents, the classic example of which would be marriage between the male sponsor and the widowed mother of the child. Indeed, Caesarius never explicitly mentioned coparents, persons whom Frankish Latin sources were calling *compatres* and *commatres* within fifty years of his death. However, his silence on this subject fits well with contemporary views, for the prohibition on such marriages was also a relatively late development in the Byzantine version of spiritual kinship. Indeed, the Byzantine sources reveal no interest in coparental marriages until 692, and it was only in the 720s that the Frankish church was prodded by the popes, who were Byzantine in outlook and political allegiance for much of the period, to prohibit

---

[56] *Regula monachorum*, ch. 10, *Sancti Caesarii opera omnia*, 2:150: "Filium de baptismum nullus excipiat."

[57] Gregory I, *Dialogi*, bk. 4, ch. 33, ed. Umberto Moricca, Istituto storico italiano per il medio evo. Fonti per la storia d'Italia, vol. 57 (Rome, 1924), p. 277.

such unions. Thus, in the form of spiritual kinship known to Caesarius of Arles, sexual prohibitions were absent, although this situation changed in the course of the eighth century as papal influence grew.[58]

Caesarius of Arles had been born in the twilight of the western Roman Empire, and when he died in 542 all of Gaul was under Frankish control. In his writings, sponsors had certainly become godparents, although the bishop focused on their religious and moral duties to the virtual exclusion of their social significance. But in the last decades of the sixth century written sources originating in the Frankish territories begin to remedy that imbalance, providing important evidence for the existence of a code of social behavior and a set of social expectations rooted in baptismal sponsorship. Indeed, Frankish sources from the sixth to the ninth centuries that refer directly to spiritual kinship are relatively abundant, as abundant as the source materials for almost any aspect of the social history of the period. In the next chapter we will survey these sources.

[58] Joseph H. Lynch, "Spiritual Kinship and Sexual Prohibitions in Early Medieval Europe," *Monumenta iuris canonici*, series C: Subsidia, vol. 7 (Vatican City, 1985), pp. 271-288.

SIX

THE SPIRITUAL FAMILY IN
FRANKISH SOCIETY

Without the *History of the Franks* by Bishop Gregory of Tours (538–
594), our knowledge of the first century of that tribe's presence on
Roman soil would be almost nil.[1] In this history, books 1 to 4 deal
primarily with events up to the year 575, while books 6 to 10 treat
contemporary events, for many of which Gregory had been a witness
or participant. Thus Gregory's *History* not only provides a detailed
framework of political history but also emerges as a treasure trove of
information about Gallo-Frankish social life, religion, and folkways.
Gregory himself was not a Frank; he was the scion of a Gallo-Roman
family that boasted six bishops in the half century before his own
election to the see of Tours. Gregory did not always understand the
doings of the Frankish kings and aristocrats about whom he wrote,
but he was an eager observer of the world in which he lived and
because of this both his *History* and his hagiographic works are irre-
placeable for our understanding of the Franks.

Gregory's *History* also begins an unbroken flow of Frankish sources
that deal with spiritual kinship as a social phenomenon. Indeed, he
mentions baptismal kinship sixteen times in that work.[2] It is significant
that he knew virtually nothing about sponsorship in Frankish history
before his own time. Hence, in every instance but one,[3] he reports on
spiritual kinship among his contemporaries. That instance was the
case of Clovis, the first Christian king of the Franks, to whom Gregory
devoted much of book 2 and whose baptism by Bishop Remigius of
Rheims was reported in detail. However, Gregory did not name, and
at ninety years' remove probably did not know, the king's sponsor.
This omission might have been an accident of Gregory's choice of
sources. However, when Clovis was baptized, between 496 and 506,

---

[1] Gregory of Tours, *Historiarum libri x*, 2nd ed., ed. Bruno Krusch, Wilhelm Levison,
and Walther Holtzmann, MGM SSRM, vol. 1, pt.1 (Hanover, 1937–1951); tr. O. M.
Dalton, *The History of the Franks by Gregory of Tours*, 2 vols. (Oxford, 1927).

[2] *Historiarum*, bk. 3, ch. 23; bk. 5, chs. 18 and 22; bk. 6, chs. 17 and 27; bk. 7, chs.
14 and 22; bk. 8, chs. 1, 9 and 37; bk. 9, chs. 4, 8, 9, and 10; bk. 10, chs. 1 and 28.

[3] Ibid, bk. 3, ch. 23, p. 122.

the liturgical sponsor was only beginning to take on the attributes of a godparent and there may have been little reason for his identity to be remembered. The Franks did, nevertheless, eagerly integrate baptismal sponsorship and spiritual kinship into their folkways and, in Gregory's day and beyond, spiritual kinsmen were prominent in the sources.

In marked contrast to Caesarius' sermons, which had been delivered only sixty or seventy years earlier, Gregory's *History* contains almost no information on the liturgical or pedagogical duties of godparents and a relatively great amount of information on their secular role. This difference in the approaches of the two bishops is at least partially rooted in the different genres in which they worked. For the sermons were intentionally edifying and pastoral, whereas the *History*, although it had religious purposes and presuppositions,[4] was intended to be a narrative of events, many of which were decidedly not edifying. The contrast in approaches is also grounded in the fact that the secular impact of the institution was greater in Gregory's day than it had been seventy years earlier and thus it impinged quite directly on his narrative.

Any evaluation of the evidence that Gregory and later Frankish writers provide about the workings of spiritual kinship must take into account two factors. First, the sources allude to such kinship only incidentally, when it touches a topic of immediate interest, and it usually serves to account for behavior between spiritual kinsmen. Such spiritual kinship had quickly become part of the Frankish Christian world view and, like the cult of the saints or the sacraments, it was more often assumed than explained. Second, the sources concentrate for the most part on persons of high social standing. And although there is abundant evidence that after the tenth century spiritual kinship functioned at all levels of society, the possibility must be kept in mind that the enhanced social role of spiritual kin may have emerged initially among the Frankish elite and only subsequently have been imitated by their social inferiors.

The relationships created by baptismal sponsorship in Frankish society had four distinct manifestations, two of which (spiritual fatherhood and spiritual siblingship) were rather perfunctory and inconsequential from a social perspective, and two of which (godparenthood and coparenthood) were important factors in shaping attitudes and behavior. First, the bishop or priest who baptized a person became

[4] J. M. Wallace-Hadrill, "The Work of Gregory of Tours in the Light of Modern Research," in his *The Long-Haired Kings* (New York, 1962), pp. 57–58.

his "spiritual father," a role that must be sharply distinguished from that of "godfather." Second, sponsorship created a vertical relationship between the sponsor and the baptizee that was comparable to that of a parent and a child and may be designated as *paternitas*, or godparenthood. Third, sponsorship created a horizontal relationship between the sponsor and the natural parents of the baptizee, which was designated in sources from the late sixth century onwards as *compaternitas*, meaning coparenthood. Fourth, the natural and spiritual children of the same person became "spiritual siblings" to one another.

The Minister of Baptism as "Spiritual Father"

In antiquity both pagans and Christians found it congenial for a disciple to call his master in religious knowledge a father.[5] Thus in Apuleius' *Metamorphoses*, a second-century pagan work, when Lucius was initiated into the cult of Isis by the priest Mithras he expressed his gratitude emotionally:

> I embraced Mithras the priest, who was now as my father [*meum iam parentem*], and clinging to his neck with many kisses I begged him to pardon me because I was unable to recompense him justly for so great favours.[6]

In writing to the unruly Christians at Corinth, Paul sounded the same theme of fatherhood through instruction:

> I am saying all this not just to make you ashamed but to bring you, as my dearest children, to your senses. You might have thousands of guardians in Christ, but not more than one father and it was I who begot you in Christ Jesus by preaching the Good News. That is why I beg you to copy me.[7]

Paul linked instruction to parenthood in 2 Corinthians 6:13, Galatians 4:19, 1 Thessalonians 2:7 and 11, and Philemon 10. It remained a deeply rooted conviction, especially in eastern Christianity, that anyone who guided, instructed, or advanced another person in religious knowledge was his "spiritual father."[8]

---

[5] Hendrik Wagenvoort, " 'Rebirth' in Profane Antique Literature," *Studies in Roman Literature, Culture and Religion* (Leiden, 1956), pp. 132–149.

[6] Apuleius, *Metamorphoses*, bk. 11, ch. 25, ed. and tr. J. Gwyn Griffiths, *The Isis-Book (Metamorphoses, Book XI)* (Leiden, 1975), pp. 102–103.

[7] 1 Cor. 4:14–15.

[8] Irénée Hausherr, *Direction spirituelle en Orient autrefois*, Orientalia christiana analecta, vol. 144 (Rome, 1955), pp. 17–55, or "Direction spirituelle chez les chrétiens orientaux,"

In the second and third centuries, there were bitter disagreements among the adherents of Christianity about the nature of Jesus and the meaning of his work. Through this controversy distinct traditions—including the Gnostic, Jewish-Christian, and Catholic—took shape, each with its own sacred writings and institutions. The victorious Christian tradition was the one that called itself "universal," using the Greek work *katholikē*. As a reaction against the other traditions, which it regarded as heretical, this Catholic church attempted to bolster unity and guard against deviant views, creating such defenses as the catechumenate, the authoritative list of scriptures that became the New Testament canon, and the establishment of a strong community leader, the bishop (*episcopos*).

By the late second or early third century, the bishop was the chief preacher, teacher, liturgist, and disciplinary figure in each local congregation. Because he was the primary teacher in matters of religion and the chief dispenser of baptism to the members of his community, he became the spiritual father par excellence to his flock, a notion that is sometimes summed up in the word *papa*,[9] which was originally used to designate any bishop. The *Didascalia*, composed in Syria about 250, exalted the office of bishop in many ways, including the following:

> But the Levite and high priest is the bishop. He is minister of the word and mediator; but to you a teacher, and your father after God, who begot you through the water.[10]

Amphilocus of Iconium, writing in the late fourth century, described baptism in the conventional way as a birth in grace with the church as the mother, but he was rather unconventional in identifying the baptizer rather than God as the father.[11] Thus, from an early date, the bishop was called a "spiritual father" or simply a "father," in recognition of his activity as teacher and baptizer within his community.

The bishop's monopoly of religious functions was possible in practice because early Christian communities were modest in size and, with the assistance of the presbyters and deacons, the bishop could

---

DSAM 3 (1957):1008–1017; Michel Dujarier, *Le parrainage des adultes aux trois premiers siècles de l'Eglise. Recherche historique sur l'évolution des garanties et des étapes catéchuménales avant 313* (Paris, 1962), pp. 345–368, discusses spiritual paternity that arose out of religious instruction and guidance.

[9] Pierre de Labriolle, "Papa," *ALMA* 4 (1928):65–69.

[10] *Didascalia*, bk. 2, ch. 26.4, in *Didascalia et Constitutiones Apostolorum*, 2 vols., ed. F. X. Funk (Paderborn, 1905), 1:104. Tr. Richard Connolly, *Didascalia apostolorum* (Oxford, 1929), p. 86.

[11] Cited in Hausherr, *Director*, pp. 27–28.

carry out all that was expected of him. But by the third century, the pressure of numbers in certain large communities forced a revision of the bishop's role. As the Greco-Roman world turned en masse to Catholic Christianity in the fourth and fifth centuries, bishops increasingly delegated or simply lost to other clergy their monopoly on teaching and baptizing. And as priests and deacons took on the tasks associated with teaching or baptizing they too were accorded the title "spiritual father" for their work. The rise of monasticism, with its pattern of younger disciples learning the ascetic life from a grizzled veteran (who was called *abba*, an Aramaic term for father) also reinforced the notion that any teacher in spiritual things was a father to his students, whether or not he had baptized them.[12]

In the Latin West, the figure of the spiritual father from instruction or baptism was familiar. Thus, in the early sixth century, Bishop Ennodius of Pavia referred to a certain Paterius as his son whom the virgin womb of the baptismal font had borne him; he claimed to be the *genitor* in Paterius' second birth and boasted of being his father in heavenly matters.[13] Similarly, in a letter of the mid-sixth century, Abbot Florianus of Romainmoutier told Bishop Nicetius of Trier that he had three heavenly patrons: Bishop Ennodius of Pavia ("Therefore he is my father from baptism, whom I believe to intervene for his son with the eternal Father through the Son"), Bishop Caesarius of Arles ("He therefore taught the alphabet to me with Latin" and "I am sure that he asks on behalf of his follower and disciple"), and Abbot Theodatus ("my abbot and archimandrite" . . . "who prays for [me] his son and disciple and successor" as abbot of Romainmoutier).[14] Nicetus' letter is a fine illustration of the spectrum of meanings for the term "spiritual father": baptizer, godfather, teacher, spiritual guide.

In the seventh-century *Life* of Saint Segolena, the heroine, a young married woman of the diocese of Albi, wishes to adopt an ascetic life of chastity and prayer; hence she welcomes a wandering holy man as her *pater spiritualis*, her guide to the ascetic life.[15] In the early eighth-century *Life* of Pope Gregory I, an anonymous Anglo-Saxon monk of Whitby describes Bishop Paulinus, who had converted, instructed,

[12] Basilius Steidle, "Heilige Vaterschaft,"*Benediktinische Monatschrift* 14 (1932):215–226; Hausherr, *Direction*, pp. 21–23, 28–29.

[13] Ennodius, *Magni Felicis Ennodi opera*, ed. F. Vogel, MGH AA, vol. 7 (Berlin, 1885), l. 28, p. 310.

[14] Abbot Florianus to Nicetius, in *Epistolae austresicae*, ed. Wilhelm Gundlach, MGH Epis, vol. 3 (Berlin, 1892), p. 116.

[15] *Vita sanctae Segolenae viduae*, AASS, July, vol. 5, p. 632.

and baptized King Edwin, as the latter's "father."[16] Bede also told of
Cadwalla, king of the West Saxons, who was baptized at Rome on 10
April 689, and was renamed Peter by Pope Sergius, his "father."[17]

It is evident from these texts that in early medieval Europe the
clergyman who instructed and/or baptized someone was that person's
spiritual father, a status not to be confused with that of a godfather.
In particular, it was rare for a spiritual father in this broad sense of
the term to contract an enduring bond with his spiritual child, a bond
with social import. The major exception was in monastic communities, where the tradition of the abbot as spiritual father in a significant
sense remained alive. Here a conscientious abbot was teacher/adviser/
father to the members of his community. In contrast, a bishop or
priest in the course of an active career became spiritual father to a
large number of people. He might remain a close adviser or an effective father figure to some of them, but certainly not to most.

The notion of a bishop or priest as a father was preserved in language and in canon law, but the institution itself became archaic and
static, ceasing to mean much except in rare cases. Thus, although the
sources continued to refer to the baptizing clergyman as a "spiritual
father," such status ordinarily possessed little emotional content or
social significance. Modern scholars have not always understood this
distinction between the broad meaning of a spiritual father (which
could embrace, depending on the context, a bishop or priest in relation
to his people, a Byzantine emperor with relation to other kings, an
abbot with relation to his monks, or a pope with relation to lay Christians)[18] and the narrower, godparental meaning of the term. In other
words, while the minister of baptism was always a "spiritual father"
to the baptizee, he was not automatically a godparent.

As the social importance of spiritual kinship increased in Frankish
society, some clergymen wished or were asked to be godparents.
Members of the secular clergy (bishops and priests) could quite properly receive a person into their arms after baptism and thereby attain
this role. Indeed, it was not uncommon for a bishop or priest to assume two kinds of spiritual parenthood at the same baptism, that is,
both to baptize and to receive the baptizee from the waters. Gregory
of Tours reports five instances in which this occurred, involving bish-

[16] *Vita Gregorii Magni Papae*, ch. 14, ed. and tr. Bertram Colgrave, *The Earliest Life of Gregory the Great* (Lawrence, Kans., 1968), p. 96.

[17] Bede, *Ecclesiastical History of the English People*, bk. 5, ch. 7, ed. and tr. Bertram Colgrave and R.A.B. Mynors (Oxford, 1969), p. 470.

[18] Franz Joseph Dölger, "Die 'Familie der Könige' im Mittelalter," *HJ* 60 (1940):397–420.

ops who had both baptized and sponsored royal infants, and two other cases in which a bishop might have assumed both roles.

The clergyman who both baptized and sponsored remained a common figure throughout Frankish history,[19] but the participation of monks or nuns in this practice was a different matter in the eyes of the ecclesiastical authorities. In the monastic tradition stemming from Caesarius of Arles, the acceptance of baptismal kinship was rejected for monks and nuns as a danger to their separation from the world. This prohibition was ratified by some monastic rules, some bishops, and by Pope Gregory I. And although the attraction of the relationship was great enough that the prohibition was occasionally violated, it certainly acted as a check on the full participation of monks and nuns in the baptismal kinship of their society.[20]

In sum, although the minster of baptism was called the baptizee's "spiritual father," the term did not necessarily imply a socially significant bond with the baptized child or its parents. However, if the clergyman went further and received the child from the font, a practice denied to monks and nuns but permitted to secular clergy until the thirteenth century,[21] he became a godparent in the same manner that anyone else did and was obligated to observe the norms of spiritual kinship.

The Godparent/Godchild Relationship (PATERNITAS)

Gregory of Tours and other Frankish sources transmit to us no abstract term for the relationship that bound a godparent and godchild together. Thus I shall use *paternitas* as a convenient designation for the vertical bond between godparent and godchild, although the word was not commonly given that meaning before the twelfth century.

In Caesarius' day, the notion that a baptismal sponsor was primarily a guarantor to a contract with God was already being challenged by

[19] Gregory, *Historiarum*, bk. 5, chs. 18 and 22; bk. 6, ch. 27; bk. 7, ch. 22; bk. 8, ch. 37; bk. 9, chs. 4, 8 and 10. *Annales regni Francorum*, year 781, ed. F. Kurze and reprinted in *Ausgewählte Quellen zur deutschen Geschichte des Mittelalters*, vol. 5 (Darmstadt, 1968), p. 40: Archbishop Thomas of Milan both baptizes and sponsors Charlemagne's daughter Gisela; *Vita Eucherii episcopi Aurelianensis*, ch. 2, MGH SSRM, vol. 7 (Hanover, 1920), p. 47: Eucherius was both baptized and sponsored by Bishop Ansbertus.

[20] Joseph H. Lynch, "Baptismal Sponsorship and Monks and Nuns, 500–1000," *ABR* 31 (1980):114-129.

[21] The earliest text I have found that forbids secular clerics to be sponsors is the Council of Albi (1254), canon 49, in Mansi 23:845. See also the Synod of Benevento (1331), canon 60, in Mansi 25:967, which contains a partial prohibition of sponsorship by secular clergy.

the rival view that a sponsor was a parent in a spiritual birth. Two generations later, Gregory of Tours' *History* reflected the victory of the godparent/godchild image. The notion of the guarantor probably remained alive in learned circles, but in Gregory's vivid, earthy stories it never appeared, having been overwhelmed by notions of spiritual birth and spiritual family.

Paternitas was created in Frankish society by service as a sponsor during the baptismal liturgy. To judge from the language used by Gregory and others to describe it, the crucial moment was the public act of receiving the child from the baptismal waters, which was perceived in a popular interpretation of high theology as the time when the spiritual birth occurred and the bond of *paternitas* was forged. In describing this rite, the sources from Caesarius' day onward made frequent use of the Latin verbs *suscipere* and *excipere*, meaning to take or to receive. The godparent was the *susceptor*, the one who received the child from the font. Often, the godparent was also called a spiritual father or mother (*pater* or *mater spiritualis*) and the godchild a spiritual son or daughter (*filius* or *filia spiritualis*).[22] However, these terms were found to be ambiguous and misleading without a clearly delineated context. The importance of *paternitas* demanded a more precise vocabulary, which first appeared in the sources in seventh- or eighth-century Gaul.

The *Ordo romanus xi*, a set of instructions or stage directions for performing baptism, occasionally identified sponsors by the traditional circumlocution "those who are going to take the infants" (*eos qui ipsos suscepturi sunt*).[23] But the *Ordo* also used neologisms, calling the male sponsor a *patrinus* and the female sponsor a *matrina*, words obviously built on the Latin terms for father (*pater*) and mother (*mater*).[24] There has been some debate about when and where this linguistic innovation occurred. Michel Andrieu, editor of the *Ordo romanus xi*, identifies it as a Roman liturgical document that "saw the light of day in the sev-

---

[22] *Vita beate Genovefae virginis*, ch. 7, in *Etude critique sur le texte de la vie latine de Sainte-Geneviève de Paris*, ed. Charles Kohler, Bibliothèque de l'Ecole des hautes études, Sciences philologiques et historiques, vol. 48 (Paris, 1881), p. 12; *Vita Amandi episcopi*, ch. 17, ed. Bruno Krusch and Wilhelm Levison, MGH SSRM, vol. 5 (Hanover and Leipzig, 1910), p. 440.

[23] *Ordo romanus xi*, chs. 2, 32, 34, 74, and 98 in vol. 2 of *Les Ordines Romani du haut moyen âge*, ed. Michel Andrieu, Spicilegium sacrum lovaniense, Etudes et documents, vol. 23 (Louvain, 1948), pp. 418, 425, 441, 446.

[24] Ibid., ch. 12, p. 420: "Item dicit diaconus: *Signate illos. Accedite ad benedictionem.* Et signent illos infantes in frontibus eorum patrini vel matrinae de policis suis, dicendo. *In nomine patris et filii et spiritus sancti.*" See also chs. 17, 20, 23, and 27, where the *patrini* and *matrinae* are instructed to bless the infants in their arms.

enth century, perhaps even in the second half of the sixth century."[25] Andrieu's great authority in such matters has precluded much subsequent discussion of the dating and origin of *Ordo romanus xi*. However, Thierry Maertens and his disciple Marie-Magdeleine van Molle argued that *Ordo romanus xi* was not in fact a Roman text, but reflected practices in Frankish Gaul in the eighth century. They argue in particular that *patrinus* and *matrina* were popular Gallic terms of the eighth century,[26] and their view is supported by several indices. First, the earliest surviving manuscripts of *Ordo romanus xi* have been dated to the early ninth century.[27] Second, aside from the *Ordo* and one ambiguous text of the seventh century,[28] the terms *patrinus/matrina* are found only in sources after the middle of the eighth century.[29] Third, Christine Mohrmann has provided linguistic arguments for dating the *Ordo* to Gaul at a relatively late period. In his *Französisches etymologisches Wörterbuch*, Walther von Wartburg agreed, noting that "the term *patrinus* is securely attested for the first time in the eighth century."[30]

Thus, by the eighth century, the technical terms for godfather and godmother had emerged in Frankish Gaul, where spiritual kinship flourished as a component of social life. The older terms *pater/mater spiritualis* did not, of course, disappear, but they were often replaced by the more precise words, especially when the context left room for

[25] Andrieu, *Les Ordines*, 2:413.

[26] Thierry Maertens, *Histoire et pastorale du rituel du catéchuménat et du baptême*, Paroisse et liturgie, Collection de pastorale liturgique, vol. 56 (Bruges, 1962), pp. 207–208; Marie-Magdeleine van Molle, "Les fonctions de parrainage des enfants, en Occident, de 550 à 900" (unpublished *mémoire*, l'Année de Pastorale Liturgique, Abbaye de Saint André, Bruges, 1961), pp. 99–115.

[27] Andrieu, *Les Ordines*, 2:365–366.

[28] Fredegar, *Chronicarum quae dicuntur Fredegarii scholastici libri iv*, bk. 2, ch. 58, MGH SSRM, vol. 2 (Hanover, 1888), p. 82: when Alaric, King of the Visigoths (d. 507), and Clovis, King of the Franks (d. 511), made peace, Alaric touched the beard of Clovis and became his *patrenus (ut Alaricus barbam tangeret Chlodovei, effectus ille patrenus)*. Here the exact meaning of *patrenus* is unclear, but it certainly does not mean baptismal godfather.

[29] The earliest uses of the terms *patrinus/matrina* that I have found are in (1) Pirminius, *Dicta abbatis Pirmini de singulis libris canonicis scarapsus*, ch. 12, in *Kirchenhistorische Anecdota*, ed. C. P. Caspari, vol. 1, (Christiania, 1883), p. 160; this source was composed about 724; the Capitulary of King Pepin (751–755), ch. 1, MGH Capitularia, vol. 1, p. 31. The oft-cited diploma of Pepin for Echternach, in *Pippini, Carlomani, Caroli Magni Diplomata*, vol. 1 of *Diplomata Karolinorum*, ed. E. Mühlbacher, A. Dopsch, J. Lechner, and M. Tangl (Hanover, 1906), pp. 42–43, which called Saint Willibrord the *patrinus* of the king, is a twelfth-century forgery, on which see E. Mühlbacher, "Urkundenfälschung im Echternach,"*MIOG* 21 (1900): 350–354.

[30] Walther von Wartburg, *Französisches etymologisches Wörterbuch*, vol. 8 (Basel, 1958), p. 23.

ambiguity. In addition, the technical terms for godson/goddaughter were *filiolus/filiola*, classical Latin words that were given new meanings by at least the eighth century and perhaps as early as the mid-seventh.[31]

In sixth-century Frankish society, the birth analogy had not yet been carried to a full imitation of natural procreation: each child had only one godparent, a male for boys and a female for girls. Gregory of Tours reveals nothing about the liturgical duties of these sponsors, beyond the act of receiving the child from the font. However, both earlier and later evidence confirms that in Frankish Gaul, as in antiquity, the sponsor acted for the child during the initiation ceremonies, carried him, blessed him, responded to questions on his behalf, and undressed and dressed him at the appropriate times. It is likely that some of these duties were still shared with the natural parents and with the officiating clergy, but the tendency was to enhance the sponsor's role at the expense of the natural parent, a process that culminated in the ninth century with the exclusion of the natural parent from any participation in the baptismal liturgy.

Although Gregory is parsimonious in his comments on the liturgical duties of sponsors, he provides precious information about the paraliturgical and nonliturgical duties of sponsors, which included a role in the naming of the child and gift-giving. Baptism and the naming of children were fully linked only in the tenth century, when it became customary for the sponsor to choose the child's name, often giving it his or her own name.[32] The evidence for the earlier period would not support the view that godparents were similarly free to name children. In fact, the principles of early medieval naming had much to do with kinship and left little initiative to the sponsor.[33] The godparent may, however, have had a role in bestowing the name that family tradition or other considerations dictated.

[31] On the classical Latin usage of *filiola*, generally as a term of affection for a young girl, see the *Oxford Latin Dictionary*, ed. P.G.W. Glare (Oxford, 1982), p. 701.

[32] In an unpublished paper ("Godparents and the Naming of Children in Late Medieval England"), Philip Niles of Carleton College examines and synthesizes the late medieval English evidence to demonstrate the godparent's right to name the child. See also Michael Bennett, "Spiritual Kinship and the Baptismal Name in Traditional European Society," in *Principalities, Powers and Estates: Studies in Medieval and Early Modern Government and Society*, ed. L. O. Frappell (Adelaide, Australia, 1979), pp. 1–13.

[33] Karl F. Werner, "Liens de parenté et noms de personne. Un problème historique et méthodologique," *Famille et parenté dans l'occident médiéval*, Collection de l'Ecole française de Rome, vol. 30 (Rome, 1977), pp. 13–18 and 25–34, delineates the rules of name-giving among the Germanic nobility prior to the eleventh century. They were marked by a strong preference for traditional family names and left little room for innovation.

In no case that I have found for the Merovingian or early Carolingian periods was a child named *for* a godparent, although some were said to have been named *by* the sponsor. Thus King Guntram sponsored his nephew, the son of the late King Chilperic, naming the child Lothar after his own father and the child's grandfather.[34] Likewise, Bishop Veranus of Cavaillon, baptizer and sponsor of a son of King Childebert, gave him the name Theuderic (*Teoderici nomen inposuit*);[35] and a son of King Childeric "was received from the font by Ragnemond, bishop of Paris, and by the king's will was named Theuderic."[36] In the middle of the seventh century, saint Eligius of Noyon named his royal godson Lothar, a traditional Merovingian family name.[37] In 688 Pope Sergius baptized the Anglo-Saxon king Cadwalla and renamed him Peter.[38] In the mid-eighth century, Wolfram of Sens named a godson for the child's father, Radbod of Frisia.[39] And finally, in a well-known case, Pope Hadrian I baptized and sponsored Charlemagne's son Carloman in 781 and changed his name to Pepin for dynastic reasons.[40] Thus the godparent played a role in the naming of children, but one that was tightly circumscribed by the customs of the time. Only in the late Carolingian period did sponsors receive freer rein to name children and then they often chose to name them after themselves.

In some societies it is difficult to refuse to be a sponsor if asked directly by a child's parent.[41] Such a refusal insults the requester and is sometimes seen as impious because it expresses a reluctance to further the salvation of the child. There is evidence from sixth-century

---

[34] Gregory, *Historiarum*, bk. 10, ch. 28, pp. 520–522.

[35] Ibid., bk. 9, ch. 4, p. 416.

[36] Ibid., bk. 6, ch. 27, p. 295; tr. Dalton, *History*, 1:257.

[37] *Vita Eligii episcopi Noviomagensis*, bk. 2, ch. 32, ed. Bruno Krusch, MGH SSRM, vol. 4 (Hanover, 1902), p. 717.

[38] Bede, *Ecclesiastical History*, bk. 5, ch. 7, p. 470.

[39] *Vita Uulfranni episcopi Senonici*, ch. 4, ed. Bruno Krusch and Wilhelm Levison, MGH SSRM, vol. 5 (Hanover, 1910), p. 664.

[40] *Annales mosellani*, year 781, ed. J. M. Lappenberg, in MGH SS, vol. 16, p. 497: "perrexit rex Karlus Romam et baptizatus est ibi filius eius qui vocabatur Karlomannus; quem Adrianus papa mutato nomine vocavit Pippinum." See also *Annales regni Francorum*, year 781, ed. F. Kurze, in *Quellen zur karolingischen Reichsgeschichte*, vol. 1, p. 40: "Et ibi baptizatus est domnus Pippinus, filius supradicti domni Caroli magni regis, ab Adriano papa, qui et ipse eum de sacro fonte suscepit."

[41] Hugo G. Nutini and Betty Bell, *Ritual Kinship: The Structure and Historical Development of the Compadrazgo System in Rural Tlaxcala*, 2 vols. (Princeton, N.J., 1980 and 1984), 1:56–57: "It [the system of inviting compadres] is regulated by two interrelated principles: no one can refuse to enter into a compadrazgo relationship of any type, and it must always be known in advance that those who are asked will accept."

Gaul that this sort of social pressure to accept an invitation was already present. Thus, the monastic rule known as the *Regula Tarnantensis*, composed in southeastern Gaul between 551 and 573, softened its stance forbidding any monk to become a "spiritual father" without the abbot's permission by declaring that the prohibition could be disobeyed "if a reason of sufficient necessity is present or if he is moved by the prayers of some faithful person and cannot avoid these forbidden things, that which is recognized as imposed on a reluctant person should be overlooked entirely for the sake of charity."[42] This text could be interpreted as referring to the spiritual direction of adults, but it has been understood as standing in Caesarius' tradition of prohibiting baptismal sponsorship. The very fact that the legislator acknowledged the difficulty a monk could experience in refusing to serve as a spiritual father suggests the social pressure that was involved.

An even more revealing example is found in Gregory's *History*. The Merovingian King Guntram (561–593) and his nephew and adopted son King Childebert (575–595) entered into a pact at Andelot on 28 November 587 to settle disputes and to regulate the succession between them in the event that one of them died without a male heir.[43] Subsequently, King Guntram agreed to sponsor the infant son of another nephew, King Chilperic, who had been assassinated. The child's mother, Fredegund, asked Guntram to do so. But King Childebert, with whom Guntram had concluded the pact at Andelot, saw in this sponsorship a threat to his position and he sent messengers to express his displeasure to his uncle. Childebert's anger was rooted in the Frankish view of baptismal *paternitas*, which was a relationship at once religious and sociopolitical. For in society's eyes, Guntram would now have a spiritual son. In his defense, Guntram responded:

> To the promise which I made to my nephew Childebert I shall not be false. He ought not to take offence if I receive from the sacred font his cousin, my own brother's son; the call to perform this office is one that no Christian should refuse. As for me, God best knoweth that I seek to act without any subtlety, but in the singleness of a pure heart, for if I do not so, I dread to incur the

[42] *Regula Tarnantensis*, ch. 3, in Fernando Villegas, "La 'Regula Monasterii Tarnantensis,' Texte, sources et datation," *RB* 84 (1974):20: "Spiritalem se fieri patrem sine abbatis imperio nullatenus adquiescat; sed si causa tantae necessitatis exstiterit, aut cuiuscumque fidelis personae precibus inclinatus interdicta non ualet effugere, quod contradicenti cognoscitur inpositum, caritatis intuitu est omnimodis omittendum."
[43] The pact of Andelot is in Gregory, *Historiarum*, bk. 9, ch. 20, pp. 434–439. See Anna M. Drabek, "Der Merowingervertrag von Andelot aus dem Jahr 587," *MIOG* 78 (1970):34–41.

divine anger. No indignity is done to our race if I take up this child. For if lords receive their servants at the sacred font, how should it be unlawful for me to receive one so near me in blood, and make him my son by the spiritual grace of baptism?[44]

In the tangled undergrowth of Merovingian family politics, it is best not to be too quick in believing what is said. Obviously, it suited Guntram's purpose to stress the compelling moral force of a request to be a sponsor, a call "that no Christian should refuse." However, Gregory of Tours reports the speech without irony and the king's position was credible because in Frankish society refusal to serve as a sponsor was not something to be done lightly. As matters turned out, Childebert's suspicions of the *paternitas* were justified. Guntram, who had no living sons, now had a spiritual one and (a factor left unmentioned in the text) he also had as a coparent Fredegund, who was a mortal enemy of Childebert. Guntram's protection of his "son" Lothar was an important factor in the boy's survival during the critical years of his minority.

In Frankish society, important events were often accompanied by the giving and receiving of gifts, which served to make feelings of good will concrete and to cement relationships.[45] Baptismal sponsorship thus became an occasion for gift-giving and a festive meal, as it still is in many cultures.[46] Indeed, Guntram's sponsorship of young Lothar at Nanterre was capped by just such a celebration:

> The ceremony ended he invited the boy to his table, and loaded him with many gifts. He was invited by his nephew in return, and departed enriched with numerous presents, deciding to return to Chalon.[47]

An even more explicit description of Frankish gift-giving and feasting on the occasion of a baptism can be found in Ermoldus Nigellus' poem in honor of Louis the Pious, written around 828.[48] In 826 Heriold, a

---

[44] Gregory, *Historiarum*, bk. 10, ch. 28, pp. 520–521; tr. Dalton, *History*, 1:465.

[45] The classic study of gift-giving remains Marcel Mauss, *The Gift: Forms and Functions of Exchange in Archaic Societies*, written in 1925 and translated by Ian Cunnison (New York, 1967), esp. pp. 59–62 on Germanic societies. See also the interesting comments on the importance of gift exchange in early medieval society in Philip Grierson, "Commerce in the Dark Ages: A Critique of the Evidence," *TRHS*, 5th series, 9 (1959):123–140.

[46] Helga Schwarz, *Das Taufgeld. Ein Beitrag zur historischen Entwicklung der Taufbräuche* (Ph.D. diss., Graz, 1950).

[47] Gregory, *Historiarum*, bk. 10, ch. 28, p. 521; tr. Dalton, *History*, 1:465.

[48] Ermoldus Nigellus, *Poème sur Louis le Pieux et épîtres au Roi Pépin*, ed. and tr. Edmond Faral, CHF, vol. 14 (Paris, 1932).

claimant to the Danish kingship, came to Mainz or Ingelheim, where he and his family accepted baptism as one element of an alliance with the Frankish Emperor Louis. The *Royal Frankish Annals* reported the matter in a spare, sober style:

> Heriold came with his wife and and great number of Danes and was baptized with his companions at St. Alban's in Mainz. The emperor presented him with many gifts before he returned home through Frisia. . . . In this province one county was given to him, the county of Rüstringen, so that he would be able to find refuge there with his possessions if he were ever in danger.[49]

Ermoldus Nigellus, a court scholar, described the same events in more detail and his poem is precious evidence on Frankish baptismal sponsorship. I shall use it here primarily to illuminate gift-giving practices.[50]

The baptismal proceedings conducted for Heriold reflected the Carolingian sense of hierarchy. According to Ermoldus, the Emperor Louis received the Dane from the font and personally clothed him in the white garments of a neophyte. The Empress Judith sponsored Heriold's wife; Louis' eldest son Lothar sponsored Heriold's son; Frankish court nobles sponsored Heriold's noble followers; and, finally, Frankish commoners sponsored the remaining Danes. Ermoldus describes in detail the gifts given by the sponsors to the godchildren. Not surprisingly, Louis gave gifts befitting his rank and that of Heriold: an outfit of Frankish clothing made of expensive materials and decorated with the jewels and precious metals that so captivated Frankish taste. Each of the other godparents also gave clothing in the Frankish style, suitable to the rank of both the giver and the receiver. After the religious services were completed, the emperor presided at a lavish banquet for the new Christians; some days later the emperor and his new godson concluded a feudal alliance, renewing a bond that had existed since 814.[51]

Royal sponsorship must not, however, mislead us. Kings were expected to behave in an open-handed way; conspicuous consumption of wealth was necessary for them and royal baptismal gifts were chosen according to this necessity. Nevertheless, in due proportion, royal behavior did reflect reality at lower rungs on the social hierarchy. The nature of the gift was a variable feature of the duties of sponsorship,

---

[49] *Annales regni Francorum*, year 826, *Quellen*, vol. 5, p. 144, and tr. Bernhard Walter Scholz, *Carolingian Chronicles* (Ann Arbor, Mich. 1972), p. 119.

[50] Ermoldus Nigellus, *Poème*, ll. 2234–2359, pp. 171–181.

[51] *Annales regni Francorum*, year 814, *Quellen*, vol. 5, p. 106.

differing by region, by time period, and by social class. But the giving of some gift was universal. Clothing seems to have been a common choice among the Franks, but cattle might do,[52] or a coin, given either to the child or to his family to help defray expenses.[53] Bishop Theodulph of Orléans commented in his diocesan statutes (composed about 813) that if they so wished, sponsors could give a gift to the baptizing priest, but the latter could not demand it.[54] Thus the baptismal feast and a gift, whatever its value and nature, remained duties of a conscientious sponsor.[55]

But sponsorship was not merely a matter for the day of the baptism and its festive aftermath. For when a baptism was completed, a spiritual kin group had been created, consisting of a child, his natural parents, his godparent, the baptizing clergyman, and all their respective spouses and children, if there were any. This new kin group became a focus of enduring loyalties. In Gregory of Tours' references to the behavior of persons joined by *paternitas*, there was an expectation, sometimes explicitly stated and at other times tacit, that respect, protection, and cooperation would govern relations between them. The *Chronicle* attributed to Fredegar calls this relationship *amor*, or love.[56] In the violent, fratricidal world of the Franks, such "love" could be very important.

One of the long-term structural features of Frankish society and indeed of all Germanic societies was the weakness of those institutions and values that promoted social peace and the strength of the contrary traits, particularly the ethic of vengeance and feud.[57] But within the limits imposed by its customs and values, Frankish society experi-

---

[52] Radulphus Glaber, *Historiarum sui temporis libri quinque*, bk. 3, ch. 7, ed. Maurice Prou, CT, vol. 1 (Paris, 1886), pp. 70–71, reported that in early eleventh-century Troyes it was customary for godparents to give a calf (*vitulus*) to their godchildren.

[53] Schwarz, *Taufgeld*, pp. 49–52.

[54] Theodulph of Orléans, *Second diocesan statute*, ch. 4, ed. Carlo de Clercq in his *La législation religieuse franque de Clovis à Charlemagne (507–814)* (Louvain and Paris, 1936), p. 324: "Quod si forte parentes illorum aut qui eos a sacris fontibus suscipiunt sponte sua et gratuito aliquid muneris vobis dare voluerint, accipite nihil haesitantes." The context of the chapter is a prohibition to priests on demanding anything for baptizing, since such demands were a form of simony.

[55] On gifts to godchildren in the twelfth to fourteenth centuries, see Jean Richard, "La donation en filleulage dans le droit bourguignon,"*Mémoires de la Société pour l'histoire du droit et des institutions des anciens pays bourguignons, comtois et romands* 16 (1954):139–142.

[56] *The Fourth Book of the Chronicle of Fredegar With Its Continuations*, ch. 42, ed. and tr. J. M. Wallace-Hadrill (London, 1960), p. 35.

[57] J. M. Wallace-Hadrill, "The Bloodfeud of the Franks," *BJRL* 41 (1959):459–487; reprinted in his *The Long-Haired Kings* (New York, 1962), pp. 121–147. This article examines the feud in Frankish society.

mented with ways to repress violence and strengthen loyalty and cooperation. It is in such a context that the luxuriant array of Frankish
institutions meant to create solidarity must be understood. Thus the
widespread use of oaths,[58] the emergence of drinking guilds[59] and
prayer confraternities,[60] the emergeance of feudalism, the attempts of
Merovingian and Carolingian rulers to settle disagreements by arbitra-
tion and treaties,[61] the pressure to end feuds by a payment of money,[62]
and similar developments had as a major purpose the creation of bonds
of trust, cooperation, and peace within specific and usually small
groups of men.

Like other Germanic peoples, the Franks idealized the kin group,
the *Sippe*.[63] Most of the time, family bonds functioned well enough,
and tightly knit groups of close kin supported, counseled, aided, and
on occasion avenged one another.[64] However, as Gregory's account

[58] Elisabeth Magnou-Nortier, *Foi et fidélité. Recherches sur l'évolution des liens personnels chez les Francs du viie au ixe siècles*, Publications de l'Université de Toulouse-Le Mirail, series A, vol. 28 (Toulouse, 1976); Wolfgang Fritze, "Die fränkische Schwurfreund-schaft der Merovingerzeit. Ihr Wesen und ihre politische Funktion," *ZSSRG*, Germanistische Abteiluung, 71 (1954):74–125.

[59] E. Coornaert, "Les ghildes médiévales (v^e–xive siècles): définition—évolution," *RH* 199 (1948):31–35; and Heinrich Fichtenau, *The Carolingian Empire: The Age of Charle-magne*, tr. Peter Munz (New York, 1964), pp. 139-140.

[60] Reinhard Schneider, *Brüdergemeine und Schwurfreundschaft*, HS, vol. 388 (Lübeck and Hamburg, 1964), pp. 75–78; Joseph Duhr, "La confrérie dans la vie de l'Eglise," *RHE* 35 (1939):451–464, traces the origin and growth of *confraternitates* in eighth- and ninth-century Francia under Anglo-Saxon influence. He identifies Archbishop Boniface as the leading figure in their spread.

[61] Eugen Ewig, *Die fränkischen Teilungen und Teilreiche (511–613)*, Mainzer Akademie der Wissenschaften und der Literatur, Abhandlungen der Geistes- und Sozialwissen-schaftlichen Klasse, vol. 9 (1952); and Margret Wielers, *Zwischenstaatliche Beziehungsfor-men im frühen Mittelalter (Pax, Foedus, Amicitia, Fraternitas)* (Ph.D. diss., Münster, West-phalia, 1959), pp. 4–34, 119–122.

[62] François L. Ganshof, *Frankish Institutions under Charlemagne*, tr. Bryce and Mary Lyon (New York, 1970), p. 96; Wallace-Hadrill, "The Bloodfeud," pp. 126–128.

[63] The extended clan or *Sippe* may not have been so important in Germanic societies as has traditionally been thought. The narrower family of parents/children/siblings was probably the "effective" family after the Germanic peoples settled in Roman territory. Laurent Theis, "Saints sans famille? Quelques remarques sur la famille dans le monde franc à travers les sources hagiographiques," *RH* 255 (1976):3–20, concludes on the basis of saints' lives that the assumption that early medieval Frankish families were "ex-tended" or "clans" has virtually no grounding. Lorraine Lancaster, "Kinship in Anglo-Saxon Society," *British Journal of Sociology* 9 (1958):375–376, concludes similarly that among the Anglo-Saxons the "circle of effective kin" was "smaller" than has usually been thought.

[64] Charles Galy, *La famille à l'époque mérovingienne. Etude faite principalement d'après les récits de Grégoire de Tours* (Paris, 1901).

vividly reminds us, the strength of kin ties was far from unlimited. Jealousy, greed, and prickly egos could still lead to intrafamilial strife that took second place to none in bloodiness and treachery. And even aside from this occasional failure to deter strife among relatives, blood kinship had a second limitation, for the kin group was the product of biology and as such did not include all the people with whom close ties would be advantageous or even crucially important for an individual or for the group itself. Of course, marriage served to extend kin bonds, but it could not do all that was wanted. Hence there was also a tradition in Germanic societies of making outsiders kinsmen by forms of adoption, a term that must be understood in a looser sense than its modern usage.[65]

Such adoptions were intended to build friendships and alliances; they imitated family structures because blood kinship was the most powerful creator of friendship and loyalty known in these societies. Ordinarily, adoption did not place the adoptee on an equal footing with the natural children of the adopter: on the crucial issue of inheritance, for example, the natural children were rarely threatened by their adopted siblings. An apparent exception was the adoption of King Childebert by his uncle King Guntram. However, Guntram had no living sons and Childebert was a close kinsman who might expect to share in his uncle's inheritance in any event. The two kings were at odds and they met for reconciliation at Pompierre in the Vosges, where the adoption took place.

> Then King Guntram said: 'It is befallen me through my sins that I am left childless; and therefore I ask that this my nephew may now be to me as a son." And setting him upon his own seat, he gave over to him his whole kingdom in these words: "Let a single shield protect us and a single spear defend! If I should yet have sons, I will none the less regard thee as one of them, that between them and thee there may abide the loving kindness which today I promise thee, calling God to witness." The chief men of Childebert made a like promise on his behalf. Then did they eat and

[65] Max Pappenheim, "Uber künstliche Verwandtschaft im germanischen Rechte," *ZSSRG*, Germanistische Abteilung, 29 (1908):315–322; Karl A. Eckhardt, "Adoption," *Studia merovingica*, Bibliotheca rerum historicarum, vol. 11 (Aalen, 1975), pp. 240–261; Jack Goody, "Adoption in Cross–Cultural Perspective," *Comparative Studies in Society and History* 11 (1969):55–78, demonstrates the wide range of motives behind acts called "adoption"; and E. N. Goody, "Forms of Pro-Parenthood: The Sharing and Substitution of Parental Roles," in *Kinship*, ed. Jack Goody (London, 1971), pp. 331–345, emphasizes the diversity of ways to create parent/child relationships.

drink together, honoring each other with worthy gifts, and so parted in peace.[66]

In this case, close kinship was reinforced by a voluntary, adoptive kinship. Through such means, kinsmen, who already had strong bonds between them, were able to reaffirm and heighten the intensity of these bonds. And when no bond of blood kinship existed, adoption took on even greater weight as the chief tie between two people.

A variety of procedures could create a parent/child relationship between persons who were not actually parent and child. For instance, the first cutting of a boy's hair or beard was an important rite of passage to manhood, and the person who cut the hair entered into a special relationship to the boy, a relationshp that was described in parental terms.[67] Such a ritual is still practiced among some South Slavic peoples.[68] The Lombard historian Paul the Deacon reported that the Frankish mayor of the palace, Charles Martel (d. 741), sent his son Pepin, later King of the Franks (751–768), to the Lombard King Liutprand (d. 744) for the hair-cutting ceremony, and "cutting his hair, he was made a father to him and sent him back to his father [Charles Martel] enriched with many royal gifts."[69] Similarly, the investing of a boy with his first weapons was an ancient Germanic manhood ceremony and from at least the sixth century it was described as the occasion for creating a parent/child relationship.[70] In short, partic-

---

[66] Gregory, *Historiarum*, bk. 6, ch. 17, pp. 286–287; tr. Dalton, *History*, 1:185–186.

[67] Pierre Riché, *Education and Culture in the Barbarian West*, tr. John J. Contreni (Columbia, S. C., 1976), pp. 233–234; Pappenheim, "Über künstliche Verwandtschaft," pp. 320–321; Eckhardt, "Adoption," pp. 254–256.

[68] M. S. Filipovic, "Forms and Functions of Ritual Kinship Among South Slavs," *VIe congrès international des sciences anthropologiques et ethnologiques*, vol. 2, pt. 1: *Ethnologie* (Paris, 1963), pp. 78–79.

[69] Paul the Deacon, *Historia Langobardorum*, bk. 6, ch. 3, ed. L. Bethmann and G. Waitz, MGH SSRG, vol. 48 (Hanover, 1878), p. 237: "Qui eius caesariem incidens, ei pater effectus est multisque eum ditatum regiis muneribus genitori misit." See also bk. 4, ch. 38, p. 167; and *Liber Pontificalis*, ch. 83, 2nd ed. Louis Duchesne, 3 vols. (Paris, 1955–1957), 1:112: the Byzantine emperor Constantine IV sent the first hair cuttings of his two sons to Pope Benedict II (684–685), to the Roman clergy, and to the Roman army as a way of encouraging them to take the boys under their protection.

[70] Tacitus, *Germania*, ch. 13, tr. Herbert Benario, in *Tacitus: Agricola, Germany, Dialogue on Orators* (Indianapolis, Ind. 1967), p. 46: "But it is not the custom for anyone to assume arms before the community has obtained evidence that he will be worthy of them. Then, in the council itself, either one of the chieftains or the father or relatives present the young man with shield and *framea*: among the Germans these are the equivalent of the toga, this is the first honor of young manhood"; Eckhardt, "Adoption," pp. 254–258; Wielers, *Zwischenstaatliche*, pp. 47–49. On the adoption of the Ostrogothic king Theoderic through the bestowal of weapons (*per arma*) by the Byzantine Emperor Zeno,

ipation in any of several rites of passage for young men created a parental bond that could endure for a lifetime.

It is clear, then, that Christian baptismal sponsorship had rivals as a mode of creating parental bonds. Nevertheless, in Frankish society it soon outdistanced the others in frequency and importance. The hair-cutting ceremony and the presentation of arms survived, but their older significance was no longer clearly understood and they were increasingly interpreted in the light of baptismal sponsorship.[71]

Baptismal sponsorship had advantages over rival modes of creating kinship. First, whereas the traditional ceremonies involved only male children, baptism was necessary for every child, boy or girl; the opportunity to choose sponsors was thus opened up with every birth. Second, as we shall see, sponsorship created ties with the child's parents (*compaternitas*), something that no other ritual did in so solemn or explicit a manner. Third, the code of behavior binding spiritual kin to proper relations with one another was sanctioned by the church as well as by community opinion: in other words, it was a sacred bond. In contrast, other adoption arrangements were strictly secular in their binding force, which might be considerable nonetheless. But in the Frankish realm, sponsorship became the preferred way to integrate outsiders into the kin group or to reinforce other personal bonds.

In the most dramatic cases, the peace and protection expected between a godparent and godchild were literally a matter of life and death. Thus when King Theuderic (d. 534) murdered his kinsman Sigwald, he sent a message to his son Theudebert to kill Sigwald's son, who was with him. But Theudebert disobeyed his father because he himself had sponsored the intended victim. Instead, he warned his godson to flee into exile until King Theuderic died. After that death, he welcomed Sigwald the Younger back, gave him gifts, and restored his property and position.[72] Similarly, the *Chronicle of Fredegar* reports that in about 613 King Lothar II (d. 629) killed his cousin Theuderic II and captured the latter's three young sons. The two older boys were executed at Lothar's command, but the youngest, Meroeus, who was six or seven years old, was his captor's godson. Lothar spared the child's life and secretly sent him into exile because of the "love" (*amor*)

---

see Eckhardt, "Adoption," pp. 257–258, and Wilhelm Ensslin, *Theoderich der Grosse* (Munich, 1947), pp. 44, 159.

[71] Eckhardt, "Adoption," pp. 255–256, notes that a ceremony having to do with "touching" a beard was interpreted in terms of becoming a *patrinus* (godfather), presumably because the old ceremony no longer was understood on its own terms.

[72] Gregory, *Historiarum*, bk. 3, ch. 23, p. 122.

he felt for the child, which was due to the baptismal tie between them.[73]

Much of the evidence for the cooperation and protection provided by baptismal *paternitas* relates to violent events, in keeping with the character of the *History of the Franks* and other early sources. But gentler and more mundane aid, which failed to attract much attention from chroniclers and hagiographers, was characteristic of the relationship as well. For example, when the parents of Saint Geneviève died in the mid-fifth century, the young orphan was sheltered at Paris by her "spiritual mother" (*mater spiritualis*).[74]

The *Life* of Balthildis (d. 680), the Anglo-Saxon wife of the Frankish king Clovis II (d. 657), exists in two recensions. In the first, written within fifteen years of the queen's death, Balthildis is described as concerned on her deathbed for the fate of her *filiola*, praying that the little girl might "go with her." The child died before Balthildis, an event the author of the *Life* saw as a manifestation of God's favor to the queen.[75] *Filiola* was an ambiguous term in a late seventh-century text: it could mean a goddaughter, a granddaughter, or even a small daughter. Thus, when the *Life of Balthildis* was reworked in the ninth century, the reviser removed the ambiguity of *filiola* by specifically describing the child as one "whom she had received from the font of holy baptism."[76] If the reviser was correct in his interpretation of the text, then we may see in it an example of godmother/goddaughter closeness, an episode not to our tastes, but explicable in terms of early medieval views of baptismal *paternitas* (in this case *maternitas*).

In another late seventh-century text, a hagiographer emphasizes the endurance of ties of *paternitas* beyond the grave. Here the corpse of Adelphius, abbot of Remiremont, is brought into the church on the feast of Saint Amatus: "For thus, by God's arrangement, it happened that on the very day on which the feast of saint Amatus was held, the godson [*filiolus*] of that saint, the holy Adelphius, was buried in that same basilica with great pomp."[77]

Aper, a seventh-century hermit, had a servant-companion who was

---

[73] *Chronicle of Fredegar*, bk. 4, ch. 42, p. 35.

[74] *Vita beate Genovefae virginis*, ch. 7, p. 12.

[75] *Vita sanctae Balthildis* (recension A), ch. 14, ed. Bruno Krusch, MGH SSRM, vol. 2 (Hanover, 1888), pp. 500–501: "Et erat aliqua quidem tunc infantula, sua filiola, quam voluit, ut secum iret, quae et ipsa subito e corpore exiit et eam ad tumulum praecessit."

[76] *Vita sanctae Balthildis* (recension B), ch. 14, ibid.: "Habebat praeterea ipsa domna Balthildis quandam infantulam, quam ex fonte sacri baptismatis susceperat."

[77] *Vita Adelphii abbatis Habendensis*, ch. 6, ed. Bruno Krusch, MGH SSRM, vol. 4 (Hanover, 1902), p. 227: "Sic namque, disponente deo, factum est, ut in die illo, quo festivitas sancti Amati agebatur, filiolus ipsius sanctus Adelphius in eadem basilica cum magno ornatu sepeliretur."

SPIRITUAL FAMILY IN FRANKISH SOCIETY 183

also his godson. When the boy went to draw water, he fell into the river Isère and was in danger of drowning. The hermit prayed to God "that You return to me the son whom I gained, Abrunculus by name, whom I have raised from infancy and have instructed in letters and have dedicated to You my Creator." The child was saved.[78]

In general, Frankish saints' lives, which often reflect popular attitudes and fantasies, show that the emotional setting of baptismal *paternitas* could be protective and concerned; at least it was expected to be so. Godparents and godchildren were depicted in such sources as teachers and disciples or companions and friends whose deep sympathy for one another was lifelong.[79] It might even go so far as to justify a strict Frankish ascetic in kissing his godchild with obvious affection. Thus Saint Richarius (d. about 645) kissed his godson and visited amiably with the child's mother, who was the saint's *cummater*.[80] Pardulf (d. 737) also kissed his godson, and the child was later rocked in his cradle by the miraculous power of the saint.[81]

Because of the nature of the sources, we know upper-class Frankish behavior best, and particularly that of the Frankish royal families, the Merovingians and the Carolingians. The intrigues, quarrels, feuds, and killings among the descendants of Clovis (d. 511) constitute a striking *leitmotiv* of Frankish history. Their thirst for revenge and the instability of their land divisions made violence seem inevitable. Yet it is clear that amidst the carnage, cooperation among kinsmen was still the ideal. Merovingian kings sought sporadically to restrain the intrafamilial mayhem that, at its most extreme, threatened the royal line with extinction. Thus treaties, succession agreements, oaths, appeals to kin ties, and adoptions of various sorts (including the creation of baptismal kinship) were employed in Merovingian, and subsequently in Carolingian, family politics to repress violence and promote solidarity.[82] Baptismal sponsorship was especially useful in gaining protectors for vulnerable youngsters. For when a royal kinsman was

---

[78] *Vita sancti Apri eremitae*, ch. 4, ed. the Bollandists, *Catalogus codicum hagiographicorum latinorum antiquiorum seculo XVI qui asservantur in Bibliotheca Nationali Parisiensi*, vol. 2 (Paris and Brussels, 1890), pp. 92–93.

[79] Bishop Gaugericus of Cambrai (ca. 585 to ca. 626) baptized, sponsored, and ordained to the diaconate and priesthood a person who was his spiritual son and long-time companion, ch. 4, *Vita sancti Gaugerici episcopi Cameracensis antiquior*, in *AB* 7 (1888):390–391.

[80] *Vita Richarii sacerdotis Centulensis Primigenia*, ch. 5, ed. Bruno Krusch, MGH SSRM, vol. 7 (Hanover and Leipzig, 1920), pp. 446–447.

[81] *Vita Pardulfi abbatis Waractensis*, ch. 20, ed. Wilhelm Levison, MGH SSRM, vol. 7 (Hanover and Leipzig, 1920), pp. 37–38.

[82] Schneider, *Brüdergemeine*, pp. 106–170; Fritze, "Die fränkische Schwurfreundschaft," pp. 74–125.

godfather to a Frankish kinglet, the bonds of blood that were so idealized in the abstract and so potentially weak in practice could be strengthened by a holy relationship; the child's life and his entry into his inheritance could depend on it.

The scanty sources for the Merovingian period preserve the memory of three intrafamilial sponsorships between 585 and 630. In 585, King Chilperic's assassination left his young son in a precarious position, with other kinsmen looking greedily at his inheritance and accusations being made abroad that the boy was not actually the dead king's son. As we have seen, Chilperic's widow Fredegund invited King Guntram, the boy's uncle, to be his baptismal sponsor and protector. After some hesitation, Guntram agreed, and the boy's position was secured, particularly against his cousin King Childebert.[83] The second recorded attempt to use baptismal *paternitas* to foster protection within the royal clan occurred in 607, when King Lothar, the same person who had been sponsored by Guntram more than twenty years earlier, sponsored Meroeus, son of King Theuderic. This tie of *paternitas* saved the boy's life in 613, when his father and two brothers were executed at Lothar's command.[84] The third example of *paternitas* within the royal kin group came in 629/30 when King Charibert (d. 630) came to Orléans to be godfather to Sigibert (d. 656), son of King Dagobert (d. 639).[85]

Since every child of the Merovingian family had a sponsor, baptism provided opportunities in each generation to create alliances of choice, both inside and outside the circle of kinsmen. And in the ninth century the Carolingian family, fragmented among the grandsons and great grandsons of Charlemagne, also used sponsorship for maintaining internal peace.[86] Nonroyal examples of such intrafamily sponsorship are rarely recorded for the Merovingian period, although ninth-

[83] Gregory, *Historiarum*, bk. 8, chs. 1 and 9; bk. 10, ch. 28, pp. 370, 376, and 520–522.

[84] *Chronicle of Fredegar*, bk. 4, ch. 42, p. 35.

[85] Ibid., bk. 4, ch. 62, p. 51. The incident is also described in ch. 24 of the ninth-century *Gesta domni Dagoberti I regis Francorum*, ed. Bruno Krusch, MGH SSRM, vol. 2 (Hanover, 1888), p. 409.

[86] Louis the Pious attempted to protect his late-born son Charles by asking the child's half-brother Lothar to be his godfather, as recounted in Nithard, *Historiarum libri iiii*, bk. 2, ch. 1 and bk. 3, ch. 3, ed. E. Müller, MGH SSRG, vol. 44 (Hanover, 1897), pp. 13–14, 33; *Annales Bertiniani*, year 853, ed. Georg Waitz and reprinted in *Ausgewählte Quellen zur deutschen Geschichte des Mittelalters*, vol., 6 (Darmstadt, 1969), p. 84: Lothar and Charles the Bald became cofathers when Lothar sponsored Charles' daughter; *Annales Bertiniani*, year 849, in *Ausgewählte Quellen*, vol. 6, p. 74: Charles the Bald spared the life of his nephew Charles, who was his godson.

century Frankish sources reveal that it was occasionally practiced within aristocratic kin groups.[87]

Paternitas was expected to endure for the lifetime of the parties, but in early medieval society life expectancies were low and infant mortality was high, with the result that many "spiritual families" did not go through their normal life cycle because one or both of the parties died prematurely.[88] However, if the godchild survived to adolescence and the godparent was still alive and active, the youngster could expect support and protection. As is usual, Gregory of Tours' information concerns persons in high social station, but on the basis of later developments we may assume that the fostering role of godparents was operative at lower social levels as well.

In this connection, the confrontation between King Chilperic (d. 584) and Bishop Praetextatus of Rouen is quite revealing. In a repetition of the conflict so often seen within the Merovingian family, Chilperic and his son Merovech (d. 578) were bitterly at odds. One of Merovech's chief supporters was Bishop Praetextatus of Rouen (d. 586), who had been the boy's baptismal sponsor. King Chilperic lodged charges of theft and disloyalty against the bishop before a council of forty of his peers meeting in Saint Peter's church at Paris in 577. Among that company was Gregory of Tours.

In this proceeding, the king first alleged that the bishop had stolen property, but the latter responded that the goods in question were held by him in safekeeping (*depositum*) for Brunhild, wife of young Merovech. To this, the king countered by asking why, if the goods were merely held in safekeeping, Praetextatus had dispensed some of them as gifts to gain supporters for the rebellious Merovech. The bishop did not deny that he had given away some of the goods, and in an explanation that reflects the Germanic gift-giving ethic he reported that he had been given gifts by visitors and was thus obliged to reciprocate. Since he had nothing handy that was appropriate, he took a belt with threads of gold from Brunhild's treasure and cut it into parts for distribution. In doing so, he argued that his actions did

---

[87] The Frankish aristocratic woman Dhuoda advised her son William to pray for his deceased godfather and uncle, who had designated the boy as his heir, in ch. 15, of *Manuel pour mon fils*, ed. Pierre Riché and tr. B. de Vregille and Claude Mondésert, SC, vol. 225 (Paris, 1975), pp. 320–322.

[88] Gregory, *Historiarum*, bk. 5, ch. 22, p. 229: Chilperic's son Samson was sponsored by the bishop of Tournai, but the child died before the age of five; *Vita Pardulfi abbatis Waractensis*, ch. 20, pp. 37–38: the saint sponsored a child and a modest miracle occurred (the cradle rocked without human hands intervening), but after a few days the infant died. For estimates of life expectancy based on archaeology and grave finds, see Josiah Cox Russell, "Recent Advances in Mediaeval Demography," *Speculum* 40 (1965):85–88.

not constitute theft because Merovech was his godson and "it seemed to me in some sort mine, because it belonged to my son Merovech, whom I had received from the font of regeneration."[89] This argument, that the bond of *paternitas* gave him a right to use goods held in safe-keeping for his godson's wife, satisfied the assembled bishops that Praetextatus was not guilty of theft.

The king then accused the bishop of disloyalty because he had used the gifts to gain oaths of support for Merovech against his father and to promote plans to assassinate the king. In replying, Praetextatus was misled by Chilperic's supporters into believing that a quick confession and a plea for mercy would gain him pardon. Thus he admitted to the charge before the council:

> I confess that I sought their friendship for him; and had it been permitted, I would have summoned not mortal man, but an angel from heaven to succour him; for, as I have often repeated, he was my spiritual son, from his baptism.[90]

For the crime of conspiring against the king, Praetextatus was deposed and exiled to the island of Jersey in the English Channel until Chilperic's death.[91]

Gregory's account is colored by the fact that he was favorable to Praetextatus and hostile to the king and his episcopal supporters. But this bias does not prevent us from seeing that while the assembled bishops disapproved of certain aspects of Praetextatus' behavior, they understood the attachment to his "spiritual son" that had motivated him. It made cultural sense to them because godparents did aid their godchildren, though rarely in such dangerous, high-stakes situations.

The case of Merovech and Praetextatus may serve as an illustration of the general rule that the code of behavior governing relations among spiritual kinsmen might take precedence over the ordinary legal and social norms of society. Anthropologists have found repeatedly in modern societies with vigorous godparent complexes, particularly in Latin America, that it is not permissible for one coparent to refuse to

[89] Gregory, *Historiarum*, bk. 5, ch. 18, p. 221: "Proprium mihi esse videbatur, quod filio meo Merovecho erat, quem de lavacro regenerationis excipi." Tr. Dalton, *History*, 1:190–191.

[90] Gregory *Historiarum*, bk. 5, ch. 18, p. 222: "Petii, fateor, amicitias eorum habere cum eo, et non solum hominem, sed, si fas fuisset, angelum de caelo evocaveram, qui esset adiutor eius; filius enim mihi erat, ut saepe dixi, spiritalis ex lavacro." Tr. Dalton, *History*, 1:191.

[91] Gregory's account of the trial of Praetextatus is in *Historiarum*, bk. 5, ch. 18, pp. 221–222. On the council in which the trial took place, see *Concilia Galliae A.511–A.695*, ed. Carlo de Clercq, CCSL, vol. 148A (Turnhout, 1963), p. 218.

accede to the request of the other, whether it be for aid in agricultural tasks or for a loan of money. The relationship of *paternitas* also made it difficult for a godfather or a godchild in Frankish society to refuse a request from the other, although the relationship tended to be asymmetrical: the godparent gave material aid and support, while the godchild reciprocated with respect and honor.[92] A royal godchild, with access to considerable wealth, might give material aid to his godfather, but that was merely one of the ways in which kings differed from ordinary folk.[93] A person who refused to honor the legitimate request of a spiritual kinsman earned the disapproval of neighbors and a smirched reputation.

Gregory of Tours recorded an incident that falls into this catetory of behavior as shaped by *paternitas*. When the daring and treacherous Duke Guntram Boso (d. 587) fell out of favor with King Childebert (d. 595), he faced execution at the king's order. To save himself, Guntram Boso asked Bishop Agericus of Verdun, the king's godfather, to intercede. The bishop approached the king and, in Gregory's revealing comment, "since the king could not deny him what he sought,"[94] that is, he could not refuse his godfather's request, Guntram Boso received a limited and grudging pardon. He was placed in Bishop Agericus' custody until the king could confer with his uncle, King Guntram. When Guntram Boso appeared before the two kings at Trier, Bishop Agericus was asked not to be present so that Childebert would not be placed in the awkward position of revoking his condemnation if his godfather intervened again. The two kings decided that Guntram Boso must die for his crimes and he was killed in a violent attempt to save himself, in the course of which he had kidnapped another spiritual kinsman of King Childebert, a *compater*, in an effort to pressure the king to relent.[95]

---

[92] Gallatin Anderson, "Il Comparaggio: The Italian Godparenthood Complex," *SJA* 13 (1957):32–53, stresses the modern Italian expectation that, while godparent and godchild would not impose on one another, they would have an enduring, fond relationship marked by small gifts on the one side and respect on the other.

[93] Clovis, the first Christian king of the Franks, was said to have made considerable gifts to his godfather, Bishop Remigius of Rheims, some of which were recorded in Remigius' will. See ch. 32 of Hincmar, *Vita Remigii episcopi Remensis*, ed. Bruno Krusch, MGH SSRM, vol. 3 (Hanover, 1896), pp. 336–339. For a defense of the authenticity of the will contained in Hincmar's *Vita Remigii*, see A.H.M. Jones, Philip Grierson, and J. A. Crook, "The Authenticity of the 'Testamentum S. Remigii,' " *RBPH* 35 (1957):356–373.

[94] Gregory, *Historiarum*, bk. 9, ch. 8, p. 421: "Tunc pontifex ad regem properat depraecaturque pro eo; cui rex cum negare nequiret quae petebat."

[95] Ibid., bk. 9, ch. 10, pp. 424–426. The king's *compater* was Bishop Magneric of

Yet another instance of social rules yielding to *paternitas* occurred in the reign of King Chilperic (d. 584). Chilperic had ordered the baptism of some Jews, to some of whom he stood as godfather. However, one prominent Jew, Priscus, refused to accept the new situation, using bribes and promises of future conformity to ward off Chilperic's anger. Priscus had a quarrel with a converted Jew named Phatyr, "who was a son of the king by reason of baptism."[96] When Priscus was proceeding unarmed to the synagogue on a certain Sabbath, Phatyr killed him in cold blood and sought refuge along with his accomplices in the church of Saint Julian at Paris. Chilperic was angered at the murder of Priscus and ordered the assassins to be dragged from the church and executed, with the exception of his godson, whom he pardoned and permitted to go away into King Guntram's realm. However, Phatyr was not spared, since Frankish Jews shared the feud ethic with their Christian neighbors; Priscus' kin avenged his death by killing the murderer.[97] But despite the outcome, Chilperic's willingness to exile rather than kill his godson is the revealing aspect here. It meant that between godparent and godchild the ordinary demands of life were (or at least should be) suspended.

In the early sixth century, Caesarius of Arles had stated the role of sponsors in such a way as to give great prominence to their teaching function. Thus Caesarius warned them to give good moral example and to teach the Lord's Prayer and the Creed to their natural and spiritual children. These exhortations retained some vitality in the flourishing Frankish *paternitas* of the sixth, seventh, and early eighth centuries, for Caesarius' sermons continued to be copied, used, and adapted, and it was through them that his influence was felt.

In a sermon attributed to Bishop Eligius of Noyon (642–660), the hearers were reminded of the pact they had made with God in baptism, either by their personal response or by the response of a *fideiussor*, a godparent. The sermon exhorted the faithful to memorize the Creed and the Lord's Prayer and teach them to their sons and daughters. To sum up these Caesarian themes, Eligius quoted freely and without attribution from Caesarius' sermon 13.2, urging his listeners to:

> memorize the Creed and Lord's Prayer and teach it to your sons.
> Instruct and admonish even the sons whom you received from

Trier, who had sponsored Childebert's son Theuderic (*Historiarum*, bk. 8, ch. 37, p. 405).

[96] Ibid., bk. 6, 17, p. 286: "qui iam regis filius erat ex lavacro."

[97] Ibid., bk. 6, ch. 17. On this episode, see Michel Rouche, "Les baptêmes forcés de juifs en Gaule mérovingienne et dans l'Empire d'Orient," in *De l'antijudaïsme antique à l'antisémitisme contemporain*, ed. V. Nikiprowetzky (Lille, 1979), pp. 111–113.

baptism, so that they may live forever with God. Be aware that you are guarantors [*fideiussores*] for them with God.[98]

Caesarius' sermons had an impact even outside of Gaul. For example, Ildephonsus of Toledo (d. 667) drew on Caesarius' sermon 200.6 in his *De cognitione baptismi*, chapter 114, to remind sponsors to admonish both before and after baptism by words and deeds those whom they had received from the font.[99] Abbot Pirminius, an early eighth-century missionary in Alemanian territory, composed a handbook for preachers and converts in which he also sounded the Caesarian theme of sponsors teaching prayers and proper behavior to the sponsored.[100] Thus the teaching role of godparents remained alive through the influence of Caesarius' sermons.

It is significant, however, that in pre-ninth-century sources I have found no instance of a godparent in ordinary circumstances instructing his godchild as Caesarius had directed. The saints' lives, in particular, are silent on the matter, and the canon law of the pre–ninth century makes no demand for instruction by godparents. The only exceptions to this general observation are to be found in saints' lives in which a child was both a godchild and a disciple of a holy man. In such cases, the instruction of the youngster was owed more to the abbot/disciple relationship than to the godparent/godchild relationship.[101]

The existence of an occasional sermon inspired by Caesarius that exhorted godparents to be teachers of religious knowledge is proof of the tenuous survival of the ideal. But the lack of any evidence that the Merovingian Frankish church vigorously promoted this practice in its

[98] Eligius of Noyon, *Predicacio*, chs. 2, 5, 6, ed. Bruno Krusch, MGH SSRM, vol. 4 (Hanover and Leipzig, 1902), pp. 751–753.

[99] Ildephonsus of Toledo, *De cognitione baptismi*, ch. 114, *PL* 96:159, "Illi sane, qui ex utero matris Ecclesiae, id est ex lavacri fonte per spiritum sanctum genitos in adoptionem filiorum religioso amore excipiunt, et ante quam baptizantur, et postquam baptizati fuerint, non solum exemplis, sed etiam verbis eos admonere prorsus oportet."

[100] Pirminius, *Dicta abbatis Pirminii de singulis libris canonicis scarapsus*, ch. 32, ed. G. Jecker and tr. Ursmar Engelmann, *Der heilige Pirmin und sein Pastoralbüchlein* (Sigmaringen, 1976), p. 76: "Simbolum et orationem dominicam et ipsi tenite et filios vel filias vestras docete, ut et ipsi teneant. Filiolus, quos in baptismo excepistis, scitote vos fide iussores pro eis apud deum extetisse, et ideo eos docete semper et castigate et corripite et illos omnes subditus vertros, ut subrii et caste et iuste vivant, sepius admonete adque corregite." Compare this with Caesarius' sermon 13.2, *Sancti Caesarii opera omnia*, 1:64.

[101] *Vita sancti Apri eremitae*, ch. 4, pp. 92–93; *Vita sancti Gaugerici episcopi Cameracensis antiquior*, ch. 4, in *AB* 7 (1888):390–391. François Kerlouegan, "Essai sur la mise en nourriture et l'éducation dans les pays celtiques d'après le témoignage des textes hagiographiques latins,"*Etudes celtiques* 12 (1968/69):101–146, argues that the Celtic institution of fosterage survived in Christian baptismal *paternitas*. He cites two saint's lives in which a child was raised by a holy man who was his godfather.

canonical or pastoral texts or that such instruction happened in real life must be taken to imply that the pedagogical component was a subordinate aspect of pre-Carolingian godparenthood. Certainly the Carolingian reformers of the ninth century criticized earlier generations' negligence in the matter.[102] They were probably too hard on their ancestors, since the Merovingian world, in which Christianity was more practiced than understood, was too stony a ground for such a custom to take root. *Paternitas* flourished in the sixth through the eighth centuries, but there is little evidence from that period to see in it an effective channel for the transmission of religious knowledge.

It is important to clarify the relationship between baptismal *paternitas* and the inheritance of property. Gifts from godparent to godchild were expected at the baptism, but there was no presumption that a godchild had a right to share in the real or movable property of a deceased godparent. However, after the twelfth century, when it became more common for people to dispose of property by written will, there is abundant evidence that testators often left something to godchildren. But these legacies were ordinarily modest in value, representing fond memories more than hard cash. And the godchild certainly could not claim a legacy as a right under law. Instead, the ordinary legal rules for the determination of heirs and the transmission of property were followed, uninfluenced by the existence of spiritual bonds.

If, on the other hand, adults were childless and hence freer to dispose of their property, *paternitas* might then take on a larger role in the determination of heirs. Such adults might favor godchildren, particularly those with whom they had close personal or kin bonds and make them the major beneficiaries of their estates. Thus the Frankish noble Theoderic left his estate in the care of his godchild's father until the boy reached maturity. But in this case, the child was Theoderic's nephew or grandnephew, a factor that probably influenced his decision to treat him "like his first-born son."[103] Such favor to a godchild was unusual, but still possible in the right circumstances. Nevertheless, the crucial point is that, like a testator leaving a silver cross or two shillings to his godchild, the gift was voluntary. In other words, the godchild had no right to demand a legacy even of a deceased, childless godparent. And only if they were very close could he expect more than a modest gift in any godparent's will.

Both Julian Pitt-Rivers and Stephen Gudeman have argued from an anthropological perspective that this absence of a title to inherit is no

[102] The Council of Paris (829), canon 6, MGH Concilia, vol. 2, pt. 2, p. 614.
[103] Dhuoda, *Manuel* ch. 15, pp. 320–322.

accident, that it is in the nature of spiritual kinship. As they see it, the spiritual bond is complementary to natural family bonds; it has those qualities that are lacking in the other. Indeed, the two forms of kinship may be understood in terms of opposites: carnal and spiritual, birth and rebirth, obligatory and free. As Gudeman puts it, "the family and *compadrazgo* are opposed as the material to the spiritual but complementary. This polarisation permits or forces each to be what the other is not."[104] Thus the spirital family is "pure" and insulated from sinful behavior. In contrast to the natural family, which is formed by sexual intercourse and based on material self-interest, the spiritual family is formed by grace and religious love and based on altruism.

The transmission of wealth is in the domain of the natural family, being a matter of law and rights and a source of strife among natural kinsmen. But spiritual kinsmen are above such matters, functioning in the realm of "friendship," as Pitt-Rivers calls it.[105] In his view, spiritual kinship draws its strength not from laws or contracts but from a voluntary union that is sanctioned by the church as well as by community values. Hence, property considerations, at least in a clearly visible way, are inappropriate for spiritual kinsmen.

The *paternitas* created by baptismal sponsorship flourished in Frankish society. Each child had one same-sex sponsor and every responsible adult in the community was a godparent, perhaps several times. The bond between adult and child was expected to be warm and nurturing, reinforced periodically by small gifts, favors, and acts of affection. The godparent also had religious and moral duties toward the growing child, in particular the obligation to teach the Creed and the Lord's Prayer and to give moral guidance, although such religious and pedagogical duties were eclipsed in importance by the more secular component.

From one perspective, godparenthood involved a patron/client relationship in which the adult sponsor protected and promoted the "adopted" child over a long period of time, perhaps even a lifetime. Such a bond could not ordinarily be symmetrical in its demands, since the godparent and godchild did not stand on an equal footing. The godparent was the authority figure, freely giving material aid and advice, while the godchild was the client, reciprocating with gratitude and respect. But *paternitas* did not always succeed in creating this kind

[104] Stephen Gudeman, "The *Compadrazgo* as a Reflection of the Natural and Spiritual Person: The Curl Prize Essay, 1971,"*Proceedings of the Royal Anthropological Institute* (1972), p. 57.

[105] Julian Pitt-Rivers, "The Kith and the Kin," in *The Character of Kinship*, ed. Jack Goody (Cambridge, 1973), pp. 89–105.

of enduring social bond; rather, the participants had to cultivate it. And it apparently functioned most effectively when it reinforced other ties, such as blood kinship or shared economic interests. However, because it created a "spiritual" kinship where there was weak kinship or no kinship, it also acted as a restraint on violence and a force for cooperation. Thus in the changed conditions of early medieval Europe, a rather modest liturgical act became a part of the social glue, a role it filled for centuries to come.

The Godparent/Natural Parent Relationship (COMPATERNITAS)

Compaternitas, or coparenthood, must be distinguished sharply from the other spiritual relationships created by sponsorship. The very idea that natural parents and their child's sponsor were united by a bond more sacred than ordinary kinship has become archaic in much of modern society. Prior to the seventeenth century, however, all Christian cultures understood and honored this bond between a child's natural and spiritual parents, who were coparents of the child. As a consequence of social changes that need to be explored, coparenthood has withered in much of modern northern Europe and North America, where godparenthood is the only recognized social consequence of sponsorship. But this effacement of coparenthood in the north has been balanced by its survival in southern[106] and eastern Europe[107] and its flourishing in Latin America,[108] the Philippines,[109] and elsewhere.[110]

[106] Gallatin Anderson, "A Survey of Italian Godparenthood," *The Kroeber Anthropological Society Papers* 15 (1956):1–110; and "Il Comparaggio: The Italian Godparenthood Complex," *SJA* 13 (1957):32–53; Leonard W. Moss and Stephen C. Cappannari, "Patterns of Kinship, Comparaggio and Community in a South Italian Village," *Anthropological Quarterly* 33 (1960): 24–32; Julian Pitt-Rivers, "Ritual Kinship in Spain," *Transactions of the New York Academy of Sciences*, 2nd series, 20 (1957–58):424–431.

[107] Eugene A. Hammel, *Alternative Social Structures and Ritual Relations in the Balkans* (Englewood Cliffs, N.J., 1968); John K. Campbell, *Honour, Family and Patronage: A Study of Institutions and Moral Values in a Greek Mountain Community* (Oxford, 1964), pp. 217–224; Paul Friedrich, "The Linguistic Reflex of Social Change: From Tsarist to Soviet Russian Kinship,"*Sociological Inquiry* 36 (1966):159–185.

[108] The bibliography on Central and South America is extensive. See Nutini and Bell, *Ritual Kinship*, 1:473–482; Stephen Gudeman, *Relationships, Residence and the Individual: A Rural Panamanian Community* (Minneapolis, Minn., 1976), pp. 190–231; Norman W. Whitten, *Class, Kinship and Power in an Ecuadorian Town: The Negroes of San Lorenzo* (Stanford, 1965), pp. 102–113.

[109] Donn V. Hart, *Compadrinazgo: Ritual Kinship in the Philippines* (Dekalb, Ill. 1977).

[110] R. L. Stirrat, "Compadrazgo in Catholic Sri Lanka," *Man*, new series, 10 (1975):589–606.

In medieval societies, the choice of a sponsor was significant to a child's parents, since they could use it not only for the child's welfare but also for their own. The godparent/godchild bond was certainly important, but many parents must have regarded it as complementary to their own alliance-building. If asked what was the more important consequence of sponsorship, many would no doubt have agreed with the ninth-century monk who wrote that "as a result of that praiseworthy rite dedicated to bringing together bonds of brotherly love among Christians" cofathers are created.[111] This coparental bond was a pervasive form of medieval kinship with social consequences as important as or more important than those flowing out of godparenthood. And its emergence in Frankish society during the early Middle Ages had an impact on the social history of the West for at least a millennium.

Beginning in the later sixth and seventh centuries, the sources permit us to glimpse a horizontal relationship among adults in Frankish society that was created by the sponsorship of a child. Unlike godparenthood, coparenthood spread in spite of the church, which was slow to recognize or sanction such a bond, and even slower to place a positive value on it. The baptismal liturgy acknowledged through prayers and gestures the link between the child and its new spiritual parent, particularly by means of the dramatic act of lifting the child from the font. But in contrast, there was no liturgical acknowledgement of the relationship between coparents. There is some evidence that the *compatres* and *commatres* kissed one another to express their bond,[112] but if this was so, it was a popular creation of a religious act to fill the void left by the formal liturgy.

The official coolness toward coparenthood was already reflected in the sermons of Caesarius, which were explicit on the religious consequences of *paternitas*, but remained silent on the corresponding consequences of *compaternitas*. Prior to the early eighth century, the

---

[111] *Vita Bertini*, ch. 19, MGH SSRM, vol. 5, p. 765: "Huic vero Waldberto et coniugi suae pater confessionum beatus fuit Bertinus necnon et compater fuit secundum laudabilem ritum, inter christianos ad coniungenda fraternae caritatis foedera consecratum."

[112] On 23 August 816 a synod at Aachen promulgated a series of canons for monks, inspired by the reform efforts of Benedict of Aniane. In canon 14, it was decreed "that [monks] not make for themselves *conpatres* or *conmatres* and that they not kiss any woman whatsoever." *Initia consuetudinis benedictinae*, ed. Joseph Semmler, CCM, vol. 1 (Siegburg, 1963), p. 460. This linking of a ban on monks entering into coparenthood with a ban on their kissing women was repeated in five other texts related to the Aachen Synod (ibid., pp. 436, 448, 519, 546, 558). I believe it reflects the custom of coparents greeting one another with a kiss, a gesture acceptable for lay people but considered inappropriate for monks.

Frankish church generally ignored *compaternitas* in its liturgy, sermons, edifying literature, and canon law. Indeed, the major explicit acknowledgments of its existence were negative ones: the prohibition for monks and nuns to participate in it because it was incompatible with their commitment to flee the world,[113] and the prohibition on marriage between coparents. It was only in the ninth century that the official church encouraged the faithful in some small measure to respect the ethical demands of coparenthood. And even then, the prohibition on marriage between coparents loomed largest in the concerns of churchmen. Thus the social code originating in coparenthood remained outside their control and generally beneath their written comment.

If the church showed no enthusiasm for the relationship, how did it originate and gain acceptance? Coparenthood seems to have grown out of a popular conclusion drawn from the church's own premises about rebirth in baptism. For early medieval theology held that before an unbaptized child entered the baptismal font it had a single set of parents, the carnal parents, and when the child emerged reborn from the water it had gained other parents. In high theology these parents were Mother Church and God the Father, but in an increasingly popular view they were the sponsor and the baptizer.

The theology of the pre-Carolingian period agreed that the sponsor was a spiritual parent, but the folk view understood this in a very literal way. Thus the natural and spiritual parents were thought to share in the creation of a full person who was alive both physically and spiritually. And the second, spiritual, birth was so real that after it the parents and the sponsor stood in relation to one another as coparents to the child, a conclusion that the church did not readily embrace. Indeed, it was a situation in which the church's theology appeared to ordinary people to have consequences that the church itself was slow to recognize.

The precocious development of technical terms to describe coparenthood is an indicator of its relative importance. In the late sixth and early seventh centuries, when godparental language was still characterized by ambiguity and circumlocution, Latin words were coined to identify precisely the bond between the sponsor and the natural parent. The abstract noun *compaternitas* and the correlative nouns *compater* (cofather) and *commater* (comother) were quite unambiguous and proved to be a successful linguistic innovation.[114]

[113] Lynch, "Baptismal Sponsorship," pp. 114–121.
[114] For *compater* see the *Fourth Book of the Chronicle of Fredegar*, continuation 2, p. 82; *Canons* of Bishop Leudgar of Autun (663–680), canon 5, ed. Carlo de Clercq, CCSL, vol. 148A, p. 319; and the *Testamentum* of Bishop Bertram of Le Mans (616), ed. Gus-

The social code of coparenthood had much in common with that of godparenthood, but it had important differences as well. Unlike godparenthood, which tended to create a relationship of patron to client, coparenthood placed adults on a roughly equal footing, even when one of the coparents was socially superior to the other. Coparents were friends in a formal way and they addressed one another as "cofather" and "comother," terms that overrode more official titles. For instance, Charlemagne and Pope Hadrian I were cofathers to one another because the pope had sponsored the king's son in 781. After that event, Hadrian always addressed Charlemagne in his letters as *compater* and, in the sole extant letter of Charlemagne to Hadrian, the Frankish king also used *compater*.[115] This implication of standing on equal footing with the pope was a modest diplomatic asset for Charlemagne, who would otherwise have been expected to address him in the traditional "father/son" language of subordination.[116]

Whether godparenthood or coparenthood is the more significant bond created by sponsorship depends on the society that is being examined. In modern English-speaking societies, godparenthood is the only bond commonly recognized and it is usually socially insignificant. In modern Italy and Spain, godparenthood is the more prominent bond, and coparenthood has been reduced to a formalized courtesy with few significant burdens.[117] But in Latin America, the primary focus of attention is on coparenthood, and godparenthood is the lesser relationship. At its most extreme in contemporary Latin America, the child can even be replaced by an object, which is "sponsored" to create coparenthood when no unbaptized child is available.[118]

---

tave Busson and Ambroise Ledru, *Actus pontificum Cenomannis in urbe degentium*, Archives historiques du Maine 2 (1901):117, 132–133. For *commater* see Pope Gregory I, *Epistolae*, bk. 4, letter 40, ed. Paul Ewald and Ludo Hartmann, MGH Epis, vol. 1, pt. 1, p. 276; *Diocesan Synod of Auxerre* (561–605), canon 25, ed. Carlo de Clercq, CCSL, vol. 148A, p. 268. For *compaternitas* see Pope Paul I to King Pepin (758), *Codex Carolinus* no. 14, ed. Wilhelm Gundlach, MGH Epis, vol. 3, p. 512. For *compateratus* (there is some doubt about this form), see the *Testamentum* of Bishop Bertram of Le Mans (616), p. 133.

[115] The letters of Pope Hadrian to Charlemagne are in *Codex Carolinus*, letters 66 to 94 (except for letter 69), pp. 594–632. The sole extant letter of Charlemagne to Hadrian was found in a palimpsest and edited by E. Munding, *Ein Königsbrief Karls des Grossen an Papst Hadrian*, Texte und Arbeiten, vol. 1, pt. 6, (Beuron and Leipzig, 1920), p. 3.

[116] Arnold Angenendt, "Das geistliche Bündnis der Päpste mit den Karolingern (754–796)," *HJ* 100 (1980):78–79.

[117] George M. Foster, "Cofradia and Compadrazgo in Spain and Spanish America," *SJA* 9 (1953):5–6; Anderson, "Il Comparaggio," pp. 45–47; Knut Weibust, "Ritual Coparenthood in Peasant Societies,"*Ethnologia Scandinavica* (1972):107.

[118] Robert Ravicz, "Compadrinazgo," in *Handbook of Middle American Indians*, vol. 6:

In Frankish society coparenthood tended to carry more social weight than godparenthood, whose participants were so unequal in power. This was because the coparents, as members of the same generation, could put their relationship to immediate use, interacting in ways that were unlikely for godchildren and godparents. Coparenthood touched directly on the conduct of adults in the context of politics, economics, and private strife. It was an important component in the shaping of alliances and in the creation of trust in a society where suspicion was the norm. The Frankish sources of the sixth and seventh centuries are not at all theoretical in their references to coparenthood, but they do permit us to identify important features of the way coparents were expected to behave.

In the first place, coparents were expected to protect one another. An example of this took place in about 587, when a conspiracy against the life of King Childebert was thwarted. After two of the chief conspirators, Ursio and Berthefred, took refuge in a fortified place, Brunhild, the king's mother, sent a message to Berthefred, telling him that his life would be spared if he abandoned Ursio. Gregory of Tours reports her motivation in the following way: "For the Queen had received his daughter from the water of baptism, and for this reason was fain to have compassion on him."[119] Berthefred did not accept Brunhild's offer, but Gregory treats the promise of safety as plausible because they were coparents, and as such were expected to treat one another generously.

Such restraint in spite of provocation by a coparent was exhibited by Gregory of Tours himself. The bishop had a series of conflicts with Eberulf, King Chilperic's treasurer, over property that Gregory claimed for the church of Saint Martin. When Eberulf fell into disgrace after Chilperic's death, he blamed Gregory for his misfortunes. However, Gregory responded in his own defense by stating that he had always refrained from reprisals:

> But God, to whom the secrets of all hearts are open, knoweth that I gave him aid in singleness of heart and to the utmost of my power. And though he had often in the time previous dealt treacherously with me in the matter of things belonging to the

---

Social Anthropology, ed. Manning Nash (Austin, 1967), pp. 242–244, surveys the numerous ways that Central American peoples use to create spiritual kinship. Nutini and Bell, *Ritual Kinship*, 1:59–61, 101–194, describe more than a dozen forms of sponsorship in contemporary Mexico in which the sponsored object is inanimate, including such items as a truck or a television set.

[119] Gregory, *Historiarum*, bk. 9, ch. 9, pp. 423–424: "Filia enim eius ex lavacro regina susciperat et ob hoc misericordiam de eo habere voluit." Tr. Dalton, *History*, 1:379.

holy Martin, yet, as I had received his son from the sacred water at his baptism, I had ever a reason to overlook his misdeeds.[120]

The implication of Gregory's comment is clear: a good person aided but did not injure his coparent.

Coparents were also expected to honor one another's requests. As noted earlier, Guntram Boso played on this rule of social behavior as it affected godparents and godchildren to obtain a grudging pardon from King Childebert through the intervention of the latter's godfather, Bishop Agericus of Verdun.[121] The reprieve was temporary, however, and kings Childebert and Guntram decided to execute Guntram Boso because of his egregious offenses. Childebert asked Bishop Agericus to stay away from the proceedings so as to preclude his being placed in the dilemma of either rejecting the intercession of his godfather or sparing a dangerous offender.

When Guntram Boso learned of the royal decision, he sought the intervention of yet another royal spiritual kinsman. In a desperate attempt to save himself, he fled to the lodging of Bishop Magneric of Trier, who was King Childebert's *compater* through his son Theudebert.[122] The fugitive threatened to kill the bishop unless he interceded with Childebert:

> Holy bishop, I know that thou art as a father to the king's son, like as he is himself [*pater communis*] and that whatsoever thou askest of him shall be granted thee, nor can he refuse thy sanctity anything which thou shalt request. Either, therefore, demand my pardon, or we die together.[123]

It is clear that Guntram Boso hoped to play upon the reluctance of any Frank to refuse the request of his *compater*. However, circumstances thwarted his maneuver, for Bishop Magneric was a hostage, unable to address directly his cofather, King Childebert. Because of this, the kings were misled by intermediaries into believing that Magneric was willingly protecting Guntram Boso. Childebert was angered by the new developments, but hesitated to act against his spiritual

---

[120] Gregory, *Historiarum*, bk. 7, ch. 22, p. 341: "Et quanquam multas nobis insidias prius de rebus sancti Martini fecisset, extabat tamen causa, ut eadem obliviscerem, eo quod filium eius de sancto lavacro suscipissem." Tr. Dalton, *History*, 1:300.

[121] Gregory, *Historiarum*, bk. 9, ch. 8, p. 421.

[122] Ibid., bk. 8, ch. 37, p. 405.

[123] Ibid., bk. 9, ch. 10, p. 425: "O sanctus sacerdos, scio enim, te patrem communem cum rege esse filio eius, et novi, quoniam quaecumque petieris ab eo obtenebis, nec negare omnino poterit sanctitate tuae quaecumque poposceris. Ideoque aut inpertire veniam, aut moriamur simul." Tr. Dalton, *History*, 1:379–380.

kinsmen. Thus King Guntram, who was not bound to the bishop, broke the impasse by commanding that the house in which the men were trapped be burned. Bishop Magneric was rescued by his clergy, and Guntram Boso was killed as he attempted to escape.

It can be seen, then, that coparenthood bound the *compatres* to cooperate, to accede to one another's wishes, and to respect one another. Affection was also an ingredient in at least some coparent relationships. Thus when Gregory's contemporary and fellow bishop, Bertram of Le Mans, drew up his testament in 616, his warmest comment was addressed not to his blood kinsmen but to his *compater* Ghiso, who was called *dulcissime*, "most-beloved."[124]

Just as spiritual kinship functions as a social safeguard in many modern societies, so too did the Frankish version repress the overt expression of hostility by creating a sacred bond that was to be free of strife, greed, lust, and other worldly faults. In the course of daily life, spiritual kin were expected to be deferential and respectful to one another. Indeed, the Latin words for spiritual kinship convey some of this social force. Such terms included "love" (*amor*),[125] "the grace of the Holy Spirit which is the benign bond of *compaternitas*" (*spiritus sancti gratia, scilicet compaternitatis affectio*),[126] "the spiritual bond of *compaternitas*" (*compaternitatis spirituale vinculum*),[127] and "friend" (*amicus*).[128] As noted earlier, the author of the mid-ninth-century *Life of Saint Bertin* (d. 697) described the practice of creating *compatres* as "a praiseworthy rite dedicated to bringing together bonds of brotherly love among Christians."[129]

Such ritualized friendship had the potential to become a burden to those obligated to observe it. Indeed, as William C. Sayres found during field work in rural Colombia, the very intimacy of the *compadrazgo* might lead to resentment that could not be articulated but was certainly felt by some peasant *compadres*. Thus some of Sayres' peasant informants had ambivalent feelings about the *compadres'* right "to watch, guide and judge his behavior and he theirs." Such a situation

[124] *Testamentum* of Bertram of Le Mans, p. 133.

[125] The *Chronicle of Fredegar*, bk. 4, ch. 42, p. 35, calls the bond between godparent and godchild *amor*, or love.

[126] Pope Stephen III to King Carloman (770), *Codex Carolinus* no. 47, p. 565.

[127] Walafrid Strabo, *Libellus de exordiis et incrementis quarundam in observationibus ecclesiasticis rerum* (written 840/42), ch. 27, ed. A. Boretius and V. Krause, MGH Capitularia, vol. 2 (Hanover, 1897), p. 512.

[128] Donatus of Metz, *Vita Trudonis confessoris Hasbaniensis*, ch. 19, ed. Wilhelm Levison, MGH SSRM, vol. 6 (Hanover, 1913), p. 290.

[129] *Vita Bertini*, ch. 19, ed. Bruno Krusch, MGH SSRM, vol. 5 (Hanover, 1910), p. 765.

could foster cooperation in a small village, but it could also be perceived as oppressive and constraining. Because of this, Sayres coined the term "negative affect" to describe the hostile emotions that were felt but repressed by some participants in the Colombian *compadrazgo*.[130]

Are there any signs of "negative affect" in the Frankish sources? Any evidence of hostility that simmered but was ordinarily unexpressed? As Sayres noted about his Colombian informants, participants in a godparent complex are reluctant to say publicly anything negative about their spiritual kinsmen because such comments run contrary to what they are expected to think. Indeed, Sayres' informants talked only privately; and often after alcohol had loosened their tongues.[131] Unfortunately, medievalists cannot give alcohol to Frankish informants in hopes of getting the true story. And as one might expect, no Franklish author whom I found wrote down explicit complaints about the sacred bond of spiritual kinship.

They did, however, record noteworthy violations of the bond, but that is an entirely different matter. Among the upper-class Franks, conflicts over property and power were practically inevitable. And no bond—whether made through blood kinship, oaths, feudalism, or spiritual kinship—was powerful enough to withstand every assault of such elemental forces as greed, jealousy, and anger. Coparents occasionally fought one another, betrayed one another, and even killed one another.[132] As in the case of a mother killing her child, such incidents involving coparents were recorded precisely because the historians and hagiographers saw in them shocking breaches of social norms. The notion of what constituted proper behavior was clear and these incidents were not proper behavior. Such spectacular violations of social expectations must not blind us to the fact that spiritual kinship shaped to some degree much ordinary behavior, which is recorded only rarely in the written sources.

Open strife among spiritual kin certainly existed in Frankish society, but this was not a reflection of Sayres' negative affect, which by definition is not overt. There may, however, be some indirect evidence for the existence of negative affect in a motif that recurs in some saints' lives. Simply stated, the motif involves the hagiographer's cast-

---

[130] William C. Sayres, "Ritual Kinship and Negative Affect," *American Sociological Review* 21 (1956):348–352.

[131] Ibid., p. 350.

[132] Gregory, *Historiarum*, bk. 7, ch. 22, pp. 340–341; *Chronicle of Fredegar*, continuation 2, p. 82; ibid, bk. 4, ch. 42, pp. 34–35; *Vita Filiberti abbatis Gemmeticensis et Heriensis*, ch. 27, ed. Wilhelm Levison, MGH SSRM, vol. 5, (Hanover, 1910), pp. 598–599.

ing of a spiritual kinsman in the role of a villain. In the tale a saint is betrayed, even killed, by his coparent, his godparent, or his godchild. I have identified three instances of this motif.

In the *Life of St. Philibert* (d. 685), written in the second half of the eighth century, a monk who was Philibert's *compater* through a son born before his conversion usurped the position of abbot while Philibert was in exile.[133] In the *Life of Dagobert III* (written about 900 near Trier), the king was slain by his godson, who was motivated by greed.[134] And in the *Life of Saint Bercharius* (d. 685/96), written by Adso, abbot of Montier-en-Der (d. 992), the saint punished a monk who was also his godson for an infraction of monastic discipline. The monk/godson (a "spiritual son" on two counts) attempted to murder Bercharius while he slept.[135] These saints' lives, late in composition and drawing heavily on clichés, may project the hidden anger that some felt about spiritual kinship, an anger they could not express openly themselves but could attribute to their hero's opponent, who compounded his wickedness by betraying even the sacred bond of baptismal kinship.

Frankish society is not often thought of as a creative one. Indeed, Robert Latouche has used words like "inertia," "stagnation," and "rot" to describe economic life among the Merovingian Franks.[136] Intellectual life was also at a low ebb in western Europe between the sixth and ninth centuries, yet that impoverished and backward society did manage to invent or reshape social institutions that had an enduring impact in the medieval West. The best known of these institutions would be feudalism, but coparenthood has a claim on our attention as well. For in building on the practice of infant baptism, Frankish Christians elaborated a social institution of great flexibility and usefulness.

Every baptism created a holy bond among the adults involved, a bond that, if cultivated by acts of kindness, could develop into a tightly knit alliance. In this alliance, the mother, the father, the priest, and the sponsor (and perhaps even the sponsor's spouse as well) became coparents to one another through the mediation of the infant. Simply put, the adults were transformed into friends, bound to treat

[133] *Vita Filiberti*, ch. 27, p. 598.
[134] *Vita Dagoberti III regis Francorum*, ch. 12, ed. Bruno Krusch, MGH SSRM, vol. 2 (Hanover, 1888), pp. 519–520.
[135] Adso of Montier-en-Der, *Vita sancti Bercharii*, ch. 26, AASS, October, vol. 7, pt. 2, p. 1017.
[136] Robert Latouche, *The Birth of Western Economy*, tr. E. M. Wilkinson (New York, 1966), pp. 123, 139.

each other generously. In later times, the sources are quite explicit about the ways in which this holy friendship was expressed. And even in the sixth and seventh centuries we can see that coparents addressed one another in a way that leveled social distinctions, protected one another, acceded to one another's requests, and trusted in one another's good will. In addition, as we shall see in a later chapter, coparents were put sexually off-limits to one another in the eighth century, a taboo that heightened the holiness and distinctivenesss of the bond. Thus, by the Merovingian period, coparenthood had become an integrative mechanism involving most adults in interlocking webs of alliance with distant kinsmen and nonkinsmen. As such, it was one of the major forces shaping personal behavior in Frankish culture.

Spiritual Siblings (SPIRITALES GERMANI)

The very notion of a spiritual family raised questions about who was to be included in it. In the early Middle Ages the spiritual family had a tendency to expand to imitate the structure of the natural family. Thus, on the biblical grounds that married persons become "one flesh" (Gen. 2:24), people tended to be absorbed into the spiritual kinship of their spouses.[137] The natural and spiritual children of the same person also came to be regarded as spiritual siblings to one another. The weight given to such spiritual siblingship was one of the ways in which Frankish and papal-Byzantine versions of spiritual kinship differed.

Byzantine Christianity knew both godparenthood and coparenthood, and the tendency to make spiritual kinship as extensive as natural kinship was very marked in the East. Hence, in the Byzantine Empire, spiritual siblingship had been recognized as early as the eighth century. Its exact importance has yet to be mapped out, but we do know that it was perceived as a relationship close enough to prevent marriage. In the influential code of Byzantine law issued by Leo III and Constantine V such marital unions are explicitly prohibited:

> Marriage is forbidden between those who are bound together by the tie of the holy and salvation bringing baptism, that is to say

---

[137] On the implications for marriage law of the notion that a married couple constitute one flesh (una caro), see Joseph Freisen, *Geschichte des kanonischen Eherechts bis zum Verfall der Glossenliteratur*, 2nd ed. (Paderborn, 1893; reprint ed., Aalen, 1963), pp. 439–489; and Derrick S. Bailey, *Sexual Relation in Christian Thought* (New York, 1959), pp. 144–146.

the sponsor and his goddaughter and her mother, and also *the son of the sponsor with the goddaughter* or her mother.[138]

Byzantine clerical discipline probably heightened the importance of spiritual siblingship, for in the Byzantine church priests were permitted to marry and a priest's children would be spiritually related to every child he had baptized. In the same law code, this sort of marriage is prohibited as well:

> Moreover any man who has baptized a woman cannot afterwards marry her, since she has thereby become his daughter, *nor can his son do so*[139]

In the eighth century, Italy was a cultural satellite of Byzantium in many ways. It is therefore no accident that the earliest allusions to spiritual siblingship in Latin sources emanate from Lombard and papal Italy. Thus in 723, Liutprand, King of the Lombards, issued a law forbidding marriage among spiritual kinsmen. And, for the first time in the West, he included in his enumeration of prohibited sexual unions a ban on marriages between spiritual siblings, whom he called *spiritales germani*.[140]

Some of the popes also shared the Byzantine view of the matter. Pope Zachary (741–752), who was a Greek, expressed his disgust at the report of a marriage between spiritual siblings in northern Italy:

> You have asked if it may be permitted for a son whose father took the daughter of another man from the holy baptism (that is, the spiritual daughter of his own father) to take that girl in marriage, a deed which is cruel even to say.[141]

And in his famous letter to the recently converted Bulgars, Pope Nicholas I (858–867) reiterated this papal-Byzantine ban on sexual unions between spiritual siblings, who were bound together by what he called *spiritalis proximitas*.[142]

---

[138] *Ecloga*, bk. 2, ch. 2, tr. Edwin H. Freshfield in *A Manual of Roman Law: The* Ecloga *Published by the Emperors Leo III and Constantine V of Isauria* (Cambridge, 1926), pp. 72–73 (my italics).

[139] Ibid., bk. 2, ch. 3, p. 73, (my italics).

[140] Liutprand, *Leges Liutprandi regis*, title 34.5, ed. F. Bluhme, in *Leges Langobardorum*, MGH Leges, vol. 4 (Hanover, 1868), p. 124: "neque filius eius presumat filiam illius uxorem ducere, qui eum de fonte suscepit, quia spiritalis germani noscuntur."

[141] Pope Zachary to Bishop Theodore of Pavia, ed. Wilhelm Gundlach, MGH Epis, vol. 3 (Berlin, 1892), p. 710.

[142] Pope Nicholas I, Letter 99, ch. 2, in *Epistolae*, ed. E. Perels, MGH Epis, vol. 6 (Hanover, 1925), p. 569.

In contrast to these developments in Italy and Byzantium, the Franks did not spontaneously recognize spiritual siblingship as a significant social institution. However, an unofficial form of this relationship did exist in Frankish society because the coparents were close to one another and their children were presumably present during the visits, feasts, and other interactions that characterized an enduring coparental relationship. As a secondary consequence of such coparental ties, the spiritual and natural children of the same person must often have been childhood friends.

An eighth-century Frankish saint's life confirms this view. In it, Bishop Lupus of Sens, who died in the early seventh century, was maligned at court because of his friendship with a nun. Fulcarius, a courtier, came to Lupus to warn him about the rumors. Reporting the visit, the hagiographer declares that Fulcarius did so because "he was a friend to the holy man particularly for this reason, that his [Lupus's] father Betto had received him [Fulcarius] from the holy fonts."[143] In Frankish society, such spiritual siblingship was an indirect consequence of sponsorship, but neither the legal nor the narrative sources prior to the eighth century contain any mention of it.

It was in the eighth century that the Frankish church's liturgy and discipline began to be reshaped along Roman lines. And one consequence of this wave of Romanization was the dissemination of the notion that spiritual siblingship carried with it a marital impediment. Later I shall discuss more fully the marital consequences of all forms of spiritual kinship. It is sufficient here to note that the Franks incorporated the papal ban on marriage between spiritual siblings into some canonical collections and penitentials,[144] but that they never wholeheartedly adopted a stress on the importance of the bond. It was only with Gratian's *Decretum* in the twelfth century that spiritual siblingship gained wider recognition, still primarily as a marital impediment.[145]

The vocabulary for spiritual siblingship, which originated in the eighth century, was quite straightforward. The baptizee was related as spiritual brother or sister (*frater/soror spiritualis*) to the natural chil-

[143] *Vita Lupi episcopi Senonici*, ch. 8, ed. Bruno Krusch, MGH SSRM, vol. 4 (Hanover and Leipzig, 1902), p. 181: "qui maxime ob hoc sancto viro erat amicus, quia Betto pater ipsius de sacris eum susceperat fontibus."

[144] *Poenitentiale Hubertense*, ch. 51, ed. F.W.H. Wasserschleben, *Die Bussordnungen der abendländischen Kirche* (Halle, 1851; reprint ed., Graz, 1958), p. 384, forbade marriage with a "sister from the holy font or from the chrism" (*sororem ex sacro fonte vel chrismate*).

[145] Freisen, *Geschichte*, pp. 523–531. Gratian treated the impact of spiritual siblingship on marriage in *Decretum, causa* 30, *questio* 3.

dren of the sponsor and probably to those of the baptizing priest as well. It was a matter of some debate among twelfth-century canonists as to whether the relationship of spiritual siblingship bound only those natural children already born to the sponsors when the baptism occurred. But such casuistry was not characteristic of the earlier Frankish sources.

Spirital siblingship made a certain logical sense within the paradigm of spiritual kinship. However, for reasons that are not clear, this logical sense was translated into social reality more readily in Mediterranean Christianity than it was in Frankish Christianity. As a result, the Franks, who did recognize the existence of a loose bond among the spiritual and natural children of a person, invested this bond with marital consequences only under papal pressure and never placed much weight on its potential to build social alliances.

Nevertheless, the spiritual family in all its complexity insinuated itself into the social and religious life of the Frankish realm, from which it spread into the entire West. Indeed, spiritual kinship became so highly valued that contemporaries thought there were not enough opportunities to create it. The solution to this dilemma, the proliferation of sponsors and of ceremonies requiring sponsorship, will be addressed in the chapter that follows.

SEVEN

THE PROLIFERATION OF
SPIRITUAL KINSMEN

The significance of spiritual kinship in Frankish society was enhanced by the fact that it was a relatively scarce commodity, although it became more abundant as time passed. Until the eighth century, there was only one religious ceremony requiring sponsorship (that is, baptism) and one sponsor for each candidate. Under such conditions, individuals did not contract spiritual kinship indiscriminately or with large numbers of people. Unfortunately, we do not know the full extent of spiritual kinship for any one person in the Frankish period. Such information becomes accessible only in the fifteenth century, when diaries and *livres de raison*, which often recorded such data, are available.[1] But we do know the parameters within which a Frankish Christian might acquire spiritual kinsmen from baptism and on that basis some rough estimates of the number of spiritual kin can be made.

The potential extent of the bond of godparenthood (*paternitas*) is easiest to grasp, for until the collapse of traditional norms in the mid-ninth century each child had one sponsor of the same sex and thus only one godparent. There was, however, a tendency to treat the godparent's spouse as a spiritual parent as well.[2] The baptizer was a spiritual father, but this bond was not the same as godparenthood. Before the ninth century, then, a Frank had one or two baptismal godparents, a fact that helps to account for the closeness of the bond. As we shall see, there is no satisfactory way to estimate the number of godchildren that any particular individual might have. That number would be in

---

[1] See, for instance, the *mémoire* of Jehan de Fynnes in I.L.A. Diegerick, "Une famille au xvie siècle," *Annales de la Société historique, archéologique et littéraire de la ville d'Ypres et de l'ancienne West Flandre* 8 (1878):138–168. Many such personal records survive from Italy in the fifteenth and sixteenth centuries. Dr. Christiane Klapisch-Zuber is investigating godparentage in Renaissance Italy, partly on the basis of these records.

[2] Joseph Freisen, *Geschichte des kanonischen Eherechts bis zum Verfall der Glossenliteratur*, 2nd ed. (Paderborn, 1893; reprint ed., Aalen, 1963), p. 539, cites a letter of Pope Nicholas I as the first authoritative declaration that one spouse was bound by a tie of spiritual kinship contracted by the other. See Nicholas I to Bishop Solomon of Constance, Letter 138, *Epistolae*, ed. E. Perels, MGH Epis 6 (Hanover, 1925), p. 657.

some proportion to the desirability of the sponsor on account of character, power, or wealth.

The potential extent of coparenthood (*compaternitas*) is more difficult to assess. There were two distinct ways to gain coparents through baptism. An individual could ask someone to sponsor a child or could be asked to be a sponsor. The first alternative is the simpler to consider. Since one sponsor of the same sex as the child was the norm until the ninth century, a parent gained one cofather for a male child or one comother for a female child. The spouse of the sponsor became a coparent to the inviter(s) as well. Obviously, the more children there were to be baptized, the more coparents a person acquired.

Family size varied greatly, both as a consequence of fertility (approximately 20 percent of all couples would be childless)[3] and of economics, because the resources available to a household conditioned the number of children it could support. Charlemagne, for instance, had at least eight sons and eleven daughters by nine women, although not all the children survived their infancy.[4] Louis the Pious had one illegitimate and four legitimate sons as well as one illegitimate and three legitimate daughters.[5] But royal families, with their abundant resources, cannot be viewed as typical. Indeed, Pierre Riché has stated categorically that in the ninth century "large families were rare."[6] The peasant households described in the polyptych of Abbot Irminon of Saint Germain des Prés, which was compiled about 820, confirm this, showing an average of slightly more than two children per family. And evidence from tenth-century Burgundy points to approximately three children per household of serfs.[7] However, such figures must be interpreted cautiously, since very young children, who had no use as agricultural laborers, were probably not counted. Nevertheless, the figures do indicate that, except for the rich, the number of coparents whom a person could gain through his own children was modest, perhaps half a dozen at most, to which he could add their spouses.

Many children died young. And although the effect this had upon the survival of the coparenthood created at baptism is not clear, it may

[3] William Petersen, *Population*, 2nd ed. (New York, 1969), pp. 180-181.

[4] Silvia Konecny, "Eherecht und Ehepolitik unter Ludwig dem Frommen," *MIOG* 85 (1977):3.

[5] Ibid., pp. 9–18; Suzanne Wemple, *Women in Frankish Society: Marriage and the Cloister, 500 to 900* (Philadelphia, 1981), pp. 100–101.

[6] Pierre Riché, *Daily Life in the World of Charlemagne*, tr. Jo Ann McNamara (Philadelphia, 1978), p. 49.

[7] Georges Duby, *Rural Economy and Country Life in the Medieval West*, tr. Cynthia Postan (Columbia, S.C., 1968), p. 13.

well be that such a relationship faded in significance, since occasions for renewing the bond were obviously not available. In some modern societies, the death of the child is taken as a sign that the godparent is unlucky.[8] If such views were held in the early Middle Ages (I know of no such evidence), then they too might cool the relationship. It is clearer, however, that some coparenthoods did not thrive, either because the participants violated the code of expectations or because long distances prevented the cultivation of the bond by mutual aid and visiting. Thus we are safe in assuming that for most people the number of coparents created at the baptism of their own children was rather restricted and that only some of those relationships remained vigorous over time.

It is much more difficult to assess properly the situation in which a person was invited to sponsor someone else's child. For each time that one served, he or she gained two coparents, the child's father and the child's mother. And in theory there was no limit to the number of times someone could be a sponsor. Indeed, in some modern societies, prominent individuals have been sponsors so often that they can no longer remember the number of their godchildren and coparents.[9]

In Frankish society, there were at least two groups of people who were often asked to be sponsors, holy men and powerful men. A *vir dei*, who was likely to be a hermit, a monk, or an especially ascetic cleric, might be asked by relative strangers to baptize and/or sponsor their child. Such "men of God" were thought to be capable of transmitting good luck, and a successful career was sometimes attributed to their sponsorship.[10] But although holy men loomed large in the

[8] On the unlucky godparent, see Marcelle Bouteiller, "Tradition folklorique et 'parentés parallèles.' Le couple parrain-marraine et ses implications dans les lignées familiales," *Echanges et communications. Mélanges offerts à Claude Lévi-Strauss à l'occasion de son 60ème anniversaire*, 2 vols. (Paris and The Hague, 1970), 1:156–157; Eugene A. Hammel, *Alternative Social Structures and Ritual Relations in the Balkans* (Englewood Cliffs, N.J., 1968), pp. 41–42.

[9] Donn V. Hart, *Compadrinazgo: Ritual Kinship in the Philippines* (DeKalb, Ill.), pp. 73–74.

[10] Jonas of Bobbio, *Vitae Columbani abbatis discipulorumque eius libri duo*, bk. 1, ch. 14, ed. Bruno Krusch, MGH SSRM, vol. 4 (Hanover and Leipzig, 1902), p. 79: a childless *dux* was granted heirs by Columban, who asked to sponsor the first son; *Vita Pardulfi abbatis Waractensis*, ch. 20, ed. Wilhelm Levison, MGH SSRM, vol. 7 (Hanover and Leipzig, 1920), p. 37; *Vita Amandi episcopi*, ch. 17, ed. Bruno Krusch and Wilhelm Levison, MGH SSRM, vol. 5 (Hanover and Leipzig, 1910), p. 440; Arbeo, *Vita Corbiniani episcopi Frisingensis*, ch. 32, ed. Bruno Krusch, MGH SSRM, vol. 6 (Hanover, 1913), p. 587; Donatus of Metz, *Vita Trudonis confessoris Hasbaniensis*, ed. Wilhelm Levison, MGH SSRM, vol. 6 (Hanover, 1913), pp. 286–287; Alcuin, *Vita Willibrordi archiepiscopi Traiectensis*, ch. 23, ed. Wilhelm Levison, MGH SSRM, vol. 7 (Hanover,

religious consciousness of late Roman and early medieval people,[11] they were in fact scarce and most individuals would not have had the opportunity to have a *vir dei* as a coparent, even if they had wished it. In ninth century Byzantium, dead saints were sometimes called upon to be sponsors, through the medium of their icons, but there is no evidence for such practices in the West until much later.[12]

It was more likely that a parent would have one of the powerful in this world as sponsor to a child and thus as coparent. Powerful individuals were often asked by their subordinates to sponsor children, in part with the hope of gaining an important friend or patron for both the child and the parent. Masters sponsored slave children, feudal lords sponsored the children of their vassals, and kings sponsored the children of their more important subjects and kinsmen.[13] Such important individuals must have been godparents and coparents to many people, probably more than they could have recalled with ease. Humbler folk were godparents to the children of their peers and social inferiors as well, but their invitations to serve were less frequent. It is thus impossible to calculate an "average" number of coparents gained through the sponsorship of others' children. All we know is that the number was a function of social standing. The powerful minority were asked often, but for others it was a rarer opportunity to create bonds. If, for the sake of argument, we assume that a person had six children and was invited to be a sponsor six times, he might then have had twenty living coparents, a number perhaps comparable to that of his brothers and sisters and their spouses.[14]

To judge from developments that are first visible in the eighth century and have continued into modern times, persons living in societies

1920), p. 133; *Virtutes Fursei abbatis Latiniacensis* ch. 10, ed. Bruno Krusch, MGH SSRM, vol. 4 (Hanover, 1902), p. 443.

[11] Peter Brown, "The Rise and Function of the Holy Man in Late Antiquity," *JRS* 61 (1971):80–101; Arnold Angenendt, "Bonifatius und das Sacramentum initiationis. Zugleich ein Beitrag zur Geschichte der Firmung," *RQCAKG* 72 (1977):164–169.

[12] Theodore the Studite (ca. 759 to 826), Letters, bk. 1, number 17, PG 99:961–964: John the Spatharius had his son sponsored by an icon of St. Demetrius; Letter of the Emperors Michael and Theophilus to Louis the Pious, ed. A. Werminghoff, MGH Concilia, vol. 2, pt. 2 (Hanover and Leipzig, 1908), p. 479: "Plerique autem linteaminibus easdem imagines circumdant et filiorum suorum de baptismatis fonte susceptrices faciebant."

[13] On masters sponsoring slaves, see Augustine, Letter 98, ch. 6, ed. A. Goldbacher, CSEL, vol. 34 (Vienna, 1895), p. 527, and Gregory of Tours, *Historiarum*, bk. 10, ch. 28, pp. 520–521.

[14] Hart, *Compadrinazgo*, pp. 73–74, found that in Caricugan women averaged ten baptismal sponsorships and men averaged six, while each sex had an additional ten sponsorships from confirmation and marriage.

with systems of spiritual kinship often feel that there are too few opportunities to gain coparents and godparents. And although the society of the early Middle Ages had not reached the stage of some modern Latin American countries, in which occasions for creating
compadrazgo have multiplied luxuriantly,[15] the impulse to elaborate on
them was already at work. There were two strategies for multiplying
spiritual kinsmen: more sponsors could be enlisted at baptism or new
occasions requiring sponsorship could be created. Both of these were
pursued in Frankish society. They began among the people and their
origins are poorly documented, but they become visible in the sources
of the eighth and ninth centuries.

The most natural way to multiply *compatres* and *commatres* was to
invite more than one person to be a sponsor. This increase in the
number of sponsors at baptism is first evident in the late ninth century. It was resisted for centuries by the official church, which had to
compromise repeatedly in the face of pressure from the laity. Thus a
council at Metz in 893 attempted to roll back the increase in sponsors
and reassert the old tradition:

> Let not two or more receive an infant from the font of baptism,
> but rather one, since an opening is given to the devil and the
> reverence due so great a ministry is soiled by a development of
> this sort. For [there is] one God, one baptism and there ought to
> be one father or mother of the infant, who receives it from the
> font.[16]

Such efforts were unsuccessful and in subsequent centuries the church
authorities had to accept three sponsors (two of the same sex as the
child),[17] even as lay pressure to further multiply such sponsors contin-

[15] Robert Ravicz, "Compadrinazgo," in *Handbook of Middle American Indians*, vol. 6:
Social Anthropology, ed. Manning Nash (Austin, 1967), pp. 242–246; Hugo G. Nutini
and Betty Bell, *Ritual Kinship: The Structure and Historical Development of the Compadrazgo
System in Rural Tlaxcala*, 2 vols. (Princeton, N.J., 1980 and 1984), 1:100–194, traces
thirty-one ways to create *compadrazgo* in Tlaxcala, Mexico.

[16] Council of Metz (893), canon 6, in Mansi 18:79: "et infantem nequaquam duo vel
plures, sed unus a fonte baptismatis suscipiat, quia in hujuscemodi secta diabolo datur
locus, et tanti ministerii reverentia vilescit. Nam unus Deus, unum baptismum, unus,
qui a fonte suscipit, debet esse Pater vel Mater infantis." See also the Council of Coblenz
(922), canon 3, in MGH Legum, sec. 4, *Constitutiones et acta publica imperatorum et regum*,
vol. 1, ed. L. Weiland (Hanover, 1893), p. 630.

[17] On the multiplication of sponsors after the ninth century, see Jules Corblet, "Parrains et marraines. Etude liturgico-historique," *Revue de l'art chrétien*, 2nd series, 14
(1881):336–341; Derrick S. Bailey, *Sponsors at Baptism and Confirmation: An Historical
Introduction to Anglican Practice* (New York, 1951), pp. 101–106; Franz Gillmann, "Das

ued. Rich members of the bourgeoisie and nobles, eager to flaunt their social superiority, had numerous sponsors for their children, in defiance of church discipline and secular sumptuary laws.[18] But in spite of much confusion and assertions to the contrary among modern authors, the multiple sponsors did *not* become coparents to one another, only to the parents of the child.[19]

There was yet another strategy for multiplying spiritual kinsmen, the creation of new occasions for sponsorship, a development that began in the eighth century. Some of these occasions were sanctioned by the church and others were not. In the West, the sacrament of confirmation and the ceremonies of the *catechismus* were chief among the former.

The appearance of sponsors at confirmation was an outgrowth of the course of liturgical development. From antiquity until the sixth century, the procedures of Christian initiation had been an integrated succession of ceremonies that took the candidate from prebaptismal preparation through baptism itself to postbaptismal anointing(s) and first communion—a full panoply of rituals that was performed whether the baptizee was an adult or a child.[20] In Byzantine Christianity this remained the pattern of initiation, and there was never a separate sacrament of confirmation. Liturgical developments in the West, however, led gradually to the separation of baptism, anointing (confirmation), and first communion into rites distinct from one another in timing and in conception.

The reasons for the "disintegration of the primitive rite of initiation" in the West are complex.[21] However, the main factor in the emergence of a separate rite of confirmation was a peculiarity of the Roman liturgy. For it was the only one of the western liturgies to have two postbaptismal anointings, one of which could be performed only by a

---

Ehehindernis der gegenseitigen geistlichen Verwandtschaft der Paten?" *AKKR* 86 (1906):697–698, n. 4.

[18] Gillmann, "Das Ehehindernis," p. 698. Berthold of Regensburg, a thirteenth-century Franciscan, in Sermon 3, *Vollständige Ausgabe seiner deutschen Predigten*, 2 vols., ed. Franz Pfeiffer (Vienna, 1862 and 1880) 1:31, complained about the presence of five, seven, nine, or twelve sponsors. There is no adequate study of late medieval and early modern attempts by the church and the public authorities to limit the number of godparents; see Hans Boesch, *Kinderleben in der deutschen Vergangenheit*, Monographien zur deutschen Kulturgeschichte, vol. 5 (Leipzig, 1900), pp. 28–31.

[19] Gillmann, "Das Ehehindernis," pp. 688–714.

[20] J.D.C. Fisher, *Christian Initiation: Baptism in the West*, Alcuin Club Collections, vol. 47 (London, 1965), pp. xi–xiii and passim.

[21] Fischer, *Christian Initiation*. This phrase is the subtitle of his book.

bishop.[22] Such a custom posed few problems in the small dioceses of Italy, where a bishop's presence at a high proportion of baptisms was possible. But in northern Europe, where dioceses were considerably larger and the presence of a bishop less likely, baptism was often administered by a priest. In the Gallican liturgy that was native to the Frankish realm, priests performed the postbaptismal anointing with chrism (olive oil mixed with some sort of aromatic substance) that had been consecrated by a bishop. Thus the episcopal participation in the anointing was indirect, through the substance used for anointing,[23] an arrangement that was upset in the eighth century by the spread of the Roman liturgy north of the Alps.

Anglo-Saxon missionaries, native Frankish Romanizers, and eventually the Carolingian house mayors and kings promoted the Romanization of the Frankish church, including its liturgy.[24] And one consequence of their work was the separation of baptism from confirmation in many cases. For if a bishop was required in order to confirm a baptism conferred by a priest, then that confirmation was often necessarily delayed until there was a bishop in the vicinity.[25] Arnold Angenendt has thus argued that the eighth- and ninth-century Carolingian stress on visitation of their dioceses by bishops was rooted in the desire to increase such opportunities for confirmation and to remedy the problem posed by reserving it for bishops.[26]

Almost everything about the early history of confirmation is vague, but it appears that by the mid-eighth century in Frankish lands it was commonly being administered later than and separate from baptism. Since it was a public rite of passage like baptism, it is not surprising that it too became an occasion for sponsorship. The technical phrase for sponsoring at confirmation was "to hold someone before the bishop" (*tenere aliquem coram* or *ante episcopo*),[27] which was quite distinct

---

[22] Damien Van den Eynde, "Les rites liturgiques latins de la confirmation," *La Maison-Dieu* 54 (1958):53–78; Angenendt, "Bonifatius," pp. 142–150.

[23] Angenendt, "Bonifatius," pp. 159–163.

[24] Cyrille Vogel, "La réforme liturgique sous Charlemagne," *Karl der Grosse. Lebenswerk und Nachleben*, vol. 2: *Das geistige Leben*, ed. Bernhard Bischoff (Düsseldorf, 1965), pp. 217–232; and "Les échanges liturgiques entre Rome et les pays francs jusqu' à l'époque de Charlemagne," *Le chiese nei regni dell'Europa occidentale e i loro rapporti con Roma sino all'800*, pt. 1, SSAM, vol. 7 (Spoleto, 1960), pp. 185–295.

[25] Angenendt, "Bonifatius," pp. 150–158.

[26] Ibid., pp. 151–152. See also Albert M. Koeniger, *Die Sendgerichte im Deutschland*, vol. 1, Veröffentlichungen aus dem Kirchenhistorischen Seminar München, vol. 3, pt. 2 (Munich, 1907), pp. 15–17, who saw in the bishop's *Firmungsreise* the core around which visitation developed.

[27] *Capitulary of Compiègne* (757), ch. 15, MGH Capitularia, vol. 1, p. 38: "Si quis

from the phrase used to identify baptismal sponsorship, "to receive someone from the font."

There are no eighth-century liturgical texts describing the unfolding of sponsorship at confirmation, but the circumlocution for it is quite clear. In the context of a liturgical ceremony, the sponsor offered the child to the bishop, who anointed it on the forehead with chrism. In the *Romano-Germanic Pontifical*, composed at Mainz about 950, the symbolization of this sponsorship was carefully worked out: each confirmand had one sponsor of the same sex; a small child was held before the bishop in the sponsor's right arm; and an older child stood with one foot on the sponsor's foot.[28]

Sponsorship at confirmation created both *paternitas* and *compaternitas*. And because of its late development, the language of this confirmation sponsorship was based squarely on that of baptismal sponsorship. Thus the godparent was designated as "godfather/godmother from the bishop's confirmation" (*patrinus/matrina de confirmatione episcopi*)[29] and the godchild was called "son/daughter at confirmation" (*filius/filia ad confirmationem*)[30] or "godson/goddaughter from conversion" (*filiolus/filiola de conversatione*).[31] Similarly, the coparents were known as "cofather/comother from the holy chrism" (*compater/commater de sacro chrismate*).[32]

Spiritual kinship from confirmation was never so important as that from baptism, but it did expand the opportunities to choose spiritual kinsmen. It also gave parents some flexibility in choosing such spiritual kin. After all, baptism was a sacrament of necessity, to be administered soon after birth lest a child die in original sin. In contrast, confirmation was a sacrament of choice, to be administered late or perhaps never, since its lack carried no clear penalty. Because of this, a family could keep an unconfirmed child in reserve, so to speak, for important opportunities to expand the circle of spiritual kin.[33]

---

filiastrum aut filiastram ante episcopum ad confirmationem tenuerit"; *Council of Chalons* (813), canon 31, MGH Concilia, vol. 2, pt. 2, p. 279; Theod I, ch. 22, p. 198. Sponsorship was described as "to lead to confirmation" (*ducere ad confirmationem*) in canon 55 of the *Council of Mainz* (813), MGH Concilia, vol. 2, part 1, p. 273; or "to hold at the bishop's hand" (*tenere ad manum episcopi*), in ch. 17 of Ghaer II, p. 362.

[28] *Ordo ad baptizandum infantes*, ch. 38, in *Le Pontifical Romano-germanique du dixième siècle*, ed. Cyrille Vogel and Reinhard Elze, ST, vol. 227 (Vatican City, 1963), pp. 163–164: "Induti vero ordinentur per ordinem et infantes quidem in brachiis dextris tenentur, maiores vero pedem ponunt super pedem patrini sui."

[29] *Capitulary of Pepin* (751–755), ch. 1, MGH Capitularia, vol. 1, p. 31.

[30] *Council of Mainz* (813), canon 55, MGH Concilia, vol. 2, pt. 1, p. 273.

[31] Haito, ch. 21, p. 365.

[32] Ghaer II, ch. 16, p. 361.

[33] In 996, Otto III sponsored the son of the Doge of Venice at his confirmation, John

Confirmation may be visualized as the amputation of the last portion of the traditional process of initiation, which then stood on its own as an independent rite. In a similar fashion, the early stages of initiation were also separated off and made into an occasion for sponsorship. Thus the preliminary rituals of baptism, which were vestiges of the ceremonies for entry into the catechumenate or competentate, could be performed as a separate entity for which a sponsor was invited. Radulphus Glaber reported such an incident that occurred in 962 when William of Dijon (962–1031), the later monastic reformer, was baptized. On this occasion, the wife of the Emperor Otto I was the sponsor of the child at baptism, but Otto held him in his arms before the baptism, when the child was made a catechumen, and it was at this point that he named him William.[34]

The ceremonies preceding baptism were called by various names, including *catechismus*, *catechumenus*, and *prima signatio*. They were first attested as an occasion for sponsorship in the *Canons of Theodore*, a penitential composed between 690 and 755. These *Canons* referred to three occasions for sponsorship that had emerged out of the breakup of the traditional procedures for initiating converts:

> If it is necessary, there can be a single father in the *catechumenus* and baptism and confirmation, but that is not the custom. Rather, separate persons receive [the candidate] in the separate rites.[35]

This provision, which reflected either Anglo-Saxon or Frankish practice, indicates that it was customary for a baptism to require three sponsors, although the author would permit one person to fill the three roles if that was necessary. The spiritual kinship derived from sponsorship during the prebaptismal ceremonies was rarely mentioned in

the Deacon of Venice, *Chronicon venetum et gradense*, ed. Giovanni Monticolo, *Cronache veneziane antichissime*, Fonti per la storia d'Italia, vol. 9 (Rome, 1890), pp. 151–152; Otto's successor, Henry II, also sponsored a ducal son at confirmation, ibid., p. 167.

[34] Radulphus Glaber, *Vita domni Willelmi abbatis*, ed. Neithard Bulst, "Rodulfus Glabers Vita domni Willelmi abbatis. Neue Edition nach einer Handschrift des 11. Jahrhunderts (Paris, Bibliothèque Nationale, lat. 5390)," *DAEM* 30 (1974): 464: "Tunc quoque isdem Rotbertus, ut erat vir prudens ac strenuus, suggessit imperatori, ut filium, quem ei uxor sua . . . pepererat, catecuminum fieri per manum imperialem preciperet. Quod ille libentissime annuens, ut monitus fuerat, impleri mandavit ac propria puerum sustulit dextera eique nomen indidit Willelmum. Quem scilicet postmodum regina, coniux illius, ex sacro fonte suscepit baptismatis."

[35] *Canones Theodori*, bk. 2, ch. 4.8, in the version attributed to the *Discipulus Umbrensium*, in Paul Finsterwalder, ed., *Die Canones Theodori Cantuariensis und ihre Überlieferungsformen. Untersuchungen zu den Bussbüchern des 7., 8. and 9. Jahrhunderts*, vol. 1 (Weimar, 1929), p. 317: "In catechumino et baptismate et confirmatione unus potest esse pater si necesse est non est tamen consuetudo sed per singula singuli suscipiunt." See also sec. 7.69 of the *Canones Cottoniani*, attributed to Theodore, ibid., p. 275.

the sources and had less social importance than baptismal or confirmation sponsorship, but it does reflect the impulse to multiply occasions for sponsorship.[36]

There is some slight evidence that other parts of the initiation ceremonies were at least proposed as occasions for sponsorship. In this connection, we have a forged decretal letter (*Pervenit ad nos*), attributed to Pope Deusdedit (615–618), which insisted that marriages between spiritual kin be dissolved. At the end of the letter, the forger reminded his reader, a Bishop Gordianus, that sponsorship at any of seven points in the initiatory rituals, from the giving of salt to the conferring of confirmation, created spiritual kinship. So far as I know, the decretal *Pervenit ad nos* appeared for the first time in book 17, chapter 44, of Burchard of Worms' *Decretum*, which was compiled in the early eleventh century. However, the forger's views on the seven occasions for sponsorship had no reflection in society, insofar as I can tell. They were apparently a liturgical fantasy derived from the very real desire to find ways to gain more spiritual kinsmen.

Sponsorship at baptism and its two clones, sponsorship at confirmation and sponsorship at *catechumenus*, were rooted directly in the liturgy and were approved by the ecclesiastical authorities, but they did not satisfy the impulse to create more spiritual kinsmen. For this there were other occasions that emerged in the shadow world of Frankish and post-Frankish popular culture. Such sponsorship was beyond the control of the official church and generally beneath its notice. Because churchmen took little interest in these phenomena, they survive to us only as brief enigmatic references in scattered sources. Their exact origin and meaning remain obscure, but their existence is a reminder that spiritual kinship was so attractive that it insinuated itself into many aspects of medieval society and popular behavior.

References to unofficial occasions for creating spiritual kinship occur in sources after the later eighth century, except for an isolated and puzzling use of what may be the term *patrinus* (godfather) in the seventh-century *Chronicle of Fredegar*. The chronicle relates that Clovis, King of the Franks, and Alaric II, King of the Visigoths, entered into

---

[36] Flodoard of Rheims, *Annales*, year 945, ed. Philippe Lauer, CT, vol. 39 (Paris, 1905), pp. 95–96: "Gerberga regina filium Lauduni peperit, qui Karolus ad catezizandum vocitatus est." See also bk. 3, ch. 21 of Flodoard, *Historia ecclesiae remensis*, ed. J. Heller and G. Waitz, MGH SS, vol. 13 (Leipzig, 1881), p. 518, which recorded a letter of Hincmar of Rheims written "on behalf of a man who was tricked into holding his own son at the catechizing" (pro quodam, qui dolo deceptus fuerat, ut infantem proprium ad catezizandum teneret).

a state of peace that was symbolized by the following rite: "that Alaric would touch the beard of Clovis, becoming his *patrenus.*"[37] Adoptions through an act involving the hair or beard are familiar enough,[38] but what did the chronicler mean when he called Alaric the *patrenus* of Clovis? As far as I can tell, the word appears nowhere else. Merovingian Latin orthography was notoriously variable and the word could be a form of, or a copyist's mistake for, *patronus* (patron) or *patrinus* (godfather). In later centuries, medieval historians of the Franks drew on the *Chronicle of Fredegar* and they too were puzzled by the term. Their perplexity was expressed by their tendency to correct it to something they understood. Thus Aimon of Fleury (d. about 1010) restated it as *adoptivus pater*, while others "normalized" the word to *patrinus*. These latter included the author of the twelfth-century *Gesta Theoderici regis.*[39]

Baptismal kinship was such a widespread and deep-rooted social custom that older forms of alliance-building were assimilated into it. Because of this, it may well be that the author of the *Chronicle of Fredegar*, writing more than a century after the treaty between Alaric and Clovis, also interpreted the bond between the two kings in terms of baptismal kinship, which was already an important institution in his society. The beard-touching ceremony was a way to create a fictive parent/child bond and it perhaps seemed natural to describe it with a term from the most common Christian mode of creating such bonds, baptismal sponsorship. Thus we see in this seventh-century text and in its subsequent medieval interpretations the impulse to understand originally independent forms of alliance-building in terms of baptismal kinship.

Other references to occasions for creating a spiritual kinship analo-

[37] Fredegar, *Chronicarum quae dicuntur Fredegarii scholastici libri iv*, bk. 2, ch. 58, ed. Bruno Krusch, MGH SSRM, vol. 2 (Hanover, 1888), p. 82: "cum pacem inire coepissent huius convenientiae, ut Alaricus barbam tangerit Chlodovei, effectur ille patrenus, perpetuam ab invicem pacem servarint."

[38] Margret Wielers, *Zwischenstaatliche Beziehungsformen im frühen Mittelalter (Pax, Foedus, Amicitia, Fraternitas)* (Ph.D. diss., Münster, Westphalia, 1959), pp. 47–49; Karl A. Eckhardt, "Adoption," *Studia merovingica*, Bibliotheca rerum historicarum, vol. 11 (Aalen, 1975), pp. 254–255.

[39] Aimon of Fleury, *Gesta regum Francorum*, bk. 1, ch. 20, in M. Bouquet, ed., *Recueil des historiens des Gaules et de la France*, 2nd ed., 24 vols. (Paris, 1869), 3:41; *Gesta Theoderici regis*, ch. 15, ed. Bruno Krusch, MGH SSRM, vol. 2 (Hanover, 1888), p. 207: "Alaricus infirmior factus, pacem peciit, et hoc ordine concordia decreta fuit, ut, quia Clodoveus intonsus barba usque in haec tempora fuit, Alaricus illi eam detonderet, et patrinus ei hoc modo effectus, perpetuam ad invicem pacem servarent"; on other medieval interpretations of Fredegar's text, see Eckhardt, "Adoption," pp. 255–256.

gous to baptismal kinship are rather laconic. For example, the *Poenitentiale Vallicellanum II*, a ninth- or tenth-century text, forbade adultery with one's *commater sentiana*,[40] a term that may represent one of the kinds of spiritual kinship recognized by the church or an otherwise unattested variety of *commaternitas*. The *Poenitentiale Merseburgense c*, edited by Wasserschleben from a ninth-century manuscript, also forbade sexual contact with one's *cummater de sancto Joh*(anne).[41] This ninth-century coparenthood of Saint John has the same name as practices that have survived into modern times in Italy and elsewhere. In the present state of the evidence, there is no way to know if the name covers a common reality, but it well could.

For centuries the feast of Saint John the Baptist (June 24) has held a special place in popular belief. Depending on the time and place, Saint John's eve has been associated with bonfires, the gathering of medicinal herbs, and the witches' Sabbath.[42] In parts of southern Italy, Saint John's feast is also the occasion for creating the *comparaggio di San Giovanni*, as described by the anthropologist Gallatin Anderson. In her work, Anderson has translated *compare/commara* as "godfather/godmother." They are etymologically the terms for cofather and comother.

> There are three godparenthood rituals in southern Italy, all associated with San Giovanni Batista . . . in which the participants bind themselves in a communally-acknowledged pact of love, friendship, or brotherhood. . . .
>
> In San Benedetto del Tronto (Marche) the relationship, which may involve two individuals of the same or opposite sex, is known as that of "compare di fiori" (godfather of the flowers). The person wishing to initiate the pact prepares two bouquets of flowers in such fashion that the stem-ends are together so that the flowers intertwine. The bouquets are placed on a decorated tray, covered with a fancy shawl or cloth, and thus carried by a friend or relative to the home of the person who it is hoped will be "compare.". . . If the person receiving the tray wishes to enter the pact he sends a similar tray in acknowledgment on the day of San Pietro (St. Peter, June 29). . . . There is no renewal of the pact

---

[40] *Poenitentiale Vallicellanum II*, ch. 18, ed. F.W.H. Wasserschleben, *Die Bussordnungen der abendländischen Kirche* (Halle, 1851; reprint ed., Graz, 1958), p. 559.

[41] *Poenitentiale Merseburgense c*, ch. 13, ibid. p. 436.

[42] Arnald van Gennep, "La Saint-Jean dans les croyances et coutumes populaires de la Savoie," *Journal de psychologie normale et pathologique* 24 (1927):26–77.

on subsequent occasions, and it lasts just as long as it is kept active by the participants. . . .

In Villa Sebastiano (Abruzzi) the relationship, which is between a boy and a girl from ten to fourteen years of age, is known as "compare del fiume" (godfather of the river). The young people go to the river bank, pledge their devotion, and join right hands. Then they kneel and dip their clasped hands in the water three times, after which they call each other "compare" and "commara.". . .

In Villanova Montelione (Sardinia) two or four people . . . enter into a "compari di fogo" (godfather of fire) or "compari di San Giovanni" (godfather of St. John) relationship. A fire is built from kindling contributed by the participants, who holding hands, sing and dance around the blaze. Then the circle is broken and one of the four takes a rectangular cloth. . . . Each person makes a knot in an opposing corner of the cloth, after which knots are passed along so that everyone ends up with another's knot. The ceremony is considered effective only if the fire continues to burn merrily.[43]

As is evident from Anderson's report, the means used to create the *comparaggio di San Giovanni* are as varied as local Italian folk traditions can make them. I have found no such description of medieval rites for creating the pact and, in view of the tradition's modern diversity, any speculation on their existence is pointless. However, in an eighth-century sermon that survives in a twelfth-century manuscript there is information about the meaning attributed to the relationship.

The sermon was composed for lay people and was couched in simple, direct Latin. After a comment on the observation of Sunday rest and before an exhortation to teach godchildren the Creed, the Lord's Prayer, and the belief in the Trinity, the preacher declares that "you must observe well the *comparato sancto Iohanni*, because you accepted faith and holy love among you; and he who corrupts that faith and love commits a serious sin."[44] Dom Germain Morin, the editor of the text, was puzzled by the phrase *comparato sancto Iohanni* and conceded that it was "*impossible pour moi de dire ce que signifient ces mots.*"[45] I believe

---

[43] Gallatin Anderson, "Il Comparaggio: The Italian Godparenthood Complex," *SJA* 13 (1957):44–45.

[44] Germain Morin, "Textes inédits relatifs au Symbole et à la vie chrétienne," *RB* 22 (1905):517: "Comparato sancto Iohanni bene debetis colere, quia fidem et caritatem sanctam accepistis inter uos; et qui ipsam fidem et caritatem corruperit, malum peccatum facit."

[45] Ibid.

that the phrase is a corruption of *compaternitas sancti Iohanni* and that the attribution of faith (*fides*) and holy love (*caritas sancta*) as its characteristics permit us to glimpse one of the variant ways to create spiritual kinship that had developed in Frankish popular culture.

The impulse to create new occasions for spiritual kinship was not exhausted by the end of the Carolingian period. (Indeed, it has not been exhausted yet in the area of modern Mexico studied by Hugo Nutini and Betty Bell.)[46] However, by then it was well established that spiritual kinsmen could be gained in many ways, all of which probably imitated baptismal sponsorship and none of which equaled or surpassed that form of sponsorship in intensity or importance. In a sense, one could have as many spiritual kinsmen as one wanted, although the strength of the bond would vary. Yet at the same time there was a price to pay, for all of the ecclesiastically sanctioned occasions for sponsorship carried with them a ban on sexual intimacy between spiritual kinsmen. This had not always been so, but in the eighth century, under papal and Byzantine influence, an incest taboo was incorporated into the flourishing Frankish spiritual family. This new development will be treated in the next chapter.

[46] Nutini and Bell, *Ritual Kinship*, 1:59–61.

EIGHT

SPIRITUAL KINSMEN AND
SEXUAL TABOOS

In the Frankish sources prior to the eighth century, one feature that has characterized both the medieval and most modern variations of spiritual kinship is strikingly absent: there is no prohibition of incest between persons related by such kinship. The absence of such a sexual taboo is unexpected, particularly when viewed against the background of what is known about the many historic and surviving variants of baptismal kinship. Anthropologists have studied dozens of extant godparent systems and none of those with any vitality lacks a sexual taboo of some sort. Indeed, in many systems it is one of the most prominent features.[1] The Frankish situation appears even more anomalous when it is noted that the Byzantine variety of baptismal kinship had such a taboo, which had been incorporated into the civil law by Justinian in A.D. 530. Because of all this, the historical process by which the Frankish church adopted a prohibition on sexual contact among spiritual kin requires some elucidation.

The Christian church was heir to the Jewish conviction, so marked in the Book of Leviticus, that the sexual behavior of Yahweh's followers was of deep concern to Him and that He had prescribed clear rules for judging the propriety of such behavior. The Christian church has historically acted on this inherited conviction, and thus the regulation of sexual behavior, including marriage, has bulked large in both the

---

[1] There is no satisfactory historical or synthetic treatment of the sexual prohibitions arising out of spiritual kinship. The following book and articles discuss aspects of the issue: Charles J. Erasmus, "Current Theories on Incest Prohibition in the Light of Ceremonial Kinship," *The Kroeber Anthropological Society Papers* 2 (1950):42–50; Knut Weibust, "Ritual Coparenthood in Peasant Societies," *Ethnologia Scandinavica* (1972):105–107, 111–114; Eva Krener, "An Evaluation of the Major Theories Concerning Compadrazgo in Latin America," *Folk* 14/15 (1972/73):103–118, esp. pp. 103 and 111; Stephen Gudeman, "The *Compadrazgo* as a Reflection of the Natural and Spiritual Person: The Curl Prize Essay, 1971," *Proceedings of the Royal Anthropological Institute* (1972):45–71; Jack Goody, *The Development of the Family and Marriage in Europe* (Cambridge, 1983), pp. 194–204.

legislation and the admonitory literature of Christianity.[2] However, the emphases within this concern about sexual behavior have varied according to culture and circumstance. One of the issues that rose in importance during the Middle Ages was incest and its prevention.

When the Christian church made its peace with the Roman Empire under Constantine and began to attempt to influence public policy, the chief problem of sexual and marital morality was divorce, a practice deemed incompatible with the Christian view of marriage and yet quite legal in Roman society and deeply rooted in customary mores.[3] The ecclesiastical concern with divorce is reflected in surviving conciliar decisions. Thus the twenty extant Gallic church councils of the Roman period (that is, from 314 to 506) regularly issued canons on divorce and remarriage, but contained nothing more than vague, sparse references to incest, specifically to the degrees of kinship within which marriage was forbidden.[4]

In contrast, the Gallic councils of the Frankish period (from 511 to 695) expended much effort to define and extend the network of affinal and consanguinal relationships that rendered a sexual union incestuous.[5] The reasons why the Frankish bishops were so concerned about incest are not easy to discern, although this preoccupation was perhaps related to Frankish customs, which encouraged marriages among relatively close kin.[6] On the other hand, some scholars have

[2] See Vern L. Bullough and James A. Brundage, *Sexual Practices and the Medieval Church* (Buffalo, N.Y., 1982).

[3] Jean Gaudemet, *L'Eglise dans l'Empire romain, ivᵉ–vᵉ siècles*, Histoire du droit et des institutions de l'Eglise en occident, vol. 3 (Paris, 1958), pp. 507–513; Pierre Nautin, "Divorce et remariage dans la tradition de l'église latine," *Recherches de science religieuse* 62 (1974):7–54; Henri Crouzel, "Le remariage après séparation pour adultère selon les Pères latins," *BLE* 75 (1974):189–204; Charles Munier, *L'Eglise dans l'Empire romain (iiᵉ–iiiᵉ siècles)*, Histoire du droit et des institutions de l'Eglise en occident, vol. 2, pt. 3 (Paris, 1979), pp. 36–55.

[4] Paul Mikat, "Die Inzestverbote des Konzils von Epaon—Ein Beitrag zur Geschichte des fränkischen Eherechts," *Rechtsbewahrung und Rechtsentwicklung. Festschrift für Heinrich Lange zum 70. Geburtstag* (Munich, 1970), p. 63. For the councils, see *Concilia Galliae A.314–A.506*, ed. Charles Munier, CCSL, vol. 148 (Turnhout, 1963).

[5] Paul Mikat, "Zu den Voraussetzungen der Begegnung von fränkischer und kirchlicher Eheauffassung in Gallien," *Diakonia et ius. Festgabe für Heinrich Flatten zum 65. Geburtstag* (Munich, 1973), p. 25. The councils were edited by Carlo de Clercq, *Concilia Galliae A.511–A.695*, CCSL, vol. 148A (Turnhout, 1963). Georges Duby, "Le mariage dans la société du haut moyen âge," *Il matrimonio nella società altomedievale*, SSAM, vol. 24, pt. 1 (Spoleto, 1977), pp. 25–29, discusses the efforts of proponents of "the ecclesiastical model of marriage" to define and enforce incest rules. He dates their success to the ninth century, but the beginnings of the effort are already evident in the sixth century.

[6] See Goody, *Development*, pp. 34–41, on marriages between close kin in Germanic society.

held that it was a reflection of eastern influence, since a similar concern is discernible there in the fourth century, particularly with Bishop Basil of Caesarea's letter to Diodorus, which disapproved a man's marriage to the sister of his dead wife, a prohibition not found in the Old Testament. Paul Mikat has argued, however, that the earliest western council to concern itself extensively with incest, that held at Epaon in 517, can be explained by indigenous developments and requires no postulation of eastern influence.[7]

The immediate intellectual inspiration for the rising tide of concern with defining and repressing incest was the Old Testament itself, particularly the holiness code in the Book of Leviticus. Raymund Kottje has examined the growing influence of the Old Testament on law and liturgy from the sixth to the eighth centuries in the West, and in the process has noted the tendency to read Old Testament provisions in a literal fashion rather than in the symbolic way in which they were interpreted after the Carolingian Renaissance. Kottje sees in this development an Irish influence, which spread on the Continent in the early Middle Ages. In particular, he points to the effort to impose Old Testament views on such matters as Sunday observance, tithing, liturgy, ritual purity and impurity, and the incompatibility of sexual activity with holiness.[8] Peter Browe also amassed extensive evidence of the influence of Old Testament notions on early medieval provisions for restricting access to holy things by those who were unclean, a category that included women who had recently given birth or were menstruating as well as individuals of either sex who had recently engaged in voluntary or involuntary sexual activity, and newly wedded persons.[9]

In this general atmosphere of reviving Old Testament norms, the concern with incest becomes comprehensible. Here Leviticus 18:5–18 was the most important scriptural passage:

> I am Yahweh your God. You must keep my laws and my customs. Whoever complies with them will find life in them. I am Yahweh. None of you may approach a woman who is closely related to him, to uncover her nakedness. I am Yahweh. You must not uncover the nakedness of your father or mother. She is your mother—you must not uncover her nakedness. You must

---

[7] Mikat, "Die Inzestverbote," pp. 64–65. Basil of Caesarea's views on incest are treated in Jean Fleury, *Recherches historiques sur les empêchements de parenté dans le mariage canonique des origines aux Fausses Décrétales* (Paris, 1933), pp. 32–36.

[8] Raymund Kottje, *Studien zum Einfluss des Alten Testamentes auf Recht und Liturgie des frühen Mittelalters (6–8 Jahrhundert)*, BHF, vol. 23 (Bonn, 1964).

[9] Peter Browe, *Beiträge zur Sexualethik des Mittelalters*, Breslauer Studien zur historischen Theologie, vol. 23 (Breslau, 1932).

not uncover the nakedness of your father's wife; it is your father's nakedness. You must not uncover the nakedness of your sister, whether she is your father's or your mother's daughter. Whether she is born in the same house or elsewhere, you must not uncover her nakedness. You must not uncover the nakedness of your own son or daughter; for their nakedness is your own. You must not uncover the nakedness of the daughter of your father's wife, born of your father. She is your sister; you must not uncover her nakedness. You must not uncover the nakedness of your father's sister; for it is your father's flesh. You must not uncover the nakedness of your mother's sister; for it is your mother's flesh. You must not uncover the nakedness of your father's brother; you must therefore not approach his wife, for she is your aunt. You must not uncover the nakedness of your daughter-in-law. She is your son's wife; you must not uncover her nakedness. You must not uncover the nakedness of your brother's wife; for it is your brother's nakedness. You must not uncover the nakedness of a woman and of her daughter too; you must not take the daughter of her son or of her daughter to uncover their nakedness. They are your own flesh; it would be incest. You must not take into your harem a woman and her sister at the same time, uncovering the latter's nakedness while the former is still alive.

In the century between the Council of Epaon (517) and the Council of Clichy (626/27), the Frankish bishops reenacted the Old Testament strictures against incest, with some additions, notably a prohibition on marriage between a man and his deceased wife's sister, a union that had not been mentioned in Leviticus. And by the time that Frankish conciliar activity petered out in 695, a Christian (always considered male in the canons) was forbidden to marry his mother, his sister or half-sister, his wife's sister, his brother's widow, his step-mother, his maternal or paternal first cousin, his maternal or paternal uncle's widow, his step-daughter, his son's widow, or his wife's mother.[10]

In view of the pronounced interest that Frankish councils took in the repression of incest, it is striking that spiritual kinship, which certainly existed, was *not* an expressed reason for declaring a sexual relationship incestuous in the sixth or seventh century. Indeed, the

[10] Fleury, *Recherches*, pp. 84–113; Mikat, "Die Inzestverbote," pp. 63–84. The Council of Tours (567), canon 22, repeated verbatim Leviticus 18:5–18.20 (*Concilia Galliae A.511–A.695*, pp. 188–191). See also canon 30 of the Council of Epaon (517), ibid., pp. 32–33; canon 18 of the Council of Orléans (511), ibid., pp. 9–10; canon 11 of the Council of Orléans (538), ibid., p. 118; canon 16 of the Council of Paris (614), ibid., p. 280; and canon 10 of the Council of Clichy (626–627), ibid., p. 293.

virtual universality of the ban on sexual contact between godparent and godchild would lead one to expect to find at least that specific restriction.

Such an omission can be traced to a feature of the Frankish sponsoring custom. For although I have found no explicit rule requiring that a sponsor be of the same sex as the sponsored, I have also found no other pattern in the Frankish or Anglo-Saxon West prior to the eighth century. In that century, the canonical tradition claiming the authority of Archbishop Theodore of Canterbury (668–690), who was a Byzantine cleric from Tarsus in Asia Minor, defended the position that cross-sexual sponsorship was permitted.[11] The very fact that such a Byzantine view required defense in the West implies that it was not the norm.

In this light, the silence of the western church on sexual prohibitions arising out of spiritual kinship becomes explicable. Prior to the eighth century, sponsor and sponsored were of the same sex and thus marriage was not a possibility. Perhaps the best way to describe the situation in pre-eighth-century Frankish Gaul is to say that a prohibition on marriage between sponsor and sponsored was implicit in the notion of spiritual kinship but did not need to be made explicit until same-sex sponsorship gave way to cross-sex sponsorship, a change that points to papal-Byzantine influence. In addition, the Franks were slow to adopt a prohibition on sexual contact between coparents. When they did, they were probably also influenced by the practices of Italy and the East.

Spiritual Kinship and Marriage in Byzantine Territory

In antiquity, the heartland of Christianity had been the shores of the eastern Mediterranean and certain of its hinterlands, notably Egypt and Anatolia. Baptismal sponsorship and its social consequences were well known in these areas, although modern scholars have largely ignored the topic. The convulsions of the early Middle Ages, including the Germanic migrations into the western Empire and the rapid spread of Islam in the Near East, changed the face of eastern Christianity, particularly since many Christian populations lived henceforth under alien religious domination. The Byzantine Empire, centered in

[11] *Discipulus Umbrensium*, bk. 2, ch. 4.10, in *Die Canones Theodori Cantuariensis und ihre Überlieferungsformen. Untersuchungen zu den Bussbüchern des 7., 8. und 9. Jahrhunderts*, ed. Paul W. Finsterwalder, vol. 1 (Weimar, 1929), p. 317: "Viro autem licet feminam suscipere in baptismo similiter et feminae virum suscipere." See also canon 180 of the *Canones Gregorii*, ibid., p. 269.

Asia Minor and Greece and with territories in Italy, sheltered and fostered Orthodox Christianity, which was a major eastern heir of the ancient church. It was in the context of this Byzantine church that the spiritual kinship arising out of baptism was first assimilated into natural kinship in such a realistic way that it demanded an incest taboo.[12]

The earliest clear evidence of a ban on sexual contact between sponsor and sponsored comes from sixth-century Byzantium. In October 530 the Byzantine Emperor Justinian (529–565) addressed a response to the Praetorian Prefect Julian, who had inquired about the legality of certain marriages. Justinian's letter was subsequently incorporated into the *Code* of the Roman civil law (book 5, title 4, law 26). The chief point at issue was the propriety of a man's marrying a girl to whom he had been a quasi-parent, although he had not legally adopted her. In Justinian's letter the girl is identified as an *alumna*, best translated as a foster-daughter, since she was not a ward (*pupilla*) in the legal sense but was being protected and raised by the man in question. Justinian had been asked whether the man might marry his *alumna* after she had been freed from his control.

Classical Roman law had a good deal to say about marriages between young girls and men in authority over them. All persons deemed incapable of managing their own economic affairs (a group that included minors, the mentally ill, and women) were legally required to have a guardian (*tutor*), whose duty was primarily to protect the financial interests of the ward (*pupillus/a*).[13] Such a position of guardianship was open to abuse, one form of which was to pressure a female ward to marry the guardian or his son so that the husband could gain permanent control of the girl's property. In order to prevent such an outcome, a tutor was flatly forbidden to marry his ward or to marry her to his son. Accordingly, Justinian's *Code* (book 5, title 6) brought together eight laws issued by his predecessors that worked out the details of such a prohibition.[14]

[12] Byzantine marriage law, as it worked out the popular repugnance felt for sexual contact between spiritual kin, is outlined by Karl Zachariä von Lingenthal, *Geschichte des griechisch-römischen Rechts*, 3rd ed. (Berlin, 1893; reprint ed., Aalen, 1955), pp. 69–71. Zachariä von Lingenthal's approach is more legal than historical and shows little interest in the cultural context of the laws. See also Fleury, *Recherches*, pp. 73–84, 139–144.

[13] On the Roman law of guardianship, see Richard W. Leage, *Roman Private Law Founded on the Institutes of Gaius and Justinian*, 3rd ed. by A. M. Prichard (London, 1961), pp. 128–142, or Joseph A. C. Thomas, *Textbook of Roman Law*, 2 vols. (Amsterdam, 1976), 2:453–468. I wish to thank Dr. John Fowler for suggesting to me the importance of the Roman law of guardianship for understanding Justinian's decision of 530.

[14] *Codex Iustinianus*, bk. 5, title 6, ed. Paul Krueger, *CIC*, vol. 2 (Berlin, 1895), pp. 199–200.

In the pre-Christian Empire, the financial rectitude of the guardian was the primary concern of legislators. The first Christian emperor, Constantine, introduced a moral element into the law when he laid down strict penalties for a guardian who sexually violated his ward (*Code*, book 9, title 9, law 10). It was within this traditional Roman legal context of safeguarding the economic and moral interests of young girls under the protection of adult males that Justinian's decision of 530 must be understood.

The actual relationship between an *alumna* and her protector could be close or distant, according to the individual circumstances. But the emperor's response presupposed that those who questioned him were troubled by the possibility that the man had treated the girl like a daughter and subsequently decided to marry her. Justinian dismissed such behavior as unlikely, but certainly reprehensible if it occurred: "No man can be found who is so wicked [*impius*] as to afterwards marry a girl who in the first place, he treated as his daughter." However, provided that "he did not originally bring her up as his daughter, but gave her her freedom, and afterwards deemed ·her worthy to be married to him," Justinian saw "nothing impious or contrary to law in such a union."[15]

Justinian's letter to the Praetorian Prefect Julian took up a second topic as well, which also touched on what constituted a proper sexual union:

> Clearly any woman should be entirely forbidden to marry a man who received her from most holy baptism, whether she was his *alumna* or not, since nothing else can so bring about paternal affection and a just prohibition of marriage as a relationship of that sort by which their souls are joined through God's mediation.[16]

The context in which this decision was rendered suggests that Justinian objected to such a sexual union because the "paternal affection" uniting the man and woman was such as to render it incestuous. In other words, they were spiritual parent and child, whose marriage would be an unclean thing. Justinian's decision is also important be-

---

[15] Bk. 5, title 4, law 26 of the *Code*, as tr. by S. P. Scott in *The Civil Law Including the Twelve Tables, the Institutes of Gaius, the Rules of Ulpian* . . . , 17 vols. (Cincinnati, 1932), 13:154.

[16] *Codex Iustinianus*, bk. 5, title 4, law 26, p. 197: "ea videlicet persona omnimodo ad nuptias venire prohibenda, quam aliquis, sive alumna sit sive non, a sacrosancto suscepit baptismate, cum nihil aliud sic inducere potest paternam affectionem et iustam nuptiarum prohibitionem, quam huiusmodi nexus, per quem deo mediante animae eorum copulatae sunt."

cause of an inference that can be drawn from it: in sixth-century Byzantium one could sponsor someone of the opposite sex or, to read the law literally, a male could sponsor a female. This custom lay at the root of the precocious development at Byzantium of attempts to regulate the sexual behavior of godparent and godchild.

Justinian's decision of 530 is the earliest reference in either the civil or the canon law to baptismal kinship as an impediment to marriage. Most modern canonists have assumed, without reference to specific evidence, that his decision was not an innovation but rather a ratification of existing Christian folk attitudes that disapproved of sexual contact between godparent and godchild.[17] Such an assumption can be supported by two pieces of sixth-century evidence that confirm the existence of a body of opinion in Byzantine territory that was hostile to the violation of baptismal kinship by sexual contact.

The first evidence comes from the pen of Procopius, Justinian's contemporary and chronicler, who in his *Secret History* recorded the scandal caused by an amorous affair between Antonina, wife of the Byzantine general Belisarius, and Theodosius, Belisarius' godson. The story is worth repeating in its entirety:

> There was a certain youth from Thrace in the household of Belisarius, Theodosius by name, who had been born of ancestors who professed the faith of those called Eunomians. Now when Belisarius was about to embark on the voyage to Libya, he bathed this youth in the sacred bath, from which he lifted him with his own hands, thus making him the adopted child of himself and his wife, as is customary for Christians to make adoptions, and consequently Antonina loved Theodosius, as she naturally would, as being her son through the sacred word, and with very particular solicitude she kept him near herself. And straightway she fell extraordinarily in love with him in the course of this voyage, and having become insatiate in her passion, she shook off both fear and respect for everything both divine and human and had intercourse with him, at first in secret, but finally even in the presence of servants of both sexes. For being by now possessed by this passion and manifestly smitten with love, she could see no longer any obstacle to the deed. And on one occasion Belisarius caught them in the very act in Carthage, yet he willingly allowed himself

[17] Franz Laurin, "Die geistliche Verwandtschaft in ihrer geschichtlichen Entwicklung bis zum Rechte der Gegenwart," *AKKR* 15 (1866):221–222; Joseph Petrovits, *The New Church Law on Matrimony* (Philadelphia, 1921), p. 279; Gaudemet, *L'Eglise*, p. 528; Fleury, *Recherches*, p. 78.

to be deceived by his wife. For though he found them both in an underground chamber and was transported with rage, she, without either playing the coward or attempting to conceal the deed, remarked "I came down here in order to hide with the aid of the boy the most valuable of our booty, so that it may not get to the knowledge of the Emperor." Now she said this as a mere pretext, but he, appearing to be satisfied, dropped the matter, though he could see that the belt which supported the drawers of Theodosius, covering his private parts, had been loosened. For under compulsion of love for the woman, he would have it that the testimony of his own eyes was absolutely untrustworthy.

Now this wantonness kept growing worse and worse until it had become an unspeakable scandal, and though people in general, observing what was going on, kept silence about it, yet a certain slavegirl named Macedonia, approaching Belisarius in Syracuse, when he had conquered Sicily, and binding her master by the most dread oaths that he would never betray her to her mistress, told him the whole story, adducing as witnesses two lads who were charged with the service of the bedchamber. Upon learning these things, Belisarius ordered certain of his attendants to destroy Theodosius. He, however, learned this in advance and fled to Ephesus. For most of the persons in attendance upon Belisarius, moved by the instability of the man's temper, were more eager to please the wife than to seem to the husband well-disposed towards him, and for this reason they betrayed the command laid upon them at that time touching Theodosius.[18]

Procopius' *Secret History* is difficult to evaluate since it is a bitter, scurrilous attack on prominent persons, including Procopius' patrons, whom he praises lavishly in other works. Procopius was not above gross distortion and fabrication in the pursuit of his underground vendetta against his social betters. He was particularly hostile to Justinian's wife Theodora and to Antonina, the lady in the account quoted above.

Elizabeth Fisher has studied Procopius' portrayal of these two prominent women and concludes that he was offended by the fact that both violated the common Byzantine assumptions about how women should behave.[19] Theodora and Antonina were hardly the dependent,

[18] Procopius, *The Anecdota or Secret History*, bk. 1, ch. 1, ed. and tr. H. B. Dewing, the Loeb Classical Library, vol. 6 (London and Cambridge, Mass., 1935), pp. 10–13.

[19] Elizabeth A. Fisher, "Theodora and Antonina in the Historia Arcana: History and/ or Fiction," *Arethusa* 11 (1978):253–279.

sheltered, intellectually subservient, and male-directed females of Procopius' ideal. Indeed, in the *Secret History* they are portrayed as independent, influential actors who exert abnormal and harmful influence
over their respective husbands. Antonina's behavior toward Theodosius, her husband's baptismal son, thus fits Procopius' pattern of de-
picting her as flouting conventional norms and ignoring natural restraints, particularly restraints on sexual behavior. In addition, Belisarius' blindness to his wife's blatant transgressions simply confirmed
Procopius' unflattering portrait of the great general.[20] We shall never
know whether Antonina actually violated social conventions and religious sensibilities by taking Theodosius as her lover. However, Procopius' use of such a transgression to taint his victim is certainly evidence of public opinion about proper sexual behavior between
godparent and godchild in sixth-century Byzantine society.

The case of Antonina has a further implication as well, since Belisarius was the actual sponsor of Theodosius and there is no reason to
believe that Antonina took part in the liturgical ceremonies of baptism
and sponsorship. Procopius' account assumes, however, that the wife
shares the spiritual parenthood with her husband: "and consequently
Antonina loved Theodosius, as she naturally would, as being her son
through the sacred word."[21] This tendency of spiritual kinship to envelop in its web the close kinsmen both of the sponsor and of the
sponsored did much to complicate the subsequent marriage laws,[22] but
it was a spontaneous popular response to the emergence of a new form
of kinship.

The second piece of evidence for sixth-century attitudes is a text
from Pope Gregory I (590–604), who, although Latin in speech, was
Byzantine in citizenship and in much of his outlook. (At this time,
central and southern Italy were outliers of the Byzantine world, a fact
too often forgotten in view of their subsequent incorporation into the
cultural orbit of the West.)[23] Gregory's *Dialogues*, composed about 594,

[20] Ibid., pp. 269–270.

[21] Procopius, *Secret History*, bk. 1, ch. 1, p. 11.

[22] On the extension of spiritual kinship to spouses, called by medieval canonists *cognatio spiritualis superveniens*, see Joseph Freisen, *Geschichte des kanonischen Eherechts bis zum
Verfall der Glossenliteratur*, 2nd ed. (Paderborn, 1893; reprint ed., Aalen, 1963), pp. 549–
555.

[23] Jeffrey Richards, *The Popes and the Papacy in the early Middle Ages, 476–752* (London,
1979), pp. 270–283. See also Jules Gay, "Quelques remarques sur les papes grecs et
syriens avant la querelle des iconoclasts (678–715)," *Mélanges offerts à M. Gustave Schlumberger*, vol. 1 (Paris, 1924), pp. 40–54; E. H. Fischer, "Gregor der Grosse und Byzanz,"
ZSSRG, Kanonistische Abteilung, 36 (1950):15–44; and W. N. Schumacher, "Byzantinisches in Rom," *RQCAKG* 68 (1973):104–124.

record a story told by Maximianus, Bishop of Syracuse, who had been abbot of Gregory's monastery at Rome.[24] According to this story, a court official in the province of Valeria, east of Rome, had raped his young goddaughter, whom he had received from the baptismal font during the Easter vigil. The next day was Easter and, for the sake of his reputation, he went unrepentant to church services, though clearly apprehensive about divine punishment. When no ill befell him he was bold enough to attend church for six days in succession. But on the seventh day he died suddenly without having taken advantage of his opportunity to repent. When he had been buried, his bones burned to ashes in his grave, an occurrence that was interpreted as an external sign of what was happening invisibly to his soul for his failure to repent so wicked a crime.

Gregory's tale was not primarily about the sexual behavior of spiritual kin, but about a sinner's failure to repent when God mercifully provided an opportunity. However, the evidence the story provides for public opinion of such behavior is precious. Thus the deed was called a "terrible thing," not only in itself but as a violation of a sacred relationship with a spiritual daughter and a betrayal of the trust of the child's parents. The implicit assumption that a girl should be safe with her godfather is shared in many contemporary Latin American societies, where one of the few adult males with whom one would trust female relatives is a spiritual kinsman.[25] Such a violation of a sacred bond was thought by Gregory to be worthy of the destruction of both body and soul.

Justinian's decision of 530 was, then, no fiat from above. Rather, it reflected widespread disapproval of the violation of the holy bond between godparent and godchild. Between the seventh and the ninth centuries, Byzantine canon and civil law extended this prohibition of sexual contact between spiritual kin, although the web of marital impediments did not yet extend to the same range of prohibited degrees of kinship that governed affinal and consanguineous kin.[26]

[24] Gregory I, *Dialogi libri iv*, bk. 4, ch. 33, ed. Umberto Moricca, Istituto storico italiano per il medio evo, Fonti per la storia d'Italia, vol. 57 (Rome, 1924), pp. 277–278.

[25] Benjamin D. Paul, "Ritual Kinship: With Special Reference to Godparenthood in Middle America," (Ph.D. diss., University of Chicago, 1942), pp. 67–68; Erasmus, "Current Theories," pp. 44–45; Eric R. Wolf, "San José: Subcultures of a 'Traditional' Coffee Municipality," in *The People of Puerto Rico*, ed. Julian H. Steward (Urbana, Ill., 1956), pp. 208–209; Norman W. Whitten, *Class, Kinship and Power in an Ecuadorian Town: The Negroes of San Lorenzo* (Stanford, 1965), pp. 102–103, 120.

[26] Laurin, "Die geistliche Verwandtschaft," pp. 222–223, briefly described the ultimate extent of Byzantine sexual prohibitions arising out of baptismal sponsorship. These prohibitions tended to imitate in extent those arising out of blood kinship. See

The earliest evidence for a prohibition on sexual contact between coparents appears in the sources more than 160 years after Justinian's law. In 692 the Emperor Justinian II convoked a church council that met in the domed hall of the imperial palace at Constantinople, called the Trullos, hence its usual designation as the Council in Trullo. This council was intended to complement the ecumenical councils of 553 and 680, which had treated only doctrinal matters.

The Council in Trullo issued 102 canons highly critical of popular practices, canons that were concerned with improving the discipline of the church.[27] In canon 53, the bishops forbade marriage between a man who had received a child from the font and the child's widowed mother because, as the canon stated, a spiritual relationship was more important than and took precedence over a physical one. Thus for the first time there was a prohibition of marriage because of the spiritual relationship of coparenthood, which was called *compaternitas* or *commaternitas* in Latin and *pneumatikē sungeneia* in Greek. According to canon 53, existing marriages between coparents were to be tolerated, but if any persons created such a union after the promulgation of the canon they were required to separate and to undergo the punishments prescribed for fornicators.[28]

In the first half of the eighth century, the Emperor Leo III and his son Constantine V issued the most ambitious codification of Byzantine law since Justinian's great *Code* of 534. The scholarly consensus has been that the new code, called the *Ecloga* ("Selection"), was issued in March of 726. Recently, however, an alternate date of 741 has been vigorously defended by Otto Kresten.[29]

Jean Dauvillier and Carlo de Clercq, *Le mariage en droit canonique oriental* (Paris, 1936), pp. 146–153.

[27] On Justinian II and his Council in Trullo, see Franz Görres, "Justinian II und das römische Papsttum," *BZ* 17 (1908):432–454; V. Laurent, "L'oeuvre canonique du concile *in Trullo* (691–692), source primaire du droit de l'Eglise orientale," *Revue des études byzantines* 23 (1965):7–41; and Constance Head, *Justinian II of Byzantium* (Madison, Wis., 1972), pp. 65–79, 132–136.

[28] Council in Trullo, canon 53, in Mansi 11:967, tr. by Henry R. Percival in *The Seven Ecumenical Councils of the Church*, vol. 14 of A Select Library of Nicene and Post-Nicene Fathers of the Christian Church, second series (New York, 1916), p. 390: "Whereas the spiritual relationship is greater than fleshly affinity; and since it has come to our knowledge that in some places certain persons who become sponsors to children in holy salvation-bearing baptism, afterwards contract matrimony with their mothers (being widows), we decree that for the future nothing of this sort is to be done. But if any, after the present canon, shall be observed to do this, they must, in the first place desist from this unlawful marriage, and then be subjected to the penalties of fornicators."

[29] Otto Kresten, "Datierungsprobleme 'isaurischer' Eherechtsnovellen I.Coll.I.26,"

Justinian's *Code*, which was the culmination of classical Roman imperial legal development, had been rendered increasingly obsolete by two centuries of momentous change. Its usefulness was further lessened by the fact that it had been written primarily in Latin, which was no longer widely understood in the predominantly Greek empire of the eighth century. Thus the *Ecloga* was composed in Greek and it incorporated many of the significant legal changes that had been introduced into practice in the centuries since Justinian's *Code*. In particular, the sections of the *Ecloga* dealing with marriage were more overtly influenced by Christian norms than had been the corresponding portions of Justinian's work.[30] Spiritual kinship arising out of baptismal sponsorship was one of the matters whose impact on marriage had burgeoned in the interval since Justinian, a development of which the *Ecloga* took account.

In the new code, three categories of relationship were recognized as impediments to a proper sexual union: relationship by blood, relationship by marriage, and relationship by baptismal kinship. Relative to the third bond, the *Ecloga* specified:

> Marriage is forbidden between those who are bound together by the tie of salvation-bringing baptism, that is to say the sponsor and his goddaughter and her mother, and also the son of the sponsor with the goddaughter or her mother.[31]

This text reaffirmed the decision of Justinian (no sexual union of godfather and goddaughter) and that of the Council in Trullo (no sexual union of coparents), but it also codified two extensions of the prohibition of sexual contact among spiritual kin. First, it forbade marriage between a natural and a spiritual child of the same person, thus recognizing "spiritual siblingship" as an impediment to marriage. Second, the law forbade marriage between a child and his parent's coparent. Thus the *Ecloga* revealed a tendency to make the impediment of spiritual kinship comparable in extent to that of blood kinship.

As in the case of Justinian's pronouncement of 530, it is prudent to assume that the new code was ratifying popular attitudes about spir-

---

Forschungen zur byzantinischen Rechtsgeschichte, vol. 7: *Fontes Minores*, vol. 4 (Frankfort am Main, 1981), pp. 48–53.

[30] *Ecloga*, tr. by Edwin H. Freshfield as *A Manual of Roman Law: The* Ecloga *published by the Emperors Leo III and Constantine V of Isauria* (Cambridge, 1926). On Christian influence in the *Ecloga*'s marriage law, see Alexander A. Vasiliev, *History of the Byzantine Empire* 2nd ed., 2 vols. (Madison, Wis., 1964), 2:242–243.

[31] *Ecloga*, ch. 2.2, pp. 72–73.

itual kinship. I have, however, found no Byzantine source from the period between Justinian and Leo III to substantiate this assumption.

The early Christians had seen the bond between baptizer and baptized as another source of spiritual kinship and the *Ecloga* also acknowledged its importance for the incest taboo:

> Moreover any man who has baptized a woman cannot afterwards marry her, since she has thereby become his daughter; nor can he marry her mother or her daughter, nor can his son do so; for the marital relations cannot be combined with the paternal. For nothing is so able to induce a paternal relationship and [so cause] a just impediment to marriage as such a bond whereby the souls are united, through God's mediation.[32]

In the theology of the eighth century, any person could baptize another in an emergency, but in ordinary circumstances baptisms were performed by the clergy. This provision of the *Ecloga* would doubtless apply to anyone who had performed a baptism, but in fact it would most vitally affect the clergy, who were thereby forbidden to marry the many spiritual kin whom they acquired over the course of a career. This was a matter of minor practical importance because priests in the Byzantine church could marry only prior to ordination and hence before they had acquired spiritual kin from baptizing.[33] Of more practical significance was the fact that a priest's children were restricted in their potential marriage partners by being forbidden to marry any person baptized by their father, a ban that could obviously pose problems in a small rural village.

The law ended by restating in Greek Justinian's conclusion to his law of 530, but it added a significant clarification: "for the marital relations cannot be combined with the paternal." In this, the *Ecloga* reflected the position that where spiritual kinship was concerned it was offensive and incestuous for the domain of paternal bonds to overlap with that of sexual union. The two spheres of life were seen as incompatible, and the law was willing to punish their confusion.

The *Ecloga* explicitly forbade marriage among baptismal kin, but the implication of the legislation was that *any* sexual contact was banned. In part 17, which concerned offenses and punishments, the *Ecloga* made this implication explicit in the treatment of the oldest and most primary spiritual relationship, that between godparent and godchild.

---

[32] *Ecloga*, ch. 2.3, p. 73.

[33] For a lucid description of the regulations governing clerical marriage in the Greek East, see Roger Gryson, *Les origines du célibat ecclésiastique du premier au septième siècle* (Gembloux, 1970), pp. 45–126.

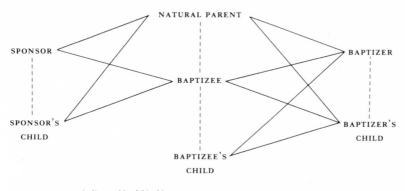

———— indicates blood kinship.

———— indicates spiritual kinship. Persons connected by this line were forbidden sexual contact by the Ecloga on the grounds of their spiritual
kinship.

Thus if a godfather had extramarital sexual intercourse with his goddaughter, "after being exiled, [they shall] be condemned to the same
punishment meted out for other adultery, that is to say both the man
and the woman shall have their noses slit."[34]

The *Ecloga*'s provisions on marriage reflected two centuries of Byzantine society's efforts to define who was a spiritual kinsman and to
decide what significance that status had. The tendency is clear: to
expand the circle of spiritual kinsmen and to prohibit them from marrying. In this the *Ecloga*'s attempt to codify Byzantine practice may be
represented graphically (see chart). Certain cautions are required in
order to read this chart correctly. First, it must be recalled that spiritual kinship was still developing in the eighth century and that the
Ecloga was, as it were, merely a snapshot from a moving picture. Byzantine canon and civil law continued to refine the marital implications
of spiritual kinship until well into the high Middle Ages, and because
of this the *Ecloga* did not represent the fullest expansion that the Byzantine church and society eventually acknowledged.[35] Further, the
Ecloga was a learned exercise and probably did not fully reflect the
popular practice of its own day. In particular, the sixth-century epi-

[34] *Ecloga*, ch. 17.25, p. 109.
[35] Zachariä von Lingenthal, *Geschichte*, p. 71, n. 140, refers to Byzantine canonists of
the twelfth to fourteenth centuries who treated the impact of spiritual kinship on marriage. See also Andreas Schmidt, "Der Traktat *Peri gamon* des Johannes Pediasmos,"
Forschungen zur byzantinischen Rechtsgeschichte, vol. 1: *Fontes Minores*, vol. 1 (Frankfort am
Main, 1976), p. 155, ll. 335–374, for a late-thirteenth- or fourteenth-century Byzantine
treatment of spiritual kinship and marriage.

sode involving Antonina, who was the spouse of the sponsor Belisarius, should serve as a warning that in popular practice the spouses of some or all of the persons represented on the chart were included in the web of spiritual kinship, even though the *Ecloga* did not explicitly state this to be the case. Thus the *Ecloga* probably understates the importance of spiritual kinship in Byzantine cultural and religious life.

From the sixth to the eighth centuries, spiritual kinship developed in parallel but not identical fashion in the Byzantine Empire and in the kingdom of the Franks. The most striking difference between the two was in the perception of how spiritual kinship affected marriage. The Franks were indifferent to the issue, whereas the Byzantines gradually placed spiritual kinship on a par with blood kinship and affinal kinship as an impediment to marriage.

The problem presented by a sexual bond between spiritual kin was posed early and starkly at Byzantium, at least in part because of the custom of cross-sex sponsorship, which carried the potential for a subsequent marriage between godparent and godchild. This sort of union was forbidden by Justinian. Similarly, as the notion of spiritual kinship enveloped coparents and spiritual siblings, they too were forbidden sexual contact. In the eighth and ninth centuries, some of these Byzantine marital taboos were grafted onto the flourishing Frankish form of spiritual kinship.

Papal and Lombard Developments

Papal Italy was a major conduit of influence for the acceptance in the Frankish West of marital impediments derived from spiritual kinship. In a fitful process beginning with the Lombard invasions of the later sixth century and culminating in the Norman conquests of the south in the eleventh, the Italian peninsula was removed from the political and cultural orbit of Byzantium. But the process was far from completed in the sixth, seventh, and eighth centuries, and during this time central and southern Italy remained part of the Byzantine political, cultural, and religious world. Even the politically independent Lombard kingdom and its principalities, centered in Pavia, Spoleto, and Benevento, were heavily influenced by Byzantine diplomacy, religion, and culture.[36]

From 678 to 752, eleven out of thirteen popes were easterners by birth. The papacy was still politically within the Byzantine Empire

[36] I. Dujcev, "Bizantini e longobardi," *Atti del Convegno Internazionale sul tema: La Civiltà dei longobardi in Europa (Roma, 24–26 maggio 1971)*. Problemi attuali, vol. 189 (Rome, 1974), pp. 45–78.

and, in spite of recurrent tension, it generally promoted Byzantine practices and interests, even in religious matters. In this, Geoffrey Barraclough has neatly summarized the attitude of the papacy prior to its eighth-century alliance with the Franks: "The popes might stand out against the emperor on questions of dogma and resist the pretensions of the patriarch of Constantinople; but politically they were loyal."[37] And despite the fact that during the late eighth and ninth centuries northern and central Italy were engulfed by the military might of the Franks and drawn into a more northerly cultural orientation, the Byzantine impress on Italian development continued to be felt for centuries.

The papacy had always been more than a Byzantine patriarchate. It had universal claims and it possessed ties with the northern and western Germanic kingdoms, in particular with those of the Franks and the Anglo-Saxons, who revered Saint Peter as the gatekeeper of heaven and at irregular intervals consulted his representative, the pope, on matters of doctrine, practice, and liturgy. Thus, during the eighth century, the papacy drew closer to the kingdom of the Franks and its rulers, the descendants of Charles Martel. This rapprochement, usually called the papal-Frankish alliance, had as a major consequence the increasing penetration of Roman norms in liturgy and canon law into the Frankish church. And it is within such a context of gradual Romanization that the transmission to the Franks of certain features of the Byzantine incest rules governing spiritual kinship must be understood. The papacy was the chief conduit for this transmission.

The coexistence of the pope and the Byzantine emperor had been uneasy since the late fifth century. Because religion was integral to imperial policy, successive rulers had attempted by flattery, by persuasion, by threat, and even by force to harness papal support to the policy of the moment. The popes, for their part, were conscious of their relative weakness in the contest with the emperor and sought relief by temporizing, by guarded concessions, and more rarely by open defiance, which was usually provoked by imperial encroachments on the papacy's traditional religious primacy.

Justinian II (685–695; 705–711) had summoned the Council in Trullo (692) to reform the church's discipline. The twenty-two-year-old emperor wished this council to be regarded as ecumenical and its

---

[37] Geoffrey Barraclough, *The Medieval Papacy* (New York, 1968), p. 30. Richards, *The Popes*, pp. 231–234, also argues that the papacy only reluctantly abandoned its stance of loyalty to the Christian empire and its emperor.

102 canons to be accepted by the entire church. Following precedents set by fourth- and fifth-century councils, the emperor had summoned the assembly, and Pope Sergius (687–701) had sent representatives without full powers to approve its deliberations. At the conclusion of the council, Justinian II sent six copies of the canons for signing by Pope Sergius, who was Syrian by birth, although he had spent part of his youth at Palermo.[38] Sergius refused to sign because he perceived an anti-Roman thrust in six or seven of the canons, which implicitly or explicitly criticized Roman practices on clerical celibacy, fasting, and liturgy. Justinian was determined to have papal assent, and negotiations escalated to threats, ending finally with an imperial order of arrest against the pope. Local resistance at Rome saved Sergius temporarily, and Justinian's deposition, mutilation (his nose was cut off), and exile to Cherson in the Crimea in 695 ended the confrontation.[39]

Justinian II's restoration to the imperial throne a decade later reopened the issue. However, by then the atmosphere had changed considerably. As *The Life of Pope John VII* in the *Liber Pontificalis* makes clear, Justinian II was now eager to compromise, and he offered John the right to reject or omit the objectionable canons, if only he would approve the rest.[40] The initial overture to Pope John VII was rejected, but in 711 Pope Constantine I (708–715) traveled to Nicomedia in Asia Minor, where a compromise was hammered out. The pope's chief adviser and negotiator in these maneuverings was the deacon Gregory, who succeeded him as Pope Gregory II (715–731).[41] The details of the negotiations are sketchy, but it may be assumed that Gregory and other theological advisers studied each canon, including canon 53 on the marriage of coparents, and analyzed its contents before accepting or rejecting it. Canon 53 was one of the canons accepted by the papal side.

The future Pope Gregory II's role in these negotiations is of considerable importance because, on his accession to the papacy, he incor-

[38] Head, *Justinian II*, pp. 72–79. On Pope Sergius, see *Liber Pontificalis*, 2nd ed., 3 vols., ed. Louis Duchesne (Paris, 1955–1957), 1:372–374.

[39] Head, *Justinian II*, pp. 92–98.

[40] Ibid., pp. 132–136. On iconographic evidence of the rapprochement of pope and emperor and of the acceptance of the Council in Trullo, see James D. Breckenridge, "Evidence for the Nature of Relations Between Pope John VII and the Byzantine Emperor Justinian II," *BZ* 65 (1972):364–374. For the papal version of the episode, see *Liber Pontificalis*, pp. 385–386.

[41] On Gregory's role at Nicomedia in 711, see Laurent, "L'oeuvre canonique," pp. 34–35; Head, *Justinian II*, pp. 135–136; Görres, "Justinian II," pp. 452–453. I have not seen Josef Dahmen, *Das Pontifikat Gregors II. nach den Quellen bearbeitet* (Düsseldorf, 1888).

porated the substance of canon 53 into the decisions of an influential Roman council of 721, and he apparently promoted the incorporation of the decision into Lombard law under King Liutprand in 723. The Roman council of 5 April 721 reflected the penetration into papal territory of the disciplinary canons of the Council in Trullo, particularly those concerning marriage and incest. In a series of brief canons, the twenty-two bishops assembled at Rome condemned marriage with a nun, with one's *commater spiritualis*, with the wife of one's brother, with one's niece, with one's stepmother or daughter-in-law, with one's cousin, and with a close kinsman or the spouse of a close kinsman. In addition, the council forbade the forcible marriage of a widow or a virgin, presumably against her will or that of her male relatives.[42]

Canon 4 declared that "if anyone takes his spiritual comother in marriage, let him be anathema. And all responded three times: 'Let him be anathema.' "[43] In spite of its brevity, this was a historic text because it was the first official acknowledgment in the West that marriage between coparents was forbidden. The canon was far more than a "first," however. A medieval text's importance must be measured by its diffusion and influence, and on that criterion canon 4 of the Roman council of 721 was a seminal text. In company with the other canons of that council, it was widely incorporated into eighth- and ninth-century Frankish canonical collections,[44] penitentials,[45] and councils.[46]

[42] The canons of the Council of Rome (721) are in Mansi 12:263–264. Gregory II's views on marriage law are surveyed in William Kelly, *Pope Gregory II on Divorce and Remarriage*, Analecta Gregoriana, vol. 203 (Rome, 1976), especially pp. 41–75.

[43] Roman Council (721) canon 4, in Mansi 12:263: "Si quis commatrem spiritalem duxerit in conjugium, anathema sit. Et responderunt omnes tertius: anathema sit."

[44] *Collectio Dionysio-Hadriana*, in *PL* 67:343c; *Collectio Herovalliana*, title LXXIIII, as described in Friedrich Maassen, *Geschichte der Quellen und der Literatur des canonischen Rechts im Abendlande*, vol. 1 (Graz, 1870), p. 831; Pseudo-Isidorian Decretals, in *Decretales Pseudo-Isidorianae et Capitula Angilramni*, ed. Paul Hinschius (Leipzig, 1863), pp. 753–754.

[45] *Poenitentiale Martenianum*, canon 30.3, in Walter von Hörmann, ed., "Bussbücherstudien VI," *ZSSRG*, Kanonistische Abteilung 4 (1914):374; *Poenitentiale Valicellanum I*, ed. Hermann J. Schmitz, *Die Bussbücher und die Bussdisciplin der Kirche*, vol. 1 (Mainz, 1883, reprint Graz, 1958), p. 246; Halitgar of Cambrai, *Penitential*, bk. 4, canon 22, ibid., p. 726; Theodore of Canterbury, *Penitential*, canon 5.(20).2, ed. F.W.H. Wasserschleben, *Die Bussordnungen der abendländische Kirche* (Halle, 1851; reprint ed. Graz, 1958), p. 584.

[46] Synod of Doucy (874) in Mansi 17:285e. See also Rabanus Maurus' Letter to Hatto, abbot of Fulda, in Rabanus Maurus, *Epistolae*, ed. Ernst Dümmler, MGH, Epis, vol. 5 (Berlin, 1899), p. 458; Pope Leo IV to the bishops of Brittany (JW 2599), ed. A. de Hirsch-Gereuth, MGH, Epis, vol. 5 (Berlin, 1899), p. 595; and Isaac, bishop of Langres, *Canones*, title 5, canon 6, in *PL* 124:1095c.

Under the authority of "Pope Gregory," it became a major proof text in the West for the prohibition of sexual contact between spiritual kin.

Gregory II also disseminated the Byzantine strictures against incest to the Lombard kingdom, which had occupied the valley of the Po and adjoining areas since the late sixth century. The Lombard king Liutprand (712–744) vigorously promoted his people's long-standing ambition to unite the entire peninsula, but the papacy, controlling a swath of territory in central Italy, was a major obstacle, just as it had been to Liutprand's predecessors. Thus Liutprand attempted by diplomacy and by the cultivation of a pro-Lombard party at Rome to win papal support, or at least acquiescence, for his plans.[47] One element of Liutprand's diplomacy was to proclaim often his Catholic orthodoxy and his respect for the papacy. Indeed, in the preamble to his laws of 721, he described himself as the "most excellent king of the divinely chosen Catholic nation of the Lombards" and in a law of 723 he called Gregory II the "head of the church of God and of priests throughout all the world."[48]

Liutprand's policy of cultivating amicable relations with the pope accorded Gregory II a certain amount of influence with his northern neighbor, and the pope used this influence in 722 or 723 to encourage Liutprand to forbid incest, including that among spiritual kin. (The Roman council of 721 specifically mentioned Lombards alongside Romans as the intended audience for the canons issued against incest.)[49]

Liutprand was the great legislator of the Lombard royal line; he issued written laws almost annually and his legal code, which collected laws issued from 713 to 735, contains 153 provisions. In 723, Liutprand issued twenty-four laws, the first five of which were intended to forbid certain sexual unions: (1) that of a nun and any man, (2) that of a free woman abducted by a man, (3) that of a man with his stepmother or stepdaughter or sister-in-law, (4) that of a man with the widow of a paternal or maternal first cousin, and (5) that of a man with his godmother or goddaughter or the daughter of his godfather.[50] It is striking how closely these prohibitions parallel those of the Ro-

[47] Louis Halphen, *Les barbares des grandes invasions aux conquêtes turques du xi° siècle*, 2nd ed. (Paris, 1930), pp. 207–209; Jan Hallenbeck, *Pavia and Rome: The Lombard Monarchy and the Papacy in the Eighth Century*, TAPS vol. 72, pt. 4 (Philadelphia, 1982), pp. 21–31.

[48] Liutprand, *Leges Liutprandi regis*, ed. F. Bluhme, in *Leges Langobardorum*, MGH, Leges, vol. 4 (Hanover, 1868), pp. 96–175, tr. Katherine Fischer Drew, *The Lombard Laws* (Philadelphia, 1973), pp. 137–214.

[49] Council of Rome (721), Mansi 12:263.

[50] Liutprand, *Leges*, chs. 30–34, pp. 123–124.

man council of 721. But they were no slavish repetition. Liutprand's laws were much fuller than the Roman canons; if the Lombard laws drew their inspiration from the canons, they also assimilated and adapted them to Lombard conditions.

Mere resemblance is not the only reason for believing that Liutprand was legislating at papal request. The third law, which forbade a man to marry his brother's wife or his wife's sister, was justified by reference to "the canons," confirming explicitly that these provisions were inspired by ecclesiastical law, though not necessarily by the Roman canons of 721. In the fourth law, which forbade a man to marry the widow of a maternal or paternal first cousin, Liutprand noted that "we have added this measure because, as God is our witness, the Pope at Rome, who is head of the church of God and of priests throughout all the world, has exhorted us through a letter that we not permit such unions to be contracted in any way."[51] This letter of Pope Gregory II is not extant; however, it seems unlikely that the pope wrote *only* about marriage to a cousin's widow. Rather, it is a reasonable hypothesis that Pope Gregory informed the king of the decisions taken by the Roman council, perhaps with more elaboration than the scanty canons provide, and asked him to support the measures as well. The king did so, but with a formulation that appears to be quite independent. In any case, the laws issued by Liutprand in 723 constitute the earliest secular legislation in the western Germanic kingdoms directed against the marriage of spiritual kin:

> We likewise decree that no one may presume to take to wife his godmother, nor that goddaughter whom he raised from the baptismal font; nor may his son presume to marry the daughter of the man who received him from the font, because such are known to be spiritual siblings.[52]

Stern civil punishments were provided for any such union, and the children from it were at a disadvantage before the law.

> He who attempts to perpetrate such an evil should lose all his possessions and the children who are born of the illicit marriage should not inherit, but rather close kinsmen should. If there are

---

[51] Ibid., ch. 33, p. 124: "Hoc autem ideo adfiximus, quia Deo teste papa urbis Romae, qui in omni mundo caput ecclesiarum Dei et sacerdotum est, per suam epistolam nos adortavit, ut tale coniugium fieri nullatinus permitteremus."

[52] Ibid., ch. 34: "Item hoc censemus adque precipimus, ut nullus presumat cummatrem suam uxorem ducere, sed nec filiam, quam de sacro fonte levavit; neque filius eius presumat filiam illius uxorem ducere, qui eum de fonte suscepit, quia spiritalis germani esse noscuntur."

no close kinsmen, the royal treasury should succeed. When, however, any persons are discovered who have contracted the above-mentioned illicit unions, they should immediately be separated and undergo the above-mentioned penalty.[53]

Even after the Frankish conquest of the Lombard kingdom in 774 and Charlemagne's assumption of the Lombard crown, the laws of the Lombard kings continued to be in force, supplemented from time to time by Frankish royal capitularies. This slowly evolving Lombard law (including Liutprand's ban on the marriage of spiritual kin) persisted in parts of Italy until the revival of Roman law in the eleventh and twelfth centuries.

Thus during the second decade of the eighth century there emerged in legal forms a loose consensus within what might be called "Mediterranean Christianity," that is, Italy and Byzantium, that baptismal sponsorship had significant sexual implications. Within a period of five years (721–726), papal, Lombard, and Byzantine law all formally forbade sexual contact along the primary axes of the godparent complex—horizontally between persons related by coparenthood and vertically between those bound by godparenthood. The Byzantines, whose priests could be married, spelled out the implications of baptism for the baptizer and his family as well, while the westerners, whose clergy were in theory unable to marry, felt no comparable need. In addition, both Liutprand's law and Leo III's *Ecloga* explicitly prohibited marriage between the natural and baptismal child of the same person, on the grounds that they were spiritual siblings. Within a generation, this prohibition had been ratified by Pope Zachary (741–752) in a letter responding to a question from Theodore, bishop of Pavia, who asked if a man was permitted to marry a girl who had been sponsored by his father.[54] Zachary called such an act a thing cruel even to be said aloud and quoted Leviticus 18 against revealing the "nakedness" of one's blood kin. In doing so, Zachary picked up the theme, which had been sounded in the Council in Trullo, that spiritual kin are in some sense even more significant than carnal kin in the matter of incest:

[53] Ibid.: "Et qui hoc malum facere temptaverit, perdat omnem substantiam suam, et filii qui de inlicito matrimonio nascuntur heredes esse non debeant, nisi parentes propinqui; et si parentes propinqui non fuerint, curtis regia succedat. Ubi autem inventi fuerint qui suprascripta inlicita coniugia contraxerint, de presenti separentur, et poenae suprascriptae subiaceant."

[54] Pope Zachary to Theodore, Bishop of Pavia (JW 2306), ed. Wilhelm Gundlach, MGH Epis, vol. 3 (Berlin, 1892), pp. 710–711.

Much more is it fitting for us with rigor to keep away completely from the spiritual daughter of our own father, with every excuse and argument thrust aside, lest if anyone, enveloped in such an offense, does not curb the reins of lust, he may fall under the anger of divine judgment. Hence, all should entirely avoid the commission of such a crime, lest they perish forever.[55]

Zachary encouraged Bishop Theodore to work for the separation and suitable penance of the offenders.

Theodore had also indicated that in his diocese there was a reluctance to allow a child born of such a union ever to marry. The denial of the right to marry was a penalty inflicted by the canon law for certain serious offences,[56] and in this case it had apparently been applied in popular practice to the offspring of baptismal kin. It may reflect a popular aversion toward the products of incest, but it was a folk reaction not ratified by learned law. Zachary explicitly disapproved of this penalty being imposed on innocent children:

But why are they kept from marriage or compelled to do penance, since they are considered without offense from this deed? For the father will not sustain torments on behalf of the son, nor will the son bear them on behalf of the father, as the Lord says through the prophet: "The father's life and the son's life, both alike belong to me. The man who has sinned, he is the one who will die [Ezekiel 18:4]."[57]

On the basis of such reasoning, Pope Zachary might also have disapproved of the civil penalty of incapacity to inherit, which Liutprand inflicted on the children of such forbidden unions, but if such disapproval existed there was no overt expression of it.

We have seen that by 750 the incorporation within the learned legal traditions of Mediterranean Christianity of a sexual taboo arising out of baptism was well advanced. This legal development was rooted in

---

[55] Ibid.: "Multo magis a spiritali patris nostri filia omnimodo omni occasione aut argumento reposito, sub nimia districtione cavere nos convenit, ne in iram divini examinis incidat, si quis tali facinore mixtus minime restrinxerit frena luxurie."

[56] Since the fourth century, public or canonical penance required the penitent to assume serious burdens, including the renunciation of marriage or, if the penitent was already married, marital intercourse. See Cyrille Vogel, *La discipline pénitentielle en Gaule des origines à la fin du viiᵉ siècle* (Paris, 1952), pp. 37–40, 102–115.

[57] Zachary to Theodore, p. 711: "Sed hi cur prohibeantur a coniugio aut pro huiusmodi poenitentiam agere compellantur, dum ex hoc absque condemnatione esse perhibentur? Quia non pater pro filio neque filius pro patre sustinebit tormenta, dicente Domino per prophetam: 'Anima patris mea est anima filii mea est; anima quae peccaverit morietur.' "

a folk aversion to such unions, whose intensity and exact distribution by region and social class we are not in a position to assess, but whose dim outlines are discernible. The export of such a taboo across the Alps, under papal aegis, was part of the great implications for world history of the papal-Frankish rapprochement of the later eighth century.

The Papal-Frankish Alliance and the Ban on the Marriage of Spiritual Kin

There is abundant evidence that the Franks had a form of baptismal kinship in the sixth century, and there is adequate evidence that the Anglo-Saxons had also adopted a version of it as Christianity spread among them in the seventh century. In both cases, a vocabulary rooted in kinship analogies expressed a religious and social code binding together godparent and godchild, as well as the coparents of a baptizee. Since both the Franks and the Anglo-Saxons practiced same-sex sponsorship, there was no danger of godparent/godchild marriage. Neither group seems independently to have recognized incest taboos based on spiritual kinship—at least, no source alludes to such a taboo before the third decade of the eighth century, when papal influence was already making itself felt north of the Alps.

The Anglo-Saxons are an important case in point. The conversion of the Germanic society of lowland Britain to Christianity had begun with Augustine of Canterbury in the late sixth century, but it was three quarters of a century before the missionary effort was secure and vigorous enough to penetrate native folkways. The Italian missionaries to the Anglo-Saxons certainly knew the traditional Mediterranean Christian practice of infant baptism and its corollary, sponsorship. However, in the mission setting of Britain, the baptism of adults regained a prominence it had not had for generations in older Christian lands. Adults acted for themselves in the baptismal ritual, but the presence of sponsors was so deeply ingrained that they participated in the rebirth of Anglo-Saxon adults as well.

In his *Ecclesiastical History of the English People*, completed about 731, the Anglo-Saxon monk Bede refers to two royal baptisms in which he mentions *susceptores*, that is, those who receive the candidate from the font. In the 650s, when Suidhelm became king of the East Saxons, he "was baptized by [Bishop] Chad in the province of the East Angles, at a royal manor which is called Rendlesham, that is, Rendel's House, and as he was ascending from the holy font, Ethelwald, king of the East Anglian people and brother of King Anna, received [*suscepit*] him."⁵⁸ In the 680s, Bishop Wilfrid, exiled because of a conflict with King Egfrid, began to preach among the still pagan South Saxons. "The king of that people, Ethelwalh, was baptized not too long before in the province of the Mercians, in the presence and at the suggestion of King Wulfhere, by whom he was received as a son [*loco filii susceptus est*] when he had emerged from the font."⁵⁹ Thus Bede was thoroughly familiar with the practice of sponsorship, even when adults were baptized, and the constitutive act in Bede's view was the traditional one of receiving the candidate from the font. In his commentary on Mark 7:29, Bede states that parents spoke the *fides* and *confessio* for their small children and thereby liberated them from the devil,⁶⁰ but it is likely that some third party received the child from the font.

In the course of the seventh century, the social code rooted in sponsorship, particularly in the bond of *paternitas*, found a place in Anglo-Saxon society. References to the godparent/godchild tie appear in Bede's *Ecclesiastical History*, as noted above, as well as in the *Anglo-Saxon Chronicle*.⁶¹ But one of the most explicit glimpses at the assimilation of baptismal kinship is provided by the laws of King Ine of Wessex (688–725), which were issued about 692. Here, in law 76, Ine provides compensation for slain spiritual kinsmen. Ine's list of such kinsmen is probably significant. It includes the godfather (*godfaeder*) as well as the godsons from both baptism (*godsunu*) and confirmation (*biscepsunu*), but it does not refer to coparents:

> 76. If anyone kills the godson or godfather of another, the compensation for the [spiritual] relationship is to be the same as that to the lord; the compensation is to increase in proportion to the wergild, the same as the compensation for his man does which has to be paid to the lord.
>
> 76.1. If, however, it is the king's godson, his wergild is to be paid to the king the same as to the kindred.

⁵⁸ Bede, *Ecclesiastical History of the English People*, bk. 3, ch. 22, ed. Bertram Colgrave and R.A.B. Mynors (Oxford, 1969), p. 284.

⁵⁹ Ibid., bk. 4, ch. 13, p. 372.

⁶⁰ Bede, *In Marci Evangelium Expositio*, bk. 2, ch. 7, verse 29, ll. 1419–1423, ed. D. Hurst, CCSL, vol. 120 (Turnhout, 1960), p. 525: "Vbi datur exemplum cathecizandi et baptizandi infantes quia uidelicet per fidem et confessionem parentum in baptismo liberantur a diabolo paruuli qui necdum per se sapere uel aliquid agere boni possunt aut mali." Cf. ibid., bk. 4, ll. 1959–1964, p. 645, where Bede states that infants believe *per alios*, a vague formulation encompassing parents and other sponsors.

⁶¹ *The Anglo-Saxon Chronicle: A Revised Translation*, by Dorothy Whitelock, David C. Douglas, and Susie D. Tucker (New Brunswick, N.J., 1961), A.D. 635 and A.D. 639, p. 18; A.D. 661, p. 21; and A.D. 688, p. 24.

76.2. If, however, he was resisting him who slew him, then the compensation to the godfather is remitted, in the same way as the fine to the lord is.

76.3. If it is a spiritual son at confirmation, the compensation is to be half as much.[62]

The early Anglo-Saxon version of spiritual kinship thus emphasized the bond of godparenthood from baptism, while giving less weight to the spiritual kinship from confirmation and ignoring coparenthood, a situation that changed after the eighth century as Frankish and papal influence grew stronger.

Although the Anglo-Saxons recognized spiritual kinship, neither Bede nor any earlier Anglo-Saxon writer alluded to a sexual prohibition resulting from baptismal sponsorship; in fact, Bede described approvingly a situation that might have given pause to his exact contemporaries in Italy or Byzantium. In 635 Bishop Birinus began to preach to the pagan West Saxons and his efforts moved King Cynegils to conversion and baptism. "It happened at that time that the most holy and victorious king of the Northumbrians, Oswald, was present and he received him [Cynegils] as he emerged from the font; and by an alliance most pleasing and acceptable to God, he [Oswald] first accepted him as son dedicated to God by a second birth, whose daughter he was going to take to wife";[63] in other words, Oswald married the daughter of his godson. At almost precisely the same time that Bede was writing of this incident, the Byzantine *Ecloga* forbade a sponsor's son to marry the mother of his spiritual sibling, and it also forbade the baptizer to marry a woman whom he had baptized or her daughter. Neither case is exactly the situation of Oswald and Cynegils' daughter, but they are analogous.

The clearest evidence for the situation among the Anglo-Saxons is

---

[62] Ine, King of Wessex, *Institutiones*, law 76, ed. Felix Liebermann, *Die Gesetze der Angelsachsen*, vol. 1 (Halle, 1903; reprint ed., Aalen, 1960), pp. 122–123. Tr. in Dorothy Whitelock, ed., *English Historical Documents*, vol. 1: *c. 500–1042*, 2nd ed. (London, 1979), p. 407. Whitelock indicates that the translation is taken from Frederick L. Attenborough, *The Laws of the Earliest English Kings* (Cambridge, 1922), but in fact it is not. Her translation is a great improvement on Attenborough's, particularly when dealing with law 76.3, where Attenborough renders *biscepsunu* as "godson of a bishop" rather than "spiritual son at confirmation." Ine's laws survived as an appendix to Alfred's laws; see Felix Liebermann, "Uber die Gesetze Ines von Wessex," *Mélanges d'histoire offerts à M. Charles Bémont* (Paris, 1913), pp. 21–42. There is a possibility that Alfred "modernized" their content, a point that needs investigation relative to law 76.

[63] Bede, *Ecclesiastical History*, bk. 3, ch. 7, p. 232: "ac pulcherrimo prorsus et Deo digno consortio, cuius erat filiam accepturus in coniugem, ipsum prius secunda generatione Deo dedicatum sibi accepit in filium."

provided by three letters of that champion of papal policies and interests, the Anglo-Saxon missionary Boniface (680–754). In the course of
a long career among Continental pagan Germanic peoples, Boniface
had relied faithfully on papal authorization and advice, and his correspondence contains detailed responses to the questions he posed to
a succession of popes.[64] In about 735, when he was a missionary
bishop of more than fifteen years experience, he was embroiled in a
controversy with native clergy in Gaul about a marriage he had permitted. The evidence for the controversy is contained in three letters
that he directed to learned Anglo-Saxons: Pehthelm, Bishop of Whithorn; Abbot Duddo; and Nothelm, Archbishop of Canterbury. To
Nothelm he wrote:

> Further, I wish to hear your advice as regards a sin which I un-
> knowingly committed by allowing a certain man to marry. It hap-
> pened in this way. A certain man, as many are accustomed to do,
> in lifting the son of another man from the font of holy baptism
> adopted him as a son. Afterward the child's mother was widowed
> and he took her to wife. The Romans say that this is a sin, indeed
> a serious sin, so that in such cases they command a divorce be
> made. They maintain that under the rule of Christian emperors
> the outrage of such a marriage must be punished by a capital
> sentence or expunged by perpetual exile.[65]

In this remarkable text, some commentators have seen the reference
to Christian emperors as a vague allusion to Justinian's law of 530.
However, I believe the correct interpretation is that Boniface's opponents, whom he calls Romans, were citing against him contemporary
practice, perhaps that provided by canon 53 of the Council in Trullo,
which had been approved by the pope about twenty years earlier, or

[64] Boniface, *Epistolae*, in *Die Briefe des heiligen Bonifatius und Lullus*, ed. Michael Tangl,
MGH Epistolae selectae, vol. 1 (Berlin, 1916). On Boniface and the papacy, see Wilhelm Levison, *England and the Continent in the Eighth Century* (Oxford, 1946), pp. 70–78.
Arnold Angenendt, "Bonifatius und das Sacramentum initiationis. Zugleich ein Beitrag
zur Geschichte der Firmung," *RQCAKG* 72 (1977):133–183, attempts to place in a cultural context Boniface's concern with the adherence to proper liturgical forms, which
in Boniface's view were the Roman ones. Angenendt succeeds in moving the discussion
of Boniface's loyalty to the papacy from the sphere of power politics to that of the
intellectual history of the eighth century, where the discussion properly belongs.

[65] Boniface, Letter 33, to Archbishop Nothelm, *Die Briefe*, pp. 57–58. Boniface asks
about the same issue in Letter 32, to Bishop Pehthelm of Whithorn, ibid., pp. 55–56,
and in Letter 34, to Abbot Duddo, ibid., pp. 58–59. See also Theodor Schieffer, *Winfrid-Bonifatius und die christliche Grundlegung Europas* (Freiburg, 1954), pp. 167–169, for
the significance of this correspondence in Boniface's career.

perhaps even the *Ecloga* of Leo and Constantine, if the promulgation date of March 726 happens to be correct. In this they were referring to the situation in Byzantine Italy, of which Rome was a part.

In the letter to Abbot Duddo, Boniface again identified his critics as *Romani*,[66] but in the letter to Pehthelm, the "Romans" were not mentioned; instead the situation is introduced by the statement: "The priests throughout the whole of Frankland and in Gaul maintain. . . ."[67] We may thus conclude that Boniface's permission for the marriage of coparents was criticized by some native Frankish clergy, as well as by some clergy who were Romans or at least perceived as spokesmen for Roman views. Their judgment was defended by reference to recent developments in Italy, notably the acceptance of the canons of the Council in Trullo and perhaps the promulgation of Leo III's *Ecloga*.

Boniface's plea to his Anglo-Saxon supporters and advisers is quite revealing. To Bishop Pehthelm he acknowledged that "up to now I knew nothing about this kind of sin—if it is truly a sin—nor was I aware that the fathers had enumerated it in the ancient canons or in the decrees of the popes, or that the apostles had enumerated it in a list of sins. Consequently, if you should find anything anywhere in ecclesiastical writings, take care to point it out to us and let us know your view of the matter."[68] To Nothelm of Canterbury, he was even stronger: "Take care to let me know if you find this counted as so serious a sin in the decrees of the Catholic fathers or in the canons or even in holy scripture. Thus in gaining understanding, I may know whose authority is in that judgment, for in no way can I understand why in one place spiritual relationship in marital intercourse should be so great a sin, when we are all known to be sons and daughters, brothers and sisters of Christ and of the Church in holy baptism."[69]

Boniface knew that traditional Christian imagery and terminology

[66] Boniface, Letter 34, *Die Briefe*, p. 59.

[67] Boniface, Letter 32, ibid., p. 56: "Adfirmant sacerdotes per totam Franciam et per Gallias. . . ."

[68] Ibid.: "Quod peccati genus, si verum est, actenus ignorabam et nec in antiquis canonibus nec in decretis pontificum patres nec in calculo peccatorum apostolos usquam enumerasse cognovi. Qua de re si aliquid uspiam in ecclesiasticis scriptis disputatum invenissetis, nobis indicare curate, et, quid vobis videatur, nosse velimus."

[69] Boniface, Letter 33, *Die Briefe*, p. 58: "Ut si hoc in catholicorum patrum decretis vel canonibus vel etiam in sacro eloquio pro tam magno peccato conputatum esse inveniretis, indicare mihi curetis, ut et ego intellegendo cognoscam, cuius auctoritas sit in illo iudicio, quia nullatenus intellegere possum, quare in uno loco spiritalis propinquitas in coniunctione carnalis copulae tam grande peccatum sit, quando omnes in sacro baptismate Christi et ecclesie filii et filiae fratres et sorores esse conprobemur."

abounded in references to spiritual brothers and sisters, fathers and mothers, sons and daughters. He also knew that no one argued that such spiritual relationships constituted impediments to marriage, because if they did they would be denying the existence of any legitimate marriage among Christians. He could not understand why baptismal kinship was so different.

Of course, Boniface was aware of the existence of baptismal kinship; to judge from his use of language, he saw it as an adoption of some sort. However, he still viewed this kinship from a traditional perspective that treated it as loose and perhaps metaphorical, without serious marital consequences. But in the Mediterranean Christianity of the eighth century such a view was archaic. It had already been replaced by a more literal conception in which one particular subset of spiritual relations, those arising out of baptism, had been separated from other less clearly defined varieties of relationships and subjected to an incest taboo. Boniface was not aware of this development and reacted negatively when he encountered it.

Boniface's resistance to the papal-Byzantine ban on marriage among coparents is rooted in his own background and society. He was in his fifties when the controversy broke out and his intellectual formation had taken place in Anglo-Saxon England between 690 and 715, that is, before the Byzantine disapproval of marriage between coparents had any significant impact in papal or Lombard Italy, and none north of the Alps. The Anglo-Saxon church of Boniface's youth certainly knew the practice of sponsorship and the important social bond created by it. But the practice of same-sex sponsorship meant that godparent/godchild marriage was not a problem. It is also clear that the Anglo-Saxon church did not recognize coparenthood as an impediment to marriage. When Boniface encountered such "modern" views in Gaul he resisted them as an innovation and sought support from his compatriots. He demanded that the "Romans" justify their position by citing *ecclesiastical* authorities, and thus rejected by implication the imperial laws that were cited for so serious a social and religious innovation. His letters reveal an angry puzzlement over the fact that "in one place" (perhaps a discreet reference to Rome) people forbade marriages and demanded the termination of existing marriages without clear warrant from scripture, canon law, or papal decretals.

Boniface was an important man, an adviser of Frankish rulers, a tireless missionary, a papal champion, and a leader of a reform party composed of Anglo-Saxons and their Continental allies. Because of this, his objection to the prohibition of marriage among coparents was a serious obstacle to its acceptance in the north. And his request for a justification from scripture, canon law, or tradition was an intellectual challenge to the proponents of the marital prohibition.

Boniface's arguments had considerable weight on their side, for spiritual kinship of a socially significant kind, as distinguished from simple baptismal sponsorship, was not older than the fifth century. Furthermore, whatever roots the marriage prohibitions might have had in Byzantine Christian custom, they had received sanction in the civil law for the first time only in 530. The canon law had expanded them in the Trullan council (692), during Boniface's own lifetime, but he exhibited no familiarity with these controversial decrees. In the West, the papal approval of the Trullan decrees was only fifteen or twenty years old, and Boniface was either not aware of the Roman council of 721 or was unwilling to accept its implications. In short, he was quite correct in his belief that the case for the sexual taboos was not securely grounded in ecclesiastical authority, particularly when weighed against the social consequences of ending long-standing marriages because of coparenthood between the spouses.

Boniface's reaction bears out the observation that a sexual taboo was not integral to the insular version of baptismal kinship. This is also confirmed by the silence of the earliest Celtic penitentials, as seen in Ludwig Bieler's edition of fifteen Latin texts relating to penance among the Irish and Welsh between the fifth and seventh centuries, as well as in Daniel Binchy's translation into English of two penitential documents composed in Old Irish. The Celtic penitentials were deeply concerned with the sexual behavior of Christians; indeed, it was perhaps the single topic they treated the most. It is striking, therefore, that they drew no link between sexual behavior and baptismal kinship. And although in the eighth and ninth centuries some Irish penitentials were reworked on the Continent to reflect papal and Frankish concerns about the purity of spiritual kin ties, such "modernization " must not obscure the fact that a vigorously articulated set of sexual prohibitions to govern the behavior of spiritual kin was not originally a part of spiritual kinship in the British isles.[70]

No reply to Boniface's letters of inquiry to his fellow Anglo-Saxons exists and the archbishop never returned to the matter in his surviving correspondence. However, the issue at stake remained a lively one in mid-eighth-century Gaul, and Boniface's views were repudiated, though without mention of his name. We may have a direct response from Pope Zachary who, while not openly criticizing the views of

[70] *The Irish Penitentials*, ed. Ludwig Bieler, with an appendix by Daniel A. Binchy, SLH, vol. 5 (Dublin, 1963).

Boniface, laid the matter to rest. This occurred when Pepin, the Carolingian mayor of the palace, sent the priest Ardobanius to Rome with a series of questions about ecclesiastical matters. In a letter from Zachary to Boniface, dated 5 January 747, the pope informed Boniface that he had responded. The pope's written reply extended to twenty-seven chapters and was sent with the instructions that it was to be read in a church council that Boniface was asked to attend.[71]

Zachary's pamphlet, addressed to Pepin and the Frankish bishops, abbots, and magnates, was a brief canonical collection, in which Pepin's questions were stated and an appropriate canon or papal letter was quoted, generally without elaboration or personal comment. The source for the quoted authorities was the *Dionysiana*, the official canonical collection in use at Rome.[72] The only exceptions to this format of quoted authorities were chapters 1 and 22. The former concerned bishops and priests who wished to observe the monastic form of life; the pope approved, but since there were no ancient texts to buttress this view he expressed his approbation in his own words. In chapter 22, Pope Zachary responded to Pepin's hesitations about the prohibition of marriage between spiritual kin. Boniface was not mentioned, but the response from the pope was probably directed against the views espoused a decade earlier by the archbishop. After some observations about the effect of carnal kinship on the right to marriage, Zachary continued:

> Nor should anyone with foolhardy boldness take as wife his spiritual comother or his spiritual daughter (may it not happen!): for such is a shocking thing and a deadly sin before God and his angels.[73]

If Zachary had followed the format used in twenty-five of the other chapters of his response to Pepin, he would have introduced authoritative texts at this point to defend his decision. But there were no

[71] Boniface, Letter 77, *Die Briefe*, pp. 159–161. The pope's reply in twenty-seven chapters (JW 2277) was incorporated as Letter 3 into the *Codex Carolinus*, ed. Wilhelm Gundlach, MGH Epis, vol. 3 (Berlin, 1892), pp. 479–487. On the circumstances surrounding the pope's reply, see Carlo de Clercq, *La législation religieuse franque de Clovis à Charlemagne. Etude sur les actes de conciles et les capitulaires, les statuts diocésains et les règles monastiques (507–814)*, Université de Louvain, Recueil de travaux publiés par les membres des conférences d'histoire et de philologie, 2nd series, vol. 38 (Louvain and Paris, 1936), pp. 125–128.

[72] De Clercq, *La législation* (1936), p. 127.

[73] Zachary to Pepin, ch. 22, MGH Epis, vol. 3, p. 485: "Sed nec spiritalem cummatrem aut filiam, quod absit, quis ducat temerario ausu uxorem; est namque nefas et perneciosum coram Deo et angelis eius."

early canons or decretals, as Boniface had insisted in his letters of 735.
And so Zachary offered a reason (or rationalization) to explain the
absence of proof texts and disarm Boniface's objection:

> This is so serious an offense that it was condemned by none of
> the holy fathers and decisions of the holy councils nor indeed
> even in the imperial laws; but, fearing the horrible judgment of
> God, they refrained from rendering a decision.[74]

Pope Zachary was a well-educated Greek from southern Italy, and
his claim that the horror of incest led the church fathers to cover the
matter in a reverential silence may indicate that he had before him the
decrees of the Council in Trullo. That council had relied on the authority of Basil of Caesarea for the condemnation of certain marital
unions, but the bishops had wished to expand the list to include
unions not explicitly condemned by Basil. They justified such an expansion in this fashion:

> The divine scriptures plainly teach us as follows: "Thou shalt not
> approach to any that is near of kin to thee to uncover their na-
> kedness." Basil, the bearer-of-God, has enumerated in his canons
> some marriages which are prohibited and has passed over the
> greater part in silence, and in both these ways has done us good
> service. *For by avoiding a number of disgraceful names (lest by such
> words he should pollute his discourse)* he included impurities under
> general terms, by which course he shewed to us in a general way
> the marriages which are forbidden. But since by such silence, and
> because of the difficulty of understanding what marriages are pro-
> hibited, the matter has become confused; it seemed good to us to
> set it forth a little more clearly.[75]

Zachary insisted, as the Council in Trullo had, that there was a good
reason for the silence of the tradition on incest among spiritual kin, a
silence that he was now filling at the request of Pepin.

Zachary's assertion that neither church councils nor imperial laws
had expressed a judgment on the subject is puzzling, for Zachary himself had issued a canon against marriage with one's spiritual comother
in a Roman council (743)[76] and his letter to Bishop Theodore of Pavia,

---

[74] Ibid.: "In tantum enim grave est, ut nullus sanctorum patrum atque sacrarum sino-
dorum adsertiones vel etiam in imperialibus legibus quippiam iudicatum sit; sed, terri-
bile Dei iudicium metuentes, siluerunt sententiam dare."

[75] Council in Trullo, canon 54, in Percival, *Seven Ecumenical Councils*, p. 390 (italics
added).

[76] Roman Council (743), canon 5, Mansi 12:383.

which betrayed no hesitation in forbidding marriage between spiritual siblings, was roughly contemporary with the letter to Pepin. In view of the archival practices of the era, it is not impossible that he was unaware of Gregory II's council of 721, but it is unlikely.

Carlo de Clercq has surmised that Zachary's puzzling response was calculated. After all, the pope was aware that the prohibition on marriage between coparents was not generally observed in Gaul and thus it would be natural for him to hesitate to call into question numerous existing marriages. In de Clercq's view, Zachary chose to present the issue as a new one, and to overlook past abuses, with the demand that in future such marriages be forbidden.[77] I suggest that Zachary also had in mind Boniface's demand for justification out of traditional ecclesiastical sources and because of this avoided citing Roman imperial legislation as irrelevant, as well as recent church councils, which did not fit his schema of basing reform squarely on ancient councils and ancient papal decisions.

In any case, Zachary made the prohibition of marriage between coparents (and between spiritual parents and children) an explicit part of the papal law that spread north of the Alps under Carolingian leadership. And in 754, his successor, Pope Stephen II, who traveled to Gaul to seek Pepin's aid against the Lombards, reiterated this papal view in a response to a question put to him by the monks of Bretigny.[78]

Boniface was martyred in Frisia in 754, by which time his hesitations over the marriage prohibitions rooted in baptismal kinship were already being forgotten. The issue had been linked by popes Gregory, Zachary, and Stephen II to papal prestige and church reform, both of which were in the ascendant in the Frankish realm. Indeed, the western canonical tradition against marriage between coparents and between spiritual siblings was built squarely on papal letters and Frankish councils of the eighth and ninth centuries.

It was common in the development of canon law that a weak case or a situation unanticipated in the ancient sources called forth forgers to create suitable precedents. And in this the imposition and expansion of marital impediments based on spiritual kinship were no exception. Thus Gratian's *Decretum*, *causa* 30, contained authentic eighth- to twelfth-century papal texts and councils mixed with apocryphal texts

[77] De Clercq, *La législation* (1936), p. 126.
[78] Pope Stephen II to the monks of Bretigny, ch. 4 (JW 2315) in Mansi 12:559: "Ut nullus habeat commatrem suam spiritalem, tam de fonte sacro quam de confirmatione, neque sibi clam in neutra parte conjugio sociatam. Quod si conjuncti fuerint, separentur."

of uncertain date that had entered the canonical tradition long before Gratian encountered them. The more important among them
included:

(1) A letter from Pope Deusdedit to Bishop Gordian, "Pervenit ad
nos" (JW 2003). Here Bishop Gordian reported that husbands and
wives had sponsored their own children and thus became coparents to
their own spouses. Could they subsequently, asked the bishop, have
sexual intercourse? The pope responded that he had done extensive
research in the "archives" of the apostolic see and had discovered that
earlier popes forbade such persons to continue as husband and wife
and ordered them to separate. He reaffirmed this decision and added
that sponsorship at any of seven points, from the giving of salt to a
catechumen to the confirmation by a bishop, created coparenthood
and prevented marriage or invalidated existing marriages.

(2) A text attributed to Zachary and Deusdedit, "Non oportet filiam" (JW 2004), in which marriage between spiritual siblings (germani) was forbidden and penalties were imposed on the couple and on
those who arranged or consented to the union.

(3) A letter from Pope Innocent I to Bishop Exsuperius of Toulouse,
"Si quis unus," which stated that if one member of a married couple
sponsored a child at baptism, confirmation, or catechumenus, both
spouses became coparents to the child's parents. Such coparenthood
by contagion was justified on the grounds that a married couple is
"one flesh." This text entered the canonical tradition and was misattributed to Innocent I in the Collectio Herovalliana, a Frankish collection of canon law compiled in the later eighth century.[79]

As a consequence of such authentic and apocryphal texts, marriage
between coparents or spiritual siblings was forbidden in western canon
law, just as it had been forbidden in Byzantine canon law.

The popes' encouragement to the Franks to bring their practices
into line with papal views was not without results. While he was still
mayor of the palace, Pepin had been warned by Pope Zachary about
the evils of marriage between coparents. And after Pepin became king
of the Franks in 751 (with the cooperation of Pope Zachary, who
sanctioned the deposition of the last Merovingian king) his first extant
capitulary prescribed stern secular penalties for several sexual
transgressions, including those involving spiritual kinsmen:

    1. Concerning incest. If a man commits incest with any of the
    following persons, he should lose his wealth, if he has any: with

[79] Hubert Mordek, Kirchenrecht und Reform im Frankenreich. Beiträge zur Geschichte
und Quellenkunde des Mittelalters, vol. 1 (Berlin, 1975), p. 137, n. 182.

a woman consecrated to God; *with the mother of his godchild*; *with his godmother from baptism or from confirmation from the bishop*; with a mother and her daughter; or with two sisters; or with his brother's daughter; or with his sister's daughter; or with a niece; or with a cousin on either side; or with an aunt on either side. If he is unwilling to correct himself, no one should receive him or offer him food. If he does this, he should pay sixty shillings in composition to the Lord King, until that man corrects himself. If he has no money and if he is a free man, he should be put into prison until he makes amends. If he is a serf or a freedman, he should be beaten by many blows. If his lord permits him to fall into this crime again, then the lord should pay sixty shillings in composition to the King.

2. Concerning churchmen, on the other hand: if he is a respectable person, he should lose his position. Lesser persons are to be beaten or imprisoned.[80]

In the capitulary of Compiègne (757), Pepin forbade anyone to sponsor a stepchild at confirmation. If an individual did so, he was required to separate from his spouse, the mother of the child, because he had become her cofather. Such a separation was not a divorce in the modern sense of the term, since neither party was permitted to remarry. Rather, it was a punishment for incest with a spiritual kinsman.[81]

Pepin was a pioneer in the effort to force Frankish spiritual kinsmen to observe the papal-Byzantine forms of sexual avoidance. However, such a policy was probably disruptive of traditional marriage practices and Pepin's successor Charlemagne drew back somewhat. Indeed, in none of his extant capitularies is the matter of marriage among spiritual kinsmen explicitly mentioned.

In Charlemagne's lifetime and for a century thereafter, bishops and compilers of penitentials continued to promote the ban on sexual contact among spiritual kin. They also continued the process of extending the ban to cover all eventualities. One example of this may suffice. Early in the ninth century, Bishop Ghaerbald of Liège (785/87–809) issued a questionnaire for his priests to use in their dealings with the laity, commanding them to inquire about the sexual behavior of spir-

---

[80] *Capitulary of King Pepin* (751–755), chs. 1 and 2, in MGH Capitularia, vol. 1, p. 31 (italics added).

[81] *Capitulary of Compiègne* (757), ch. 15, in MGH Capitularia, vol. 1, p. 38: "Si quis filiastram aut filiastrum ante episcopum ad confirmationem tenuerit, separetur ab uxore sua et alteram non accipiat. Similiter et femina alterum non accipiat."

itual kinsmen under their supervision. Ghaerbald recognized only two occasions for sponsorship, baptism and confirmation, each of which created marital impediments. (If other forms of sponsorship existed, they fell outside the bishop's concern.) He instructed his priests to determine whether anyone had married a comother from baptism or confirmation and if so, whether he had publicly married the woman or had entered into an informal union. He also instructed the priests to identify men who had entered into a marriage or some other sexual relationship with goddaughters from baptism or confirmation. Finally, Ghaerbald told his priests to bring before him any man who had spon- sored a stepchild in confirmation and had remained married to the child's mother.[82] Ghaerbald's silence about spiritual siblings was char- acteristic of the failure of the Frankish church to pay much attention to that aspect of papal-Byzantine practice, perhaps because such a bond would have put too many marital unions out of reach.

The reshaping of marriage law and practice was necessarily a slow process, since it touched on a fundamental social institution. Further- more, some Carolingian legislation implies that the complexities of the law on incest were hazy to the clergy as well as to the laity. Thus Bishop Haito of Basel (807–823) expressed his frustration over the matter in a detailed instruction to his priests: "There are other things that could be written about the crime of incest, . . . and cases almost without number that have not occurred to the one writing this."[83] In time, however, the emphasis on sexual avoidance among spiritual kin became a key feature of western marriage law.

It is not accidental that the infiltration of papal-Byzantine views sparked quarrels and legislation about the marriage of coparents, for such unions had been quite possible in the context of traditional Frankish spiritual kinship. In contrast, there was less upheaval caused by the papal-Byzantine ban on marriage between godparent and god- child. After all, so long as Frankish society maintained the custom of males sponsoring males and females sponsoring females, the likelihood of such a marriage was nil. Papal letters and papally influenced canon- ical collections forbade the marriage of godparent and godchild, but this prohibition did not correspond to any pressing situation in the north and it was accepted rather passively. Only in the ninth century did Frankish councils and episcopal statutes begin to repeat the ban on godparent/godchild unions.[84] These prohibitions imply that the

[82] Ghaer II, chs. 3, 16, and 17, pp. 357–362.
[83] Haito, ch. 21, p. 365.
[84] Ghaer II, ch. 16, pp. 361–362; Haito, ch. 21, p. 365.

custom of same-sex sponsorship was changing or that the spouse of a sponsor was sharing in the godparenthood, creating the possibility that in the event of the sponsor's death the surviving spouse might marry the godchild.

Italian custom is discernible in the slow disintegration of the practice of same-sex sponsorship in the north. Indeed, the two earliest cross-sex sponsorships of Frankish children that I have found both involve Italy.

In 758 Pope Paul I was eager to win Pepin's protection against the Lombards. Paul's predecessor and brother, Pope Stephen II (752–757), had been Pepin's cofather and Paul wished to renew that bond.[85] In 758 Pepin had no unbaptized son, but he did have a newborn daughter, Gisela. Pope Paul was well acquainted with cross-sex sponsorship and he went to some lengths to sponsor Gisela in order to add a bond of spiritual kinship to his political ties to her father. It was not feasible for Pope Paul to go to the kingdom of the Franks or for Gisela to be brought to Italy. Hence the baby was baptized at home and the pope was her sponsor by proxy, the earliest example of that procedure. The towel (*sabanum*) with which she had been received from the font was sent to Rome. There Pope Paul gathered a crowd in the church of Saint Petronilla and celebrated a Mass at which he received the *sabanum* "with great joy." He later told Pepin in a letter that "through that *sabanum* we rejoice to have received her [Gisela] as if she were right here."[86] The point to be stressed in this context is that for political reasons the pope sponsored the baby girl in conformity with papal-Byzantine custom, which was quite unknown north of the Alps.

In 781 a similar incident occurred, although it was overshadowed by a more conventional same-sex sponsorship. In this instance, Charlemagne went to Rome, where Pope Hadrian sponsored his son Carloman, then about seven years old, whose name was changed to Pepin for dynastic reasons. On the journey back to the north, Charles stopped in Milan, where his infant daughter, also named Gisela, was baptized and sponsored by Archbishop Thomas of Milan. [87] Here too

---

[85] Stephen II addressed Pepin as *compater noster spiritualis* in letters 6, 7, 8, and 11 of the *Codex Carolinus*, pp. 488–507 passim.

[86] Paul II to Pepin, ibid., letter 14, pp. 511–512.

[87] *Annales regni Francorum*, year 781, ed. F. Kurze and reprinted in *Ausgewählte Quellen zur deutschen Geschichte des Mittelalters*, vol. 5 (Darmstadt, 1968), p. 40: "Et inde revertente domno Carolo rege, Mediolanis civitate pervenit, et ibi baptizata est filia eius domna Gisola ab archiepiscopo nomine Thoma, qui et ipse eam a sacro baptismo manibus suscepit."

a Frankish king was introduced to Italian sponsoring customs in the course of creating desirable political alliances.

Such contact with Italy opened the way for cross-sex sponsorship, which was legitimized by its uncontroversial use in the pope's immediate neighborhood. However, the northern custom of same-sex sponsorship yielded only slowly, and the evidence with which I am familiar argues overwhelmingly for its predominance in the ninth century. Cross-sex sponsorship in the strict sense of the term—that is, one sponsor of the opposite sex to the child—usually occurred in the West for political reasons.[88] But other developments, particularly the multiplication of sponsors at baptism, also eased the transition to cross-sex sponsorship. Eventually, each infant had both male and female sponsors. Once this happened, the possibility of marriage between godparent and godchild increased and the ban on such marriages became a normal feature of official pronouncements on spiritual kinship.

The major religious development in the Frankish church during the eighth and ninth centuries was the establishment of close bonds between Continental and Mediterranean Christianity. The papal-Frankish alliance opened the northern churches to papal influence, which in practice included much that was shared with Byzantine Christianity. Thus the Frankish church was increasingly Romanized in its structures, liturgy, and canon law.[89]

One feature of Mediterranean Christianity that found fertile soil in the north was the incest taboo among spiritual kinsmen, which was grafted onto the flourishing Frankish spiritual kinship system in the space of a single lifetime (ca. 730 to ca. 800). But changes in so fundamental a social institution as marriage cannot merely be commanded, and it was several generations before the mass of western Christians actually took spiritual kinship into account in contracting marriage. Nevertheless, the combined impact of papal decretals, councils, royal capitularies, episcopal statutes, canonical collections, peni-

[88] In 853 the Emperor Lothar sponsored the daughter of his half-brother Charles the Bald: *Annales Bertiniani*, year 853, ed. Georg Waitz and reprinted in *Ausgewählte Quellen*, vol. 6, p. 84; in 943 Duke Hugh sponsored the daughter of King Louis IV: Flodoard, *Annales*, year 943, ed. Philippe Lauer, CT, vol. 39 (Paris, 1905), p. 89; and in 948 Duke Conrad the Red of Lorraine sponsored another daughter of the same king, ibid., p. 116.

[89] On the Romanization of the Frankish liturgy, see Cyrille Vogel, *La réforme cultuelle sous Pepin le Bref et sous Charlemagne* (Graz, 1965), pp. 171–242; and on the Romanization of Frankish canon law, particularly through the official acceptance and dissemination of the Roman canonical collection called the *Dionysio-Hadriana*, see Paul Fournier and Gabriel Le Bras, *Histoire des collections canoniques en occident depuis les Fausses Décrétales jusqu'au Décret de Gratien*, 2 vols. (Paris, 1931), 1:92–120.

tentials, and sermons eventually remade the popular perception of spiritual kinsmen and put them sexually off limits to one another. Thus, from the ninth to the sixteenth centuries, spiritual kinship with a prominently delineated sexual taboo was an important feature of social life in the West.

NINE

THE CULTURAL ROOTS OF THE
BAN ON SEXUAL CONTACT BETWEEN
SPIRITUAL KINSMEN

By the mid-eighth century, the sibling Christian cultures of Byzantium and the Latin West had adopted significant restrictions on sexual behavior between spiritual kin, restrictions that were buttressed by the canon and civil law. These sexual taboos were an innovation of the sixth and seventh centuries that had their basis in a perception of baptismal kinship as real kinship that was binding on all participants; to superimpose a sexual relationship on this spiritual kinship was perceived as an unclean act, a form of incest.

Legislative texts, saints' lives, and other written sources permit the modern scholar to trace the formal aspects of the unfolding of the taboo and, very imperfectly, the informal, popular aspects of the movement. But to ask *why* this innovation occurred is to venture onto slippery terrain, that of human feelings and emotions in a culture that is not our own. Any explanation must attempt to account for a shift in sensibilities that led to a significant adaptation of the social institutions governing sexual behavior. Thus, to respond that the book of Leviticus or any other literary source caused the development will not suffice because such an explanation overestimates the power of high literate culture to effect changes in mores and underestimates the strength of feeling necessary to influence so basic an institution as marriage. Furthermore, it must be recalled that Leviticus treated consanguinity and affinity but not spiritual kinship, a notion unknown to Old Testament Judaism and only vaguely delineated in the first five centuries of Christianity. Finally, it is clear that while Leviticus and the other books of the Pentateuch gave many commands and prohibitions, only some of these were observed in early medieval society. It is necessary, therefore, to seek to identify the conditions in early medieval Christian culture that favored the acceptance of heightened concern about incest, purity, and sexual restraint.

There are many ways to approach so complex an issue, some of which are useful but not adequate by themselves. Most modern studies of marital impediments have been conducted by canonists, whose unraveling of the subtle intricacies of the topic has been thorough. However, in the canonistic studies with which I am familiar, there has been little attempt to investigate the historical origins of the various prohibitions.[1] In recent years, social historians and at least one anthropologist have explained the proliferation of marital impediments in terms of the church's efforts at social control. In this they do not deny that other factors may have influenced medieval attitudes, but they nevertheless point to the institutional self-interest of the church as the key factor.

Georges Duby has argued that in themselves many of the elaborate marital prohibitions were inexplicable to contemporaries and that the arguments used to justify them were often *post factum* rationalizations. However, the impediments make sense when seen from another perspective, that of the church's implementation of social control. Thus Duby delineated two medieval visions of what a proper marriage should be, a "lay model" and an "ecclesiastical model." The two had much in common, but at important points they were in conflict. In the lay model, marriage was a family matter, bound up with property, family interests, and family pride, and was not to be tampered with by churchmen. But according to Duby's interpretation, this is just what the church attempted to do in its elaboration of marital prohibitions and its concern with "incestuous" marriages, all of which were elements of a strategy to impose the church's model of marriage on society. The multiplication of impediments made marriages "public" and subject to scrutiny and approval by the church, and the very complexity of marriage law demanded adjudication, thereby promoting the church's claim to regulate a fundamental social institution.[2]

Recently the British anthropologist Jack Goody has also detected a link between marital impediments and ecclesiastical control, but in his analysis it is given an economic twist. Thus Goody argues that extensive marriage prohibitions were part of an ecclesiastical strategy to accumulate property since they restricted the ways in which families

---

[1] Jean Fleury, *Recherches historiques sur les empêchements de parenté dans le mariage canonique des origines aux Fausses Décrétales* (Paris, 1933), pp. 266–271, concludes that it was the Levitical law of purity that stimulated the early medieval elaboration of marital impediments.

[2] Georges Duby, "Le mariage dans la société du haut moyen âge," *Il matrimonio nella società altomedievale*, pt. 1, SSAM, vol. 24 (Spoleto, 1977), pp. 28–29. Duby also explores the relationship between incest impediments and ecclesiastical control in *Medieval Marriage: Two Models from Twelfth-Century France*, tr. Elborg Forster (Baltimore, 1978), pp. 17–20.

could provide themselves with heirs, thereby undermining their hold on property. In earlier days, marriages with close kin had served to keep property within the wider family, with dowries and bridewealth passing from one part of the kin group to another. Goody sees the church's negative attitude toward a whole series of family matters—including concubinage, adoption, divorce, and marriages with close kin—as intended to deny many families such easy ways to find legal heirs, particularly male heirs. The net result of the marriage regulations was to increase the chances that some of an heirless family's property would be given to the church as a pious donation.[3] His conclusion was that:

> for the Church to grow and survive it had to accumulate property, which meant acquiring control over the way it was passed from one generation to the next. Since the distribution of property between generations is related to patterns of marriage and the legitimisation of children, the Church had to gain authority over these so that it could influence the strategies of heirship.[4]

Such explanations are interesting and illuminating, but the assessment of their validity must wait for more research. It is one thing to describe what happened as a result of the increasing complexity of marriage law, but it is quite another to demonstrate that the church *intended* such results or even understood the cause and effect relationship that apparently increased its power and wealth. In any case, without denying the multiplicity of causes and results, I shall look elsewhere to account for the growth of a specific set of marital taboos, those between spiritual kin.

An explanation for these sexual taboos that stresses ecclesiastical or secular legislation would, however, also be inadequate, for in the rudimentary state of premodern governments mere legislative command could not create *ex nihilo* a strong sentiment about incest. But if such a sentiment existed already, the law could channel it, reinforce it, diffuse it to new groups or areas, fix its contours, and settle disputes about its limits. The early medieval written law on the matter was basically a reaction rather than a cause. In other words, anxiety about sexual contact among spiritual kin arose in a particular time and place, among the Christian peoples of the Mediterranean in the sixth and seventh centuries. This anxiety was influenced by biblical injunctions,

[3] Jack Goody, *The Development of the Family and Marriage in Europe* (Cambridge, 1983), pp. 59, 95, 103–156.
[4] Ibid., p. 221.

legislators' strictures, and perhaps the political and material interests of the church, but it was not created by them.

The roots of the sexual taboos that came to be an integral element of spiritual kinship must be sought in two other areas: first, in late ancient and early medieval attitudes toward sexuality, and second, in the contrast that Christians perceived between carnal and spiritual birth, between the realms of the flesh and the spirit. The incest taboo makes cultural sense when it is seen as flowing out of the confrontation between a pessimistic view of sexual activity and a conviction that baptism created a spiritual family, which had to be kept free from the taint inherent in sexuality.

The great Semitic religions, Judaism, Christianity, and Islam, have been marked by a vigorous effort to direct the sexual behavior of their adherents, primarily by limiting such activities. As a consequence of its allegiance to the Old Testament and to the ethics of normative Judaism, early Christianity condemned with little hesitation a wide range of sexual activities, including homosexuality, bestiality, fornication, adultery, and incest. These prohibitions were probably reinforced by trends in the culture of late antiquity. In the course of the third century, Catholic Christianity entered more and more into contact with the main currents of Greco-Roman life. And one of the strongest of these currents, at least among the educated classes to whose opinions we have access, was a growing "spiritualization" of thought and values, a stress on spirit to the disadvantage of matter, a sharpening of the dualism inherent in much of Greek thought, and an almost boundless admiration for ascetics who denied the body: in short, a flight from the world of sense and matter to a realm where men would be angels.

The place of Christianity in this epoch-making change has often been exaggerated. For it was not a Christian phenomenon, although Christians shared in it. Thus the familiar figure of the fierce Christian ascetic given over to a struggle against his body and its earthly yearnings must be balanced by references to pagan philosophers who also taught renunciation. For example, the Neo-Platonic philosopher Plotinus (ca. 205–270) was described by his disciple Porphyry as a person who seemed to be ashamed to be in a body. Plotinus was a vegetarian, reluctant to pamper himself with baths, and reticent about such earthly matters as his parents or his native country.[5] This example warns us that the shift in sensibilities about the relative value of matter

---

[5] Porphyry, *Life of Plotinus*, chs. 1–2, ed. Emile Bréhier, *Plotin. Ennéades*, 6 vols. (Paris, 1924), 1:1–3.

and spirit crossed religious lines. Christians, Jews, and many of late antiquity's finest representatives of traditional Greco-Roman religious and philosophical values all experienced the attraction of this spiritualization of life and thought. The thrust toward denigrating matter took on varied hues and degrees of intensity, but it is striking how widespread it was.[6]

One consequence of this shift in attitudes was an increasingly pessimistic view of human sexual functions, which were identified with the material, animalistic side of reality. In the most extreme forms of this pessimism, manifested primarily within Gnostic Christian circles, sexuality and all sexual activity were condemned as inherently evil.[7] In fact, several Gnostic systems of thought regarded material creation, including the human body and all its physical functions, as the product of an evil power, to be avoided as far as possible by enlightened believers.[8] However, the Catholic tradition of Christianity, the strand that was to dominate the future development of the movement, rejected such an extreme stance as part of its more general repudiation of Gnostic notions of an evil creator who was distinct from the good God. Thus in the credal statments of the early church, there was the vigorous assertion of the existence of one God, who was creator of heaven and earth, and the accompanying assertion that his creation, including the human body, was inherently good.

This legitimation of human sexuality and reproduction on theological grounds was, however, grudging in the extreme. And the late

[6] The spiritualization of values in the later Roman Empire and its practical consequences have not received a sufficiently broad and synthetic treatment, although there is a huge bibliography dealing with specific aspects of the topic. For a brief, illuminating approach to the alienation from the material world that was so common among late antique intellectuals, see Eric R. Dodds, "Man and the Material World," *Pagan and Christian in an Age of Anxiety* (Cambridge, 1965), pp. 1–36.

[7] On the rejection of sexuality by some early Christian groups, see Arthur Vööbus, *Celibacy: A Requirement for Admission to Christian Baptism in the Early Syrian Church*, Papers of the Estonian Theological Society in Exile, vol. 1 (Stockholm, 1951); Georges Blond, "Encratisme," *DSAM* 4 (1959):628–642; and Charles Munier, *L'Eglise dans l'Empire romain (iie–iiie siècles)*, Histoire du droit et des institutions de l'Eglise en Occident, vol. 2, pt. 3 (Paris, 1979), pp. 7–16.

[8] On the rejection of material creation and its creator by second-century Gnostics, see Hans Jonas, *The Gnostic Religion*, 2nd ed. (Boston, 1963), pp. 42–46; Robert M. Wilson, *The Gnostic Problem: A Study of the Relations Between Hellenistic Judaism and the Gnostic Heresy* (London, 1958), pp. 202–228. On the Manichaean doctrine that spread into the Roman Empire from Persia in the fourth century and for a time counted Augustine among its adherents, see John J. O'Meara, *The Young Augustine: The Growth of Augustine's Mind Up to His Conversion* (London, 1954), pp. 69–79, and Gerald Bonner, *St. Augustine of Hippo: Life and Controversies* (London, 1963), pp. 161–172.

antique culture's increasing spiritualization, as well as the church's struggles with rigorists within its own ranks, left an enduring mark on Christianity's ethical teaching. Christians clearly shared in the widespread feelings of disgust and shame over the human body and its physical functions, particularly sexuality. Indeed, by the fourth century, when the church entered into an alliance with the Roman Empire, the Christian ethical system was marked by a stern ascetic component that would dominate theory and practice until the thirteenth century. And although scholastic theologians tempered the theory somewhat, common practice retained much of this rigidity into the modern era.[9]

According to the new ascetic ethic, virginity was a highly prized, indeed recommended state, although marriage was admitted to be a good, if second class, status for most Christians.[10] All sexual activity outside of marriage was forbidden, and even within marriage rigorous moralists like Augustine of Hippo argued that sexual intercourse was legitimate only *causa liberorum procreandorum*, "for the procreation of children." If the desire for sexual gratification motivated sexual intercourse within marriage, then the act was tainted by sin, though Augustine conceded that such sin was not mortal and could be redeemed by alms-giving and prayer.[11] Some early medieval theologians saw in Psalm 50:7 ("For behold I was conceived in iniquities: and in sin did

[9] Josef G. Ziegler, *Die Ehelehre der Pönitentialsummen von 1200–1350*, Studien zur Geschichte der katholische Moraltheologie, vol. 4 (Regensburg, 1956), pp. 259–274.

[10] Gennadius, *Liber sive Definitio ecclesiasticorum dogmatum*, chs. 29–31, ed. Charles Turner, *JTS* 7 (1906):95–96: "XXVIIII. Bonae sunt nuptiae, sed causa filiorum et conpescendae fornicationis obtentu. XXX. Melior est continentia; sed non sibi sufficit ad beatitudinem, si pro solo amore pudicitiae retinetur, sed si cum hoc affectu causa vacandi Domino elegatur. . . . XXXI. Virginitas utroque bono praecelsior est, quia et naturam vincit et pugnam, naturam corporis integritate, pugnam castimoniae pace." Compare Augustine, *Contra Faustum*, bk. 30, ch. 6. ed. J. Zycha, CSEL, vol. 25 (Vienna, 1891), pp. 754–755, and *De nuptiis et concupiscentia*, bk. 1, ch. 4 (5), ed. C. F. Urba and J. Zycha, CSEL, vol. 42 (Vienna, 1902), pp. 215–216. On the esteem accorded virginity, see John Bugge, *Virginitas: An Essay in the History of a Medieval Ideal* (The Hague, 1975), especially pp. 67–75; Ton H. C. Van Eijk, "Marriage and Virginity, Death and Immortality," *Epektasis. Mélanges patristiques offerts au Cardinal Jean Daniélou* (Paris, 1972), pp. 209–235.

[11] Augustine, *De bono coniugali*, ch. 6, ed. J. Zycha, CSEL, vol. 41 (Vienna, 1900), p. 195; and sermon 9.18 in *PL* 38:88. For a synthetic treatment of Augustine's views on sex within marriage, see Michael Müller, *Die Lehre des hl. Augustinus von der Paradiesehe und ihre Auswirkung in der Sexualethik des 12. und 13. Jahrhunderts bis Thomas von Aquin*, Studien zur Geschichte der katholischen Moraltheologie, vol. 1 (Regensburg, 1954), pp. 29–32, or Dominikus Lindner, *Der Usus Matrimonii. Eine Untersuchung über seine sittliche Bewertung in der katholischen Moraltheologie alter und neuer Zeit* (Munich, 1929), pp. 57–66.

my mother conceive me") a confirmation of their conviction that even marital intercourse was, for all practical purposes, never free from some taint of impurity and sin.[12] And Augustine himself expressed the view, echoed by others, that virtually no one could honestly say that he or she had intercourse solely for the sake of children.[13] Thus all sexual activity was tainted to some degree by sin and surrounded by emotions of revulsion and shame.

Such restrictive and negative evaluations of sexual activity were not confined by any means to Christians, but they were reinforced by a specifically Christian view of human nature. Christian intellectuals discussed human nature from two distinct perspectives, that of humans in Paradise before the Fall and that of humans after the Fall. From the first perspective, a scholar could treat human nature as God had intended it to be, in a state of relative perfection. Thus the consensus by the fourth century was that mankind had been created to be immortal and free from pain, labor, sorrow, and irrational passion.

Many of the church fathers of the third, fourth, and fifth centuries could not bring themselves to believe that so perfect a creature as man-in-Paradise had reproduced in the way that they and much of their culture perceived as degrading, lustful, and shameful. That is, they could not believe that the sexuality of Paradise had much in common with that which characterized fallen mankind in the empirically observable world around them.[14] The daring third-century theologian Origen even went so far as to deny that humans in Paradise had a physical body at all.[15] This view was rejected by the main ecclesiastical tradition, but some of the church fathers, notably Gregory of Nyssa and John Chrysostom, argued that even though Adam and Eve had physical bodies they did not engage in sexual reproduction. In other words, before the Fall immortal human beings had no need for offspring to replace them and hence no need for sexual reproduction. Sexuality had entered the world as a consequence of sin, when mankind forfeited immortality and so needed a way to carry on the race.[16]

[12] Pope Leo I (d. 461), Second Christmas Sermon, ch. 3, ed. René Dolle in *Sermones*, SC, vol. 22 (Paris, 1947), pp. 80–81, declared that every human conception, except that of the Virgin Mary, involved sin. See Müller, *Die Lehre*, pp. 33–34, and Lindner, *Der Usus*, pp. 66–72.

[13] Augustine, *De bono coniugali*, ch. 13.(15), p. 208.

[14] Bugge, *Virginitas*, pp. 12–29.

[15] Müller, *Die Lehre*, pp. 11–13; and Jean Daniélou, *Origène* (Paris, 1948), pp. 215–217.

[16] Müller, *Die Lehre*, pp. 13–19; Gregory of Nyssa, *De hominis opficio*, ch. 17, ed. J. Laplace, SC, vol. 6 (Paris, 1944), pp. 30–31; John Chrysostom, *La virginité*, chs. 14–15, ed. Herbert Musurillo and B. Grillet, SC, vol. 125 (Paris, 1966), pp. 137–147. On

Augustine of Hippo, whose influence was enormous in the West, had held similar views in his early years as a bishop, but in his maturity he argued that human beings in Paradise had indeed reproduced, perhaps even by sexual intercourse, although not in the distasteful way that fallen humanity subsequently did. In Paradise the intellect and will had controlled the reproductive organs in the same way that they still guided the action of a foot or hand. Hence reproduction in Paradise had, in Augustine's view, been orderly, decorous, rational, and free from any degrading taint of lust.[17]

Discussions of humanity in Paradise were, however, merely interesting speculations, for by the fourth century it was a fundamental tenet of Christianity that mankind was no longer in a paradisiacal state.[18] Adam's disobedience had cost him Paradise and had severely damaged his nature and that of his descendants, who were subject to pain, disorder, and death. In particular, the disorderly and disgusting aspects of sexuality, summed up in the Latin terms *libido* or *concupiscentia*, were among the consequences of Adam's sin.[19] In the observable state of humankind, that is, the fallen state, the human will was incapable of controlling lust, which clouded the powers of reason. Thus in the late Roman and early medieval Christian world, sex was perceived as good in its creation for the purposes of propagating the race, but so disoriented by the original sin of Adam that it was, in its real existing state, a problem, a disorderly power, a strong inducement to sin.[20] This theoretical proposition was colored by strong feelings of aversion and shame, at least among the elite whose voices are still discernible, and very likely among the silent masses as well.

The conviction that sin and shame hung around sexuality was closely allied to a belief that sexual activity was incompatible with access to holy persons, places, and things. This was not, however, a peculiarly Christian idea, for there had been an undercurrent in

the view that mankind needed sexual reproduction as a substitute for immortality, see Van Eijk, "Marriage," pp. 220–234.

[17] Augustine, *De civitate Dei*, bk. 14, chs. 21–24, ed. B. Dombart and A. Kalb, CCSL, vol. 48 (Turnhout, 1955), pp. 443–448; and *De nuptiis et concupiscentia*, bk. 1, ch. 6. 7, pp. 218–219, and bk. 22, ch. 37, p. 291. See also Bugge, *Virginitas*, pp. 24–29.

[18] See J.N.D. Kelly, *Early Christian Doctrines*, 5th ed. (London, 1977), pp. 346–352, on the fourth-century Greek Fathers and pp. 353–372 on the Latin Fathers. Jaroslav Pelikan, *The Christian Tradition: A History of the Development of Doctrine*, vol. 1: *The Emergence of the Catholic Tradition (100–600)* (Chicago, 1971), pp. 298–302.

[19] On Augustine's views, see Bonner, *St. Augustine*, pp. 398–401.

[20] Ibid., pp. 375–378; Müller, *Die Lehre*, pp. 32–41; and for the views of Caesarius of Arles, see Henry G. J. Beck, *The Pastoral Care of Souls in South-East France during the Sixth Century*, Analecta Gregoriana, vol. 51 (Rome, 1950), pp. 233–235.

Greco-Roman paganism that demanded temporary sexual abstinence by a person who intended to enter a sacred precinct or to approach a god with prayer or sacrifice. The motivation for such behavior was not clearly moral; rather, the worshipper had to avoid pollution if he or she were to please the deity.[21] Christianity might have imbibed such views from its Greco-Roman milieu, but far more important was the influence of the Old Testament, in which the idea was clearly expressed that sexual activity polluted its participants for a time, making them unfit in a moral and physical sense to approach Yahweh.

In Exodus 19:15, Yahweh commands the Israelites to abstain sexually for three days in preparation for His revelation to them; similarly, Deuteronomy 23:9–11 records the command of Moses that any soldier in camp who experiences a nocturnal emission must leave the area until sunset and wash before returning, for "Yahweh must not see anything improper among you." A series of texts in Leviticus also supported the view that a loss of semen or menstrual blood made a person temporarily unclean and that he or she should be shunned by fellow Israelites and was certainly not fit to approach Yahweh.[22] These biblical texts did not *create* the feelings of unease that late Roman and early medieval people felt toward sex—such feelings already existed—but they did give divine sanction to them, reinforced them, and very likely diffused them through sermons and the like.

The New Testament also contributed (although on a lesser scale) to the system of values and behavior that tightly restricted sexual activity. Paul had explicitly approved of marriage, with the reservation that if possible his followers should remain unmarried like him. But in 1 Corinthians 7:5, he wrote to married couples: "Do not refuse each other except by mutual consent, and then only for an agreed time, to leave yourselves free for prayer." Many early medieval exegetes took this text to imply that sexual activity and prayer, understood in a broad way as any holy activity, were incompatible and should be kept separate.[23]

[21] Eugen Fehrle, *Die kultische Keuschheit im Altertum*, Religionsgeschichtliche Versuche und Vorarbeiten, vol. 6 (Giessen, 1910), esp. pp. 54–64, 222–238.

[22] Leviticus 15:16–18, 19–31; Leviticus 12:1–8. See also Exodus 19:15 and 1 Kings 12:4–5. For a brief anthropological assessment of notions of pollution in the Old Testament, see Mary Douglas, *Purity and Danger: An Analysis of the Concepts of Pollution and Taboo* (London, 1966), pp. 41–57.

[23] Peter Browe, *Beiträge zur Sexualethik des Mittelalters*, Breslauer Studien zur historischen Theologie, vol. 23 (Breslau, 1932), pp. 36–79; Henri Crouzel, "Le célibat et la continence ecclésiastique dans l'Eglise primitive: leurs motivations," *Sacerdoce et célibat. Etudes historiques et théologiques*, Bibliotheca ephemeridum theologicarum lovaniensium, vol. 28 (Louvain and Gembloux, 1971), pp. 345–352.

In view of such attitudes, ratified by the Old Testament and to a more limited extent by the New Testament, it is not surprising that sexual activity of any kind—marital or extramarital, voluntary or involuntary—was perceived as incompatible with religious acts. To approach holy things or to enter holy places while unclean as a result of sexual activity was perceived as irreligious, as an insult to the Deity, and dangerous to the perpetrator.

Between the fourth and the seventh centuries, this view was translated by custom and legislation into norms governing the behavior of Christians. Accordingly, married persons were advised or commanded to abstain from sexual intercourse for a suitable length of time when they intended to receive the Eucharist or even enter a church.[24] And during holy times, such as Lent or the vigil of an important religious holiday, sexual abstinence was enjoined strictly on all.[25] In southern Gaul in the sixth century, newly married couples were encouraged to abstain from sexual relations for three nights out of reverence for the nuptial blessing they had received.[26] A celibate cleric who had experienced a nocturnal emission was sometimes commanded and sometimes advised to avoid religious acts the following day because he was unclean,[27] and menstruating women were sometimes forbidden to enter a church or to receive the Eucharist.[28] In short, Christianity had erected a barrier between the sexual and religious aspects of human life.

The demand for sexual abstinence was considerable and may rarely have been fully observed in practice, but at least in theory the laity could have complied with it. Married couples could, for example, alternate times of abstinent holiness with times of sexual activity. This sort of scheduling led to lay people taking the Eucharist ever more infrequently, in part because of the demand for several days of sexual purity as a precondition for its reception.

But the demand for careful segregation of sexuality from holy acts had more direct consequences for the clergy. So long as the Eucharist was celebrated infrequently, with Sunday as the usual occasion, married clergy could plan their lives so as to accommodate both sexual

[24] Browe, *Beiträge*, pp. 36–79.

[25] In addition to Browe, *Beiträge*, pp. 36–79, see Beck, *Pastoral Care*, p. 234, and Lindner, *Der Usus*, pp. 76–78, 86–87.

[26] Browe, *Beiträge*, pp. 114–120; P. Santyves, "Les trois nuits de Tobie ou la continence durant la première nuit ou les premières nuits du mariage," *Revue anthropologique* 44 (1934):266–296.

[27] Browe, *Beiträge*, pp. 80–113.

[28] Ibid., pp. 1–14.

intercourse and their liturgical duties. Such has, in fact, been the practice among the lower clergy of the Greek church since late antiquity. However, in the West this balance did not endure.

In the late fourth century at Rome, liturgical changes led to a demand for a completely celibate clergy. Roger Gryson has argued persuasively that the Eucharist came to be celebrated more frequently at Rome, perhaps even daily. This meant that the clergy were required to perform religous ceremonies and handle consecrated objects so often that permanent sexual abstinence was imposed on them so as to avoid the ritual impurity that fourth- and fifth-century Christians feared.[29] Thus it was quite usual for the behavior of both laymen and clergy to be molded in response to the aversion to sexual activity, except within strict constraints.

By the fifth century, Christianity had assimilated from its Greco-Roman milieu and its Judaic origins the conviction that sexual activity, legitimate though it might be from a theoretical perspective, was ordinarily sinful and defiling, incompatible with anything holy. Within the context of such views, the processes of conception and birth were regarded with particular anxiety because they were associated with uncleanness, with a pollution that was both ritual and physical. Leviticus 12:1–8 was the primary biblical text that validated these preexisting attitudes:

> Yahweh spoke to Moses; he said, "Speak to the sons of Israel and say: 'If a woman conceives and gives birth to a boy, she is to be unclean for seven days, just as she is unclean during her monthly periods. On the eighth day the child's foreskin must be circumcized, and she must wait another thirty-three days for her blood to be purified. She must not touch anything consecrated nor go to the sanctuary until the time of her purification is over.
>
> 'If she gives birth to a girl, she is to be unclean for two weeks, as during her monthly periods; and she must wait another sixty-six days for her blood to be purified.
>
> 'When the period of her purification is over, for either boy or girl, she is to bring to the priest at the entrance to the Tent of Meeting a lamb one year old for a holocaust, and a young pigeon or turtle dove as a sacrifice for sin. The priest is to offer this

[29] Roger Gryson, *Les origines du célibat ecclésiastique du premier au septième siècle* (Gembloux, 1970), pp. 197–204. On the innovation of the daily Eucharist in some western churches in the later fourth century and its consequences for the celibacy of the clergy, see Raymund Kottje, "Das Aufkommen der täglichen Eucharistiefeier in der Westkirche und die Zölibatsforderung," *ZKG* 82 (1971):218–228.

before Yahweh, perform the rite of atonement over her, and she will be purified from the flow of her blood.' "

In the ancient and early medieval church there was considerable difference of opinion among theologians about the status of such Old Testament prescriptions. The main question was whether they had continuing validity or had been abrogated by the coming of Christ. In Byzantine Christianity, they were taken seriously and women were treated as ritually unclean while menstruating or until they had been purified after giving birth to a child.[30]

In the western church there was significant wavering on the matter. Learned comment tended to be lenient, while practice tended to be strict. In his *Ecclesiastical History*, Bede reproduced the *Libellus responsionum*, which he believed contained Pope Gregory the Great's answers to questions put to him by Augustine of Canterbury about the year 600.[31] In question 8, Augustine had asked about the religious status of women in certain circumstances, notably immediately after childbirth and during menstruation. It is clear from the tone of the response that Gregory (or whoever wrote it) consciously intended to mitigate literal interpretations of Old Testament texts that put severe religious disabilities on persons in a ritually unclean state. His moderate approach is evident from the following excerpts, but so are the rigorous attitudes against which he was reacting:

> When a woman is delivered, after how many days she may come into the church, you have been informed by reading the Old Testament, viz. that she is to abstain for a male child thirty-three days and sixty-six for a female. Now you must know that this is to be taken in a mystery; for if she enters the church the very hour that she is delivered, to return thanks, she is not guilty of any sin; because the pleasure of the flesh is in fault, and not the pain; but the pleasure is in the copulation of the flesh, whereas there is pain in bringing forth the child. Wherefore it is said to the first mother of all, 'In sorrow thou shalt bring forth children.' If, therefore, we forbid a woman that has brought forth, to enter the church, we make a crime of her very punishment.

[30] Browe, *Beiträge*, pp. 15–35.
[31] For a review of the controversy about the authenticity of the *Libellus responsionum*, which survives in three versions in more than 130 manuscripts, see Paul Meyvaert, "Bede's Text of the *Libellus Responsionum* of Gregory the Great to Augustine of Canterbury," *England Before the Conquest: Studies in Primary Sources Presented to Dorothy Whitelock* (Cambridge, 1971), pp. 15–33.

. . . the Law condemns to death any man that shall approach unto a woman during her uncleanness. Yet the woman, nevertheless, must not be forbidden to come into church whilst she has her monthly courses; because the superfluity of nature cannot be imputed to her as a crime; and it is not just that she should be refused admittance into the church, for that which she suffers against her will.

She must not, therefore, be forbidden to receive the mystery of the holy communion during those days. But if any one out of profound respect does not presume to do it, she is to be commended; yet if she receives it, she is not to be judged. For it is the part of noble minds in some manner to acknowledge their faults, even where there is no offence; because very often that is done without a fault, which, nevertheless, proceeded from a fault. Therefore, when we are hungry, it is no crime to eat; yet our being hungry proceeds from the sin of the first man. The monthly courses are no crime in women, because they naturally happen; however, because our nature itself is so depraved, that it appears to be so without the concurrence of the will, the fault proceeds from sin, and thereby human nature may herself know what she is become by judgment. And let man, who wilfully committed the offence, bear the guilt of that offence. And, therefore, let women consider with themselves and if they do not presume, during their monthly courses, to approach the sacrament of the body and blood of our Lord, they are to be commended for their praiseworthy consideration; but when they are carried away with love of the same mystery to receive it out of the usual custom of religious life, they are not to be restrained, as we said before.

. . . For though several nations have different opinions concerning this affair [ritual impurity after intercourse], . . . it was always the custom of the Romans, from ancient times, for such an one to be cleansed by washing, and for some time respectfully to forbear entering a church. Nor do we, in so saying, assign matrimony to a fault; but forasmuch as lawful intercourse cannot be had without the pleasure of the flesh, it is proper to forbear entering the holy place, because the pleasure itself cannot be without a fault.[32]

---

[32] Bede, *Ecclesiastical History*, bk. 1, ch. 27, ed. Bertram Colgrave and R.A.B. Mynors (Oxford, 1969), pp. 91–97, tr. J. A. Giles, *The Venerable Bede's Ecclesiastical History*, 2nd ed. (London, 1849), pp. 46–49.

These views were, however, generally submerged in the wave of opposing attitudes that were spread on the Continent by Irish missionaries and their books during the sixth to eighth centuries. The Irish had an intense interest in the Mosaic Law, and revived many of its features, including those that placed barriers between sex and holiness and treated women as ritually impure following childbirth or during menstruation.[33] Such convictions were expressed in varied ways: liturgical ceremonies for the purification of women after childbirth were elaborated, and ritually impure women were discouraged from approaching the Eucharist or entering a church. Some churchmen even felt scruples about granting full burial rites to a woman who died in childbirth and hence was unpurified. It was only in the twelfth century that views similar to those of Gregory began successfully to counteract the purity/impurity syndrome, but the fading away of earlier attitudes and customs was slow.[34]

A newborn child was also in a dangerous condition because it had not been baptized. It had no name and little or no standing in society.[35] It was also vulnerable to attack by demons, a fear that lay at the origin of stories about changelings. Such widespread views of birth as a ritually impure, dangerous event were reinforced by the specifically Christian doctrine of original sin, which had been developing since the mid-third century. According to this doctrine, Adam's disobedience to God had been disastrous for his descendants. His "original sin," as the disobedience came to be called, was hereditary: every human child was born with it. Carrying this one step further, some theologians—among them Augustine, Gregory of Nyssa, and John Chrysostom—believed that the original sin was transmitted precisely by sexual relations, by the "polluted seed."[36]

Baptism was able to undo much of the damage done by Adam's sin. It was the second birth in the life of every Christian, a spiritual birth that was pure in a ritual sense and purifying in a religious sense. In a sermon to *competentes* preparing for baptism, Augustine briefly delineated these contrasted births: "We have a father and mother on earth,

---

[33] Raymund Kottje, *Studien zum Einfluss des Alten Testamentes auf Recht und Liturgie des frühen Mittelalters (6–8 Jahrhundert)*. BHF, vol. 23 (Bonn, 1964), pp. 11–43.

[34] Browe, *Beiträge*, pp. 15–21; Ziegler, *Die Ehelehre*, pp. 243–271.

[35] In northern Germanic societies, in both their pagan and their Christian phases, until an infant was named it was not protected against abandonment or death. See Ursula Perkow, *Wasserweihe, Taufe und Patenschaft bei den Nordgermanen* (Ph.D. diss., Hamburg, 1972), pp. 21–27.

[36] Julius Gross, *Geschichte des Erbsündendogmas. Ein Beitrag zur Geschichte des Problems vom Ursprung des Übels*, 4 vols. (Munich and Basel, 1960), 1:113–255 and, on Augustine's views, 1:257–376.

so that we may be born to labors and death; we find other parents, God the Father and Mother Church, from whom we are born to eternal life."[37] By the sixth century in Gaul, the sponsors had emerged as the parents in the second birth and, at least in the popular view, had replaced or perhaps stood beside God the Father and Mother Church. The second birth was a mirror image of the first, precisely because it was free from the polluting factors that made the latter objectionable to much of contemporary opinion.

The contrast in births was deeply felt. Faustus of Riez (ca. 400 to ca. 490), an abbot and bishop in southern Gaul, expressed the views of many intellectuals on the issues of birth and sexuality in his *De gratia*, written in 473/474 against the opinions of Lucidus, a champion of extreme Augustinian views on grace, free will, and predestination.[38] Faustus belonged to that circle of monks, churchmen, and intellectuals in fifth-century Gaul who have been called semi-Pelagians, although they might with equal justice be called semi-Augustinians. They were deeply influenced by Augustine, but could not follow the North African theologian to the rigorous, systematic views on grace, free will, and predestination that he and some of his followers held. Faustus' writings illuminate the southern Gallic monastic milieu that two generations later would produce the earliest literary evidence on baptismal kinship. So far as the records reveal, Faustus did not know a taboo on sexual contact between spiritual kin, but his ideas reflect the matrix out of which they arose.

Faustus wrote *De gratia* against extreme forms of Augustinianism, but he had no sympathy for the views traditionally ascribed to Pelagius (who flourished between 400 and 415).[39] Hence in *De gratia*, book 1, chapter 2, Faustus attempted to refute these views. In the course of his argument, he also reveals the opinions of his milieu on sexual relations, birth, and rebirth.

In Faustus' literary dialogue, Pelagius begins by denying that infants need baptism. He defends this view by making the logical point that if baptism takes away original sin it cannot be possible for a baptized man and woman to pass on that sin to their child, since presumably they no longer have it to give. Faustus responds that "there are two births, from one of which sin is passed on from the lust of the begetter [*ex generantis voluptate*], while from the other sanctification is

[37] Augustine, Sermon 57, *PL* 38:387. Compare Sermon 121 and Sermon 216 in *PL* 38:680 and 1081.
[38] Faustus of Riez, *De gratia*, ed. A. Engelbrecht, CSEL, vol. 21 (Vienna, 1891), pp. 3–98.
[39] On Pelagius and his views, see Bonner, *St. Augustine*, pp. 352–393.

given from the choice of the second begetter [*de regenerantis adoptione*]."⁴⁰ The two births correspond to two realms, one of nature and the other of grace, and Pelagius' error lies in confusing them: "Most unwisely Pelagius believes that the purity of innocence is given to children through their parents. The second birth does not pertain to the activity of parents."⁴¹

As Faustus states it, the second birth in baptism is a task of God, not of parents. Furthermore, "there is no doubt that the original sin passes over from parents, even baptized ones, to their children through the very creation of flesh [at this point he cites Psalm 50:7, which was part of the liturgy], for we say every day with the prophet, 'For behold I was conceived in iniquities and in sins did my mother conceive me,' just as the Apostle confirms that the incurable fault passed from one man [Adam] to all men [Romans 5:15]."⁴² Thus Faustus affirms a dichotomy between births, carnal and spiritual, and connects the transmission of original sin with the sexual nature of carnal birth, just as he connects the transmission of grace to the spiritual birth.

As the dialogue continues, Pelagius is made to counter that the desire of begetting (*concupiscentia generationis*), that is, the human sexual drive, is derived from God and thus should not be blamed for the transmission of original sin. In reply, Faustus expresses the common deprecation of human sexual urges, as they exist among fallen humanity, asserting that sexual reproduction is indeed the mechanism by which original sin is passed from one generation to the next, "without doubt through the driving ardor of wicked begetting and through the filthy embrace of each parent."⁴³ Faustus further cites the examples of the three persons whom he thinks to have been free from the original sin—Jesus, Adam, and Eve—in each of whom the freedom from sin is linked causally to an asexual conception or creation.

In the case of Jesus, Faustus attributes sinlessness to the fact that he had been conceived "not by the flesh but by the spirit, and not by

⁴⁰ Faustus, *De gratia*, bk. 1, ch. 2, p. 12: "quibus facile respondetur duas esse natiuitates, de quarum una peccatum ex generantis uoluptate transmittitur, ex alia sanctificatio de regenerantis adoptione donatur."

⁴¹ Ibid.: "inprudentissime per parentes filiis innocentiae puritatem Pelagius dari credit. ad parentum ministerium natiuitas secunda non pertinet."

⁴² Ibid.: "originale autem peccatum ex parentibus etiam baptizatis per carnis originem ad filios transire non dubium est dicentibus nobis cotidie cum propheta: ecce enim in iniquitatibus conceptus sum et in delictis peperit me mater mea, sicut et apostolus istud insanabile piaculum ex uno in omnes homines pertransisse confirmat."

⁴³ Ibid., p. 13: "sine dubio per incentiuum maledictae generationis ardorem et per inlecebrosum utriusque parentis amplexum."

shameful lust but by an astounding blessing."[44] Such a view was not
an original one, for there had been a persistent theological argument
in the fourth and fifth centuries that the virgin birth was a precondition and guarantee of Jesus' holiness.[45] In a similar vein, Faustus main-
tains that Adam and Eve had been free from sin in their origin because
direct creation by God had removed any hint of sexuality. Furthermore, Adam and Eve had lived without sexuality (or at least without
passion) until their pride and disobedience plunged them into sin,
which was characterized precisely by an incapability to master sexuality: "He who wished to be a god came to be the slave of lust."[46]

Such views could be interpreted as an attack on marriage itself, a
position that orthodox theology in the fifth century would not con-
done. To avoid such an interpretation, Faustus agreed that marriage
had been good in its origin, but as a consequence of Adam's fall it was
corrupted, though not entirely so: "I praise whatever [relationship] the
divine precept instituted between begetting and desire; I deplore
whatever human dereliction has added."[47] To express his point, he
used the analogy of a white garment with a dark stain: the owner
would not blame the garment or cease using it for some purposes, but
it had lost its respectability (*dignitas*).[48] The present human situation
was not what had been intended by God: if Adam and Eve had not
disobeyed, "begetting would without doubt have been chaste and hon-
orable." But in fact mankind had lost the "gift to purity" along with
the "privilege of immortality."[49]

Faustus' views were not unique, for Mediterranean Christian culture had elaborated, largely from preexisting elements, a thought
world and a corresponding pattern of behavior that were postulated
on the existence of a realm of unclean, polluting, and dangerous activ-

[44] Ibid.: "nam cum illum solum uideas ab originali inmunem esse contagione, qui non
carne, sed spiritu, nec erubescenda passione, sed stupenda benedictione conceptus est,
agnosce causam mali originalis de oblectamento natum conceptionis et de uitio
uoluptatis."
[45] Pelikan, *Emergence*, pp. 286–290.
[46] Faustus, *De gratia*, bk. 1, ch. 2, p. 13: "diuinitatis ambitiosus libidinis coepit esse
captiuus."
[47] Ibid., p. 14: "inter generationem et concupiscentiam quidquid praeceptio diuina
constituit, hoc laudo, quidquid humana praeuaricatio adiecit, hoc reprobo."
[48] Ibid.: "quomodo si aliquis atro inquinamento candorem niueae uestis aspergat, non
displicet factura, sed macula. uestimenti non amisit usum, etsi perdidit dignitatem."
[49] Ibid.: "futura erat indubitanter casta et sincera generatio, si non intercessisset in-
imica transgressio. sed inmaculatos thoros caro maledictioni addicta maculauit et per
superbiae spiritum simplicem corrupit affectum et sicut inmortalitatis priuilegium, ita
donum perdidit puritatis."

ities. This realm was not strictly sexual, at least as modern biology understands that term, because it included such things as menstruation, birth, and the shedding of blood by the clergy, but the sexual theme was heavily stressed. A person rendered unclean by a polluting activity was considered temporarily unfit for contact with the "holy," that is, with holy buildings, holy persons, holy actions, and holy relationships. The higher clergy, whose entire occupation was with the holy in one form or another, were obviously the group most tightly enmeshed in restrictions intended to keep them pure, restrictions that demanded, in particular, strict sexual continence and a ban on shedding blood. But the laity were also encouraged to respect holy things with which they had contact, a policy that had as practical consequences such developments as infrequent approach to the Eucharist, sexual abstinence during holy seasons, and temporary avoidance of physical contact by married couples during the wife's menstruation and after she gave birth.

The notion that sexual activity is incompatible with holiness is a key to understanding the emergence of a taboo on sexual activity between spiritual kin. Carnal birth through sexual reproduction and spiritual birth through grace were contrasted as the impure and the pure, the earthly and the heavenly, the temporal and the eternal. This deeply felt dichotomy had little discernible social impact so long as the "spiritual" parents were perceived to be God the Father and Mother Church. But when the traditional sponsors began to be described as the spiritual parents and the baptizees as their spiritual children, new possibilities opened up. The use of the word "spiritual" here must not be misconstrued: the spiritual family was no less real than the carnal family, but it was thought to originate and function in a higher realm, that of grace and purity.

The sixth century marks a watershed in the development of the spiritual family and its attendant sexual taboos. Caesarius' sermons, Justinian's law, Procopius' *Secret History*, Gregory of Tours' *History*, and Pope Gregory's *Dialogues* all demonstrate, each in its own way, that the development was uneven in pace, but far advanced. Thus in both the popular and the official view, baptism was the occasion for the creation of a web of kinship, a family that was the mirror image of the natural family.

If one keeps in mind what "pure" and "spiritual" meant in the context of Mediterranean Christianity—most notably that the pure or spiritual thing was shielded from contact with sexuality—then the taboo on sexual contact among spiritual kin has a compelling logic to it; it makes cultural sense. The working out of this demand that the

spiritual kin be kept pure was gradual. Initially the spiritual parents
were perceived as related to the baptizee in a pure way, through divine
grace and not through carnal begetting. Subsequently, in the late seventh and eighth centuries, the baptismal parents' relationship to the
child's natural parents was also drawn into the realm of the spiritual.
Thus the spiritual and natural parents shared the child and were
bound together by ties of grace, which demanded that they not also
be bound by ties of sex. Sexual acts between spiritual kin were inappropriate because they moved the participants from the realm of grace
to that of fallen nature; they did not accord to the bond the respect it
deserved; they sullied a holy relationship. The *Ecloga* of Leo III expresses this in a terse but clear way when it explains, relative to sexual
contact between godparent and godchild, that "the marital relations
cannot be combined with the paternal."[50]

Such a breach of proper behavior was sometimes called incest, although the meaning of that term in early medieval society had a
slightly different content than it has in our own. In modern usage,
incest is defined as sexual access to those persons whom society and
its law declare to be close kin and hence unsuitable marriage partners.
In early medieval usage, "incest" also referred to sexual access to kin,
but it had other meanings as well.

One can slip too easily into the assumption that *incestum* in an early
medieval text implies incest in a modern legal sense. However, early
medieval vocabulary referring to marriage was notoriously imprecise
and the term *incestum* was no exception. An often ignored clue to a
somewhat wider meaning of the term lies in the fact that sexual relations with a woman dedicated to God, a nun, were described as incest
from at least the seventh century in Gaul.[51] The liturgical ceremonies
for veiling virgins were modeled closely on marriage ceremonies and
the nun was thus married to God in some sense.[52] But sexual relations
with a nun were not castigated as adultery or fornication, as such
relations with one's neighbor's wife would be: they were criticized as
incestuous. The explanation for this seemingly anomalous use of the

[50] *Ecloga*, ch. 2.3, tr. Edwin H. Freshfield, *A Manual of Roman Law: The* Ecloga *Published by the Emperors Leo III and Constantine V of Isauria* (Cambridge, 1926), p. 73.

[51] Canon 16 of the Council of Paris (614), *Concilia Galliae A.511–A.695*, ed. de Clercq,
CCSL, vol. 148A (Turnhout, 1963), p. 280; ch. 18 of the Edict of Chlothar II (614),
ibid., p. 285; and ch. 1 of the Capitulary of Pepin (751–55), MGH Capitularia, vol. 1,
p. 31.

[52] René Metz, *La consécration des vierges dans l'Eglise romaine. Etude d'histoire et de la
liturgie*, Bibliothèque de l'Institut de droit canonique de l'Université de Strasbourg, vol.
4 (Paris, 1954), pp. 117–124.

term is that incest did not refer only to illicit relations with kin; it designated sexual relations with any person who was outside the range of potential sexual partners, a person who could never under any circumstances be a legitimate spouse. These sorts of people happened mostly to be close kin (hence the confusion of meaning), but they were also nuns, who by their dedication to God were permanently removed from earthly sexual activity. They were also persons related by the spiritual bond contracted in baptism and, by the mid-eighth century in the West, in confirmation. Sexual relations with such spiritual kin, as with any other of the prohibited persons, were shameful and filthy, which was the root meaning of *incestum/incastum*.

One crucial result of the separation of spiritual kin from sexual relations was the elimination of parents as sponsors to their own children. In Christian antiquity, the ordinary pattern was for a parent to act as sponsor for his or her own child at baptism. But this practice had been on the wane since at least the sixth century, in part because there were practical advantages in inviting an outsider with whom both child and parents would thereafter have a potentially close relationship. However, if they wished to do so, parents could still choose to sponsor their own children. As late as 735, the Anglo-Saxon Bede noted without comment that parents responded for their children in baptism, although a nonparent might have lifted the child from the font.[53] But if a man was forbidden to have sexual relations with his comother, what would happen if that same man sponsored his own child and became a coparent to his wife? The Council in Trullo had declared that a spiritual relationship takes precedence over a carnal one: it was not permitted to maintain both.[54] Thus, because spiritual kinship was perceived as so sacred that it was incompatible with a defiling sexual relationship, spouses who became coparents to one another by sponsoring their own child were forbidden to continue conjugal life together.

Such views had their first discernible impact in Frankish lands in the second quarter of the eighth century. At that time, the Anglo-Saxon Boniface had opposed their spread and defended himself against the charge that he had erred when he allowed a man to marry his comother; in that case, however, the man and woman were not the natural parents of the child. Nevertheless, the first western instance in which reluctance to allow coparents to have sexual relations was

[53] Bede, *In Marci Evangelium Expositio*, bk. 2, ch. 7, v. 29, ed. D. Hurst, CCSL, vol. 120 (Turnhout, 1960), p. 525.
[54] Council in Trullo, canon 53, Mansi 11:967.

applied to husband and wife was also contemporaneous with Boni-face's letters. Indeed, it may well reflect the opinions of circles that were hostile to him.

The *Book of the History of the Franks (Liber historiae Francorum)* was composed about 727 by an anonymous Neustrian historian, perhaps a monk of Saint Denis, just north of Paris.[55] In chapter 31, the author reports an apocryphal tale concerning three late sixth-century figures, King Chilperic and his wives Audovera and Fredegund. According to the tale, while King Chilperic was on campaign against the Saxons, his wife Audovera gave birth to a daughter. Fredegund, a scheming palace servant, encouraged the queen to have the baby baptized before the king's return. Audovera therefore commanded a bishop to prepare the baptistery for the ceremony. But when the baptism was to take place, the *matrona* (could it be *matrina*, godmother?) who was to re-ceive the child was absent. Fredegund convinced Audovera to sponsor the child herself. Thus when the victorious Chilperic returned he was greeted by Fredegund, who said, "Praises be to God since our lord king received victory over his enemies and because a daughter has been born to you. With whom will you sleep tonight, my lord king, seeing that my lady the Queen is your *commater* through your daugh-ter Childesinda?" The king then had angry words with Queen Au-dovera: "Because of your stupidity, you have done a shameful thing; now you can no longer be my wife." Chilperic subsequently gave Audovera and the child a generous gift to take the nun's veil; he exiled the bishop who had permitted this offense to occur and made Frede-gund his queen.[56]

The tale is a fiction, of no value as evidence for events or beliefs in the late sixth century. It does, however, reflect views held in the early eighth century in the Frankish kingdom; furthermore, it has the rare merit of deriving neither from canonical nor from official sources. The premise of the tale is clear: a man may not sleep with his wife if they have become coparents through their own child. The author appar-ently believed that the separation amounted to a divorce, since he did not disapprove of Chilperic's decision to take a new wife. In subse-quent, more explicit statements, the separation of spouses who became coparents was demanded, but the remarriage of either party while the other was living was a matter of debate until the twelfth century.[57]

---

[55] *Liber historiae Francorum*, ed. Bruno Krusch, MGH SSRM, vol. 2 (Hanover, 1888), pp. 215–328. There is an English translation by Bernard Bachrach, *Liber historiae Fran-corum* (Lawrence, Kan., 1973).

[56] *Liber historiae Francorum*, ch. 31, ed. Krusch, pp. 292–293.

[57] Joseph Freisen, *Geschichte des kanonischen Eherechts bis zum Verfall der Glossenliteratur*,

By the early ninth century, the view that baptismal sponsorship was incompatible with natural parenthood of the same child had triumphed, spelling the end of the seven-hundred-year tradition of parental sponsorship. The Carolingian poet and theologian Walafrid Strabo summarized the situation in about 840:

> A father or mother must not receive their own offspring, so that there may be a distinction between spiritual and carnal generation. If by chance that [sponsorship] happens, they who have taken the spiritual bond of coparenthood in their common child will not henceforth have the sharing of carnal intercourse.[58]

At the council of Mainz, one of five regional reform councils summoned by the aged Charlemagne in 813, the assembled bishops, abbots, and other dignitaries made official the change that seemed to follow inevitably from the principle that spiritual kinship and sexual relationship were incompatible:

> Therefore no one should receive his own son or daughter from the font of baptism nor should he take as wife his goddaughter or comother, nor should he take as wife a woman whose son or daughter he led to confirmation. Where this has been done, they should be separated.[59]

The practice of ending the marriages of couples who became coparents to one another had unexpected results, for lay people have occasionally drawn conclusions from theological premises that church authorities have neither forseen nor wanted. Thus some people saw in spiritual kinship a way to obtain a divorce. In the same year that the Council of Mainz forbade parents to sponsor their own children, the bishops meeting in council at Chalons reported:

> It has been said to us that some women have held their own children before the bishop at confirmation; some did it out of

---

2nd ed. (Paderborn, 1893; reprint ed., Aalen, 1963), p. 514; Adhemar Esmein, *Le mariage en droit canonique*, 2 vols. (Paris, 1891), 1:362–374.

[58] Walafrid Strabo, *Libellus de exordiis et incrementis quarundam in observationibus ecclesiasticis rerum*, ch. 27 in MGH Capitularia, vol. 2 (Hanover, 1897), p. 512: "Non autem debet pater vel mater de fonte suam suscipere sobolem, ut sit discretio inter spiritalem generationem atque carnalem: quodsi casu evenerit, non habebunt carnalis copulae deinceps ad invicem consortium, qui in communi filio compaternitatis spiritale vinculum susceperunt."

[59] Council of Mainz (813), canon 55, MGH Concilia, vol. 2 pt. 1 (Hanover, 1906), p. 273: "Nullus igitur proprium filium vel filiam de fonte baptismatis suscipiat nec filiolam nec commatrem ducat uxorem nec illam, cuius filium aut filiam ad confirmationem duxerit. Ubi autem factum fuerit, separentur."

negligence but others did it deceitfully, in order that they might be separated from their husbands.[60]

These women must have concluded that if it was not permitted to marry a coparent, then they could escape an unhappy marriage by sponsoring their own child in confirmation (or in baptism) and thus turn an unwanted husband into a cofather, whether he wished it or not.

The bishops attempted to check the practice:

Hence we have held it fitting that if any woman has held her own son before the bishop for confirmation, whether out of negligence or deceit, she should do penance because of her trick, but let her not be separated from her husband.[61]

The bishops' solution was not the last word on this thorny issue that pitted the permanence of marriage against the sanctity of coparenthood. But the important point is that at least some lay people used spiritual kinship in a way that went beyond what the authorities thought proper.

A parallel development occurred in Byzantine Christianity at almost the same time. Canon 53 of the Council in Trullo had forbidden any man to marry his comother, and this prohibition had been ratified in book 2, chapter 2, of the *Ecloga*. In the eighth century, some men and women came to the same conclusion as their western counterparts, finding that sponsorship of one's own child offered a quick, easy way to dissolve a marriage, a way that was especially useful if one party to the union was unwilling to grant a divorce on other legal grounds. Not surprisingly, such do-it-yourself divorce was unacceptable to the authorities.

Dieter Simon has edited a Byzantine imperial *novella* that was concerned with the legal and social problems posed by such divorces. In contrast to the Frankish bishops' terse and almost illogical decision to punish the offending women while preserving the offending sexual union, the Byzantine *novella* was a complex, well-crafted response.[62] The law was issued by emperors named Leo and Constantine, whom Simon identifies as Leo III and Constantine V, the promulgators of the *Ecloga*. Simon also argues that the law was issued within a year of the *Ecloga*, that is, in 727. However, Otto Kresten has recently de-

---

[60] Council of Chalons (813), canon 31, MGH Concilia, vol. 2 pt. 1, p. 279.

[61] Ibid.

[62] Dieter Simon, "Zur Ehegesetzgebung der Isaurier," *Forschungen zur byzantinischen Rechtsgeschichte*, vol. 1: *Fontes Minores*, vol. 1 (Frankfurt am Main, 1976), pp. 30–33.

fended the position that the emperors in question were Leo V the Armenian and his son Constantine, who issued the law between 25 December 819 and 10 July 820.[63]

In spite of its disapproval of such divorces, the Byzantine *novella* conceded the main point: coparents cannot marry or remain married. Thus the legal strategy pursued by the Byzantine authorities was to make such an avenue to divorce very unattractive. The guilty party or parties were punished by fines (if they were rich), by torture (if they were poor), and by legal and financial penalties, including the loss of the right to remarry.

From all this it can be seen that both western and eastern Christianity had decisively accepted spiritual kinship as incompatible with sexual contact. And while the working out of the implications of this acceptance was not free of pitfalls, the direction it took proved to be irreversible. The keenly felt contrast between carnal and spiritual generation provided a favorable climate in which marital taboos could grow. Indeed, the ban on the marriage of spiritual kin was a particular case of the general proposition that the sexual and the holy were to be kept apart. Such attitudes and the behavior patterns they encouraged were exported as part of Christianity to northern and northwestern Europe by the Latin church and to Slavic lands by the Orthodox church.[64] Thus, from the eighth century onward, spiritual kinship became a constituent element of Christianity: to be Christian meant the adoption of the consequences of sponsorship, including the sexual consequences.

[63] Otto Kresten, "Datierungsprobleme 'isaurischer' Eherechtsnovellen I.Coll.I.26," *Forschungen zur byzantinischen Rechtsgeschichte*, vol. 7: *Fontes Minores*, vol. 4 (Frankfort am Main, 1981), pp. 76–82.

[64] Evelyne Patlagean, "Christianisation et parentés rituelles: le domaine de Byzance," *AESC* 33 (1978):628.

PART FOUR

THE CAROLINGIAN SYNTHESIS

TEN

THE GODPARENT AND THE
BAPTISMAL LITURGY

The Carolingian dynasty provided kings to the Franks from 751 until 911 in the East and until 987 in the West. During this period, the Franks continued to practice spiritual kinship. Indeed, the proliferation of the numbers of sponsors and of the occasions for sponsorship that had begun under the Merovingians steadily grew. But at the same time, coparenthood was treated differently than godparenthood, particularly by the Frankish church. The former had traditionally been beyond the control of the church and it remained so, except that the ecclesiastical and lay authorities insisted on the prohibition of marriage between coparents. Otherwise, coparenthood continued to function as an important form of solidarity-building, used at every level of society and in Carolingian diplomacy as well.[1]

Godparenthood, which was tied closely to the liturgy and was more open to ecclesiastical control, changed considerably as a result of Carolingian policies. In particular, the baptismal liturgy was reshaped to lay greater stress on sponsorship, and the godparent was made a key figure in the Carolingian quest for the dissemination of basic religious

---

[1] On the diplomatic uses of sponsorship, see Gerd Tellenbach, "Vom Zusammenleben der abendländischen Völker im Mittelalter," *Festschrift für Gerhard Ritter zu seinem 60. Geburtstag* (Tübingen, 1950), pp. 4–5; Margret Wielers, *Zwischenstaatliche Beziehungsformen im frühen Mittelalter (Pax, Foedus, Amicitia, Fraternitas)* (Ph.D. diss., Münster, Westphalia, 1959), pp. 47–59; Arnold Angenendt, "Taufe und Politik im frühen Mittelalter," *FS* 7 (1973);143–168. After my book was in galley proofs, I obtained a copy of Arnold Angenendt's *Kaiserherrschaft und Königstaufe. Kaiser, Könige und Päpste als geistliche Patrone in der abendländischen Missionsgeschichte*. Arbeiten zur Frühmittelalterforschung, vol. 15 (Berlin, 1984). It is an important contribution to the study of sponsorship, although I was not able to incorporate its conclusions into my book. However, I was able to use Angenendt's articles published between 1973 and 1980, which foreshadowed some of his conclusions. I believe that our approaches complement one another well. Angenendt sees in baptismal sponsorship a religious ceremony whose most important consequences are political and diplomatic. Although I give some attention to the diplomatic and political uses of sponsorship and spiritual kinship, I treat them primarily as "domestic" institutions, which influenced such matters as the choice of marriage partners, the creation of formal friendship, the protection of the young, the religious education of the laity, and the social structures of Frankish society.

knowledge. The liturgical reform will be taken up in this chapter and the rejuvenation of the sponsor's educational role in the next.

For approximately a century, the royal power passed at each succession or soon thereafter into the hands of a single ruler. Pepin (mayor of the palace from 741 and king from 751 to 768) was succeeded by two sons, one of whom died within three years, thus opening the way to Charlemagne's long and important reign (768–814). He in turn was succeeded by his only surviving adult son Louis (814–840). Louis has often been dismissed as an ineffectual ruler ("the Pious" is both a nickname and an implied criticism), but he carried on the tradition of his famous ancestors until the last decade of his reign, when quarrels with his sons undermined his power. After Louis' humiliating deposition and reinstatement and the accession of his three sons in 840, it is conventional to see the history of the Carolingian dynasty as one of family bickering punctuated by civil war, territorial fragmentation, and the erosion of royal power to the advantage of the great landed magnates. The last century of Carolingian rule contrasted unfavorably with the first.

Although cultural and religious developments are influenced by political realities, they do not move according to precisely the same rhythms. Indeed, societies in political decline can be marked by high cultural attainments, and the Carolingian period is a case in point. The first seventy-five years of the dynasty were marked by political success and by the laying of foundations for a cultural revival, called the Carolingian Renaissance, but the actual achievements in art, architecture, and letters during these early years were quite modest. Hence, although Charlemagne did much to foster a cultural and religious renewal among his people, he never saw the mature phase of Carolingian Frankish culture. For in the middle decades of the ninth century there was a literary, artistic, and religious flowering of a high order, even as the political structures of the Carolingian empire disintegrated.

The Carolingian rulers and their ecclesiastical allies promoted an ambitious reform program in which baptismal sponsorship and godparenthood found a place. And even when the weakened monarchy, increasingly preoccupied with its own problems, pulled back from the promotion of church reform, the reform itself did not vanish. Instead it found champions in the ranks of the bishops and monks, many of whom had benefited from earlier efforts to raise the intellectual and moral standards of the clergy. Thus in the deteriorating political conditions of the middle and later ninth century, efforts continued to elevate the behavior and religious knowledge of the lower clergy and of the laity. Baptismal sponsorship and spiritual kinship were part of this reform program and were disseminated through every channel that was available.

The secular, alliance-building aspects of spiritual kinship needed no promotion by the clergy, since they were already an integral part of the Frankish social fabric. Indeed, some of the clergy were uneasy about the way in which secular considerations threatened to overwhelm religious duties. After quoting a sermon of Caesarius of Arles, which was attributed to Augustine, Bishop Jonas of Orléans (818–843) chided his lay readers:

> We are instructed by these texts of so great a teacher that we should guide all whom we can by our words and deeds to the uprightness of a holy life, and we should challenge them by good deeds to persevere. In particular, we should act with greater vigilance with respect to those whom we have received from the holy font. In fact, many perform this saving reception not for the sake of the salvation of the one received but rather for worldly ends. Whether such people should really be called "spiritual father," they themselves must decide. Whoever is made a spiritual father in baptism must strive as best he can that the one whom he received remain a spiritual son and not become once again by evil living the son of that one [Satan] from whose service he was snatched by the grace of baptism and was made an adoptive son of God.[2]

Jonas' circumspect criticism of the worldly motives of some sponsors was unusual, for the ecclesiastical authorities had no quarrel with the social uses to which their contemporaries put sponsorship and spiritual kinship. They did, however, wish to foster a greater awareness of the pedagogical responsibilities of godparenthood. Thus the Carolingian church created a form of sponsorship and spiritual kinship in which liturgical and pedagogical functions coexisted with social functions. This synthesis influenced the social and religious history of the West even into modern times.

Carolingian society has been called a liturgical civilization because of the central position that the liturgy held in the interests both of the church and of the society's rulers. Intellectuals expended great efforts on liturgical creativity and society spent lavishly on the buildings, books, objects, and personnel needed to carry out the liturgy in a proper way. It is a matter of great significance that the inherited bap-

---

[2] Jonas of Orléans, *De institutione laicali*, bk. 1, ch. 6, in *PL* 106:133.

tismal liturgy was remade by the Carolingian church to emphasize the importance of sponsors and to impress on them the seriousness of their duties. However, some background is needed in order to understand the reasons why such a liturgical reform was essential.

By the fourth century, Christians had worked out a complex pattern for the initiation of adults, a pattern in which sponsors played a small role by testifying to the adult candidate's worthiness both to begin the initiatory process and to bring it to completion. It was possible for infants and young children to be initiated as well, and on their behalf a parent spoke and acted. But unlike the sponsor for an adult, these parent/sponsors did not testify to the infant's worthiness. Instead, their role looked to the future, when the infant would be old enough to absorb moral and religious education. The growth in the percentage of baptismal candidates who were infants, coupled with the conservatism so characteristic of liturgy, led to a situation in which generations of infants were initiated *as if* they were adults, with parents and clergy compensating for the infant's inability to speak or act for itself.

When parents began to relinquish their sponsoring duties to invited outsiders, the liturgical act of sponsorship was dramatically enhanced in social value. The baptismal sponsor became a spiritual parent to the child as well as a coparent to the child's father and mother. These spiritual kinsmen were bound to one another in an alliance that demanded altruistic behavior and, eventually, sexual avoidance.

This change in the importance of sponsorship took place between the fifth and the eighth centuries, when one civilization died in the West and another was in the process of birth. The secular role of the sponsor grew vigorously; indeed, the very disorder of society made the creation of spiritual kinship seem all the more desirable, with its potential for sacred friendship. Thus the spiritual parent and coparent became prominent figures in social life, figures whose existence was reflected in law, in mores, and in many genres of literature. But in contrast to the lively expansion of the sponsors' social roles, their liturgical duties remained relatively modest in baptismal rites that were increasingly fixed, ritualized, and out of touch with reality.

In fact, the baptismal liturgy in these centuries approached a state of ritual for its own sake. The ancient catechumenate for adults had been functionally oriented: it prepared adults for baptism. In the fourth century, the flood of converts overwhelmed the capacity of this traditional catechumenate to test and train them, but the briefer competentate still served the purpose of preparing baptismal candidates in a serious way. Both the catechumenate and the competentate had included teaching, even though initiation into Christianity was never conceived in purely intellectual terms. The baptismal candidate was in the grip of sin and had to journey from darkness to light, from sin to grace, from death to life. In this journey, dramatic exorcisms to expel demonic forces from the candidates had an important place, as did blessings to invite the Holy Spirit to dwell in them.

The growing number of infant candidates made the testing and teaching elements of the catechumenate increasingly nonfunctional. In fifth-century North Africa and Italy, this situation prompted a modest reformulation of the process of Christian initiation. There was, however, no wholesale elimination of the traditional adult-oriented prayers and rites. Instead, there was a relative increase in the weight given to exorcisms and blessings performed on the passive candidates. The didactic elements survived, but in a ritualized form, comparable to fossils embedded in rock.

The new rituals that reshuffled the traditional materials were called *scrutinia*, probably because the exorcisms scrutinized the inner state of the candidate. These scrutinies were liturgical services distributed over several weeks prior to Easter or Pentecost. There were originally three scrutinies at Rome, but by the seventh century that number had grown to seven.[3]

Ancient liturgical books do not survive in great numbers, either because they wore out from use or were discarded when they became outmoded by liturgical change. The oldest detailed description of any western baptismal liturgy is commonly thought to be *Ordo romanus xi*.[4] The *ordines romani*, of which there are about fifty extant, were produced primarily in eighth-century Gaul when Roman liturgical ceremonies began to be imported and the native clergy needed detailed instructions on how to carry them out. Such *ordines* were necessary because the Gallican clergy had never seen the Roman services. The liturgical books used by a bishop or priest, called sacramentaries, contained prayer texts but few directions about the proper way to perform a liturgical service (when to stand, sit, bless, pray silently or aloud, and so on). It is not an oversimplification to say that in the performance of public liturgical rites, the sacramentary contained the spoken word and the *ordo* contained the stage directions.[5] Later in the evolution of the western liturgy, the prayers and directions were in-

---

[3] A. Dondeyne, "La discipline des scrutins dans l'église latine avant Charlemagne," *RHE* 28 (1932):5–32, 751–787.

[4] *Ordo romanus xi*, ed. Michel Andrieu, vol. 2 of *Les Ordines Romani du haut moyen âge*, Spicilegium sacrum lovaniense, Etudes et documents, vol. 23 (Louvain, 1948), pp. 365–447. There is an English translation in E. C. Whitaker, *Documents of the Baptismal Liturgy* (London, 1960), pp. 186–194.

[5] On the *ordines romani*, see Theodor Klauser, *A Short History of the Western Liturgy*, 2nd ed., tr. J. Halliburton (Oxford, 1979), pp. 59–72.

tegrated into one book, but in the eighth and ninth centuries the *ordines* were separate booklets, often gathered together in collections.

Michel Andrieu, the great editor of the *ordines romani*, has argued that *Ordo romanus xi* originated at Rome in the late sixth or seventh century to describe the seven scrutinies and their culmination in solemn baptism at Easter or Pentecost. In his view, it was composed to be used with a sacramentary of the Gelasian type, similar to the text of the eighth-century Vatican manuscript Reginensis 316.[6] But Thierry Maertens and Marie-Magdeleine van Molle disagree with Andrieu's early dating of *Ordo xi*, as well as with his insistence on its Roman character, arguing that it was a gallicanized text that took its present form in the eighth century.[7] However, both Andrieu and his critics agree that *Ordo romanus xi* was used in Frankish territory during the eighth and ninth centuries. It can therefore illuminate the liturgical function of the sponsor prior to its enhancement in the ninth and tenth centuries.

In *Ordo romanus xi*, several centuries of development tending to undermine the functional significance of the ancient pattern of initiation had come to fruition. Because the compiler of the *ordo* was reluctant to discard traditional prayers and gestures, his efforts resulted in a solemn, complex, long-winded, and occasionally garbled set of services. The initiates were infants, but they were treated as if they were adults, being addressed directly as "*electi*" and commanded to pray, kneel, rise, and speak. This procedure posed the practical problem of arranging for the little *electi* to respond to and participate in the liturgy, a problem solved by parents, sponsors, and clergy, who spoke and acted for the infants at points in the service where in earlier times an adult would have spoken and acted for himself.

The seven scrutinies took place over the course of about a month. The first occurred on Wednesday of the third week of Lent. In the fourth century, it had been customary for a catechumen who wished to be baptized to "give in his name" near the beginning of Lent. If he was accepted by the bishop, he became a *competens* or *electus*, and participated in the intense preparation for Easter baptism. In *Ordo xi*, this ceremony of giving in a name had become a recording of the names of the candidates and of "those who are going to receive them" (*qui*

---

[6] Andrieu, *Les Ordines*, 2:389, 404–405, 409–413.

[7] Thierry Maertens, *Histoire et pastorale du rituel du catéchuménat et du baptême*, Paroisse et liturgie, Collection de pastorale liturgique, vol. 56 (Bruges, 1962), pp. 207–208; Marie-Magdeleine van Molle, "Les fonctions de parrainage des enfants, en occident, de 500 à 900," (unpublished mémoire, Année de Pastorale Liturgique, Abbaye de Saint André, Bruges, 1961), pp. 99–115.

ipsos suscepturi sunt), which was a circumlocution for sponsors. After
the recording of the names, each child was made a catechumen by
means of the traditional ceremonies of signing with the cross, laying
on hands, and placing salt in the mouth.[8] Thus in a single ceremony
the infant became a catechumen and an *electus*, although the compiler
no longer understood their significance, since he reversed the proper
order and made them *electi* before they were made *catechumeni*.

After these somewhat garbled ceremonies of admission, the *electi*
were sent out of the church for a brief interval. When they returned,
the scrutiny proper began, which was repeated verbatim at the second, fourth, fifth, and sixth meetings. At each scrutiny, the *electi* were
solemnly exorcised and blessed. Then the meeting concluded with a
Eucharistic celebration from which they were excluded because they
were not yet baptized. During the scrutinies, the infants were carried
by someone, but it is not always clear from the rubrics who this person was. At some points, the child was in his sponsor's arms,[9] at
others in his parent's arms,[10] at still others in a clergyman's arms,[11]
and finally, during the Mass that concluded each scrutiny, he was
outside, presumably with a babysitter, while his parents and sponsor
were inside the church.[12] At the Eucharist that concluded each of the
five identical scrutinies, *Ordo xi* directed that the offering be made
either by the parent or by the sponsor.[13] During each scrutinal Mass,
the names of the sponsors were recited aloud in the prayer *Memento*
and the names of the candidates were recited in the prayer *Hanc igitur*.[14] The rubrics directed that all take communion at the Mass, although this did not include the unbaptized infants.[15] The parents and
the sponsor of each child attended all seven scrutinies.

The third and seventh scrutinies differed markedly from the other
five. The third contained the instruction that survived from the catechumenate, although in a heavily ritualized form. Here the infants
underwent the traditional ceremonies to open their ears (*in aurium
apertione*) to the religious mysteries. And in the course of a long service
they experienced the handing over (*traditio*) of the four gospels, the

---

[8] *Ordo romanus xi*, chs. 2–6, pp. 418–419.
[9] Ibid., chs. 12, 17, 20, 23, 98, pp. 420, 421, 422, 423, and 446.
[10] Ibid., chs. 73, 104, pp. 441 and 447.
[11] Ibid., chs. 62, 63, 64, 66, 97, pp. 434, 435, and 446.
[12] Ibid., chs. 7, 30, 73, 74, pp. 419, 425, and 441.
[13] Ibid., chs. 32, 74, pp. 425, and 441.
[14] Ibid., chs. 34, 35, pp. 425, and 426.
[15] Ibid., chs. 36, 75, pp. 426 and 441.

Creed, and the Lord's Prayer.[16] The children were arranged in two groups according to sex and were addressed directly in the sermons and explanations.

The handing over of the gospels consisted of a sermon on their origin and nature, followed by the reading aloud in Latin (indeed, all of this was in Latin) of the opening verses of each gospel, with an explanation of the symbol appropriate to each evangelist (Matthew, a man; Mark, a lion; Luke, an ox; John, an eagle).[17] Because the city of Rome had a considerable Greek-speaking population in the seventh century, the handing over of the Creed took place in Greek as well as in Latin. Acolytes repeated the Creed aloud four times, in Greek for boys and then girls and in Latin for boys and then girls.[18] Next, after a brief introductory statement, a priest recited and explained succinctly, verse by verse, the Lord's Prayer.[19] The third scrutiny then concluded with the usual Eucharist at which the *electi* were not present. It is important to note that the clergy took the entire burden of instruction and recitation. Parents and sponsors were silent during most of the ceremonies.

The seventh and final scrutiny took place on Holy Saturday and was followed almost immediately during the Easter vigil by the baptism, first communion, and confirmation of the candidates. In earlier times, the adults who had received the Creed and the Lord's Prayer had to give them back (*redditio*) by reciting them publicly. The symmetry of handing over and receiving back (*traditio-redditio*) was no longer complete, since there was no *redditio* of the Lord's Prayer. There was, however, a giving back of the Creed. The infant who had been "given" the Creed could not, of course, give it back. But *Ordo xi* did not entrust the task to the child's parent or sponsor; instead it was given to a priest who recited the prayer once over the males and once over the females.[20] In this way, the traditional ceremonies were preserved, but with no effort to use them to teach the Creed or the Lord's Prayer to parents, sponsors, or infants.

After the *redditio* of the Creed, the candidates were dismissed with

[16] The *traditio/redditio* of the Creed was first attested by Augustine of Hippo. See Robert de Latte, "Saint Augustin et le baptême. Etude liturgico-historique du rituel baptismal des adultes chez Saint Augustin," *QLP* 56 (1975):199–203. Maertens, *Histoire*, pp. 135–137, notes that the *traditio* of the four gospels probably originated at Rome and that there was a *traditio* of the psalms at Naples.

[17] *Ordo romanus xi*, chs. 44–60, pp. 428–433.

[18] Ibid., chs. 61–67, pp. 433–437.

[19] Ibid., ch. 69, pp. 437–440.

[20] Ibid., ch. 86, p. 443.

instructions to return at the hour of baptism. In the interval, the clergy prepared the font for the ceremony. *Ordo xi* was reticent about the baptism itself, perhaps because the ceremony was well described in the sacramentary.[21] However, the rite of baptism can probably be seen in the provisions of the Gelasian sacramentary (Reginensis 316). According to this source, the baptizer asked each baptizee if he or she believed in the articles of the Creed and the response was "I believe" (*credo*), probably given by the sponsor on behalf of his little charge.[22] After the triple immersion in the water, the child was handed to a priest for an anointing on the head. It was then that the sponsor performed the key symbolic act of sponsorship, taking the child from the priest's hands: "And those who are to receive them are ready with towels in their hands and they accept them from the bishop or deacons who baptize them."[23]

The neophytes, as the newly baptized were called, were immediately confirmed by the bishop and permitted to take communion for the first time. During the week following baptism, they came to Mass each day and their parents were instructed to make the eucharistic offering for them. At the end of the week, during which they wore their white baptismal robes, the infants were fully initiated members of the church.[24]

From this it can be seen that the compiler of the fully developed scrutinies in *Ordo romanus xi* had worked out a way to initiate helpless infants while at the same time respecting venerable usages. And so the traditional ceremonies, intended originally for adults, were accumulated and organized into an elaborate, ritualistic structure. Although the infants were treated as adults, they were in fact not capable of responding and at various moments a parent, a sponsor, or a cleric compensated for their weakness. The entire ceremony was centered on the clergy, who were the chief actors and speakers. The parents and sponsors had only to perform a few acts (mostly carrying) and say an occasional "*amen*" or "*credo*" or "*in nomine patris*. . . ."

Ordo romanus xi was an imperfect compromise between the realities of infant baptism and a reluctance to tamper with the venerable liturgical forms handed down from antiquity. These forms had once served a function, that of preparing adults for baptism, but they were

---

[21] Andrieu, *Les Ordines*, 2:401–402.

[22] *Liber sacramentorum Romanae Ecclesiae*, bk. 1, no. 44, ed. H. A. Wilson (Oxford, 1894), pp. 86–87; tr. in Whitaker, *Documents*, p. 178.

[23] *Ordo romanus xi*, ch. 98, p. 446: "Et sunt parati qui eos suscepturi sunt cum linteis in manibus eorum et accipiunt ipsos a pontifice vel a diaconibus qui eos baptizant."

[24] Ibid., chs. 100–104, pp. 446–447.

decidedly nonfunctional in *Ordo xi*. The child could not, on an observable level, absorb or respond to the traditional modes of preparation, and the liturgical service made no effort to equip either parents or sponsors for the future formation of the child, nor did it impress on them the seriousness of their role in the moral and religious shaping of that child. Thus, from the perspective of what it accomplished on a human level, *Ordo romanus xi* was solemn ritual for its own sake, ill-adapted to the task of instructing young Christians, their parents, or their sponsors.

Ordo romanus xi had another drawback as well, since it was a particularly solemn form of initiation that could be carried out fittingly only in urban churches with numerous clergy over whom a bishop presided. But in the eighth century many baptisms were being performed by ordinary priests in rural settings, and circumstances in such places required an adaptation or curtailment of the full panoply of services.

Indeed, the liturgical situation in eighth-century Gaul was confusing in the extreme, both to contemporaries and to us. For generations, Roman liturgical practices had been imported piecemeal and adapted to the tastes and needs of the local Christians. These liturgical changes and experiments, directed by no central authority and guided by no readily discernible general principles, had resulted in numerous hybrid rituals that combined Gallican and Roman elements.[25] Thus, as Michel Andrieu pointed out, every surviving liturgical text from eighth-century Gaul represents merely an episode in the remarkable flux:

> We are aware of the alterations and reworkings which liturgical books underwent from one copying to another, particularly in Frankish territory, where practices changed ceaselessly in accord with the fortunes of the conflict in every church and monastery that pitted the varied native traditions against the practices which were spread by texts brought from Rome.[26]

With regard to the baptismal liturgy, two conflicting tendencies are discernible in the late eighth and ninth centuries. On the one hand, the revisers were reluctant to be too bold in discarding venerable rit-

---

[25] On the vicissitudes of the Romanization of the Gallican liturgy during the eighth century, see Cyrille Vogel, "Les échanges liturgiques entre Rome et les pays francs jusqu'à l'époque de Charlemagne," *Le chiese nei regni dell'Europa occidentale e i loro rapporti con Roma sino all'800*, SSAM, vol. 7 (Spoleto, 1960), pt. 1, pp. 185–295; and "La réforme liturgique sous Charlemagne," *Karl der Grosse. Lebenswerk und Nachleben, vol. 2: Das geistige Leben*, ed. Bernhard Bischoff (Düsseldorf, 1965), pp. 217–232.

[26] Andrieu, *Les Ordines*, 2:380.

uals and prayers. This impulse to conflate earlier texts led to elaborate, not to say overloaded, liturgical services, of which *Ordo romanus xi* is an outstanding example. On the other hand, there was also a tendency to telescope ceremonies, to perform them in rapid succession without observing the traditional intervals.[27] Long services with babies in attendance must have been a great burden on parents, sponsors, and even on the clergy. In fact, since Caesarius' day there had been complaints about parents who avoided the preparation entirely and merely presented their infants for baptism on Holy Saturday.

The pressure to speed things along must have been very great. Indeed, Andrieu describes a version of *Ordo romanus xi* in the eighth-century Gelasian sacramentary that could be carried out in two meetings. It consisted of a single scrutiny followed some days later by the services on Holy Saturday. Andrieu doubts that the *ordo* was ever used, but it still illustrates well the urge to compress ceremonies with little effort at simplification.[28]

Charlemagne's friend and adviser Alcuin (d. 804) may have contributed his own liturgical skills to the quest for a brief service. In 801/04 he probably composed a supplement for the Gregorian sacramentary that Pope Hadrian had sent to Charlemagne about 785.[29] This so-called *Hadrianum* was a book for papal use and was not suitable for an ordinary priest because it lacked provisions for many services. Alcuin added these missing liturgical rituals, including a baptismal service that was intended to be performed in a single session on healthy candidates. Of course, it had always been possible to baptize the seriously ill in a brief service, which was a concession to the emergency.[30] But the new service was more significant as an illustration of the struggle between compilation and brevity that would be played out in many of the period's surviving texts.

There were other forces at work on the baptismal liturgy as well. Ancient practice, to which *ordo xi* subscribed, had required that baptism take place on Easter or Pentecost.[31] Such a policy made sense when there was so much to be accomplished before the actual immersion in the font. However, a simplified service with little prior prep-

[27] Maertens, *Histoire*, pp. 181ff.
[28] Andrieu, *Les Ordines*, 2:396–400.
[29] Klauser, *A Short History*, pp. 72–75, accepts the traditional view that Alcuin composed the supplement to Pope Hadrian's sacramentary; in contrast, J. M. Wallace-Hadrill, *The Frankish Church* (Oxford, 1983), pp. 212–213, suggests that the compiler was not Alcuin but Benedict of Aniane.
[30] Vogel, "La réforme," pp. 224–229.
[31] S. G. Hall, "Paschal Baptism," *Studia evangelica* 6 (1973):239–251.

aration did not have to be tied to fixed times. Thus in many places baptism was tending to become a ceremony that could be performed whenever it was needed, at almost any time of the year. The Carolingian church did attempt to reintroduce the prescribed times, but with only modest success in the long run.

In the rural countryside of Francia and Germania, a service like *Ordo romanus xi* must have been beyond the ability of many priests. Here the primitive conditions tended to simplify ceremonies, sometimes brutally. During his four decades of missionary work, Archbishop Boniface reported to Popes Gregory II, Gregory III, and Zachary on the problems with baptism that he encountered in the Frankish territories as well as in the missionary lands east of the Rhine. Quite frequently, he sought papal advice on the proper course of action that should be taken.

Boniface, who was very scrupulous about such matters, was troubled by the lack of proper ritual. In 726 Pope Gregory II had to assure him that a baptism was valid even if the officiating priest omitted the traditional questions based on the Creed, provided that the baptismal formula was trinitarian in expression.[32] And in 746 Pope Zachary reprimanded Boniface for ordering the rebaptism of persons baptized by an ignorant priest who had literally baptized them "in the name of the fatherland and the daughter and the Holy Spirit" (*in nomine patria et filia et spiritus sancti*). The pope advised that so long as the priest intended to introduce neither heresy nor error, his ignorance of Latin did not invalidate the baptism.[33] It is a safe surmise that there were no elaborate scrutinies preceding a baptism performed by a priest incapable of reciting correctly a Latin formula of nine words. Under such conditions, the elaborate prayers and rituals of the traditional baptismal liturgy must have been seriously deformed or omitted altogether.

Whether an eighth-century baptism was carried out in a stone cathedral after three weeks of preparation or in a rural wooden church with a dirt floor in the space of an hour, it is certain that every effort would have been made to have in attendance someone to "receive" the child from the font. But the role of that sponsor during the liturgy was modest, passive, and almost silent, which was quite a contrast with the importance accorded to the sponsor by society. Thus during

[32] Gregory II to Boniface, Letter 26, in *Die Briefe des heiligen Bonifatius und Lullus*, ed. Michael Tangl, MGH Epistolae selectae, vol. 1 (Berlin, 1916), p. 46.

[33] Zachary to Boniface, Letter 68, ibid., p. 141; Gregory III to Boniface, Letter 45 (29 October 739), ibid., p. 73, assured Boniface that a vernacular baptismal formula did not invalidate the sacrament.

the later ninth and tenth centuries, the Carolingian church restructured the baptismal liturgy to reflect the importance of these figures.

The ninth century was a great age in the history of the western liturgy, although liturgical diversity remained a fact of life. Indeed, the intense interest in liturgy shared by the Carolingian kings, bishops, and abbots contributed to this diversity. As Theodor Klauser put it, "during the eighth and ninth centuries, the Franks boldly developed the liturgy they had inherited, exercising at the same time a high degree of creative ability."[34] The Franks' liturgical concern was focused particularly on baptism, which was discussed, regulated, and revised to an extent unmatched by any other contemporary liturgical activity. However, the exercise of creativity can be messy, and because of this there was considerable flux within the baptismal liturgies of the ninth century.

Yet in spite of the many cross currents, the direction of development of the sponsor's role is clear and striking, for the sponsor emerged as the primary nonclerical participant in a baptism, eventually ousting parents from every liturgical act. In a paradoxical way, the sponsor even came to overshadow the infant who was being baptized. The point has already been made that by this period *Ordo romanus xi* had lost its functionality, that it did not really train or form anyone. But, as Thierry Maertens has recognized, the Carolingian church succeeded in recreating a function for the baptismal liturgy, recasting the services to educate, test, and impress the godparents, who in turn were entrusted with the future religious formation of their godchildren.[35] This reorientation of the liturgy, with its unmistakable enhancement of the sponsor's role, was not a simple process and took more than a century and a half to consolidate.

The western eucharistic liturgy achieved stability early, as a consequence of Alcuin's successful supplement to the sacramentary sent by Pope Hadrian to Charlemagne. However, other aspects of the liturgy, including the sacrament of baptism, continued to develop throughout the ninth century. The Carolingian form of the noneucharistic liturgy received its definitive redaction between 950 and 962 at Mainz, where a team of anonymous liturgical scholars at the monastery of Saint Alban gathered and edited the achievements of preceding generations. The two monumental syntheses produced at Mainz were the *Ordo romanus L* and the *Romano-Germanic Pontifical*.[36] The

---

[34] Klauser, *A Short History*, p. 78.

[35] Maertens, *Histoire*, pp. 229–278.

[36] *Ordo romanus L* was edited by Michel Andrieu in vol. 5 of *Les Ordines romani du haut moyen âge*, (Louvain, 1961), pp. 83–365, and reedited by Cyrille Vogel and Reinhard

German political hegemony in Italy during the late tenth and eleventh centuries spread the Mainz texts, which served as primary models for the subsequent medieval and modern Roman liturgy.

At first glance, the baptismal liturgy in *Ordo romanus L* seems very familiar, since it is based squarely on *Ordo romanus xi*, with its seven scrutinies culminating in baptism, confirmation, and first communion at Easter or Pentecost. But this familiarity is deceiving, for the compilers of *Ordo L* modified *Ordo xi* to take account of two centuries of liturgical change that had increased the role of the sponsor. Christian initiation in *Ordo L* remains a complex, solemn procedure and I shall not attempt to trace it in detail. Instead, I shall follow the sponsor's activities in the course of initiation as carried out in *Ordo L*, comparing it to *Ordo xi*, in order to demonstrate the systematic enhancement of the sponsor's part in the drama of initiation.

One striking change is the virtual disappearance of the child's parents from the liturgy. When *Ordo xi* was used in eighth-century Gaul, there was as yet in the canon law no prohibition on a parent's sponsorship of his own child. But at Mainz in late spring of 813, a council of bishops formally forbade anyone to receive his own child from the font,[37] an act that was the key to creating baptismal kinship. Eventually, this ban was extended to confirmation and to the *catechismus*, resulting in an explicit exclusion of parents from sponsorship that was grounded in the contrast between carnal and spiritual birth and their respective consequences. Such a ban was symptomatic of the parent's growing exclusion from the entire baptismal liturgy.

For the first six scrutinies, the compilers of *Ordo L* were conservative in their treatment of the sponsors, copying the following rubrics more or less verbatim from *Ordo xi*:

> Ch. 87 (*Ordo xi*, ch. 2): an acolyte recorded the names of the infants and "of those who are going to receive them."
>
> Chs. 94, 98, 102, 106, 108 (*Ordo xi*, chs. 12, 17, 20, 23, 27): godfathers or godmothers (*patrini vel matrinae*) made the sign of the cross on the child's forehead while saying "In the name of the Father and of the Son and of the Holy Spirit."
>
> Ch. 112 (*Ordo xi*, ch. 32): either the parents or the sponsors of the candidates offered the bread and wine during the scrutinal Mass.

Elze in *Le Pontifical Romano-germanique du dixième siècle*, ST, vol. 227 (Vatican City, 1963), pp. 1–141. I shall cite the Vogel and Elze edition.

[37] Council of Mainz, (813), canon 55, MGH Concilia, vol. 2, pt. 2, p. 273.

Ch. 114 (*Ordo xi*, ch. 34): at each scrutinal Mass the names of the sponsors were read aloud during the prayer for the living, which is called the *Memento*.

Ch. 153 (*Ordo xi*, ch. 74): both the parent and the sponsor offered the *oblatio* for the candidate during the scrutinal Mass following the third scrutiny in which the gospels, the Creed, and the Lord's Prayer had been "handed over."

Ordo romanus L also copied the sole rubric of *Ordo romanus xi* in the first six scrutinies that was directed to parents alone:

Ch. 153 (*Ordo xi*, ch. 73): parents were to take their infants out of church after the third scrutiny and leave them *in custodia* when they returned to church for Mass.

Ordo L incorporated one accretion of sponsoring responsibility in its version of the first six scrutinies. After the names of candidates and sponsors had been recorded at the beginning of the first scrutiny, the priest asked each candidate by name to renounce Satan and express belief in the main articles of the Creed. At that moment, the infants were lined up with their sponsors and one may surmise that each sponsor responded three times with the words "*abrenuntio*" and *credo*." One manuscript (Munich 6425, written between 1006 and 1039) made the point explicitly when it instructed the priest to ask the *patronum infantis* about the Creed.[38]

The conservatism of *Ordo L* in treating the first six scrutinies is in marked contrast to its approach to the seventh scrutiny on Holy Saturday. There are several possible explanations for this, but the most likely is that the first six scrutinies were rarely used, that they were indeed archaic and therefore not so prone to be modernized at the hand of users and revisers. By the tenth century most infants were in fact baptized in one session, without preceding scrutinies.

The rubrics of *Ordo L* may reveal unintentionally what must have been the ordinary state of affairs. On Holy Saturday, the clergy were busy for a time with the blessing of a great candle and the baptismal fonts, ceremonies involving processions, prayers, and liturgical gestures. While these were going on, the compilers of *Ordo L* directed that "priests should catechize infants who have not been catechized and prepare them for baptism."[39] Here the verb "catechize" refers to the preparation for baptism, particularly the acts that made a person a catechumen, such as the laying on of hands, the signing with the

[38] Andrieu, *Les Ordines*, 5:131, l. 23.
[39] *Ordo romanus L*, no. 99, ch. 363, p. 101.

cross, and the placing of salt on the tongue. The rubric indicates that infants were being brought forward on Holy Saturday and, although they had not participated in the scrutinies, they were briefly "cate-chized" and then permitted to be baptized. Hence, even though *Ordo L* retained the first six scrutinies, it is clear that many infants were present only for the seventh. And it was this final session that revealed the impress of Carolingian liturgical creativity.

For the events on Holy Saturday, the compilers of *Ordo L* were more independent of *Ordo xi*, more intent on enhancing the role of the sponsor. Indeed, there was only a single reference to the activity of parents and even that allowed for the possibility that a sponsor might perform it. The youngsters to be baptized were even brought to the church by their sponsors:

> After the third hour of the sabbath, those who are to be baptized, together with godfathers and godmothers, proceed to the church and are arranged by an acolyte in the order in which they were written down, males on the right side, females on the left.[40]

When the infants and their sponsors were lined up, *Ordo L* called for the *redditio* of the Lord's Prayer and the Creed. In *Ordo xi*, chapter 86, a priest had recited the Creed, once over the boys and once over the girls. But by the early ninth century this responsibility was being shifted to the sponsors.

About 812 Amalar of Metz explained to Charlemagne that "we teach the Lord's Prayer to the godfathers and godmothers in order that they do the same to those whom they are going to receive from holy baptism. In a similar way we teach the Creed. . . . Later we examine the godfathers and godmothers, to see if they are able to recite the Lord's Prayer and the Creed, as we warned them before-hand."[41] It is possible that in Amalar's day such repetition of the two prayers took place outside the liturgy, as a test before a person was permitted to sponsor. But in *Ordo L* the testing had been incorporated into the liturgy. Adults or older children would respond for them-selves, and the godparents responded for the infants:

> And next those who are able to do so give back the Lord's Prayer and the Creed or the godfathers and godmothers (those who are going to receive them) give [them] back on their behalf.[42]

[40] *Ibid.*, no. 99, ch. 337, p. 93.

[41] Amalar, *Epistula ad Carolum imperatorem de scrutinio et baptismo*, chs. 10 and 40, ed. J. M. Hanssens, *Amalari episcopi opera liturgica omnia*, vol. 1, ST, vol. 138 (Vatican City, 1948), pp. 238, 246.

[42] *Ordo romanus L*, no. 99, ch. 337, p. 93: "et tunc qui possunt reddunt orationem

After the baptismal font had been blessed and the late-comers catechized, the bishop proceeded to the baptism, during which the sponsor carried the child and spoke in its name.

> Next the bishop baptizes one or two or as many of the infants as
> he wishes; and while he by whom it is to be received is holding
> the infant the bishop asks thus: "What is your name?" and he
> responds, "So-and-so." The bishop thus asks if they renounce
> Satan and if they hold the Creed firmly in God: "Do you re-
> nounce Satan?" and the cofather or comother responds thus "I
> renounce."[43]

The sponsors also renounced Satan's works and pomps and answered
three questions based on the Creed.

At this point in the manuscript tradition of *Ordo Romanus L*, there
is a divergence about how to proceed. Andrieu classified nine manuscripts as the alpha recension and five manuscripts as the beta recension, arguing that alpha was the original version of *Ordo L*, but that
beta was revised at Mainz within a few years of alpha: "somme toute,
les deux recensions sont également authentiques."[44] Both recensions
are worth examining, because each in its way shows the prominence
of sponsors.

In the alpha recension of *Ordo L*, after the sponsor expressed belief
in the Creed the bishop asked, "Do you wish to be baptized?" and the
sponsor replied, "I wish it" (*volo*). Since antiquity, it had been customary for a child to be offered for baptism by a parent, in whose physical
possession the child was.[45] It is therefore significant that in *Ordo L* the
formal liturgical request for baptism was made in the child's name by
the sponsor who had ousted the parent from the task. After this request, the bishop baptized some infants and handed each one back to
the godfathers and godmothers. Priests and deacons (and acolytes, if
needed) baptized the rest of the infants, whose sponsors were quizzed
about the infants' names, belief, and desire for baptism. At this point,
Ordo xi had assumed that parents handed the child to the baptizer. But
the compilers of *Ordo L* expanded the rubric to read "and having taken
the infants from their parents or godfathers,"[46] thus sharing with spon-

---

dominicam et simbolum, sive patrini pro ipsis atque matrinae eorum qui eos suscepturi
sunt."

[43] *Ibid.*, no. 99, chs. 370–372, pp. 104–105.

[44] Andrieu, *Les Ordines*, 5:46. The alpha recension is in the right-hand column of the
Vogel and Elze edition, pp. 105–109; the beta recension is in the left-hand column on
the same pages.

[45] Van Molle, "Les fonctions," pp. 47–55.

[46] *Ordo romanus L*, no. 99, ch. 375, p. 106: "Et acceptis infantibus a parentibus vel a
patrinis eorum, baptizant eos. . . ."

sors the sole task of parents explicitly mentioned for Holy Saturday. After the infants had been baptized, "those who are to receive them are ready with towels in their hands and they take them from the bishop and priests and deacons who baptize them."[47]

When the infants had been reclothed, *Ordo L* ordered that "they be arranged in a circle just as they were written down and let the infants be held in the right arms [of the sponsors], but let the bigger children place a foot on the right foot of their godfather."[48] The bishop then proceeded to confirm the youngsters and to celebrate Mass, at which they received their first communion.

The proceedings as described in the beta recension of *Ordo L* are slightly different. Here, after the sponsor's expression of belief on behalf of the child, the bishop or priest anointed the candidate. "Next let him take the infants from godfathers or godmothers and baptize [them]."[49] Baptism was preceded immediately by the question, "Do you wish to be baptized?" and the sponsor answered affirmatively on behalf of the child.

After the infants were lifted from the font, the beta recension described a previously unattested ceremony in which the sponsors held the infant above the font, with its feet dangling in the water, while the bishop or priest applied a postbaptismal anointing. The clergyman then placed a white cloth on the child's head, a vestige of the ancient custom that neophytes wore white robes.[50] The infants were next dried off by the sponsors, and confirmation was carried out as in the alpha recension, with little babies in the sponsor's right arm and older children standing on the sponsor's right foot.[51] At this point, the two recensions flowed together once again.

In *Ordo L*'s account of the services on Holy Saturday, there is no mistaking the conscious enhancement of the sponsor's role, which had eclipsed that of the natural parents and even encroached on that of the clergy. Thus the liturgy had been adapted to social reality, for in the interval since the formulation of *Ordo romanus xi* in the sixth or seventh century, the baptismal sponsor had become a major figure in the social

[47] *Ibid.*, no. 99, ch. 379, p. 107.

[48] *Ibid.*, no. 99, ch. 382, p. 108.

[49] *Ibid.*, no. 99, ch. 375, p. 106: "Deinde accipiat infantes a patrinis vel matrinis, baptizat masculos, deinde feminas."

[50] *Ibid.*, no. 99, ch. 377, pp. 106–107: "Cum autem infantes elevati fuerint a fonte, patrini vel matrinae singulorum accipientes eos habeant intra baptismum pedibus infantum adhuc in aqua consistentibus donec episcopus vel presbiter chrisma requirens faciat crucem cum pollice in vertice eorum."

[51] *Ibid.*, no. 99, ch. 382, p. 108.

life of Frankish Europe. In other words, *Ordo romanus L* represented the full acceptance of the godparental bond in liturgical act and symbol. In contrast, the coparental bond was not celebrated in the liturgy and retained its popular coloring and independence from ecclesiastical control.

The ninth-century liturgy varied from region to region, indeed from one service book to another. And although *Ordo romanus L* was a successful synthesis, it did not incorporate every liturgical variant that touched on sponsorship. In other ninth- and tenth-century texts there are allusions to further liturgical and nonliturgical tasks that had been attached to sponsorship in some places. This evidence is symptomatic of the general tendency to aggrandize the responsibilities of sponsors. For instance, *Ordo L* had instructed parents to bring their newly baptized infant to church daily during the week after baptism, called the week *in albis* (in white garments).[52] But in the statute issued about 866 by Bishop Rodulph of Bourges, even that task was assigned to the godfather, who brought the child to church in a little procession:

> And for as long as they are in white robes, let them be led by the godfathers to church daily with lights and let them all with equal right strive to receive the body and blood of Christ until the eighth day [after the baptism].[53]

The sponsor also seems to have assumed some financial obligations connected with baptism. In parts of modern Latin America, the godparents help the child's father to pay for the ceremony and its accompaniments, including such things as the church fee and the party for relatives and friends.[54] There is evidence of such sharing of costs in ninth-century Francia.

The charging of fees for church services was viewed ambivalently by the ecclesiastical authorities. If the fees were demanded, they were simoniacal; but if they were offered "freely," they were acceptable. In his second diocesan statute, Bishop Theodulph of Orléans (798–818) warned his priests to demand nothing from baptizees or their parents. And in an aside, the bishop shed a little light on the sponsor's role:

---

[52] *Ibid.*, no. 99, ch. 396, p. 111.

[53] Rodulph of Bourges, *Capitula*, ch. 20, in *PL* 119:713: "Et quandiu in albis sunt, quotidie a patrinis ad ecclesiam cum luminaribus deducantur, et corpus et sanguinem Christi usque in diem octavam aequali jure cuncti percipere studeant."

[54] John M. Ingham, "The Asymmetrical Implications of Godparenthood in Tlayacapan, Morelos," *Man*, 2nd series, 5 (1970):281; Hugo G. Nutini and Betty Bell, *Ritual Kinship: The Structure and Historical Development of the Compadrazgo in Rural Tlaxcala*, 2 vols. (Princeton, 1980 and 1984), 1:63–64.

"But if by chance the parents or those who receive [the baptizees] from the font wish to give some sort of gift to you voluntarily and freely, take it with no hesitation."[55] At least in the diocese of Orléans, sponsors were apparently helping their cofather to pay for the baptism, and perhaps for other things as well that were not of interest to the bishop as he instructed his priests.

Similarly, it had long been customary for sponsors to give a gift to their new spiritual child. Thus, in two instances of the baptism of adult Vikings, the royal or aristocratic sponsors gave clothing, arms, and jewelry.[56] Tenth-century sources also alluded to land and cattle as gifts, and even indicated that such gifts had a special name, being called a *filiolagium* or *filioladium*, words obviously based on *filiolus*, the term for godchild.[57]

From all this we can see that liturgy caught up with life in the Carolingian period, at least in regard to godparents. During this era, the sponsors took a prominent—perhaps the most prominent—role in the baptismal liturgy, which was recast to emphasize their importance. They brought the infant to church, asked that it be baptized, recited the Creed on its behalf, carried it and spoke for it at every turn, brought it to Mass for a week after the baptism, and gave it and its parents financial help or gifts. The Carolingian church also attempted to make godparents accept responsibility for the subsequent moral and religious instruction of their godchildren, a topic that will be treated in the next chapter.

[55] Theod II, ch. 4, p. 324; "Quod si forte parentes aut qui eos a sacris fontibus suscipiunt sponte sua et gratuito aliquid muneris vobis dare voluerint, accipite nihil haesitantes."

[56] Ermoldus Nigellus, *Poème sur Louis le Pieux et épitres au Roi Pépin*, bk. 4, ll. 2230–2279, ed. Edmond Faral, CHF, vol. 14 (Paris, 1932), pp. 170–175; Notker the Stammerer, *Gesta Caroli*, bk. 2, ch. 19, ed. Hans F. Haefele, MGH SSRG, new series, vol. 12 (Berlin, 1959), pp. 89–90, reported that Viking converts received Frankish clothes, arms, and jewelry from their godparents.

[57] *Recueil des chartes de l'Abbaye de Cluny*, 6 vols., ed. Auguste Bernard and Alexandre Bruel (Paris, 1880), 2:35, no. 924 (*filoladium*); Ademar of Chabannes, *Chronique*, bk. 3, ch. 11, ed. J. Chavanon, CT, vol. 20 (Paris, 1897), p. 126 (*filiolatus*); see also Jean Richard, "La donation en filleulage dans le droit bourguignon," *Mémoires de la Société pour l'histoire du droit et des institutions des anciens pays bourguignons, comtois et romands* 16 (1954):139–142.

ELEVEN

THE GODPARENT AND RELIGIOUS
INSTRUCTION

During the ninth and tenth centuries, sponsors took the central role in the baptismal liturgy, replacing the natural parents entirely, reducing the role of the clergy, and rivalling in attention the infant for whom they spoke and acted. This enlarged liturgical role was one of the consequences of the Carolingian church's effort to make Christianity understood and practiced by every group in society. Godparentage was a popular institution, one in which virtually everyone participated, and the ecclesiastical authorities attempted with considerable success to harness it to their policy of religious instruction for the laity. In other words, they sought to make the very popularity of baptismal sponsorship an encouragement for religious education.

The church's policy had several facets. Sponsors were reminded regularly in sermons, at confession, and in visitations of their duty to educate their godchildren as well as to educate themselves in preparation for that task. In addition, the church claimed the right to determine who might be a sponsor and threatened to deny such a role to those who could not pass a simple test of religious knowledge. Thus the Carolingian reformers attempted to create a dutiful godparent who was capable of and willing to instruct his godchild, a person who was a model of proper lay religious behavior. How and why this impulse came about can be understood only in the larger context of the Carolingian religious and intellectual renewal known as the Carolingian Renaissance.

We know from the writings of the pseudo-Dionysius and Caesarius of Arles that in late antiquity the sponsor had been encouraged to take part in the religious and moral education of the sponsored. But in the disrupted and illiterate society of the early Middle Ages this role had atrophied to such a degree that it might simply have disappeared, leaving the sponsors' liturgical actions as the only explicitly religious deeds they performed. They might, in short, have come to resemble the participants in Gallatin Anderson's description of *il comparaggio*, the modern Italian godparent complex, in which the godparent's educational role has generally become nonexistent, or those in Robert Ravicz's delineation of the *compadrazgo* in modern Central American Indian cultures, where it is a lively social institution whose role in formal religious instruction is virtually invisible.[1] Something analogous to this process was occurring in the Merovingian period, and the Carolingian church labored mightily to oppose it.

In 789 Charlemagne was about forty-seven years old, secure on the Frankish throne and governing a kingdom greatly enlarged by two decades of warfare. At this midpoint in his long reign, he embraced the religious and cultural renewal that was to distinguish him from so many of his warrior predecessors. The new phase of his reign was inaugurated by the promulgation of his first systematic reform capitulary, the *Admonitio generalis*.

The first sixty chapters of the *Admonitio* were based on the *Dionysio-hadriana*, a collection of canons sent to Charlemagne by Pope Hadrian, the king's cofather. The canons in this latter collection had been formulated in late Roman Mediterranean society and generally reflected the conditions of that society. Thus they did not address themselves to certain important ecclesiastical problems in the Frankish world, including the education of the laity. In order to deal with these problems, Charlemagne and his ecclesiastical advisers added chapters 61 to 82 to the *Admonitio*, providing original formulations that were intended to supplement the traditional canons.[2] The *Admonitio* expressed the general principles that were to animate Carolingian reform efforts for a century to come: promoting order in church and kingdom, obedience to rules, and adherence to the traditions of the late Roman imperial church; strengthening the office of bishop; and enforcing behavior patterns proper for the groups that constituted both church and society, notably the secular clergy, the monks, and the laity.

One of the subthemes of reform, which lay at the very heart of the Carolingian cultural renewal, was the desire that both the lower clergy and the laity *understand* the fundamental beliefs and moral imperatives of Christianity.[3] This didactic urge runs prominently through Carolin-

---

[1] Gallatin Anderson, "Il Comparaggio: The Italian Godparenthood Complex," *SJA* 13 (1957):40–41; Robert Ravicz, "Compadrinazgo," in *Handbook of Middle American Indians*, vol. 6: *Social Anthropology*, ed. Manning Nash (Austin, 1967), p. 239, note 8.

[2] *Admonitio generalis*, in MGH Capitularia, vol. 1, pp. 52–62; for a brief analysis of the text, see Carlo de Clercq, *La législation religieuse franque de Clovis à Charlemagne. Etude sur les actes de conciles et les capitulaires, les statuts diocésains et les règles monastiques (507–814)* (Louvain, 1936), pp. 172–174.

[3] Rosamond McKitterick, *The Frankish Church and the Carolingian Reforms, 789–895* (London, 1977), pp. 1–44.

gian religious and cultural life and was expressed clearly in the *Admonitio generalis*, which commanded "that the Catholic faith be carefully taught by bishops and priests and be preached to the entire people, since in the Law this is the first command of the Lord God Almighty: 'Hear, O Israel, that the Lord your God is one God. And He should be loved with your whole heart and whole mind and all your soul and all your might.' "[4]

The insistence that ordinary priests preach about the basic beliefs and behavior patterns of Christianity was an innovation of the Carolingian church, since in earlier times preaching had generally been reserved for the bishop.[5] To that end, the final chapter of the *Admonitio generalis* was, in effect, a self-contained tract on preaching. As such, it expressed well the reformers' desire that all laymen understand a simple version of Christian belief and morality.

To All. You must see to it, beloved and venerable pastors and rulers of the churches of God, that the priests whom you dispatch throughout your diocese to govern and preach to the people serving God in various churches should preach correctly and honestly; and you should not permit anyone to invent from his own fancy new, uncanonical and unscriptural things and to preach them to the people. But you yourselves should also preach useful, honest and correct views which lead to eternal life and you should instruct the others so that they may preach these same things.

First of all, it should be preached generally to all Christians that they should believe the Father, the Son and the Holy Spirit to be one almighty God, eternal and invisible, Who created heaven and earth, the sea and all that is in it; and that there is one Godhead, Substance and Majesty in three persons: Father, Son and Holy Spirit.

Likewise, you ought to preach how the Son of God became flesh from the Holy Spirit and through the Virgin Mary, for the salvation and repair of the human race; and how He suffered, was buried and on the third day rose and ascended into heaven; and how He will come again in divine majesty to judge all men according to their own merits; and how the impious will be placed along with the devil in eternal fire because of their misdeeds, and the just will be sent into eternal life with Christ and the holy angels.

Likewise, you ought to preach carefully about the resurrection

4 *Admonitio generalis*, ch. 61, p. 58.
5 McKitterick, *The Frankish Church*, pp. 87–88.

of the dead, so that the people may know and believe that they are going to receive just rewards in the very same bodies in which they now live.

Likewise, with all care you should preach to all that for certain crimes they will be handed over to eternal suffering with the devil. For we read where the Apostle says, "When self-indulgence is at work the results are obvious: fornication, gross indecency and sexual irresponsibility; idolatry and sorcery, feuds and wrangling, jealousy, bad temper and quarrels; disagreements, factions, envy; drunkenness, orgies and similar things. I warn you now, as I warned you before: those who behave like this will not inherit the kingdom of God [Gal. 5:19–21]." Therefore, zealously forbid these same crimes which the great preacher of the Church named one by one and understand how terrifying that is which he said: "He who does such things will not attain to the kingdom of God."

Ceaselessly warn them about the need for love of God and of neighbor, about faith and hope in God, about humility and patience, about chastity and continence, about kindness and mercy, about almsgiving and the confession of their sins and that they should forgive their debts to their debtors as the Lord's Prayer recommends. They should know with assurance that those who do these things will possess the kingdom of God.

Therefore, we enjoin this diligently to your charity, since we know that in these last days there will come false teachers, just as the Lord himself predicted in the gospel [Matt. 24:11] and as the Apostle Paul gave witness in his letter to Timothy [1 Tim. 4:17]. Therefore, beloved, let us prepare ourselves wholeheartedly in the knowledge of the truth so that we may be able to stand fast against those attacking the truth and with God's grace may the word of God increase and spread and be multiplied to the profit of the holy Church of God and to the salvation of our souls and to the praise and glory of the name of our Lord Jesus Christ. Peace be to the preachers, divine favor to the obedient and glory be to Our Lord Jesus Christ, amen.[6]

This urge to make Christian belief and moral demands comprehensible to the laity was a major underlying motive for the Carolingian Renaissance. Indeed, Rosamond McKitterick has argued that the "newly-defined pedagogic function of the priesthood was to become the dominant feature of all succeeding legislation" of the Carolingian

---

[6] *Admonitio generalis*, ch. 82, p. 61–62.

ecclesiastical reformers.[7] However, only a literate, informed clergy
would be capable of carrying out the instruction of the laity. Thus the
rebirth of learning among the clergy began as, and in great measure
remained, a means to the end of creating a society in which all persons
believed and lived as Christians.

At its most sophisticated levels, the Carolingian Renaissance was
the achievement of an elite of clergy, monks, and aristocratic laymen.
It was marked by the religious preoccupations of that elite, who promoted the copying of biblical and patristic texts, the appropriation of
some aspects of patristic thought, and an increase in the production of
original work in certain genres, particularly scriptural commentary,
sermons, hagiography, poetry, and history. In other words, the revival was preoccupied almost entirely with the needs of a religious
culture.

In spite of the attention accorded by modern scholars to the survival
of the pagan classics in the Carolingian period, only a tiny group of
scholars copied manuscripts of the Latin pagan authors and cultivated
an interest in the literary style of such writers as Cicero, Virgil, and
Suetonius. The impact of the Carolingian Renaissance on high literary
culture was very significant for the future, but it was restricted to a
few hundred people at any one moment and it was, in the larger
perspective, little more than a by-product of the effort to raise the
level of the rural clergy and the laity. We must not allow its splendor,
which contrasted sharply with the cultural decline of the immediately
preceding period, to blind us to the enduring importance of the less
striking efforts to christianize the lower clergy and the laity in belief
and behavior. It is at this relatively humble level of society that we
must look for evidence of the revival of the godparent's pedagogical
role.

The education of the clergy was a major undertaking in so poor a
society, but its impact was considerable. Modern scholars have made
much of the ninth-century encouragement of the founding of cathedral, monastic, and even parish schools for the training of the clergy.[8]
But although such schools were important for the success of the Carolingian Renaissance, most of the thousands of ninth-century rural
clergy learned their profession not through formal schooling but
through apprenticeship, entering the service of a particular church at

[7] McKitterick, *The Frankish Church*, p. 6.

[8] Max. L. W. Laistner, *Thought and Letters in Western Europe, A.D. 500 to 900*, 2nd
ed. (Ithaca, N.Y., 1957), pp. 207–210; Peter Brommer, "Die bischöfliche Gesetzgebung
Theodulfs von Orléans," ZSSRG, Kanonistische Abteilung, 60 (1974):57–62.

an early age and passing slowly through the ranks of holy orders.[9] If they were judged fit by a bishop, they could be ordained to the priesthood at age thirty.

The efforts of the reformers to improve the quality of the clergy have never been adequately assessed.[10] However, Carolingian diocesan statutes are precious evidence because they delineate the contemporary ideal of clerical knowledge and behavior. These statutes demanded that in the course of his apprenticeship the young cleric master Latin, canon law, the ecclesiastical calendar, the relevant liturgical services, and the rudiments of preaching.[11] He was also expected to live according to a demanding code of moral behavior and taboos that were to characterize the clerical caste, including a ban on the company of women and on sexual activity,[12] as well as a prohibition on bearing weapons,[13] wearing layman's clothing,[14] loaning money at interest,[15] acting as an oath helper,[16] and performing such nonclerical services as those of a notary or a bailiff.[17]

The clergy were tested on their knowledge and behavior prior to their ordination and thereafter at the annual diocesan synod during Lent.[18] In this connection Robert Amiet has edited a sermon that gives precious insight into the instruction offered to priests at a Carolingian diocesan synod.[19] The *Admonitio synodalis*, as the sermon is known, had a great success, surviving in many manuscripts, repeatedly revised, adapted, and supplemented. In spite of its attribution to various

[9] Guy Devailly, "La pastorale en Gaule au ixe siècle," *RHEF* 59 (1973):34–37.

[10] The more than thirty extant Carolingian *capitula episcopi* are an important source for the efforts to raise the level of the diocesan clergy. Brommer, "Die bischöfliche Gesetzgebung," pp. 1–120, treats these *capitula*. McKitterick, *The Frankish Church*, pp. 45–79, surveys the *capitula* insofar as they touch on the instruction of the clergy.

[11] E. Vykoukal, "Les examens du clergé paroissial à l'époque carolingienne," *RHE* 14 (1913):89–91.

[12] Cap sac, ch. 15; Vesoul, ch. 29; Cap Fris, ch. 5; Haito, ch. 9; Ghaer I, chs. 1–2; Theod I, ch. 12; Admon, ch. 8; Ps-Bon, ch. 17; Ps-Son, ch. 17; Riculf, ch. 14; Rodulph, ch. 16; Cap oc, ch. 7; Walter, ch. 3.

[13] Walter, ch. 1; Admon, ch. 37; Herard, chs. 50, 113; Rodulph, ch. 19; Cap Fris, ch. 19; Ghaer I, ch. 3; Cap sac, ch. 17.

[14] Admon, ch. 67; Cap Fris, ch. 19.

[15] Theod II, ch. 51; Cap ott, ch. 24; Vesoul, ch. 32; Herard, ch. 5; Walter, ch. 10; Cap Fris, ch. 10; Cap prim, ch. 9; Riculf, ch. 17.

[16] Haito, ch. 11; Cap sac, ch. 16; Ghaer I, ch. 17; Rodulph, ch. 19; Walter, ch. 10.

[17] Cap ecc, ch. 13.

[18] Vykoukal, "Les examens," pp. 81–96; Brommer, "Die bischöfliche Gesetzgebung," pp. 42–56.

[19] Robert Amiet, "Une 'Admonitio Synodalis' de l'époque carolingienne. Etude critique et édition," *MS* 26 (1964):12–82. For more manuscripts of the *Admonitio*, see Brommer, "Die bischöfliche Gesetzgebung," p. 35, n. 221.

prestigious religious figures, Amiet concluded that the text must be regarded as anonymous, composed initially in the first half of the ninth century in Carolingian Lorraine or the Rhineland.[20]

The *Admonitio synodalis* is a clear, basic collection of disciplinary commonplaces, almost all derived from earlier canonical collections, but condensed and simplified for oral presentation. It was an all-purpose address to remind priests of the practical elements of sacramental theology, morality, and penance. But within the context of Carolingian society the *Admonitio synodalis*, coupled with the diocesan statutes, contained a weighty series of aspirations for the clergy to meet. Their success at doing so was not easily assured.

The task of christianizing the laity was even more daunting. In early medieval society, religious knowledge and religious practice were quite separable, and religious practice seems to have been easier to regulate than religious knowledge. Carolingian secular rulers and ecclesiastical authorities expended a great deal of effort to impose on the laity a clear pattern of religious behavior,[21] the main components of which were (1) the observance of Sunday rest and attendance at Mass;[22] (2) proper and timely recourse to the sacraments of baptism, the Eucharist, and penance; (3) the observance of the liturgical seasons, particularly the several periods of fasting each year; (4) the payment of tithes on all income;[23] (5) the observance of marriage law and periods of sexual abstinence;[24] (6) the performance of works of practical charity, such as almsgiving; and (7) the avoidance of overtly pagan practices.

A minuscule lay elite of kings, their families, and a few pious aristocrats received personal guidance from spiritual advisers. However, for the masses Christianity was more practiced than understood, and

---

[20] Amiet, "Une 'Admonitio,' " pp. 69–74.

[21] For a contemporary description of the behavior prescribed for the laity, see the sermon edited by Germain Morin, "Textes inédits relatifs au Symbole et à la vie chrétienne," *RB* 22 (1905):515–519; see also Jean Chelini, "Les laïcs dans la société ecclésiastique carolingienne," *I laici nella 'Societas Christiana' dei secoli XI et XII*, Miscellanea del Centro di Studi medievali, vol. 5 (Milan, 1968), pp. 23–50.

[22] Jean Chelini, "La pratique dominicale des laïcs dans l'Eglise franque sous le règne de Pépin," *RHEF* 42 (1956):161–174.

[23] Giles Constable, *Monastic Tithes from Their Origins to the Twelfth Century*, Cambridge Studies in Medieval Life and Thought, new series, vol. 10 (Cambridge, 1964), pp. 31–56.

[24] Peter Browe, *Beiträge zur Sexualethik des Mittelalters*, Breslauer Studien zur historischen Theologie, vol. 23 (Breslau, 1932), pp. 1–35; Raoul Manselli, "Vie familiale et éthique sexuelle dans les pénitentiels," *Famille et parenté dans l'Occident médiéval*, Collection de l'Ecole française de Rome, vol. 30 (Rome, 1977), pp. 363–378.

their religious education in any sophisticated sense of that term was beyond the capabilities of the church. In particular, the Frankish church had no tradition of catechisms, that is, no compendia of basic religious knowledge upon which to formulate the instruction of the laity.[25] The summaries of belief and practice that were composed were often intended for the instruction of the clergy, in particular the rural clergy, or else for use by the clergy to instruct adult pagan converts in border regions.[26]

The difficulty of instructing the masses did not, however, mean that nothing was done. The need for clear, simple, and accessible formulations of belief for the laity was certainly felt, and various approaches were taken. Bishop Jonas of Orléans recommended to Count Matfrid that a layman seek religious knowledge in the Bible, but he conceded that for most it was sufficient to know the commandment to love one's neighbor, to recite the Creed, and to be able to explain the significance of baptism.[27] Indeed, Jean-Paul Buhot and Susan Keefe have drawn attention to the proliferation of explanations of baptism as one of the important pedagogical innovations of the ninth century. Such brief and simple documents were intended to enable both the clergy and the laity to understand the meaning of the traditional ceremonies, as well as the seriousness of the engagements undertaken by the baptizee and the sponsor.[28]

The Carolingian church found a workable formula for the basic religious instruction of the laity in the practices of the late imperial church. In Christian antiquity, the Lord's Prayer and the Creed had played a prominent part in the prebaptismal instruction of adults, who had been given the prayers to memorize during the competentate. These two prayers were seen as ideal models because the Lord's

---

[25] J. C. Didier, "Une adaptation de la liturgie baptismale au baptême des enfants dans l'église ancienne," *MSR* 22 (1965):80; Paul Fournier, "Notices sur trois collections canoniques inédites de l'époque carolingienne," *RSR* 6 (1926):514; Jean-Paul Buhot, "Explications du rituel baptismal à l'époque carolingienne," *REA* 24 (1978):300–301, argues that the numerous brief explanations of the baptismal liturgy reflected a widespread mode of catechesis in the ninth century, on which see Susan A. Keefe, "Carolingian Baptismal Expositions: A Handlist of Tracts and Manuscripts," in *Carolingian Essays*, ed. Uta-Renate Blumenthal (Washington, D.C., 1983), pp. 169–237.

[26] Joseph M. Heer, *Ein karolingischer Missions-Katechismus*, Biblische und Patristische Forschungen, vol. 1 (Freiburg, Breisgau, 1911), pp. 77–88, identified the ninth-century manuscript 33 of St. Emmeram (now Munich, Clm 14410) as a handbook for missionaries working among Avar or Germanic pagans.

[27] Jonas of Orléans, *De Institutione laicali*, bk. 1, ch. 8, in *PL* 106:135.

[28] Buhot, "Explications," pp. 300–301.

Prayer taught what to pray for and the Creed taught what to believe.[29] Their pedagogical usefulness was also enhanced because they were not transmitted to catechumens in bald, naked fashion. Rather, between the third and the sixth centuries, there emerged a genre of sermon in which the Lord's Prayer or the Creed was explicated verse by verse at sometime during the weeks preceding baptism. And even after infant baptism came to predominate, the *traditio-redditio* of the Lord's Prayer and the Creed, as well as the explications of each, were preserved in the liturgy in fossilized form.[30]

The Carolingian church set out to restore the Creed and the Lord's Prayer to a central place in lay religious life and to guarantee that every lay Christian knew and understood these prayers. In a deceptively simple canon, the Synod of Frankfort (June 794), stated the policy that was to guide church effort for a century and, in the process, deeply influence western lay piety: "That the Catholic faith in the Holy Trinity and the Lord's Prayer and the Creed of faith be taught and preached to all."[31]

A council at Friuli (796/97) in northern Italy under Paulinus of Aquileia stated the goal even more emphatically: "Every Christian— no matter his age, sex or condition of life, that is, men, women, young, old, slave, free, married boys and unmarried girls—should know the Creed and the Lord's Prayer by memory, because without this blessing no one can receive a share in the Kingdom of Heaven."[32]

The Carolingian reformers made these two prayers a key element— perhaps it is not too strong to say *the* key element—in their efforts to instruct lay men and women. For although the most brilliant achievements of the Carolingian Renaissance were realized in monasteries, cathedrals, and royal courts, as one moved away from these centers cultural brilliance faded rapidly in a poor and highly traditional rural society. Yet even in the rural hamlets of the Frankish kingdom the cultural and religious renewal was felt, and not least in the diffusion

[29] Friedrich Wiegand, *Die Stellung des apostolischen Symbols im kirchlichen Leben des Mittelalters*, vol. 1: *Symbol und Katechumenat*, Studien zur Geschichte der Theologie und der Kirche, vol. 4, pt. 2 (Leipzig, 1899).

[30] Wiegand, *Die Stellung*, pp. 42–145, summarizes expositions of the Creed by Augustine, Rufinus, Niceta of Remesiana, Peter Chrysologus, Maximin of Turin, and some anonymous bishops. In *Ordo romanus xi*, the exposition of the Creed and of the Lord's Prayer took place during the third scrutiny. *Ordo romanus xi*, chs. 61–71, in Michel Andrieu, *Les Ordines Romani du haut moyen âge*, vol. 2, Spicilegium Sacrum lovaniense, Etudes et documents, vol. 23 (Louvain, 1948), pp. 433–440.

[31] Synod of Frankfort (794), canon 33, MGH Capitularia, vol. 1, p. 77.

[32] Council of Friuli (796/97), preface, MGH Concilia, vol. 2, pt. 1, p. 189.

of knowledge of the words and meaning of the Creed and the Lord's Prayer.

The most important of the ancient Christian writers whose works contributed to this Carolingian strategy of lay instruction was Caesarius of Arles (502–542), whose clear, comprehensible sermons had long been attractive to churchmen dealing with simple rustic audiences. Caesarius had laid great emphasis on the centrality of the Creed and the Lord's Prayer for lay piety, and he had chided individuals in his congregation for claiming that they could not memorize these prayers. In Sermon 19, which passed under Augustine's name but was restored to Caesarius by Dom Germain Morin, the bishop spoke bluntly to such people: "You yourselves learn especially the Creed and the Lord's Prayer, and teach them to your children. Indeed, I do not know whether a person should even be called a Christian if he neglects to learn the few words of the Creed. Perhaps someone will say that he cannot remember it. How great is the misery of the human race, if both men and women can learn dissolute songs, and do not blush to say them to their own and others' sin, but their conscience cannot learn these few words!"[33]

The prayers were intended to be woven into the lives of believers, and Caesarius recommended the recitation of one or the other of them when performing certain activities: reciting both when setting out on a journey, reciting the Lord's Prayer to gain forgiveness of lesser sins (*peccata minora*), or reciting it as a preparation for receiving the Eucharist.[34] Caesarius also emphasized that the teaching of the prayers was a major responsibility for all persons in domestic authorilty: parents should teach their children, masters their servants, and sponsors their godchildren.

The Carolingians seized on Caesarius' views as a means toward the ends they wished to achieve. From the late eighth century, these Caesarian themes reappeared in many places, far too many to be quoted here. For instance, Theodulph of Orléans (798–818) composed a much copied set of statutes in which he instructed the priests of his diocese that "the faithful are to be warned that all, from the least to the greatest, should learn the Lord's Prayer and the Creed. They ought to be told the entire basis of the Christian faith rests on these two prayers; and that no one can be Catholic unless he has memorized those prayers

---

[33] Caesarius, Sermon 19.3 in *Sermones*, ed. Germain, Morin, *Sancti Caesarii episcopi Arelatensis opera omnia* (Maredsous, 1937), vol. 1, p. 86; tr. Mary M. Mueller, *The Sermons of Saint Caesarius of Arles*, FC, vol. 31 (Washington, D.C., 1956), p. 100.

[34] Caesarius, Sermon 54.1, *Sermones*, p. 226; Sermon 35.1, p. 144; and Sermon 63.1, p. 261.

and believes them with all his heart and repeats them in prayer very frequently."[35] Like Caesarius, Carolingian churchmen never tired of saying that no one was so lazy or ignorant that he could not memorize the two crucial prayers, which were brief in words but profound in meaning.[36] Thus a sermon attributed to Archbishop Boniface exhorts its hearers to learn the prayers and explains why they are particularly appropriate for a layman:

> Memorize the Lord's Prayer because in it in brief form every need of the present and the future life is contained. Christ taught it (for that reason it is called "the Lord's") and he commanded that we pray thus. Learn the Creed willingly since it is written: It is not possible to please God without faith. Consequently you yourselves should believe as it is expressed there and should hand on this same faith to your sons and to those whom you received in baptism, for you were guarantors for them that they would believe thus with you as their teachers.[37]

The campaign to disseminate the Lord's Prayer and the Creed to every Christian has left many traces in the sources, not least of which was their translation or paraphrasing into vernacular languages. In the polyglot Carolingian Empire, this issue of languages posed serious theoretical and practical problems. The western church had maintained Latin as the language of its liturgy and theology. It also acknowledged that Hebrew and Greek were sacred languages but made no significant use of them. Religious knowledge was thus carried in a language quite inaccessible to the masses, particularly those whose mother tongue was Germanic. And by the ninth century even the Romance vernaculars had evolved far enough away from Latin that the Carolingian revival of grammatically correct classical Latin made the church's idiom incomprehensible to speakers of these languages as well.

A few theorists, drawing on the views of Isidore of Seville, had argued that the religious monopoly for the sacred tongues was right and necessary: the three sacred languages were the only proper vehi-

---

[35] Theod I, ch. 22; Peter Brommer, "Die Rezeption der bischöflichen Kapitularien Theodulfs von Orléans," ZSSRG, Kanonistische Abteilung, 61 (1975):147, found that ch. 22 of Theodulph's capitulary had been incorporated into nine subsequent episcopal statutes and canonical collections, including Rodulph, ch. 22; Ruotger, ch. 22; Hildegar; and Atto, ch. 97.

[36] Jonas of Orléans, De institutione laicali, bk. 1, ch. 8, in PL 106:135; Exhortatio ad plebem christianam, ed. K. Muellenhoff and W. Scherer, Denkmäler deutscher Poesie und Prosa aus dem VIII–XII Jahrhundert, vol. 1 (Berlin, 1892), p. 200.

[37] Boniface, Sermon 5.5, in PL 189:853.

cles with which to approach God.[38] But the Carolingian church, with
its desire to extend comprehension of Christian belief and practice
among the faithful, preferred a compromise. The official liturgical,
legal, and theological texts were not rendered into languages accessible
to the masses or to the poorly educated among the clergy. They remained always the possession of the educated elite. However, for the
lower clergy simplified manuals and statutes, also in Latin, were produced and disseminated. And for the laity the vernacular languages
were sanctioned as the ordinary vehicles of religious instruction, including sermons, the Creed, the Lord's Prayer, and simple texts relating to baptism.[39]

At the Synod of Frankfort in 794 Charlemagne and his bishops
rejected the notion that the three sacred languages (Hebrew, Greek,
and Latin) had any monopoly in *personal* prayer, declaring that "no
one should believe that God must be addressed only in the three languages. God is adored in every language and a man is heard if he
seeks just things."[40] Similarly, at the Council of Tours (813) the assembled bishops ordered their clergy to deliver sermons in the Germanic (*lingua theodisca*) or Romance (*lingua romana*) vernaculars so that
their hearers could understand them.[41]

Because of their central position in Carolingian lay piety, the Creed
and the Lord's Prayer shared in the policy of vernacular dissemination. It was perhaps considered best if the laity memorized the texts
in Latin, but the emphasis on comprehension is a sign that the vernacular was simply assumed in many cases.[42] About 858 Archbishop

[38] On the three sacred tongues, see Arno Borst, *Der Turmbau von Babel. Geschichte der
Meinungen über Ursprung und Vielfalt der Sprachen und Völker*, vol. 2, pt. 1 (Stuttgart,
1957), p. 454, 497–501; Philippe Wolff, *Western Languages A.D. 100–1500*, tr. F. Partridge (London, 1971), pp. 99–114; and Robert E. McNally, "The 'tres linguae sacrae'
in Early Irish Bible Exegesis," *Theological Studies* 19 (1958):395–403.

[39] Werner Betz, "Karl der Grosse und die Lingua Theodisca," *Karl der Grosse. Lebenswerk und Nachleben*, vol. 2: *Das geistige Leben*, ed. Bernard Bischoff (Düsseldorf, 1965),
pp. 300–306, argues that Charlemagne's concern for comprehension (*intelligentia*) in religious matters provided the initial impulse to translate or paraphrase the Creed, the
Lord's Prayer, and other religious texts into Germanic vernaculars. Francesco Del
Bono, "La letteratura catechetica di lingua tedesca," *La conversione al cristianesimo
nell'Europa dell'alto medioevo*, SSAM, vol. 14 (Spoleto, 1967), pp. 697–741, reduces Charlemagne's role and argues that the surviving vernacular religious texts were produced in
the later ninth century and were often the result of local episcopal initiatives. Mc-
Kitterick, *The Frankish Church*, pp. 184–205, also stresses local initiatives.

[40] Synod of Frankfort (794), canon 52, MGH Capitularia, vol. 1, p. 78.

[41] Council of Tours (813), canon 17, MGH Concilia, vol. 2, pt. 1, p. 288.

[42] Theod I, ch. 22; Ghaer II, ch. 3; Cap sac, ch. 5; Ps-Bon, ch. 26; Hinc I, ch. 1;
Vesoul, ch. 5; Cap ex, ch. 14.

Herard of Tours commanded explicitly that "no one should receive anyone from the font unless he holds the Lord's Prayer and the Creed according to his own tongue and powers of comprehension."[43] And the ninth-century diocesan statutes attributed to Saint Boniface ordered the resignation of any priest who could not or would not plainly ask baptizees "in the very language in which they had been born" about the renunciations and professions of belief they made in baptism, "so that they may understand what they are renouncing or what they are confessing."[44]

The extant vernacular texts from the ninth century intended for popular religious instruction are quite modest in number, but they represent only the random survivals of a more extensive effort. There are Saxon and Frankish versions of the promises made at baptism; translations or paraphrases of the Lord's Prayer, known as the St. Gall, Freising, and Weissemburg texts; translations or paraphrases of the Apostles' Creed from the same manuscripts; and a translation of the Athanasian Creed known only from the so-called Weissemburg Catechism. Finally, there survives in two manuscripts a sermon translated from Latin into the Bavarian dialect, known as the *Exhortatio ad plebem christianam*, which told its hearers to learn by heart the *calaupa* (*glaube*, or Creed) and the *frono gapet* (Lord's Prayer) and to teach them to their *fillol* (godchildren).[45] It is clear that the transmission and explanation of the two prayers in the vernacular, usually in oral form, was encouraged in the ninth century and was more common than the few surviving texts might indicate.

The Carolingian emphasis on the Lord's Prayer and the Creed as the vehicles of religious knowledge for the laity revivified a practice of the late Roman imperial church that had survived tenuously in the intervening period. In stressing these particular prayers, the churchmen were also reinforcing a form of Christian folk magic. Magical songs and formulas had played an important part in pre-Christian folk medicine, in providing protection against malign forces. Such customs

[43] Herard, ch. 55, p. 768; "Ut nemo a sacro fonte aliquem suscipiat, nisi orationem dominicam et symbolum juxta linguam suam et intellectum teneat."

[44] Ps-Bon, ch. 27; see also Haito, ch. 2, p. 363; all should learn the Creed and the Lord's Prayer "tam latine quam barbarice, ut quod ore profitentur corde credatur et intelligatur." On the baptismal promises and renunciations in the Saxon language, see A. Lasch, "Das altsächsische Taufgelöbnis," *Neuphilologische Mitteilungen* 35 (1935):92–133.

[45] The texts are available in Elias von Steinmeyer, ed. *Die kleineren althochdeutschen Sprachdenkmäler* (Berlin, 1916). For a discussion of the texts, see John Knight Bostock, *A Handbook on Old High German Literature*, 2nd ed. by K. C. King and D. R. McLintock (Oxford, 1976), pp. 108–118.

proved to be stubborn elements of folk life and, after a long struggle, the ecclesiastical authorities often settled for a policy of providing Christian alternatives when eradication proved impossible. Thus the church developed its own panoply of blessings for crops, fertility, favorable weather, good health, and the like. In this strategy of replacing pagan magic with Christian magic, the Lord's Prayer and the Creed often became the Christian incantations used to fill the void left by the suppression of pagan rites.

Martin, the missionary bishop of Braga in Portugal (d. 580), contrasted the forbidden incantations of the pagans with the permissible incantations of the Christians, as embodied in the Creed and the Lord's Prayer.[46] Similarly, an eighth-century sermon forbade any Christian to recite "the songs and incantations of the pagans" either to cure animals and people or to drive away serpents and crop diseases, recommending that the Creed and the Lord's Prayer be used in their stead.[47] Certain Frankish penitentials approved the recitation of the Christian prayers to meet needs for which pagan songs had traditionally been used—for example, an accompaniment to the gathering of medicinal herbs.[48] Carolingian promotion of the two prayers thus found support in the twilight world where Christian and pagan elements mingled. From the late eighth century, the Creed and the Lord's Prayer were intended by the Carolingian rulers and bishops to be a firm point in the sea of religious ignorance, the basic minimum of religious knowledge for the laity.

Thus far, I have outlined a general Carolingian policy that was intended for all lay Christians who had reached the age of reason. The Carolingian church did, however, direct this policy toward baptismal sponsors in particular, and in an especially vigorous way. In so doing, it fixed the pedagogical role of sponsors for centuries.

Here too Caesarius of Arles provided the inspiration. He had encouraged every Christian to know the two prayers, but in several im-

[46] Martin of Braga, *De correctione rusticorum*, ch. 16, ed. Claude Barlow, *Martini episcopi Bracarensis opera omnia*, Papers and Monographs of the American Academy in Rome, vol. 12 (New Haven, 1950), p. 199.

[47] *Homilia de sacrilegiis*, ch. 4.14, ed. C. P. Caspari, *Eine Augustin fälschlich beilegte Homilia de sacrilegiis* (Christiania, 1886), p. 9; the *Homilia* also recommended recitation of the Creed and the Lord's Prayer as a substitute for seeking omens in the flights of birds, astrology, and the like, ibid., ch. 8.27, p. 16.

[48] Halitgar of Cambrai, *Penitential*, bk. 4, ch. 26, ed. Hermann J. Schmitz, *Die Bussbücher und die Bussdisciplin der Kirche*, vol. 1 (Mainz, 1883), p. 285; *Poenitentiale Hubertense*, ch. 54, ed. F. W. H. Wasserschleben, *Die Bussordnungen der abendländischen Kirche* (Halle, 1851, reprint Graz, 1958), p. 385; *Poenitentiale Merseburgense b*, ch. 11, *Die Bussordnungen*, p. 430.

portant sermons he had also impressed on sponsors their special responsibility to teach these prayers to their spiritual children when the
latter reached a suitable age. In addition, he had encouraged sponsors
to participate in the moral growth of their godchildren by setting a
living example of good moral behavior and by rebuking them when
they went astray.[49] Caesarius warned the members of his congregation
that they should teach older baptismal candidates to recite the Creed
and that they or someone else should be prepared to recite it on behalf
of the younger candidates, threatening that "whoever has done otherwise should know that he is going to suffer great shame [*grandis
verecundia*]."[50]

In the late eighth and ninth centuries, the Carolingian church took
up this congenial Caesarian theme and promoted it avidly. Caesarius'
formulation of the godparent's pedagogical role, which included moral
guidance and the teaching of the Creed and the Lord's Prayer, thus
became the classic western view. Caesarius had merely expressed a
wish that all sponsors know and teach the prayers. But in the favorable
climate of the Carolingian Empire the church set out to force them to
do so by making knowledge of the the Lord's Prayer and the Creed a
prerequisite for sponsorship. Prior to the ninth century, I have found
only one attempt to set canonical requirements to be a sponsor, that
of Caesarius forbidding monks or nuns to serve. There were probably
other criteria or disqualifications for sponsorship, but they were apparently informal and folk-oriented and have left no traces in the pre-
ninth-century sources.

The Carolingian church promulgated both positive and negative requirements to be met before a person could be a sponsor. After the
Council of Mainz (813), parents could no longer sponsor their own
children. In addition, the Carolingian bishops attempted to prevent
notorious sinners who refused to perform public penance from sponsoring at baptism or confirmation. The major positive criterion was
that the potential sponsor know the Creed and the Lord's Prayer. All
this is relatively straightforward, except for the attempt to prevent
public sinners from sponsoring, which needs further elucidation.

With the decline of royal power after Charlemagne's reign, the burden of reform fell increasingly on the willing shoulders of the episcopate, whose members possessed a growing sense of their corporate
power as well as a streak of independence that occasionally proved
troublesome for the monarchy. In the late 820s, the clerical reform

---

[49] Caesarius, Sermon 130.5, in *Sermones*, p. 515 and Sermon 229.6, ibid., p. 865.
[50] Caesarius, Sermon 130.5, ibid., p. 515.

party appeared to have gained the upper hand at the court of Louis the Pious. The emperor himself supported these clerics, and they had high hopes of effecting the changes they desired.

The reformers' ascendancy was expressed in a burst of activity. Between 827 and 829, royal emissaries investigated abuses at all levels of society and subjected the empire to a collective examination of conscience. As his father had done in 813, Louis summoned four concurrent regional councils in 829 to translate the findings of these investigators into canons.[51] Only the canons from the council at Paris, formulated in June by twenty-five bishops, survive. They are elaborate and wordy, divided into two books of fifty-four and thirteen canons respectively, with an appendix of twenty-seven canons.[52] Their scope and tone reflect the independent mood of the episcopate, critical of the contemporary church and of the secular government. In them the bishops offer much advice to the emperor, while avoiding direct attacks on him. Thus the Council of Paris' canons emerge as both a manifesto of reform and a list of grievances.

The Council of Paris was the high point of official attempts to control access to sponsorship, for in chapter 54 the bishops took the unprecedented step of denying the office to certain morally unfit persons. In particular, they barred from sponsorship those who were under the obligation to do public penance for a serious public sin and had not yet done so:

> In this particular chapter we have decided that those persons who have been punished by public penance for some sin should be barred from those duties. That is, until they earn reconciliation through a fitting penance, they should neither receive others from the font of holy baptism nor be sponsors of others before the bishops in the reception of the gift of the Holy Spirit. There is nothing surprising in this, because those whom the divine law [Deuteronomy 23:10] excluded from the war camp lest they injure the people and whom canonical authority excluded from the church are certainly excluded quite correctly from performing the above-named duties until they do penance and receive a fitting reconciliation.[53]

[51] On the reform movement of the late 820s and early 830s, see Carlo de Clercq, *La législation religieuse franque de Louis le Pieux à la fin du ixe siècle (814–900)* (Antwerp, 1948), pp. 51–86.

[52] Council of Paris (829), MGH Concilia, vol. 2, pt. 2, pp. 605–680; see de Clercq, *La législation* (1948), pp. 60–79.

[53] Council of Paris (829), bk. 2, canon 54, pp. 648–649.

The canon seems to threaten more than it actually does. After all, sponsorship was a cornerstone of lay social alliances and was too vital an institution to be summarily denied to ordinary sinners. Thus the persons barred by this canon did not fall in such a category. Rather, they were recalcitrant public sinners who were under a formal demand for penance, a group that would have included few people. In short, the bishops did not wish—and perhaps did not dare—to set too strict a moral standard for sponsors.

Other canons of the Council of Paris expressed well the Carolingian church's concern with making baptism and sponsorship an opportunity for lay religious education. The hand of Bishop Jonas of Orléans is much in evidence, particularly in the canon that traced the historical development of baptism from the early practice of baptizing adults after instruction and testing, through the rise of infant baptism, and on to contemporary Frankish customs.

In this canon, the bishops complained that contemporary instruction by sponsors had almost disappeared and "it can not be said with sufficient force how much negligence and danger exist because that practice has dropped out of the custom of the Christian religion through the carelessness of some."[54] They also complained that some sponsors were inadequately instructed in the faith and in the comprehension of the significance of baptism and "therefore they are quite incapable of teaching those whom they receive and whom they are obligated to teach, according to the testimony of the holy fathers. There is no doubt that this situation is attributable to the negligence of the priests and also of the faithful." They went on to cite Caesarius' Sermon 204.3 (attributing it to Augustine of Hippo), concluding that "it is not proper for anyone to be unaware how far matters have deviated in this matter [of instruction of and by sponsors] from the Christian religion."[55]

The bishops believed that their measures were reviving an older practice, but they were in fact innovating as well. They attempted to restore the traditional prescribed times for baptism by commanding that, except in the case of the seriously ill, all such ceremonies be reserved for Easter or Pentecost, presumably to gain greater control over the proceedings. And in canon 9, based on Jonas' *De institutione laicali*, they warned the laity that in baptism a person took weighty obligations, a true pact with God that must not be broken by sin: "It

---

[54] Ibid., bk. 1, canon 6, p. 614. On Jonas' role in formulating the canons, see de Clercq, *La législation* (1948), p. 74.

[55] Council of Paris, bk. 1, canon 7, pp. 614–615.

is very dangerous and alien to the Christian religion that after the reception of so great a gift [baptism] any believer should neglect to learn and to understand the mystery of baptism when he reaches the age of reason; and after he knows it, it is dangerous and alien to the Christian religion that he does not live in accord with it."[56] In line with this, canon 10 encouraged the clergy to preach more often about baptism and its meaning, in terms that were comprehensible to laymen.[57]

Within three months, the bishops prepared a harmonization (*relatio*) of the canons of the four councils, in which they presented a united front to the Emperor Louis. Chapter 35 summarized the essential features of their program to use baptism and sponsorship in religious instruction and to exclude serious public sinners from the honor of being sponsors, perhaps to pressure them to seek reconciliation with the church because the ineligibility to sponsor would close important avenues of alliance-building.[58] The bishops were encouraged to transmit these conciliar decisions to their diocesan clergy, and Wilfried Hartmann has recently published canons from an anonymous bishop, perhaps Halitgar of Cambrai (817–831), who did just this, adapting and simplifying certain of the Parisian canons for his own priests.[59]

The ban on sponsorship by parents had far-reaching effects, but otherwise the negative measures to control access to sponsorship were quite limited in scope. By far the most significant positive qualification for sponsorship was the demand that every sponsor know the Lord's Prayer and the Creed and be prepared to recite them to the satisfaction of the priest.[60] This requirement, which emerged in early ninth-century sources, was repeated often in the succeeding decades and affected everyone who wished to be a sponsor. Such a policy was potentially effective because failure to know the prayers could frustrate the social alliance that the natural parent and the potential godparent had agreed to initiate. The church's test was a hurdle that had to be jumped if the pact was to come to fruition.

A particularly vivid illustration of the impact of such a test is to be

[56] Ibid., bk. 1, canon 9, pp. 615–616.

[57] Ibid., bk. 7, canon 10, pp. 616–617.

[58] *Relatio episcoporum*, ch. 35, MGH Capitularia, vol. 2, p. 39.

[59] Wilfried Hartmann, "Neue Texte zur bischöflichen Reformgesetzgebung aus den Jahren 829/31," *DAEM* 35 (1979):368–394. Rodulph, ch. 22 in *PL* 119:714 also forbade those in public penance to be sponsors until they had been reconciled with the church.

[60] Cap ex, ch. 14, p. 110: "Ut nullus infantem vel alium ex paganis de fonte sacro suscipiat, antequam simbolum et orationem dominicam presbitero suo reddat"; Amalar, *Epistula*, ch. 10, p. 238.

found in a letter of Charlemagne himself to Bishop Ghaerbald of Liège, written near Easter of some year between 802 and 805. Charlemagne's capital at Aachen probably lay in the diocese of Liège and the proximity of the reform-minded emperor must often have been a burden to the bishop.

> We believe that your holiness remembers well that we have often given commands in our assembly and in our council concerning preaching in God's holy Church: that is, that each of you must preach and teach in accord with the authority of the holy canons. First, you should preach about the Catholic faith, so that the person who is incapable of grasping anything more may at least be able to hold and to recite from memory the Lord's Prayer and the Creed of the Catholic faith, just as the apostles taught. No one should dare to receive anyone from the font of holy baptism before he recites the Lord's Prayer and the Creed in your presence or in the presence of your clerical subordinates. For, see what we discovered recently. At Epiphany[61] there were many persons with us who wished to receive infants from the holy font of baptism. We commanded that each of them be carefully examined and asked if they know and have memorized the Lord's Prayer and the Creed, as we said above. There were many who had neither of the prayers memorized. We commanded them to hold back and not to dare to receive anyone from the font of holy baptism before they knew and could recite the prayer and the Creed. They were quite mortified because of this, and they wished to promise that, if they were allowed, they would in time remove this shame from themselves. We decided in this matter that they were not permitted and, as you can find in our capitulary,[62] we decided how long each one should hold back from this action until he can be a suitable sponsor in this business. Either he should find some other person right now to be godparent or, if sickness does not prevent it [by threatening the child's life], he should wait from Easter to Pentecost, until he learns those things which were declared above. Now once again we warn that you

[61] Wilhelm A. Eckhardt, *Das Kapitulariensammlung Bischof Ghaerbalds von Lüttich*, Germanenrechte, Neue Folge, Deutschrechtliches Archiv, vol. 5 (Göttingen, 1955), edited the letter from Berlin Hs. Lat F. 626. On pp. 43–47 he argues that the reference to Epiphany (*in die apparitionis Domini*) is incorrect, that it was not customary in Gaul to baptize on that date. He argued instead for Good Friday, 802.

[62] This capitulary is not extant. Eckhardt, *Das Kapitulariensammlung*, p. 97, argues that four brief titles (see note 66 below) in Berlin manuscript Lat. F. 626, f.28ʳ may represent the outline of the capitulary.

should hold a meeting with your priests and carefully seek out and examine the whole truth of the matter.[63]

This letter of Charlemagne to Bishop Ghaerbald survives in a context that emphasizes the centrality of sponsorship to Carolingian lay religious knowledge and behavior. It is preserved in a Berlin manuscript (Hs. Lat. F. 626, ff. 24ʳ-33ʳ) that Wilhelm A. Eckhardt believed to be part of a collection of capitularies and letters put together around 806 when Bishop Ghaerbald served as imperial *missus* for Charlemagne.[64] There are now fourteen items in the collection, numbered 58 to 71; Eckhardt suggested that fifty-seven items, probably capitularies or a Frankish law code, have been lost. The surviving material is a precious testimony to what a conscientious Frankish bishop might have had at his disposal in the early ninth century concerning contemporary sponsorship.

Item 59 was a capitulary from the emperor to guide the *missi* of March 806, among whom Ghaerbald served. In it, chapter 30 instructed the *missi* to provide "that the entire Christian people memorize the Creed and the Lord's Prayer."[65]

Item 63 consisted of four brief titles that constitute the outline of a lost imperial capitulary on baptism, perhaps the very capitulary to which Charlemagne referred in the letter quoted above. Chapter 1 of the lost capitulary was listed as "concerning baptism or the reception at the font," and chapter 2 as "concerning the teaching of faith. That all from his [their?] parish should learn there." Chapter 4 was listed as concerning preaching.[66]

Item 66 was a letter of Ghaerbald to his subjects in four Germanic-speaking districts (*pagi*) of the diocese. Here the bishop stressed the importance of the Creed and the Lord's Prayer, warning that no one, "high status or low status, men, women and children," should be ignorant of them. And in what was probably a reaction to Charlemagne's critical letter, Ghaerbald also advised the laity that "those who hereafter are intending to receive sons and daughters from the holy font on Easter or Pentecost should be aware that they are going to give an account of the Lord's Prayer and the faith of the Apostles'

---

[63] *Epistola* of Charlemagne to Ghaerbald, MGH Capitularia, vol. 1, pp. 241–242; Eckhardt, *Das Kapitulariensammlung*, pp. 113–114.

[64] Eckhardt, *Das Kapitulariensammlung*, pp. 66–70.

[65] Ibid., p. 84: "Ut omnis populus christianus fidem catholicam et dominicam orationem memoriter teneat."

[66] Ibid., p. 97: "c. 1 De baptisma uel susceptione fontis. c. 2 De fide docenda. Ut omnes de parochia sua ibi discant. c. 4 De predicatione."

Creed, so that we may find out what sort of true guarantor each one would be to the person whom he is going to take from the font."[67]

Item 67 was Charlemagne's letter to Ghaerbald, translated above, a letter that expressed his displeasure at the inability of so many sponsors in the diocese of Liège to recite the two prayers in his presence. In response, item 68 was a letter from Ghaerbald to his priests in which he told them that the emperor's letter of rebuke reflected on their collective negligence and laziness: "Therefore, we must command and exhort you through the awesome majesty of the Almighty that you no longer be negligent in this matter, but that each of you in his church or in however many churches he celebrates Mass preach and instruct in accord with his capacity to do so, from the command of God Almighty and from the word of our Lord Emperor and our own unimportant person." Ghaerbald threatened that continued negligence would mean punishment for the guilty.[68]

Item 70 was a diocesan statute of seventeen canons addressed to the clergy and through them to the laity. Four of these *capitula* concerned sponsorship in some way:

1. In the first place, therefore, we mention those matters which are in opposition to the Christian law, i.e., make a record of those who do not memorize the Lord's Prayer and the Creed of the faith of Christianity as well as those who do not wish to learn them, and let them come into our presence. Everyone, whether important or humble, noble or common, should come before [you] and recite the Lord's Prayer and the Apostles' Creed, where the fullness of the Catholic faith is contained, since without faith it is impossible to please God.

3. [Inquiry should be made] as to whether the godfathers and godmothers who receive infants, either boys or girls, from the font know the Creed and the Lord's Prayer; and whether they have fully taught the spiritual sons and daughters whom they received from the font about the faith concerning which they were guarantors for the children.

16. [Inquiry should be made] concerning those who marry their comothers from baptism or from the holy chrism blessed by the bishop, that is, confirmation, as to whether they have them openly or they have a secret relationship. Likewise [inquiry should be made] concerning goddaughters: who has received them from the font and then corrupted her [*adulterauit cum ea*]

[67] Ibid., pp. 106–112.
[68] Ibid., pp. 112–114.

and who has held her at the hand of the bishop and afterward married her or corrupted her.

17. If any man has held his stepson or stepdaughter at the hand of a bishop, that is, confirmation, where the seven-fold grace of the Holy Spirit is given and if he involves himself in such a marriage or irregular union [with the child's mother], you should force that person to come before us.[69]

Finally, item 71 was a diocesan statute whose sixth chapter commanded that "each priest teach carefully the Lord's Prayer and the Creed to the people entrusted to him; and he should also reveal to their minds the study of the entire religion and the mode of Christian worship."[70]

It is remarkable how often Ghaerbald's brief collection of texts returned to the theme of the religious instruction of the laity, especially by means of the Creed and the Lord's Prayer, and to the role of baptismal sponsors in that instruction. These frequent allusions are a faithful mirror of the importance attributed by the Carolingian church to the matter.

In Caesarius' model, as it had been revived by the Carolingians, sponsors were required to know the Creed and the Lord's Prayer not only because they had to recite them on behalf of the baptizee during the liturgy but also because they were expected to teach the prayers to their godchildren when the latter were capable of understanding. Caesarius had also exhorted sponsors to see themselves as moral guides to their spiritual and natural children:

Remember that you stood as surety before God for the sons you received in baptism, so always reprove and rebuke those whom you adopted at the font just as you do those who were born of you, so that they may live chastely, justly, and soberly. Do you yourself live in such a way that, if your children want to imitate you, they will not burn with you in the fire but together with you obtain eternal rewards.[71]

Some Frankish writers took up this theme of the sponsor as moral teacher and guide, and Caesarius' sermons on the topic were also used with light adaptation by Carolingian preachers. Thus Jonas of Orléans reminded sponsors to lead their godchildren "by words and examples

[69] Ibid., pp. 120–124.
[70] Ibid., p. 125.
[71] Caesarius, Sermon 13.2, *Sermones*, p. 64; tr. Mueller, p. 76.

to the probity of a holy life."[72] Bishop Haito of Basel also wished sponsors to be told by their priests that they should explain to their godchildren what they had done for them in baptism and that they should demand in full from them the renunciation of the devil that had been promised on their behalf.[73]

Thus the most sophisticated understanding of the sponsor's pedagogical role included an exhortation to be a spiritual guide. However, the stress on good moral example and advice was perhaps too ill-defined for widespread practical application in so primitive a society. It remained, therefore, a subordinate theme in the sources. In the majority of those that survive, the Carolingian churchmen hewed to the more concrete obligation to teach the Creed and the Lord's Prayer, an obligation that, if carried out, would fulfill the responsibility contracted in sponsorship.

But while ignorant godparents could be detected by requiring that they recite the prayers prior to sponsorship, there were few effective sanctions to hold over the head of a person who neglected the teaching obligation that came due five or ten years after the baptism. The weapons to hand were primarily rhetorical: the exhortation to do one's duty and the threat of consequences that willful failure would bring.

Both themes are found in ninth-century exhortations to the laity. For example, in one sermon that survives both in Latin and in the Bavarian dialect of Old High German there was an appeal to sponsors to do what they had promised:

> Beloved children, you who have received the Christian name, listen to the rule of faith which you should hold memorized in your heart; it is a sign of your Christianity; it has been inspired by the Lord and laid down by the Apostles. There are only a few words in this [rule] of faith, but great mysteries are held within it. For the Holy Spirit dictated those words to the holy Apostles, teachers of the Church, with such brevity that everyone can understand and commit to memory that which must be believed and continually professed by all Christians. How does anyone say he is a Christian if he does not wish to learn or memorize those few words of faith by which he must be saved or the few words of the Lord's Prayer, which the Lord himself laid down for prayer? Or how can anyone be a sponsor of faith for someone else if he himself does not know that faith? Therefore, you ought to be

---

[72] Jonas of Orléans, *De institutione laicali*, bk. 1, ch. 6, *PL* 106:133.

[73] Haito, ch. 25: "et quod illi qui pro eis spoponderant ab eis eadem ex integro exigant."

aware, my children, that until each one of you has taught his godson, whom he received from baptism, to understand that faith, he is liable for that promise of faith. He who neglects to teach his godson this prayer will render account on the day of judgment. As a consequence everyone who wishes to be a Christian should strive with all haste both to learn this [rule] of faith and the Lord's Prayer and to teach those whom he received from the font, lest he be compelled before the judgment seat of Christ to make excuse for himself—for to do those things is a command of God and is our salvation as well as a commandment of our rulers, nor can we obtain forgiveness of sins in any other way.[74]

Such exhortations to godparents were reinforced in the second half of the ninth century by inquiries during sacramental confession and during episcopal visitations. The Carolingian church attempted to revive ancient penitential practices, but in the process it unalterably reshaped the way western Christians sought the forgiveness of sins. By 700 the rigorous public penance of the ancient church had fallen into desuetude in most places. It had been available to a sinner only once and its requirement that the penitent abandon ordinary life was more heroic than most people were willing or able to be. Thus when the Carolingian reformers attempted to revive public penance, at least for serious and notorious sinners, they had only temporary success. The old practices remained too rigorous to serve as the way in which most Christians made their peace with God and the church.[75]

However, a concurrent mode of penance proved to be more successful. It was a method that had been developed by Irish and Anglo-Saxon monks, and it was one that was quite different from the traditional public penance. This form was repeatable and private, could be administered by any priest or holy man, and was based on a notion of redeeming sins by specific acts of penance. During the seventh and eighth centuries, the missionaries from the British isles spread such practices on the Continent, where they found a favorable audience. Indeed, the proliferation of penitentials (handbooks to guide confessors in fitting an appropriate penance to each sin) was proof of the system's popularity.[76] Thus the private encounter between priest and penitent became the ordinary way in which penance was adminis-

---

[74] *Exhortatio ad plebem christianam*, pp. 200–201.

[75] On public penance and its decline, see Cyrille Vogel, *La discipline pénitentielle en Gaule des origines à la fin du viie siècle* (Paris, 1952); on the insular and Carolingian innovations in the administration of penance, see Cyrille Vogel, *Les 'Libri Paenitentiales,'* Typologie des sources du moyen âge occidental, vol. 27 (Turnhout, 1978), pp. 34–43.

[76] Vogel, *Les 'Libri,'* pp. 60–84, surveys and classifies the surviving insular and Continental penitentials of the seventh to tenth centuries.

tered, emerging also as a potent instrument for instruction and social control.

The penitentials were intended to be used by the confessor, not by the penitent. But if private penance was to be taken seriously, it became apparent that the penitent might also benefit from written texts to arouse compunction and stimulate thought. Hence, in the ninth century, brief texts were drawn up to guide penitents in their examination of conscience in preparation for confession. These *Beichte*, as they are called in modern German scholarship, listed the sins that a layman or cleric might commit. In the reign of Louis the Pious, some of them were translated into the Germanic vernaculars to make them more useful to laymen and poorly educated clergy.[77]

The formulas for the examination of conscience were heavily influenced by the sermons of Caesarius of Arles.[78] And in view of Caesarius' interest in sponsorship, which was seconded by Carolingian concerns for lay religious knowledge, it comes as no surprise that the confession texts asked laymen to consider whether they had fulfilled their pedagogical obligations toward their godchildren. A typical confession formula in Latin from Tours, copied about 900, puts it this way:

> I have not taught my godsons and goddaughters, whom I received in the baptism of Christ . . . the belief in the Holy Trinity or the Lord's Prayer or the Creed or good works, as God commands and as I solemnly guaranteed on their behalf to God and I promised that I would do.[79]

Confession formulas in the vernacular also confronted penitents with their obligation to godchildren, who were designated as *fillulos, fillola*, or *funtdiuillola*.[80] Thus the spread of private penance, with its interrogation of the penitent by the priest, reminded many ordinary Chris-

---

[77] The vernacular *Beichte* were edited by von Steinmeyer in *Die kleineren*, pp. 309–364. Some confession formulas in Latin were edited by Edmond Martène in vol. 1 of *De antiquis ecclesiae ritibus libri quatuor* (Antwerp, 1736). See also Georg Baesecke, "Die altdeutschen Beichten," *Beiträge zur Geschichte der deutschen Sprache und Literatur* 49 (1924–25):268–355, and Hans Eggers, "Die altdeutschen Beichten," ibid., 77 (1955):89–123; 80 (1958):372–403; and 81 (1959):78–122.

[78] Franz Hautkappe, *Über die altdeutschen Beichten und ihre Beziehungen zu Cäsarius von Arles* (Münster, Westphalia, 1917).

[79] Martène, *De antiquis*, 1:278: "Filiolos meos et filiolas quos in baptismo Christi suscepi . . . fidem sanctae Trinitatis non docui nec orationem dominicam nec symbolum nec bona opera, sicut Deus praecipit et sicut Deo pro ipsis spopondi meque facturum esse promisi."

[80] *Bamberger Beichte*, in von Steinmeyer, *Die kleineren*, p. 145; *Sächische Beichte*, ibid., p. 319; and *Reichenauer Beichte*, ibid., p. 332.

tians of their obligation as godparents and sensitized them to the religious dimensions of an institution they already knew for its social impact.[81]

Penance worked on godparents one by one, impressing on them the need to fulfill their promises. But the Carolingians also used group techniques. One was the sermon, about which enough has been said to emphasize its importance. A second was the visitation of baptismal churches by the bishop or his representative.

A visitation was a formal inspection of the spiritual and economic condition of a religious establishment, that is, of a monastery, a hospital, or a parish. It was a traditional disciplinary tool, one that had been a responsibility of bishops since late antiquity, but the Carolingian reformers promoted its regular performance and prescribed many details of its nature and frequency.[82] In particular, the Carolingian insistence that bishops confer confirmation on those who had been baptized by a priest encouraged visitation. It was often during a bishop's confirmation visit that disciplinary, financial, and judicial matters were handled, relating both to the clergy and to the laity of the churches in the immediate neighborhood.[83]

During the ninth century, the bishop's role as judge during visitations was accentuated. Thus by midcentury a distinct variety of visitation, the *judicium synodale*, had emerged in the dioceses of Carolingian Germany.[84] In the early tenth century Regino of Prüm described the procedures of such a visitation in texts he attributed to an otherwise unknown council of Rouen.[85] These texts present an idealized picture, but they do reflect the Carolingian creation of a framework to regulate and educate the laity and the rural clergy.

According to Regino, the *judicium synodale* was preceded by an an-

[81] Cyrille Vogel, *Le pécheur et la pénitence au moyen-âge* (Paris, 1969), pp. 20–21.
[82] On Carolingian visitation, see Georges Baccrabère, "Visite canonique de l'évêque," *DDC* 7 (1965):1512–1517, and "Visite canonique du vicaire forain," *DDC* 7 (1965):1606–1608; Albert M. Koeniger, *Die Sendgerichte in Deutschland*, vol. 1, Veröffentlichungen aus dem kirchenhistorischen Seminar München, vol. 3, pt. 2 (Munich, 1907), pp. 11–57; Noël Coulet, *Les visites pastorales*, Typologie des sources du moyen âge occidental, vol. 23 (Turnhout, 1977).
[83] Arnold Angenendt, "Bonifatius und das Sacramentum initiationis. Zugleich ein Beitrag zur Geschichte der Firmung," *RQCAKG* 72 (1977):150–158.
[84] Koeniger, *Die Sendgerichte*, pp. 28–190.
[85] Emil Seckel, "Die ältesten Canones von Rouen," *Historische Aufsätze Karl Zeumer zum sechsigsten Geburtstag als Festgabe dargebracht von Freunden und Schülern* (Weimar, 1910), pp. 611–635, argued that four of Regino's canons attributed to Rouen might be authentic; Paul Fournier, "L'oeuvre canonique de Réginon de Prüm," *BEC* 81 (1920):22–24, saw the canons as a tendentious forgery of the later ninth century, perhaps by Regino himself.

nouncement from the archdeacon or the archpriest, who gave the congregation news of the bishop's coming and threatened with excom-
munication anyone who stayed away from the assembly in his
presence. The archdeacon or archpriest also tried to settle any minor
problems beforehand, so as to expedite the bishop's stay and reduce
the expense of his visit. When the bishop arrived, he gave a sermon
and then placed seven reliable men of the parish under oath on relics
to inform him of all transgressions that had occurred in the area.[86] In
Regino's account, there followed eighty-nine questions which were
put to the sworn witnesses concerning the behavior of laymen.[87]

Since the records of actual visitations are extremely rare for the
early Middle Ages, Regino's questionnaire is precious testimony to the
concerns of local visitation. It drew heavily upon the century and a
half of Carolingian reform efforts and embodied the traditional concerns of the Frankish church for the laity, including its pronounced
interest in baptismal sponsorship, spiritual kinship, and the teaching
of the Creed and the Lord's Prayer.[88]

Regino's questionnaire reveals that the investigation of the sexual
and pedagogical aspects of spiritual kinship had become fixed in the
tradition of visitation. Thus the lay witnesses were asked "if anyone
has fornicated with his spiritual mother or has married her; likewise
has anyone done such things with his goddaughter from baptism or
confirmation?"[89] They were also asked "if godfathers teach their godchildren the Creed and the Lord's Prayer or arrange for them to be
taught?"[90] (In a tenth-century set of visitation questions from Cologne,
the sworn witnesses were asked if anyone had corrupted his spiritual
mother or goddaughter.)[91]

Regino also recorded a text attributed to an apocryphal council of
Rheims, which was in fact based on Benedict the Levite's collection
of false capitularies. It provides an excellent summary of the Carolingian program of religious education for the laity, illustrating the prominent role of sponsors. Thus the canon commanded every priest (a) to

---

[86] Regino of Prüm, *Libri duo de synodalibus causis et disciplinis ecclesiasticis*, bk. 2, chs. 1–
3, ed. F.G.A. Wasserschleben (Leipzig, 1840), pp. 206–208; Fournier, "L'oeuvre canonique," pp. 5–44, argued that Regino's *libri* were composed for use during the *judicium synodale*. See also W. Hellinger, "Die Pfarrvisitation nach Regino von Prüm. Der Rechtsinhalt des I. Buches seiner 'Libri duo de synodalibus causis et disciplinis ecclesiasticis',"
ZSSRG, Kanonistische Abteilung, 48 (1962):1–116, and 49 (1963):76–137.

[87] Regino, *Libri*, bk. 2, ch. 5, pp. 208–216.

[88] On Regino's sources, see Fournier, "L'oeuvre canonique," pp. 11–24.

[89] Regino, *Libri*, bk. 2, ch. 5.33, p. 211.

[90] Ibid., bk. 2, ch. 5.74, p. 215.

[91] *Cologne Sendordnung*, in Koeniger, *Die Sendgerichte*, p. 198.

teach his parishioners the Creed and the Lord's Prayer; (b) to demand that they recite the prayers to him at confession during Lent; and (c) to deny communion to any parishioner who could not recite the prayers from memory. It also forbade anyone from being a sponsor before he had recited the two prayers to the priest, and it ordered the priest to inform all godparents that they were bound in duty to teach the prayers to their godchildren when the latter reached the age of reason.[92]

Regino's handbook for the clergy, written late in the Carolingian period, summarized much of the preceding generations' work. It revealed a policy that was not so ambitious as to be doomed to failure in an impoverished and illiterate society, a policy in which the Carolingian church attempted to define and disseminate a minimum of religious knowledge for the laity. This program was centered on the traditional prayers of petition and belief, the Lord's Prayer and the Creed, and it involved a carefully calculated use of godparents.

To serve as a sponsor had long been an honor and a social necessity in Frankish society, a reality that was used by the church to create a checkpoint where many laymen could be tested on their religious knowledge. Furthermore, in sermons, during visitations, and in confession laymen were reminded of their duty to carry out the promise to guide and teach that they had made as sponsors. Thus the Carolingian church grafted onto the flourishing institutions of sponsorship and spiritual kinship a significant pedagogical component.

[92] Regino, *Libri*, bk. 1, ch. 275, pp. 128–129; on the sources of the text, see Fournier, "L'oeuvre canonique," p. 21, n. 5, and Hellinger, "Die Pfarrvisitation," pp. 115–116.

TWELVE

SPIRITUAL KINSHIP IN
WESTERN SOCIETY

Between the third and the ninth centuries, the Christian world acquired a new form of kinship, which took its place alongside those of
blood and marriage. Spiritual kinship, as it was called, was originally
created by baptismal sponsorship, and this method of initiating the
bond always remained the most important. However, other occasions
for sponsorship, which were modeled on baptismal sponsorship, arose
as well. They too created spiritual kinship, although its degree of intensity and sometimes its duration were usually less than that created
by baptism.

Spiritual kinship took deep root in all premodern Christian societies
and became a fixture of private life, with important public consequences. In the West it particularly influenced marriage and personal
relationships. In the high and late Middle Ages, the institution of
sponsorship and the spiritual kinship that flowed out of it flourished
and proliferated in new ways, adapting to changing circumstances. In
modern times, the importance of sponsorship in society has differed
according to region. Although it has waned in northern Europe and
North America, it still remains vigorous among the peoples of southern Europe, eastern Europe, and Latin America. But in all cases a
knowledge of the origins and early development of western sponsoring
practices is important, since the later medieval and modern developments have been variations on the pattern that was set in the early
Middle Ages.

Baptismal sponsorship, which originally developed in the third century to meet the needs of the contemporary Christian church, involved
two distinct practices that have traditionally been lumped together
under the rubric of sponsorship. In the adult form, those wishing to
join a particular church were required to find Christians in good standing within the community who would attest to their sincerity and
readiness to hear the mysteries of salvation. Such character witnesses
had a role to perform in the elaborate preparations that preceded baptism, being called upon for testimony at two moments in the process,
entry to the catechumenate and entry to the competentate. But they

apparently had no formal obligations to the candidate after he or she was baptized.

At almost the same time, Christian families began to seek baptism for their infants, at first only for the sickly ones but eventually for all of them. And, in a choice fraught with implications for the future, Christian communities continued to use the adult-oriented liturgical rites for these infants. Since the babies could not readily participate, they needed surrogates to speak and act for them. Ordinarily this role was fulfilled by a parent who carried, spoke, and promised for the child—in short, who sponsored it. However, unlike the sponsors for adults, parents did not attest to their helpless child's fitness for baptism; instead they assumed a postbaptismal responsibility to see to the growing child's Christian upbringing.

Sponsorship of either kind was a liturgical detail in ancient Christianity, without significant social implications. Thus the responsibilities of the sponsor for an adult ended when the candidate had been enrolled by baptism in the number of the faithful. And the parent/sponsor of an infant was merely reinforcing the already weighty duties of parenthood. In neither case did contemporaries recognize the creation of new and enduring relationships; in neither was the sponsor yet a godparent.

But between the fourth and the sixth centuries, there occurred one of those great changes that leave their mark on a society for centuries. For in this period the Roman world, from Britain to Egypt, became Christian in law and to a large degree in fact. And in spite of the persistence of many features of pre-Christian society, the inhabitants of the Mediterranean littoral and its hinterlands made Christianity a central feature of their cultures. One of the customs of the triumphant religion was universal infant baptism. Of course, there continued to be baptism of adults, both within the Roman Empire and outside of it, particularly as Christianity spread beyond the borders of the classical world. However, the normative pattern gradually became that of infant baptism, and even adults were baptized to some degree as if they were infants.

In this new Christian society, baptism held a central position as the rite of entry not only to the church but also to full citizenship in the state. In theology, every human being was thought to need two births, the first a carnal one to carnal life and the second a spiritual one to spiritual life. Baptism was understood as the second birth, which carried a human being from the death of sin to the life of grace.

This notion of two births proved to be a popular one, and as it came to influence the era's thinking it had an impact that was far more than theological. The baptismal sponsor gradually was conceived as a parent in the second birth of the child, and since the two births were so radically different many felt the need to distinguish in a similar fashion between the two kinds of parents, to separate the spiritual parents from the carnal parents. Natural parents thus began to invite outsiders to sponsor their children, and the presence of such invited sponsors opened the institution to significant social uses.

The Christian church welcomed and promoted this kind of parent-hood in God. In fact, the liturgy and pastoral literature of the early Middle Ages not only acknowledged the new situation but also at-tempted to shape its religious role. Encouraged by the church, the sponsors (whom we can now call godparents) compensated for the child's weakness and helped it to be baptized in a liturgy created for adults. In the course of this liturgy, the godparents performed many actions and spoke many words on behalf of their godchild, but it was one action in particular that caught the eye of their contemporaries. For in a gesture reminiscent of the midwife's lifting of a newborn from its mother's womb, the sponsor lifted the child from the baptismal font and thereby became its parent.

The duties of sponsorship did not end at the completion of the baptism. In the years that followed, godparents were expected to take an interest in the growing child's spiritual and material welfare. The bond was kept alive by gifts, visits, and acts of kindness, and without them it apparently did not reach its potential as a source of social solidarity. Children were expected to treat their godparents with re-spect and affection. In return, the godparents had an enduring obli-gation to their spiritual offspring, one whose religious content was emphasized by such prelates as Caesarius of Arles, who warned them to teach their godchildren the Creed and the Lord's Prayer, to en-courage them to do good, and to rebuke them when they sinned.

Although the godparental bond often had practical material conse-quences, it was thought by the participants to be of a spiritual order, pure and holy. Because of this, from the sixth century on, its special character was reinforced by a ban on sexual contact between godpar-ent and godchild, since in the uncontested belief of the age sexual activity and holiness were incompatible. In the West, where godparent and godchild were initially of the same sex, such concern for preserv-ing the sanctity of godparenthood was muted. But in the East, where the participants could be of the opposite sex, the prohibition on sexual contact was a more lively matter, one with definite social conse-quences. However, although varying circumstances might determine the intensity and endurance of the bond, every Christian shared in the demands and rewards of godparenthood.

The Carolingian church's role in fixing the enduring shape of god-parenthood in the West was crucial. It was an activist church, committed to influencing society to a degree that the Merovingian church had not been. And although their success must not be exaggerated, the Carolingian church and its rulers were nevertheless committed to remaking society along Christian lines.

A key part of their plans was the effort to disseminate basic religious knowledge. In other words, the Carolingian religious reformers sought to instruct each of the church's constituent groups, or *ordines*, in the beliefs and lifestyle that were proper to it. As a result, both the secular clergy and the regular clergy were subjected to ever stricter regulation and examination with the purpose of encouraging—or forcing—them to live as they should and to know what they should. The reformers' aspirations for the laity were modest, as well they might be for an illiterate and impoverished population. But they *were* concrete. Thus the laity were encouraged to pattern their lives according to certain demands and prohibitions and were also expected to master a minimum of religious knowledge. As good Christians they must know and understand the Creed, which was the basic statement of faith, as well as the Lord's Prayer, the classical prayer of praise and petition.

It was for its potential usefulness in disseminating the basic religious knowledge proper to the laity that godparenthood attracted the attention of the authorities. However, it must also be acknowledged that godparenthood was already a centuries-old institution in Frankish society, practiced by virtually everyone; the reformers did not need to invent it, only to modify it. In particular, they sought to revivify the traditional pedagogical obligations of godparents.

Because both of the basic prayers were already closely connected with the role of godparents, the institution was well suited to be integrated into the effort to instruct the laity. Thus the reformers sought to use the desire on the part of lay men and women to be sponsors, a role highly valued for social purposes, to motivate them to learn the prayers. They denied the privilege of sponsorship to those who were ignorant of them and also sought to use the traditional obligation of a godparent to teach them to godchildren as a means of carrying out the church's larger plan that every lay person know them by heart. God-parents were reminded frequently of this pedagogical duty. Thus god-parenthood was coopted by the Carolingian Renaissance, particularly at the humbler levels where it touched the lives of ordinary Frankish Christians.

The ninth and early tenth centuries were a crucial period in the incorporation of a religiously significant godparenthood into the enduring institutions of western ecclesiastical life, for it was at this time that the Carolingian church recast its inherited liturgy to give prominence to the sponsor. It grafted onto its canon law a ban on sexual contact between spiritual kin, and it integrated into the ordinary means of religious instruction—such as sermons, visitations, and the administration of penance—a heightened concern for the long-term responsibility of the godparent to teach and admonish the godchild. In short, it encouraged the image of the godparent as a model of the good lay Christian, a knowledgeable and responsible person.

Such sponsorship created not one but two relationships because the sponsor was linked to both the baptizee and his parents. In an easily grasped piece of folk theology, the natural parents of the one who had been sponsored saw themselves as sharing the life of their child with the sponsor, who was quite literally their coparent. This sense of sharing in the life of the child proved to have important social consequences.

Coparenthood emerged at least by the sixth century as the heart of a system of personal alliances among adults. It was used at all levels of Frankish society and involved both the laity and the clergy, although there was a persistent undercurrent of uneasiness about the participation of monks and nuns. In this society, kinship was the primary form of positive human relationships and extrafamilial bonds were weak. But although blood kinsmen were one's most reliable friends and supporters, there was a disadvantage in that such kinship was contingent on the vagaries of biology and was inflexible when it came to integrating important or useful outsiders into the group. Various mechanisms to turn outsiders into kinsmen, including marriage alliances, were commonly used, but of all these spiritual kinship was the most popular.

Spiritual kinsmen were especially prized because the bond created with them was a sacred one, rooted in God's grace. Furthermore, it was a bond of choice, made by mutual agreement. Such a holy and voluntary bond was a valuable asset and adaptable to many uses. It could intensify existing bonds and make a friend or relative even closer. It could also reach out to integrate an outsider into the circle of kin. It could serve a king as a diplomatic tool, and it could also enable socially humble people to create positive bonds with their peers or their social betters. Thus in the choice of a sponsor for one's child, the advantages of turning that person into a coparent weighed heavily in the parents' deliberations.

Dutiful coparents observed a simple but powerful code of behavior in dealing with one another. They were expected to be friends, ready to place confidence in the other person's altruism, to aid one another, to grant one another's requests, and to promote one another's interests. Like the bond of godparenthood, coparenthood was holy and demanded respect, which included the need to avoid the polluting effect of sexual contact. First in the Byzantine world and subsequently in the West, coparents were forbidden to have sexual intercourse. Hence, although coparenthood created friends and spiritual kinsmen, it also complicated marriage strategies, a fact that gave it much prominence in the law and custom of marriage. For every adult Christian had a group of coparents who, along with blood and affinal kinsmen, constituted the network of friends who rendered aid and counsel in the great and small matters of life.

Coparenthood had a different course of development than that experienced by godparenthood. To put it succinctly, it was neither controlled nor coopted by the church. Godparenthood was that consequence of sponsorship most valued by churchmen, while coparenthood was the consequence most valued by laymen.

The early medieval church did not welcome or promote coparenthood, although it did not actively discourage it either. Preachers did not exhort coparents to observe the traditional code of behavior, nor did they discourage them from doing so. Fundamentally, the church ignored coparenthood in its canon law, its pastoral literature, and its liturgy. And because it was in most respects beyond the control of the church, coparenthood therefore developed more freely.

There was, however, one great exception to ecclesiastical indifference to coparenthood. Beginning in the eighth century, and under papal prodding, the Frankish church promoted a ban on sexual contact between coparents, declaring that it could not sanction such unions as marriages—and occasionally going so far as to permit the erring man and woman to marry others after their cohabitation had ended. But beyond the effort to enforce a ban on marriage between coparents, the Carolingian church did little directly to shape coparenthood, which originated in an ecclesiastical practice but remained beyond ecclesiastical supervision. Indirectly, of course, the ecclesiastical efforts to determine who could be a sponsor did subtly influence coparenthood, making knowledge of the Creed and the Lord's prayer a precondition for creating the relationship.

Spiritual kinship in both its godparental and its coparental forms was a desirable relationship, and there was more demand for it than baptismal sponsorship alone could supply. Thus, in various ways, the number of spiritual kinsmen grew in Frankish society. In particular, there was a tendency to extend such kinship to include the relatives of the principal participants, with the spouses and children of the sponsor and sponsored becoming spiritual kinsmen to one another. But even this did not fill the demand.

Reluctantly, the Carolingian church accommodated the desire of the laity to invite more sponsors for the baptism of each child. Hence, during the later ninth century, multiple sponsors replaced the traditional single sponsor of the same sex as the child. The Carolingian church also sanctioned the creation of entirely new occasions for sponsorship, most notably at confirmation and *catechismus*. And, building on this precedent, the laity went on to create other, less formally religious occasions for sponsorship, about which we know less than we would like. Such a process of expanding the number of sponsors as well as the occasions for sponsorship continued after the Carolingian period, but along the lines the Carolingians had laid down.

The social history of the Christian West was thus permanently influenced by the emergence of spiritual kinship out of religious sponsoring practices. Relations among adults and children, among peers, among social superiors and inferiors, and among potential and actual spouses were all shaped to a considerable degree by its demands and taboos. In working out the main lines of this spiritual kinship the early Middle Ages created solidly, for the end of the Carolingian period did not see a fossilization of the institution. Instead, change has continued, even while every subsequent western variation has borne the recognizable impress of its early medieval ancestor.

BIBLIOGRAPHY

Primary Sources

Ademar of Chabannes. *Chronique.* Ed. J. Chavanon. Collection de textes pour servir à l'étude et à l'enseignement de l'histoire, vol. 20. Paris, 1897.

Admonitio generalis. Monumenta Germaniae historica. *Leges,* sec. 2: *Capitularia regum Francorum,* vol. 1. ed. A. Boretius and V. Krause, pp. 52–62. Hanover, 1883.

Admonitio synodalis. Ed. Robert Amiet. "Une 'Admonitio Synodalis' de l'époque carolingienne. Etude critique et édition." *Mediaeval Studies* 26 (1964):12–82.

Adso of Montier-en-Der. *Vita sancti Bercharii. Acta sanctorum,* October, vol. 7, pt. 2, pp. 1010–1018.

Aimon of Fleury. *Gesta regum Francorum.* Ed. M. Bouquet. *Recueil des historiens des Gaules et de la France,* 24 vols., 2nd ed., 3:21–139. Paris, 1869.

Alcuin. *Epistolae.* Ed. Ernst Dümmler. Monumenta Germaniae historica. *Epistolae,* vol. 4, pp. 18–481. Berlin, 1895.

———. *Vita Vedastis episcopi Atrebatensis.* Ed. Bruno Krusch. Monumenta Germaniae historica. *Scriptores rerum Merovingicarum,* vol. 3, pp. 414–427. Hanover, 1896.

———. *Vita Willibrordi archiepiscopi Traiectensis.* Ed. Wilhelm Levison. Monumenta Germaniae historica. *Scriptores rerum Merovingicarum,* vol. 7, pp. 81–141. Hanover, 1920.

Amalar. *Epistula ad Carolum imperatorem de scrutinio et baptismo.* Ed. J. M. Hanssens. *Amalari episcopi opera liturgica omnia,* vol. 1. Studi e testi, vol. 138, pp. 236–251. Vatican City, 1948.

The Anglo-Saxon Chronicle: A Revised Translation. Tr. Dorothy Whitelock, David C. Douglas, and Susie D. Tucker. New Brunswick, N.J., 1961.

Annales Bertiniani. Ed. Georg Waitz. Monumenta Germaniae historica. *Scriptores rerum Germanicarum,* vol. 5, pp. 11–154. Hanover, 1883. Reprinted in *Ausgewählte Quellen zur deutschen Geschichte des Mittelalters,* vol. 6, pp. 12–287. Darmstadt, 1969.

Annales Mosellani. Ed. J. M. Lappenberg. Monumenta Germaniae historica. *Scriptores,* vol. 16, pp. 494–499. Hanover, 1859.

Annales regni Francorum. Ed. F. Kurze. Monumenta Germaniae historica. *Scriptores rerum Germanicarum,* vol. 6, pp. 3–115. Hanover, 1895. Reprinted in *Ausgewählte Quellen zur deutschen Geschichte des Mittelalters,* vol. 5, pp. 10–155. Darmstadt, 1968.

Ansegisus. *Capitularium collectio.* Monumenta Germaniae historica. *Leges,* sec. 2: *Capitularia regum Francorum,* vol. 1, pp. 394–450. Ed. A. Boretius and V. Krause. Hanover, 1897.

Apuleius, *Metamorphoses XI*. Ed. J. Gwyn Griffiths. *The Isis-Book (Metamorphoses, Book XI)*. Leiden, 1975.

Arbeo. *Vita Corbiniani episcopi Frisingensis*. Ed. Bruno Krusch. Monumenta Germaniae historica. *Scriptores rerum Merovingicarum*, vol. 6, pp. 560–593. Hanover, 1913.

Atto of Vercelli. *Capitulare*. *Patrologia latina*, vol. 134, cols. 27–52.

Augustine. *Confessions*. Tr. R. S. Pine-Coffin. Baltimore, 1969.

——. *Contra Faustum*. Ed. J. Zycha. Corpus scriptorum ecclesiasticorum latinorum, vol. 25, pp. 251–797. Vienna, 1891.

——. *De baptismo libri vii*. Ed. M. Petschenig. Corpus scriptorum ecclesiasticorum latinorum, vol. 51, pp. 145–375. Vienna, 1908.

——. *De bono coniugali*. Ed. J. Zycha. Corpus scriptorum ecclesiasticorum latinorum, vol. 41, pp. 187–231. Vienna, 1900.

——. *De catechizandis rudibus*. Ed. I. B. Bauer. Corpus christianorum, series latina, vol. 46, pp. 115–178. Turnhout, 1969.

——. *De civitate Dei*. Ed. B. Dombart and A. Kalb. Corpus christianorum, series latina, vols. 47–48. Turnhout, 1955.

——. *De natura et origine animae*. Ed. C. F. Urba and J. Zycha. Corpus scriptorum ecclesiasticorum latinorum, vol. 60, pp. 303–419. Vienna, 1913.

——. *De nuptiis et concupiscentia*. Ed. C. F. Urba and J. Zycha. Corpus scriptorum ecclesiasticorum latinorum, vol. 42, pp. 209–319. Vienna, 1902.

——. Letter 98, to Bishop Boniface. Ed. A. Goldbacher. *S. Aureli Augustini Hipponiensis episcopi epistulae*. Corpus scriptorum ecclesiasticorum latinorum, vol. 34, pp. 520–533. Vienna, 1895. Tr. Sister Wilfrid Parsons. *Saint Augustine: Letters (83–130)*. Fathers of the Church, vol. 18, pp. 129–138. New York, 1953.

——. *Sermones*. *Patrologia latina*, vols. 38–39.

Aurelian. *Regula ad monachos*. *Patrologia latina*, vol. 68, cols. 385–398.

——. *Regula ad virgines*. *Patrologia latina*, vol. 68, cols. 399–406.

Auxerre, Diocesan Synod of. Ed. Carlo de Clercq. *Concilia Galliae A.511–A.695*. Corpus christianorum, series latina, vol. 148A, pp. 265–272. Turnhout, 1963.

Bede. *Ecclesiastical History of the English People*. Ed. Bertram Colgrave and R.A.B. Mynors. Oxford, 1969. Tr. J. A. Giles. *The Venerable Bede's Ecclesiastical History of England*, 2nd ed. London, 1849.

——. *In Marci Evangelium Expositio*. Ed. D. Hurst. Corpus christianorum, series latina, vol. 120, pp. 427–648. Turnhout, 1960.

Benedict the Levite. *Capitularia*. Ed. F. H. Knust. Monumenta Germaniae historica. *Leges*, vol. 2, pt. 2, pp. 39–158. Hanover, 1837.

Berthold of Regensburg. *Vollständige Ausgabe seiner deutschen Predigten*, 2 vols. Ed. Franz Pfeiffer. Vienna, 1862 and 1880.

Bertram of Le Mans. *Testamentum.* Ed. Gustave Busson and Ambroise Ledru. *Actus pontificum Cenomannis in urbe degentium.* Archives historiques du Maine, vol. 2, pp. 102–141. Maine, 1901.

Boniface. *Die Briefe des heiligen Bonifatius und Lullus.* Ed. Michael Tangl. Monumenta Germaniae historica. *Epistolae selectae,* vol. 1. Berlin, 1916.

———. *Sermones. Patrologia latina,* vol. 189. cols. 843–879.

Burchard of Worms. *Decretum. Patrologia latina,* vol. 140, cols. 537–1058.

Caesarius of Arles. *Sermones.* Ed. Germain Morin. In *Sancti Caesarii episcopi Arelatensis opera omnia,* 2 vols. Maredsous, 1937 and 1942. Reprinted in Corpus christianorum, series latina, vols. 103 and 104. Turnhout, 1953. Tr. Mary M. Mueller. *The Sermons of Saint Caesarius of Arles.* Fathers of the Church, vols. 31, 47, 66. Washington, D.C., 1956–1973.

———. *Statuta sanctarum virginum.* Ed. Germain Morin. In *Sancti Caesarii Arelatensis episcopi Regula sanctarum virginum aliaque opuscula ad sanctimoniales directa.* Florilegium patristicum, vol. 34, pp. 18–27. Bonn, 1933. Tr. Maria Caritas McCarthy, *The Rule for Nuns of St. Caesarius of Arles: A Translation with a Critical Introduction.* Catholic University of America. Studies in Mediaeval History, new series, vol. 16. Washington, D.C., 1960.

Calvin, John. *Institutes of the Christian Religion.* Tr. F. L. Battles. Library of the Christian Classics, vol. 21. Philadelphia, 1960.

Les Canons d'Hippolyte. Ed. R. G. Coquin. *Patrologia Orientalis,* vol. 31, pt. 2. Paris, 1966.

Capitularia regum Francorum, 2 vols. Ed. A. Boretius and V. Krause. Monumenta Germaniae historica. *Leges,* sec. 2. Hanover, 1883 and 1897.

Catechismus romanus. Ed. Pedro Martin Hernandez. *Catecismo romano.* Biblioteca de autores cristianos, vol. 158. Madrid, 1956.

The Civil Law Including the Twelve Tables, the Institutes of Gaius, the Rules of Ulpian, the Opinions of Paulus, the Enactments of Justinian, 17 vols. Tr. S. P. Scott. Cincinnati, 1932.

Codex Carolinus. Ed. Wilhelm Gundlach. Monumenta Germaniae historica. *Epistolae,* vol. 3, pp. 476–657. Berlin, 1892.

Collectio Dionysio-Hadriana. Patrologia latina, vol. 67, cols. 135–346.

Concilia, 2 vols. Ed. F. Maassen and A. Werminghoff. Monumenta Germaniae historica, *Leges,* sec. 3. Hanover and Leipzig, 1893–1908.

Concilia Galliae A.314–A.506. Ed. Charles Munier. Corpus christianorum, series latina, vol. 148. Turnhout, 1963.

Concilia Galliae A.511–A.695. Ed. Carlo de Clercq. Corpus christianorum, series latina, vol. 148A. Turnhout, 1963.

Conciliorum oecumenicorum decreta, 3rd. ed. Ed. Joseph Alberigo. Bologna, 1973.

Constitutiones et acta publica imperatorum et regum, 7 vols. Monumenta Germaniae historica. *Leges,* sec. 4. Hanover and Leipzig, 1893–1927.

Cyprian of Carthage. *Epistulae.* Ed. W. Hartel. Corpus scriptorum ecclesiasticorum latinorum, vol. 3, pt. 2. Vienna, 1871. Tr. Rose B. Donna.

Saint Cyprian: Letters. Fathers of the Church, vol. 51. Washington, D.C., 1964.

Cyprian of Toulon, Firminius, Viventius, Messianus, and Stephanus. *Vita Sancti Caesarii.* Ed. Germain Morin. *Sancti Caesarii episcopi Arelatensis opera omnia,* vol. 2, pp. 296–345. Maredsous, 1942.

Cyril of Jerusalem. *The Works of Saint Cyril of Jerusalem.* Tr. L. P. McCauley and A. A. Stephenson. Fathers of the Church, vols. 61 and 64. Washington, D.C., 1969–1970.

Decretales Pseudo-Isidorianae et Capitula Angilramni. Ed. Paul Hinschius. Leipzig, 1863.

Dhuoda. *Manuel pour mon fils.* Ed. Pierre Riché. Tr. B. de Vregille and Claude Mondésert. Sources chrétiennes, vol. 225. Paris, 1975.

Didascalia et Constitutiones Apostolorum, 2 vols. Ed. F. X. Funk. Paderborn, 1905. Tr. Richard Connolly. *Didascalia apostolorum.* Oxford, 1929.

Dionysiaca, 2 vols. Ed. P. Chevallier. Bruges, 1937 and 1950.

Dionysius the Areopagite. *De hierarchia ecclesiastica.* Ed. P. Chevallier, *Dionysiaca,* vol. 2, pp. 1069–1476. Bruges, 1950. Tr. Thomas L. Campbell. *Dionysius the Pseudo-Areopagite: The Ecclesiastical Hierarchy.* Lanham, Md., 1981.

Diplomata Karolinorum, vol. 1: *Pippini, Carlomani, Caroli Magni Diplomata.* Ed. E. Mühlbacher, A. Dopsch, J. Lechner, and M. Tangl. Monumenta Germaniae historica. *Diplomata.* Hanover, 1906.

Discipulus Umbrensium. Ed. Paul W. Finsterwalder. *Die Canones Tœ dori Cantuariensis und ihre Überlieferungsformen. Untersuchungen zu den ɪsbüchern des 7., 8. und 9. Jahrhunderts,* vol. 1, pp. 285–334. Weimar, 1929.

Documents of the Baptismal Liturgy. Ed. E. C. Whitaker. London, 1960.

Donatus of Besançon. *Regula ad virgines. Patrologia latina,* vol. 87, cols. 273–298.

Donatus of Metz. *Vita Trudonis confessoris Hasbaniensis.* Ed. Wilhelm Levison. Monumenta Germaniae historica. *Scriptores rerum Merovingicarum,* vol. 6, pp. 264–298. Hanover, 1913.

Ecbasis cuiusdam captivi per Tropologiam. Ed. and tr. Edwin H. Zeydel. University of North Carolina Studies in the Germanic Languages and Literatures, vol. 46. Chapel Hill, 1964.

Ecloga. Tr. Edwin H. Freshfield. *A Manual of Roman Law: The* Ecloga *Published by the Emperors Leo III and Constantine V of Isauria.* Cambridge, 1926.

Egeria. *Itinerarium.* Ed. A. Franceschini and R. Weber. Corpus christianorum, series latina, vol. 175, pp. 29–103. Turnhout, 1965. Ed. and tr. John Wilkinson. *Egeria's Travels.* London, 1971.

Eligius of Noyon. *Predicacio.* Ed. Bruno Krusch. Monumenta Germaniae historica. *Scriptores rerum Merovingicarum,* vol. 4, pp. 751–761. Hanover and Leipzig, 1902.

English Historical Documents, vol. 1: *c.500–1042,* 2nd ed. Dorothy Whitelock. London, 1979.

Ennodius. *Magni Felicis Ennodi opera*. Ed. F. Vogel. Monumenta Germaniae historica. *Auctores Antiquissimi*, vol. 7. Berlin, 1885.

Epistolae langobardicae collectae. Ed. Wilhelm Gundlach. Monumenta Germaniae historica. *Epistolae*, vol. 3. Berlin, 1892.

Ermoldus Nigellus. *Poème sur Louis le Pieux et épîtres au Roi Pépin*. Ed. Edmond Faral. Les Classiques de l'histoire de France au moyen âge, vol. 14. Paris, 1932.

Exhortatio ad plebem christianam. Ed. K. Muellenhoff and W. Scherer. *Denkmäler deutscher Poesie und Prosa aus dem VIII–XII Jahrhundert*, vol. 1, pp. 200–201. Berlin, 1892.

Faustus of Riez. *De gratia*. Ed. A. Engelbrecht. Corpus scriptorum ecclesiasticorum latinorum, vol. 21, pp. 3–98. Vienna, 1891.

Ferreolus of Uzès. *Regula*. Patrologia latina, vol. 66, cols. 959–976.

Flodoard of Rheims. *Annales*. Ed. Philippe Lauer. Collection de textes pour servir à l'étude et à l'enseignement de l'histoire, vol. 39. Paris, 1905.

———. *Historia ecclesiae remensis*. Ed. J. Heller and G. Waitz. Monumenta Germaniae historica. *Scriptores* in folio, vol. 13, pp. 409–599. Leipzig, 1881.

Florianus. Letter to Nicetius. Ed. Wilhelm Gundlach. *Epistolae austresicae*. Monumenta Germaniae historica. *Epistolae*, vol. 3, pp. 116–117. Berlin, 1892.

The Fox and the Wolf. Ed. J.A.W. Bennett and G. V. Smithers. *Early Middle English Verse and Prose*, pp. 65–76 and 297–303. Oxford, 1974.

Fredegar. *Chronicarum quae dicuntur Fredegarii scholastici libri iv*. Ed. Bruno Krusch. Monumenta Germaniae historica. *Scriptores rerum Merovingicarum*, vol. 2, pp. 18–168. Hanover, 1888.

———. *The Fourth Book of the Chronicle of Fredegar With Its Continuations*. Ed. and tr. J. M. Wallace-Hadrill. London, 1960.

Fulgentius of Ruspe. *Fulgentii episcopi Ruspensis opera*. Ed. J. Fraipont. Corpus christianorum, series latina, vols. 91 and 91A. Turnhout, 1968.

Gennadius of Marseilles. *Liber sive Definitio ecclesiasticorum dogmatum*. Ed. Charles Turner. *Journal of Theological Studies* 7 (1906):78–99; 8 (1907):103–114.

Gerhard, Johannes. *Loci theologici*, 20 vols. Ed. Johannes Cotta. Tübingen, 1768.

Gesta domni Dagoberti I regis Francorum. Ed. Bruno Krusch. Monumenta Germaniae historica. *Scriptores rerum Merovingicarum*, vol. 2, pp. 399–425. Hanover, 1888.

Gesta Theoderici regis. Ed. Bruno Krusch. Monumenta Germaniae historica. *Scriptores rerum Merovingicarum*, vol. 2, pp. 202–210. Hanover, 1888.

Ghaerbald of Liège. *Capitulary Collection*. Ed. W. A. Eckhardt. *Die Kapitulariensammlung Bischof Ghaerbalds von Lüttich*. Germanenrechte, Neue Folge. Deutschrechtliches Archiv, vol. 5. Göttingen, 1955.

———. *First Diocesan Statute*. Ed. Carlo de Clercq. *La législation religieuse fran-*

que de Clovis à Charlemagne (507–814), pp. 352–356. Louvain and Paris, 1936.

———. *Second Diocesan Statute*. Ed. Carlo de Clercq. *La législation religieuse franque de Clovis à Charlemagne (507–814)*, pp. 357–362. Louvain and Paris, 1936.

Gratian. *Decretum*. Ed. Emil Friedberg. *Corpus iuris canonici*, vol. 1. Leipzig, 1879.

Gregory I. *Dialogi libri iv*. Ed. Umberto Moricca. Istituto storico italiano per il medio evo. Fonti per la storia d'Italia, vol. 57. Rome, 1924.

———. *Epistolae*. Ed. Paul Ewald and Ludo Hartmann. Monumenta Germaniae historica. *Epistolae*, vols. 1 and 2. Berlin, 1887 and 1899.

Gregory IX. *Decretales*. Ed. Emil Friedberg. *Corpus iuris canonici*, vol. 2. Leipzig, 1879.

Gregory of Nazianzus. Sermon 40. Tr. Charles Browne and James Swallow in *The Nicene and Post-Nicene Fathers*, 2nd series, vol. 7, pp. 360–377. New York, 1893. Reprint Grand Rapids, Mich., 1955.

Gregory of Nyssa. *De hominis opficio*. Ed. J. Laplace. Sources chrétiennes, vol. 6. Paris, 1944.

Gregory of Tours. *Historiarum libri x*, 2nd ed. Bruno Krusch, Wilhelm Levison, and Walther Holtzmann. Monumenta Germaniae historica. *Scriptores rerum Merovingicarum*, vol. 1, pt. 1. Hanover, 1937–1951. Tr. O. M. Dalton. *The History of the Franks by Gregory of Tours*, 2 vols. Oxford, 1927.

Haito of Basel. *Capitula Ecclesiastica*. Ed. A. Boretius and V. Krause. Monumenta Germaniae historica. *Leges*, sec. 2: *Capitularia regum Francorum*, vol. 1, pp. 362–366. Hanover, 1897.

Halitgar of Cambrai. *Pentitential*. Ed. Hermann J. Schmitz. *Die Bussbücher und die Bussdisciplin der Kirche*, vol. 1, pp. 465–489. Mainz, 1883. *Die Bussbücher und das kanonische Bussverfahren*, vol. 2, pp. 252–300. Mainz, 1898.

Herard of Tours. *Capitula*. Patrologia latina, vol. 121, cols. 763–774.

Hildegar of Meaux. *Capitula*, 2nd ed. Jean Mabillon. *Vetera analecta*, p. 412. Paris, 1723.

Hincmar of Rheims. *Capitula presbyteris data anno 852*. Patrologia latina, vol. 125, cols. 773–778.

Hincmar. *Vita Remigii episcopi Remensis*. Ed. Bruno Krusch. Monumenta Germaniae historica. *Scriptores rerum Merovingicarum*, vol. 3, pp. 239–349. Hanover, 1896.

Hippolytus. *The Apostolic Tradition*. Ed. Bernard Botte. *La tradition apostolique d'après les anciennes versions*. Sources chrétiennes, vol. 11bis. Paris, 1968.

———. *La liturgie d'Hippolyte. Documents et études*. Ed. Jean M. Hanssens. Rome, 1970.

Homilia de sacrilegiis. Ed. C. P. Caspari. *Eine Augustin fälschlich beilegte Homilia de sacrilegiis*. Christiania, 1886.

Ildephonsus of Toledo. *De cognitione baptismi*. Patrologia latina, vol. 96, cols. 111–172.

Ine, King of Wessex. *Institutiones*. Ed Felix Liebermann. *Die Gesetze der Angel-sachsen*, vol. 1, pp. 89–123. Halle, 1903. Reprint Aalen, 1960.

Initia consuetudinis benedictinae. Ed. Joseph Semmler. Corpus consuetudinum monasticarum, vol. 1. Siegburg, 1963.

The Irish Penitentials. Ed. Ludwig Bieler with an appendix by Daniel A. Binchy. Scriptores latini Hiberniae, vol. 5. Dublin, 1963.

Isaac of Langres. *Canones. Patrologia latina*, vol. 124, cols. 1075–1110.

Jacobus Diaconus. *Vita sanctae Pelagiae*. Ed. Hermann Usener. *Die Legenden der heiligen Pelagia*, pp. 3–16. Bonn, 1879.

John Chrysostom. *Huit catéchèses baptismales inédites*. Ed. Antoine Wenger. Sources chrétiennes, vol. 50. Paris, 1957. Tr. Paul Harkins. *John Chrysostom: Baptismal Instructions*. Ancient Christian Writers, vol. 31. Westminster, Md., 1963.

———. *La virginité*. Ed. Herbert Musurillo and B. Grillet. Sources chrétiennes, vol. 125. Paris, 1966.

John the Deacon. Letter to Senarius. In André Wilmart, "Un florilège carolingien sur le symbolisme des cérémonies du baptême, avec un Appendice sur la lettre de Jean Diacre." *Analecta Reginensia*. Studi e testi, vol. 59, pp. 153–179. Vatican City, 1933.

John the Deacon of Venice. *Chronicon venetum et gradense*. Ed. Giovanni Monticolo. *Cronache veneziane antichissime*. Fonti per la storia d'Italia, vol. 9. Rome, 1890.

Jonas of Bobbio. *Vitae Columbani abbatis discipulorumque eius libri duo*. Ed. Bruno Krusch. Monumenta Germaniae historica. *Scriptores rerum Merovingicarum*, vol. 4, pp. 61–152. Hanover and Leipzig, 1902.

Jonas of Orléans. *De institutione laicali. Patrologia latina*, vol. 106, cols. 121–278.

Justinian. *Codex*. Ed. Paul Krueger. *Corpus iuris civilis*, vol. 2. Berlin, 1895.

The Laws of the Earliest English Kings. Ed. and tr. Frederick L. Attenborough. Cambridge, 1922.

Legislatio Aquisgranensis. Ed. Joseph Semmler. Corpus consuetudinum monasticarum, vol. 1, pp. 423–582. Siegburg, 1963.

Leo I. *Sermones*. Ed. René Dolle. Sources chrétiennes, vol. 22. Paris, 1947.

Leo IV to the bishops of Brittany. Ed. A. de Hirsch-Gereuth. Monumenta Germaniae historica. *Epistolae*, vol. 5, pp. 593–596. Berlin, 1899.

Leudgar of Autun. *Canons*. Ed. Carlo de Clercq. *Concilia Galliae A.511–A.695*. Corpus christianorum, series latina, vol. 148A, pp. 318–320. Turnhout, 1963.

Liber historiae Francorum. Ed. Bruno Krusch. Monumenta Germaniae historica. *Scriptores rerum Merovingicarum*, vol. 2, pp. 215–328. Hanover, 1888. Tr. Bernard Bachrach. *Liber historiae Francorum*. Lawrence, Kans., 1973.

Liber Pontificalis, 2nd ed., 3 vols. Ed. Louis Duchesne. Paris, 1955–1957.

Liber sacramentorum Romanae Ecclesiae. Ed. H. A. Wilson. Oxford, 1894.

Liebermann, Felix. *Die Gesetze der Angelsachsen*, 3 vols. Halle, 1903–1916. Reprint Aalen, 1960.

Liutprand. *Leges Liutprandi regis*. Ed. F. Bluhme. Monumenta Germaniae historica. *Leges*, vol. 4: *Leges Langobardorum*, pp. 96–175. Hanover, 1868. Tr. Katherine F. Drew. *The Lombard Laws*. Philadelphia, 1973.

Ludolph of Saxony. *Vita Jesu Christi*. Paris, 1865.

Luther, Martin. *The Babylonian Captivity of the Church*. Tr. A. T. W. Steinhauser and rev. F. C. Ahrens and A. R. Wentz. *Luther's Works*, vol. 36. Philadelphia, 1956.

Macarius. *Regula*. Ed. Helga Styblo. *Wiener Studien* 76 (1963):151–158.

Martène, Edmond, ed. *De antiquis ecclesiae ritibus libri quatuor*, 4 vols. Antwerp, 1736–1738.

Martin of Braga. *De correctione rusticorum*. Ed. Claude Barlow. *Martini episcopi Bracarensis opera omnia*. Papers and monographs of the American Academy in Rome, vol. 12, pp. 183–203. New Haven, 1950.

Maximus of Turin. *Maximi episcopi Tauriensis sermones*. Ed. Almut Mutzenbecher. Corpus christianorum, series latina, vol. 23. Turnhout, 1962.

Michael and Theophilus. Letter to Louis the Pious. Ed. A. Werminghoff. Monumenta Germaniae historica. *Leges*, sec. 3. *Concilia*, vol. 2, pt. 2, pp. 475–480. Hanover and Leipzig, 1908.

Morin, Germain, ed. "Textes inédits relatifs au Symbole et à la vie chrétienne." *Revue bénédictine* 22 (1905):505–524.

Munding, E., ed. *Ein Königsbrief Karls des Grossen an Papst Hadrian*. Texte und Arbeiten, vol. 1, pt. 6. Beuron and Leipzig, 1920.

Nicholas I. *Epistolae*. Ed. E. Perels. Monumenta Germaniae historica. *Epistolae*, vol. 6, pp. 257–690. Hanover, 1925.

Nithard. *Historiarum libri iiii*. Ed. E. Müller. Monumenta Germaniae historica. *Scriptores rerum Germanicarum*, vol. 44. Hanover, 1897.

Notker the Stammerer. *Gesta Caroli*. Ed. Hans F. Haefele. Monumenta Germaniae historica. *Scriptores rerum Germanicarum*, new series, vol. 12. Berlin, 1959.

Ordo romanus xi. Ed. Michel Andrieu. *Les Ordines Romani du haut moyen âge*, vol. 2. Spicilegium sacrum lovaniense. Etudes et documents, vol. 23, pp. 365–447. Louvain, 1948.

Ordo romanus xv. Ed. Michel Andrieu. *Les Ordines Romani du haut moyen âge*, vol. 3. Spicilegium sacrum lovaniense. Etudes et documents, vol. 24, pp. 95–125. Louvain, 1951.

Ordo romanus L. Ed. Michel Andrieu. *Les Ordines Romani du haut moyen âge*, vol. 5. Spicilegium sacrum lovaniense. Etudes et documents, vol. 29, pp. 5–403. Louvain, 1961. Ed. Cyrille Vogel and Reinhard Elze. *Le Pontifical Romano-germanique du dixième siècle*. Studi e testi, vol. 227, pp. 1–141. Vatican City, 1963.

Paul the Deacon. *Historia Langobardorum*. Ed. L. Bethmann and G. Waitz. Monumenta Germaniae historica. *Scriptores rerum Germanicarum* in usum scholarum, vol. 48. Hanover, 1878.

Petrus Lombardus. *Libri iv sententiarum*. Ed. Patres Collegii S. Bonaventurae. Quarrachi, 1916.

Pirminius. *Dicta abbatis Pirminii de singulis libris canonicis scarapsus*. Ed. G. Jecker. German tr. Ursmar Engelmann. *Der heilige Pirmin und sein Pastoralbüchlein*. Sigmaringen, 1976. Also ed. C. P. Caspari. *Kirchenhistorische Anecdota*, vol. 1, pp. 151–193. Christiania, 1883.

Poenitentiale Hubertense. Ed. F.W.H. Wasserschleben. *Die Bussordnungen der abendländischen Kirche*, pp. 377–387. Halle, 1851. Reprint Graz, 1958.

Poenitentiale Martenianum. Ed. Walter von Hörmann. "Bussbücherstudien VI." *Zeitschrift der Savigny-Stiftung für Rechtsgeschichte*, Kanonistische Abteilung, 4 (1914):358–453.

Poenitentiale Merseburgense b. Ed. F.W.H. Wasserschleben. *Die Bussordnungen der abendländischen Kirche*, pp. 429–433. Halle, 1851. Reprint Graz, 1958.

Poenitentiale Merseburgense c. Ed. F.W.H. Wasserschleben. *Die Bussordnungen der abendländischen Kirche*, pp. 435–437. Halle, 1851. Reprint Graz, 1958.

Poenitentiale Vallicellanum I. Ed. Hermann J. Schmitz. *Die Bussbücher und die Bussdisciplin der Kirche*, vol. 1, pp. 227–342. Mainz, 1883. Reprint Graz, 1958.

Poenitentiale Vallicellanum II. Ed. F.W.H. Wasserschleben. *Die Bussordnungen der abendländischen Kirche*, pp. 551–566. Halle, 1851. Reprint Graz, 1958.

Le Pontifical Romano-germanique du dixième siècle. Ed. Cyrille Vogel and Reinhard Elze. Studi e testi, vols. 226 and 227. Vatican City, 1963.

Porphyry. *Life of Plotinus*. Ed. Emile Bréhier. *Plotin. Ennéades*, vol. 1, pp. 1–31. Paris, 1924.

Procopius. *The Anecdota or Secret History*. Ed. and tr. H. B. Dewing. The Loeb Classical Library. London and Cambridge, Mass., 1935.

Rabanus Maurus. *Epistolae*. Ed. Ernst Dümmler. Monumenta Germaniae historica. *Epistolae*, vol. 5, pp. 381–530. Berlin, 1899.

————. *Homiliae de festis praecipuis, item de virtutibus. Patrologia latina*, vol. 110.

Radulphus Glaber. *Historiarum sui temporis libri quinque*. Ed. Maurice Prou. Collection de textes pour servir à l'étude et à l'enseignement de l'histoire, vol. 1. Paris, 1886.

————. *Vita domni Willelmi abbatis*. Ed. Neithard Bulst. "Rodulfus Glabers Vita domni Willelmi abbatis. Neue Edition nach einer Handschrift des 11. Jahrhunderts (Paris, Bibliothèque Nationale, lat. 5390)." *Deutsches Archiv für Erforschung des Mittelalters* 30 (1974):450–487.

Recueil des chartes de l'Abbaye de Cluny, 6 vols. Ed. Auguste Bernard and Alexandre Bruel. Paris, 1876–1903.

Regesta pontificum romanorum. Ed. P. Jaffé and 2nd ed. G. Wattenbach, S. Löwenfeld, F. Kaltenbrunner, and P. Ewald. 2 vols. Leipzig, 1885–1888.

Regino of Prüm. *Libri duo de synodalibus causis et disciplinis ecclesiasticis*. Ed. F.G.A. Wasserschleben. Leipzig, 1840.

Regula Tarnantensis. Ed. Fernando Villegas. "La 'Regula Monasterii Tarnantensis.' Texte, sources et datation." *Revue bénédictine* 84 (1974):7–65.

Richer of Rheims. *Historiarum libri iiii*. Ed. G. H. Pertz. Monumenta Germaniae historica. Scriptores, vol. 3, pp. 561–657. Hanover, 1839.

Riculf of Soissons. *Statuta*. Patrologia latina, vol. 131, cols. 15–24.

Rodulph of Bourges. *Capitula*. Patrologia latina, vol. 119, cols. 703–726.

Le Roman de Renart. Branches II–VI. Ed. Mario Roques. Les classiques français du moyen âge, vol. 79. Paris, 1951.

Rufinus of Aquileia. *Apologia contra Hieronymum*. Ed. M. Simonetti. Corpus christianorum, series latina, vol. 20, pp. 19–123. Turnhout, 1961.

Ruotger of Trier. *Canones*. Ed. M. Blasen. "Die Canonessammlung des Erzbischofs Ruotger von Trier vom Jahre 927. Ein Beitrag zur Rechtsgeschichte der Diözese Trier." *Pastor Bonus* 52 (1941):61–72.

Schmitz, Hermann J. *Die Bussbücher und die Bussdisciplin der Kirche*. Mainz, 1883. Reprint Graz, 1958.

———. *Die Bussbücher und das kanonische Bussverfahren*. Düsseldorf, 1898. Reprint Graz, 1958.

The Seven Ecumenical Councils of the Church. Tr. Henry R. Percival. A Select Library of Nicene and Post-Nicene Fathers of the Church, 2nd series, vol. 14. New York, 1916.

Statuta ecclesiae antiqua. Ed. Charles Munier. *Concilia Galliae A.314–A.506*. Corpus christianorum, series latina, vol. 148, pp. 162–188. Turnhout, 1963.

Steinmeyer, Elias von, ed. *Die kleineren althochdeutschen Sprachdenkmäler*. Berlin, 1916.

Stephen II. *Responsa* to the monks of Bretigny. *Sacrorum conciliorum nova et amplissima collectio*. Ed. J. D. Mansi. vol. 12, cols. 558–563. Florence, 1766.

Tacitus. *Germania*. Tr. Herbert Benario. *Tacitus: Agricola, Germany, Dialogue on Orators*. Indianapolis, Ind., 1967.

Tertullian. *De baptismo*. Ed. R. F. Refoulé. French tr. M. Drouzy. Sources chrétiennes, vol. 35. Paris, 1952. Tr. Ernest Evans. *Tertullian's Homily on Baptism*. London, 1964.

Testamentum domini nostri Jesu Christi. Ed. I. E. Rahmani. Mainz, 1899.

Theodore of Canterbury. *Canones*. Ed. Paul W. Finsterwalder. *Die Canones Theodori Cantuariensis und ihre Überlieferungsformen. Untersuchungen zu den Bussbüchern des 7., 8. und 9. Jahrhunderts*, vol. 1, pp. 239–252. Weimar, 1929.

———. *Penitential*. Ed. F.W.H. Wasserschleben. *Die Bussordnungen der abendländischen Kirche*, pp. 566–622. Halle, 1851. Reprint Graz, 1958.

Theodore of Mopsuestia. *Commentary of Theodore of Mopsuestia on the Lord's Prayer and on the Sacraments of Baptism and the Eucharist*. Tr. Alphonse Mingana. Woodbrooke Studies, vol. 6. Cambridge, 1933.

Theodore of Mopsuestia. *Les homélies catéchétiques de Théodore de Mopsueste*. Ed. and French tr. Raymond Tonneau and Robert Devreesse. Studi e testi, vol. 145. Vatican City, 1949.

Theodore the Studite. *Epistolae. Patrologia graeca*, vol. 99, cols. 903–1679.

Theodulph of Orléans. *First diocesan statute. Patrologia latina*, vol. 105, cols. 191–208.

———. *Second diocesan statute*. Ed. Carlo de Clercq. *La législation religieuse franque de Clovis à Charlemagne (507–814)*, pp. 323–351. Louvain and Paris, 1936.

Vesoul, Diocesan Statute of. Ed. Carlo de Clercq. *La législation religieuse franque de Clovis à Charlemagne (507–814)*, pp. 367–374. Louvain and Paris, 1936.

Virtutes Fursei abbatis Latiniacensis. Ed. Bruno Krusch. Monumenta Germaniae historica. *Scriptores rerum Merovingicarum*, vol. 4, pp. 440–449. Hanover, 1902.

Vita Adelphii abbatis Habendensis. Ed. Bruno Krusch. Monumenta Germaniae historica. *Scriptores rerum Merovingicarum*, vol. 4, pp. 225–228. Hanover, 1902.

Vita Amandi episcopi. Ed. Bruno Krusch and Wilhelm Levison. Monumenta Germaniae historica. *Scriptores rerum Merovingicarum*, vol. 5, 395–449. Hanover and Leipzig, 1910.

Vita sancti Apri eremitae. Ed. the Bollandists. *Catalogus codicum hagiographicorum latinorum antiquiorum seculo XVI qui asservantur in Bibliotheca Nationali Parisiensi*, vol. 2, pp. 89–93. Paris and Brussels, 1890.

Vita sanctae Balthildis, recensions A and B. Ed. Bruno Krusch. Monumenta Germaniae historica. *Scriptores rerum Merovingicarum*, vol. 2, pp. 475–508. Hanover, 1888.

Vita Bertini. Ed. Bruno Krusch. Monumenta Germaniae historica. *Scriptores rerum Merovingicarum*, vol. 5, pp. 729–786. Hanover, 1910.

Vita Dagoberti III regis Francorum. Ed. Bruno Krusch. Monumenta Germaniae historica. *Scriptores rerum Merovingicarum*, vol. 2, pp. 511–524. Hanover, 1888.

Vita sancti Desiderii episcopi Cadurcensis. Ed. Bruno Krusch. Monumenta Germaniae historica. *Scriptores rerum Merovingicarum*, vol. 4, pp. 547–602. Hanover, 1902.

Vita Eligii episcopi Noviomagensis. Ed. Bruno Krusch. Monumenta Germaniae historica. *Scriptores rerum Merovingicarum*, vol. 4, pp. 663–741. Hanover, 1902.

Vita Eucherii episcopi Aurelianensis. Ed. Wilhelm Levison. Monumenta Germaniae historica. *Scriptores rerum Merovingicarum*, vol. 7, pp. 46–53. Hanover, 1920.

Vita Filiberti abbatis Gemmeticensis et Heriensis. Ed. Wilhelm Levison. Monumenta Germaniae historica. *Scriptores rerum Merovingicarum*, vol. 5, pp. 583–604. Hanover, 1910.

Vita sancti Gaugerici episcopi Cameracensis antiquior. Analecta bollandiana 7 (1888):387–398.

Vita beate Genovefae virginis. Ed. Charles Kohler. *Etude critique sur le texte de la vie latine de Sainte-Geneviève de Paris.* Bibliothèque de l'Ecole des hautes études. Sciences philologiques et historiques, vol. 48. Paris, 1881.

Vita sancti Gildardi episcopi Rothomagensis. Ed. Albert Poncelet. "Vita sancti Gildardi episcopi Rothomagensis et ejusdem Translatio Suessiones anno 838–840 Facta." *Analecta bollandiana* 8 (1889):389–405.

Vita Gregorii Magni Papae. Ed. and tr. Bertram Colgrave. *The Earliest Life of Gregory the Great.* Lawrence, Kans. 1968.

Vita Lupi episcopi Senonici. Ed. Bruno Krusch. Monumenta Germaniae historica. *Scriptores rerum Merovingicarum,* vol. 4, pp. 179–187. Hanover and Leipzig, 1902.

Vita Pardulfi abbatis Waractensis. Ed. Wilhelm Levison. Monumenta Germaniae historica. *Scriptores rerum Merovingicarum,* vol. 7, pp. 19–40. Hanover and Leipzig, 1920.

Vita Richarii sacerdotis Centulensis primigenia. Ed. Bruno Krusch. Monumenta Germaniae historica. *Scriptores rerum Merovingicarum,* vol. 7, pp. 438–453. Hanover and Leipzig, 1920.

Vita sanctae Segolenae viduae. Acta sanctorum, July, vol. 5, pp. 630–637.

Vita Uulfranni episcopi Senonici. Ed. Bruno Krusch and Wilhelm Levison. Monumenta Germaniae historica. *Scriptores rerum Merovingicarum,* vol. 5, pp. 657–673. Hanover, 1910.

Walafrid Strabo. *Libellus de exordiis et incrementis quarundam in observationibus ecclesiasticis rerum.* Ed. A. Boretius and V. Krause. Monumenta Germaniae historica. *Leges,* sec. 2: *Capitularia regum Francorum,* vol. 2, pp. 473–516. Hanover, 1897.

Wasserschleben, F.W.H. *Die Bussordnungen der abendländischen Kirche.* Halle, 1851. Reprint Graz, 1958.

Ysengrimus. Ed. Ernst Voight. Halle, 1884.

Zachary to Pepin. (*Codex Carolinus,* 3). Ed. Wilhelm Gundlach. Monumenta Germaniae historica. *Epistolae,* vol. 3, pp. 479–485. Berlin, 1892.

Zachary to Theodore of Pavia. Ed. Wilhelm Gundlach. Monumenta Germaniae historica. *Epistolae,* vol. 3, pp. 710–711. Berlin, 1892.

Secondary Sources

Ahlstrom, Sydney. *A Religious History of the American People.* New Haven, 1972.

Aland, Kurt. *Die Säuglingstaufe im Neuen Testament und in der Alten Kirche. Eine Antwort an Joachim Jeremias.* Theologische Existenz Heute, Neue Folge, vol. 86. Munich, 1961. Tr. G. R. Beasley-Murray. *Did the Early Church Baptize Infants?* London, 1961.

Altaner, Berthold, and Alfred Stuiber. *Patrologie,* 8th ed. Freiburg, 1978.

Amiet, Robert. "Une 'Admonitio Synodalis' de l'époque carolingienne. Etude critique et édition." *Mediaeval Studies* 26 (1964):12–82.

Anderson, Gallatin. "Il Comparaggio: The Italian Godparenthood Complex." *Southwestern Journal of Anthropology* 13 (1957):32–53.

———. "A Survey of Italian Godparenthood." *The Kroeber Anthropological Society Papers* 15 (1956):1–110.

Andrieu, Michel. *Les Ordines Romani du haut moyen âge*, 5 vols. Spicilegium sacrum lovaniense. Etudes et documents, vols. 11, 23, 24, 28, 29. Louvain, 1931–1961.

Angenendt, Arnold. "Bonifatius und das Sacramentum initiationis. Zugleich ein Beitrag zur Geschichte der Firmung." *Römische Quartalschrift für christliche Altertumskunde und Kirchengeschichte* 72 (1977):133–183.

———. "Das geistliche Bündnis der Päpste mit den Karolingern (754–796)." *Historisches Jahrbuch* 100 (1980):1–94.

———. "Taufe und Politik im frühen Mittelalter." *Frühmittelalterliche Studien* 7 (1973):143–168.

Anson, John. "The Female Transvestite in Early Monasticism: The Origin and Development of a Motif." *Viator* 5 (1974):1–32.

Arnold, Carl F. *Caesarius von Arelate und die Gallische Kirche seiner Zeit*. Leipzig, 1894.

Aschenbrenner, Stanley. "Folk Model vs. Actual Practice: The Distribution of Spiritual Kin in a Greek Village." *Anthropological Quarterly* 48 (1975):65–86.

Baccrabère, Georges. "Visite canonique de l'évêque." *Dictionnaire de droit canonique*, vol. 7 (1965), cols. 1512–1594.

———. "Visite canonique du vicaire forain." *Dictionnaire de droit canonique*, vol. 7 (1965), pp. 1606–1619.

Baesecke, Georg. "Die altdeutschen Beichten." *Beiträge zur Geschichte der deutschen Sprache und Literatur* 49 (1924–25):268–355.

Baetke, Walter. "Die Aufnahme des Christentums durch die Germanen. Ein Beitrag zur Frage der Germanisierung des Christentums." *Die Welt als Geschichte* 9 (1943):143–166.

———. "Christliche Lehngut in der Sagareligion." *Berichte über die Verhandlungen der Sächsischen Akademie der Wissenschaften*. Phil.-hist. Klasse, vol. 98, pt. 6 (1952):24–30.

Bailey, Derrick S. *Sexual Relation in Christian Thought*. New York, 1959.

———. *Sponsors at Baptism and Confirmation: An Historical Introduction to Anglican Practice*. New York, 1951.

Barion, Hans. *Das fränkisch-deutsche Synodalrecht des Frühmittelalters*. Kanonistische Studien und Texte, vols. 5 and 6. Bonn, 1931.

Barraclough, Geoffrey. *The Medieval Papacy*. New York, 1968.

Barré, Henri. *Les homélaires carolingiens de l'école d'Auxerre*. Studi e testi, vol. 225. Vatican City, 1962.

Bastiaensen, A.A.R. *Observations sur le vocabulaire liturgique dans l'Itinéraire d'Egérie*. Latinitas christianorum primaeva, vol. 17. Nijmegen and Utrecht, 1962.

Bastow, A. "Peasant Customs and Superstitions in Thirteenth Century Germany." *Folklore* 47 (1936):313–328.

Beck, Henry G. J., *The Pastoral Care of Souls in South-East France During the Sixth Century*. Analecta Gregoriana, vol. 51. Rome, 1950.

Bedard, Walter. *The Symbolism of the Baptismal Font in Early Christian Thought*. Catholic University of America. Studies in Sacred Theology, 2nd series, vol. 45. Washington, D.C., 1951.

Bell, Clair Hayden. *Peasant Life in Old German Epics*. New York, 1931.

Bennett, Michael. "Spiritual Kinship and the Baptismal Name in Traditional European Society." In *Principalities, Powers, and Estates: Studies in Medieval and Early Modern Government and Society*, ed. L. O. Frappell, pp. 1–13. Adelaide, Australia, 1979.

Berg, Karl. *Die Werke des hl. Caesarius von Arles als liturgiegeschichtliche Quelle*. Excerpta ex Dissertatione ad Lauream in facultate theologica Pontificiae Universitatis Gregorianae Urbis. Munich, 1946.

Berthet, Abbé. "Un réactif social: le parrainage. Du xvie siècle à la Révolution: Nobles, bourgeois et paysans dans un bourg perché du Jura." *Annales. Economies, sociétés, civilisations* 1 (1946):43–50.

Besse, Jean-Martial. *Les moines de l'ancienne France. Période gallo-romaine et mérovingienne*. Archives de la France monastique, vol. 2. Paris, 1906.

Betz, Werner. "Karl der Grosse und die Lingua Theodisca." *Karl der Grosse. Lebenswerk und Nachleben*, vol. 2: *Das geistige Leben*, ed. Bernhard Bischoff, pp. 300–306. Düsseldorf, 1965.

Binder, G. "Geburt II (religionsgeschichtlich)." *Reallexicon für Antike und Christentum* 9 (1976):43–171.

Bingham, Joseph. *The Works of the Learned Joseph Bingham, M.A.*, 2 vols. London, 1762.

Blond, Georges. "Encratisme." *Dictionnaire de spiritualité, d'ascétique et de mystique* 4 (1959):628–642.

Boesch, Hans. *Kinderleben in der deutschen Vergangenheit*. Monographien zur deutschen Kulturgeschichte, vol. 5. Leipzig, 1900.

Bonini, I. "Lo stile nei sermoni di Cesario di Arles." *Aevum* 36 (1962):240–257.

Bonner, Gerald. *St. Augustine of Hippo: Life and Controversies*. London, 1963.

Borst, Arno. *Der Turmbau von Babel. Geschichte der Meinungen über Ursprung und Vielfalt der Sprachen und Völker*. 4 vols. in 6 pts. Stuttgart, 1957–1963.

Bossy, John. "Blood and Baptism: Kinship, Community and Christianity in Western Europe from the Fourteenth to the Seventeenth Centuries." *Sanctity and Secularity: The Church and the World*, ed. D. Baker, pp. 129–143. Oxford, 1973.

———. "The Counter-Reformation and the People of Catholic Europe." *Past and Present* 47 (1970):51–70.

Bostock, John Knight. *A Handbook on Old High German Literature*, 2nd ed. K. C. King and D. R. McLintock. Oxford, 1976.

Botte, Bernard. Review of Michel Dujarier, *Le parrainage des adultes aux trois premiers siècles de l'Eglise.* In *Bulletin de théologie ancienne et médiévale* 9 (1962–65):319.

———. *La tradition apostolique d'après les anciennes versions*, 2nd ed. Sources chrétiennes, vol. 11bis. Paris, 1968.

———. *La tradition apostolique de saint Hippolyte. Essai de reconstitution.* Münster, 1963.

Bouteiller, Marcelle. "Tradition folklorique et 'parentés parallèles.' Le couple parrain-marraine et ses implications dans les lignées familiales." *Echanges et communications. Mélanges offerts à Claude Levi-Strauss à l'occasion de son 60 ème anniversaire*, 2 vols., 1:153–161. Paris and The Hague, 1970.

Breckenridge, James D. "Evidence for the Nature of Relations Between Pope John VII and the Byzantine Emperor Justinian II." *Byzantinische Zeitschrift* 65 (1972):364–374.

Bromiley, Geoffrey W. *Baptism and the Anglican Reformers.* London, 1953.

Brommer, Peter. "Die bischöfliche Gesetzgebung Theodulfs von Orléans." *Zeitschrift der Savigny-Stiftung für Rechtsgeschichte*, Kanonistische Abteilung, 60 (1974):1–120.

———. "Die Rezeption der bischöflichen Kapitularien Theodulfs von Orléans." *Zeitschrift der Savigny-Stiftung für Rechtsgeschichte*, Kanonistische Abteilung, 61 (1975):113–160.

Browe, Peter. *Beiträge zur Sexualethik des Mittelalters.* Breslauer Studien zur historischen Theologie, vol. 23. Breslau, 1932.

Brown, Elizabeth A. R., "The Tyranny of a Construct: Feudalism and Historians of Medieval Europe." *American Historical Review* 79 (1974):1063–1088.

Brown, Peter. "The Rise and Function of the Holy Man in Late Antiquity." *Journal of Roman Studies* 61 (1971):80–101.

Browne, Henry. "Sponsors." *Dictionary of Christian Antiquities*, vol. 2, pp. 1923–1925. Hartford, 1880.

Brusselmans, Christiane. "Les fonctions de parrainage des enfants aux premiers siècles de l'Eglise (100–550)." Ph.D. diss. Catholic University of America, 1964.

Bugge, John. *Virginitas: An Essay in the History of a Medieval Ideal.* The Hague, 1975.

Buhot, Jean-Paul. "Explications du rituel baptismal à l'époque carolingienne." *Revue des études augustiniennes* 24 (1978):278–301.

———. "Le sermon *Dominus et Salvator*. Première forme dérivée d'un sermon perdu de saint Césaire." *Revue bénédictine* 80 (1970):201–212.

Buisson, Ludwig. "Formen normannischer Staatsbildung (9. bis 11. Jahrhundert)." *Studien zum mittelalterlichen Lehenswesen.* Vorträge und Forschungen, vol. 5, pp. 95–184. Lindau and Konstanz, 1960.

Bullough, Vern L., and James A. Brundage. *Sexual Practices and the Medieval Church.* Buffalo, N. Y., 1982.

Campbell, John K. *Honour, Family and Patronage: A Study of Institutions and Moral Values in a Greek Mountain Community.* Oxford, 1964.

Campbell, Thomas L. *Dionysius the Pseudo-Areopagite: The Ecclesiastical Hierarchy*. Lanham, Md., 1981.

Capelle, B. "L'introduction du catéchuménat à Rome." *Recherches de théologie ancienne et médiévale* 5 (1933):129–154.

Chadwick, Owen. *The Reformation*. Pelican History of the Church, vol. 3. Harmondsworth, Eng., 1964.

Chelini, Jean. "Les laïcs dans la société ecclésiastique carolingienne." *I laici nella 'Societas Christiana' dei secoli XI e XII*. Miscellanea del Centro di Studi medievali, vol. 5, pp. 23–50. Milan, 1968.

———. "La pratique dominicale des laïcs dans l'Eglise franque sous le règne de Pépin." *Revue d'histoire de l'Eglise de France* 42 (1956):161–174.

Clercq, Carlo de. *La législation religieuse franque de Clovis à Charlemagne. Etude sur les actes de conciles et les capitulaires, les statuts diocésains et les règles monastiques (507–814)*. Université de Louvain. Recueil de travaux publiés par les membres des conférences d'histoire et de philologie, 2nd series, vol. 38. Louvain and Paris, 1936; and volume two, *La législation religieuse franque de Louis le Pieux à la fin du ixe siècle (814–900)*. Antwerp, 1958.

Connolly, Richard H. *The So-Called Egyptian Church Order and Derived Documents*. Texts and Studies, vol. 8, pt. 4. Cambridge, 1916.

Constable, Giles. *Monastic Tithes from Their Origins to the Twelfth Century*. Cambridge Studies in Medieval Life and Thought, new series, vol. 10. Cambridge, 1964.

Coornaert, E. "Les ghildes médiévales (v^e–xive siècles): définition—évolution." *Revue historique* 199 (1948):22–55, 208–243.

Corblet, Jules. "Parrains et marraines. Etude liturgico-historique." *Revue de l'art chrétien*, 2nd series, 14 (1881):336–353; 15 (1881):26–54. Reprinted in his *Histoire dogmatique, liturgique et archéologique du sacrement de Baptême*, 2 vols. Paris, 1881–1882.

Coulet, Noël. *Les visites pastorales*. Typologie des sources du moyen âge occidental, vol. 23. Turnhout, 1977.

Courreau, J. "Saint Césaire d'Arles et les Juifs." *Bulletin de littérature ecclésiastique* 71 (1970):92–112.

Crehan, Joseph. *Early Christian Baptism and the Creed: A Study in Ante-Nicene Theology*. London, 1950.

Crouzel, Henri. "Le célibat et la continence ecclésiastique dans l'Eglise primitive: leurs motivations." *Sacerdoce et célibat. Etudes historiques et théologiques*. Bibliotheca ephemeridum theologicarum lovaniensium, vol. 28, pp. 333–371. Louvain and Gembloux, 1971.

———. "Le remariage après séparation pour adultère selon les Pères latins." *Bulletin de littérature ecclésiastique* 75 (1974):189–204.

Dahmen, Josef. *Das Pontifikat Gregors II. nach den Quellen bearbeitet*. Düsseldorf, 1888.

Dahood, Mitchell J. "Hebrew Studies in the Christian Church." *New Catholic Encyclopedia*, vol. 6, pp. 976–978. New York, 1967.

Daniélou, Jean. *Origène*. Paris, 1948.

Daniélou, Jean, and Henri Marrou. *The Christian Centuries*, vol. 1: *The First Six Hundred Years*. London, 1964.

Dauvillier, Jean, and Carlo de Clercq. *Le mariage en droit canonique oriental*. Paris, 1936.

Del Bono, Francesco. "La letteratura catechetica di lingua tedesca." *La conversione al cristianesimo nell'Europa dell'alto medioevo*. Settimane di studio del Centro italiano di studi sull'alto medioevo, vol. 14, pp. 697–741. Spoleto, 1967.

Depoin, Joseph. "Les relations de famille au moyen âge." *Société historique et archéologique de l'arrondissement de Pontoise et du Vexin* 32 (1914):27–85.

Devailly, Guy. "La pastorale en Gaule au ixᵉ siècle." *Revue d'histoire de l'Eglise de France* 59 (1973):23–54.

Devreesse, Robert. *Essai sur Théodore de Mopsueste*. Studi e testi, vol. 141. Vatican City, 1948.

Dick, Ernst. "Das Pateninstitut im altchristlichen Katechumenat." *Zeitschrift für katholische Theologie* 63 (1939):1–49.

Didier, J. C. "Une adaptation de la liturgie baptismale au baptême des enfants dans l'église ancienne." *Mélanges de science religieuse* 22 (1965):79–90.

———. "Observations sur la date de la lettre 98 de Saint Augustin." *Mélanges de science religieuse* 27 (1970):115–117.

———. "Le pédobaptisme au ivᵉ siècle. Documents nouveaux." *Mélanges de science religieuse* 6 (1949):233–246.

Diegerick, I.L.A. "Une famille au xviᵉ siècle." *Annales de la Société historique, archéologique et littéraire de la ville d'Ypres et de l'ancienne West Flandre* 8 (1878):126–168.

Dodds, Eric R. "Man and the Material World." *Pagan and Christian in an Age of Anxiety*, pp. 1–36. Cambridge, 1965.

Dölger, Franz Joseph. "Die 'Familie der Könige' im Mittelalter." *Historisches Jahrbuch* 60 (1940):397–420.

———. "Die Garantiewerk der Bekehrung als Bedingung und Sicherung bei der Annahme zur Taufe. Die Zertrümmerung eines Mithras–Heiligtums durch den Stadtpräfeckten Gracchus und ähnliche Vorkommnisse in kultgeschichtlicher Beleuchtung." *Antike und Christentum* 3 (1932):260–277.

Dondeyne, A. "La discipline des scrutins dans l'église latine avant Charlemagne." *Revue d'histoire ecclésiastique* 28 (1932):5–32, 751–787.

Douglas, Mary. *Purity and Danger: An Analysis of the Concepts of Pollution and Taboo*. London, 1966.

Drabek, Anna M. "Der Merowingervertrag von Andelot aus dem Jahr 587." *Mitteilungen des Instituts für österreichische Geschichtsforschung* 78 (1970):34–41.

Drews, Paul. "Taufpaten." *Realencyklopaedie für protestantische Theologie und Kirche* 19 (1907):447–450.

Duby, Georges. "Le mariage dans la société du haut moyen âge." *Il matrimonio nella società altomedievale*, pt. 1. Settimane di studio del Centro italiano di studi sull'alto medioevo, vol. 24, pp. 13–39. Spoleto, 1977.

———. *Medieval Marriage: Two Models from Twelfth-Century France*. Tr. Elborg Forster. Baltimore, 1978.

———. *Rural Economy and Country Life in the Medieval West*. Tr. Cynthia Postan. Columbia, S.C., 1968.

Duhr, Joseph. "La confrérie dans la vie de l'Eglise." *Revue d'histoire ecclésiastique* 35 (1939):439–478.

Dujarier, Michel. *A History of the Catechumenate: The First Six Centuries*. New York, 1979.

———. *Le parrainage des adultes aux trois premiers siècles de l'Eglise. Recherche historique sur l'évolution des garanties et des étapes catéchuménales avant 313*. Paris, 1962.

Dujcev, I. "Bizantini e longobardi." *Atti del Convegno Internazionale sul tema: La Civiltà dei Longobardi in Europa (Roma, 24–26 maggio 1971)*. Problemi attuali, vol. 189, pp. 45–78. Rome, 1974.

Eckhardt, Karl A. "Adoption." *Studia merovingica*. Bibliotheca rerum historicarum, vol. 11, pp. 240–261. Aalen, 1975.

Eggers, Hans. "Die altdeutschen Beichten." *Beiträge zur Geschichte der deutschen Sprache und Literatur* 77 (1955):89–123; 80 (1958):372–403; 81 (1959):78–122.

Engelhardt, Isrun. *Mission und Politik in Byzanz. Ein Beitrag zur Strukturanalyse byzantinischer Mission zur Zeit Justins und Justinians*. Miscellanea byzantina monacensia, vol. 19. Munich, 1974.

Ensslin, Wilhelm. *Theoderich der Grosse*. Munich, 1947.

Erasmus, Charles J. "Current Theories on Incest Prohibition in the Light of Ceremonial Kinship." *The Kroeber Anthropological Society Papers* 2 (1950):42–50.

Esmein, Adhemar. *Le mariage en droit canonique*, 2 vols. Paris, 1891.

Etaix, R. "Nouveau sermon pascal de Saint Césaire d'Arles." *Revue bénédictine* 75 (1965):201–211.

Ewig, Eugen. *Die fränkischen Teilungen und Teilreiche (511–613)*. Mainzer Akademie der Wissenschaften und der Literatur. Abhandlungen der Geistes- und Sozialwissenschaftlichen Klasse, vol. 9 (1952).

Faber, Johannes Henricus. *Dissertatio inauguralis juridica exhibens quaestiones aliquot de muneribus patrinorum, Germanice Vom Paten- oder Göttel-geld*. Strasbourg, n.d. [1715].

Fehrle, Eugen. *Die kultische Keuschheit im Altertum*. Religionsgeschichtliche Versuche und Vorarbeiten, vol. 6. Giessen, 1910.

Fel, Edit, and Tamas Hofer. *Proper Peasants: Traditional Life in a Hungarian Village*. Chicago, 1969.

Fichtenau, Heinrich. *The Carolingian Empire: The Age of Charlemagne*. Tr. Peter Munz. New York, 1964.

Filipovic, M. S. "Forms and Functions of Ritual Kinship Among South

Slavs." *VIe congrès international des sciences anthropologiques et ethnologiques*, vol. 2, pt. 1: *Ethnologie*, pp. 77–80. Paris, 1963.

Finn, Thomas M. *The Liturgy of Baptism in the Baptismal Instructions of St. John Chrysostom*. Catholic University of America. Studies in Christian Antiquity, vol. 15. Washington, D.C., 1967.

Fischer, E. H. "Gregor der Grosse und Byzanz." *Zeitschrift der Savigny-Stiftung für Rechtsgeschichte*, Kanonistische Abteilung, 36 (1950):15–44.

Fisher, Elizabeth A. "Theodora and Antonina in the Historia Arcana: History and/or Fiction." *Arethusa* 11 (1978):253–279.

Fisher, J.D.C. *Christian Initiation: Baptism in the West. A Study in the Disintegration of the Primitive Rite of Initiation*. Alcuin Club Collections, vol. 47. London, 1965.

———. *Christian Initiation: The Reformation Period*. Alcuin Club Collections, vol. 51. London, 1970.

Fleury, Jean. *Recherches historiques sur les empêchements de parenté dans le mariage canonique des origines aux Fausses Décrétales*. Paris, 1933.

Fojtik, Karel. "Die Inhalts- und Funktionswandlungen der Gevatterschaft in Böhmen, Mähren und Schlesien vom XIV. bis zum XX. Jahrhundert." *Kontakte und Grenzen. Festschrift für Gerhard Heilfurth zum 60. Geburtstag*, pp. 337–343. Göttingen, 1969.

Foster, George M. "Cofradia and Compadrazgo in Spain and Spanish America." *Southwestern Journal of Anthropology* 9 (1953):1–28.

Fournier, Paul. "Notices sur trois collections canoniques inédites de l'époque carolingienne." *Revue des sciences religieuses* 6 (1926):78–92, 217–230, 513–532.

———. "L'oeuvre canonique de Réginon de Prüm." *Bibliothèque de l'Ecole des Chartes* 81 (1920):5–44.

Fournier, Paul, and Gabriel Le Bras. *Histoire des collections canoniques en occident depuis les Fausses Décrétales jusqu'au Décret de Gratien*, 2 vols. Paris, 1931.

Freisen, Joseph. *Geschichte des kanonischen Eherechts bis zum Verfall der Glossenliteratur*, 2nd ed. Paderborn, 1893. Reprint Aalen, 1963.

Friedrich, Paul. "The Linguistic Reflex of Social Change: From Tsarist to Soviet Russian Kinship." *Sociological Inquiry* 36 (1966):159–185.

Fritze, Wolfgang. "Die fränkische Schwurfreundschaft der Merovingerzeit. Ihr Wesen und ihre politische Funktion." *Zeitschrift der Savigny-Stiftung für Rechtsgeschichte*, Germanistische Abteilung, 71 (1954):74–125.

Gager, John. *Kingdom and Community: The Social World of Early Christianity*. Englewood Cliffs, N.J., 1975.

Galy, Charles. *La famille à l'époque mérovingienne. Etude faite principalement d'après les récits de Grégoire de Tours*. Paris, 1901.

Ganshof, François L. "Charlemagne et l'usage de l'écrit en matière administrative." *Le moyen âge* 57 (1951):1–25.

———. *Frankish Institutions under Charlemagne*. Tr. Bryce and Mary Lyon. New York, 1970.

———. *Recherches sur les capitulaires*. Paris, 1958.

Gaudemet, Jean. *L'Eglise dans l'Empire romain, ive–ve siècles*, vol. 3 of *Histoire du droit et des institutions de l'Eglise en occident*. Paris, 1958.

Gay, Jules. "Quelques remarques sur les papes grecs et syriens avant la querelle des iconoclasts (678–715)." *Mélanges offerts à M. Gustave Schlumberger*, vol. 1, pp. 40–54. Paris, 1924.

Gennep, Arnald van. "La Saint-Jean dans les croyances et coutumes populaires de la Savoie." *Journal de psychologie normale et pathologique* 24 (1927):26–77.

Ghellinck, Joseph de. "Le développement du dogme d'après Walafrid Strabon à propos du baptême des enfants." *Revue des sciences religieuses* 29 (1939):481–486.

Gillmann, Franz. "Das Ehehindernis der gegenseitigen geistlichen Verwandtschaft der Paten?" *Archiv für katholisches Kirchenrecht* 86 (1906):688–714.

Göbl, Peter. *Geschichte der Katechese im Abendlande vom Verfalle des Katechumenats bis zum Ende des Mittelalters*. Kempten, 1880.

Görres, Franz. "Justinian II und das römische Papsttum." *Byzantinische Zeitschrift* 17 (1908):432–454.

Goetz, Johann Jacob. *De iuribus patrinorum, vom Rechte der Gevattern*. Jena, 1678.

Goody, E. N. "Forms of Pro-Parenthood: The Sharing and Substitution of Parental Roles." *Kinship*, ed. Jack Goody, pp. 331–345. London, 1971.

Goody, Jack. "Adoption in Cross-Cultural Perspective." *Comparative Studies in Society and History* 11 (1969):55–78.

————. *The Development of the Family and Marriage in Europe*. Cambridge, 1983.

Green, Roger L. "Shakespeare and the Fairies." *Folklore* 73 (1962):89–103.

Grierson, Philip. "Commerce in the Dark Ages: A Critique of the Evidence." *Transactions of the Royal Historical Society*, 5th series, 9 (1959):123–140.

Grimm, Jacob. "Über Schenken und Geben." *Kleinere Schriften*, vol. 2: *Abhandlungen zur Mythologie und Sittenkunde*, pp. 173–210. Berlin, 1865.

Grimm, Wilhelm. "Altdeutsche Gespräche. Nachtrag." *Kleinere Schriften*, vol. 3, pp. 495–515. Berlin, 1883.

Gross, Julius. *Geschichte des Erbsündendogmas. Ein Beitrag zur Geschichte des Problems vom Ursprung des Übels*, 4 vols. Munich and Basel, 1960–1972.

Gryson, Roger. *The Ministry of Women in the Early Church*. Collegeville, Minn., 1976.

————. *Les origines du célibat ecclésiastique du premier au septième siècle*. Gembloux, 1970.

Guchteneëre, Bernard de. *Le parrainage des adultes aux ive et ve siècles de l'Eglise*. Excerpta ex dissertatione ad Lauream in facultate theologica Pontificiae Universitatis Gregorianae. Louvain, 1964.

Gudeman, Stephen. "The *Compadrazgo* as a Reflection of the Natural and Spiritual Person: The Curl Prize Essay, 1971." *Proceedings of the Royal Anthropological Institute* (1972):45–71.

————. *Relationships, Residence and the Individual: A Rural Panamanian Community*. Minneapolis, Minn., 1976.

Hall, S. G. "Paschal Baptism." *Studia evangelica* 6 (1973):239–251.

Hallenbeck, Jan. *Pavia and Rome: the Lombard Monarchy and the Papacy in the Eighth Century*. Transactions of the American Philosophical Society, vol. 72, pt. 4. Philadelphia, 1982.

Halphen, Louis. *Les barbares des grandes invasions aux conquêtes turques du xie siècle*, 2nd ed. Paris, 1930.

Hammel, Eugene A. *Alternative Social Structures and Ritual Relations in the Balkans*. Englewood Cliffs, N.J., 1968.

Hanssens, Jean Michel. *La liturgie d'Hippolyte: Documents et études*. Rome, 1970.

———. *La liturgie d'Hippolyte. Ses documents, son titulaire, ses origines et son caractère*. Orientalia christiana analecta, vol. 155. Rome, 1959.

Harmening, Dieter. *Superstitio. Überlieferungs- und theoriegeschichtliche Untersuchungen zur kirchlich-theologischen Aberglaubensliteratur des Mittelalters*. Berlin, 1979.

Hart, Donn V. *Compadrinazgo: Ritual Kinship in the Philippines*. DeKalb, Ill., 1977.

Hartmann, Wilfried. "Neue Texte zur bischöflichen Reformgesetzgebung aus den Jahren 829/31." *Deutsches Archiv für Erforschung des Mittelalters* 35 (1979):368–394.

Hausherr, Irénée. "Direction spirituelle chez les chrétiens orientaux." *Dictionnaire de spiritualité, d'ascétique et de mystique* 3 (1957):1008–1060.

———. *Direction spirituelle en Orient autrefois*. Orientalia christiana analecta, vol. 144. Rome, 1955.

Hautkappe, Franz. *Über die altdeutschen Beichten und ihre Beziehungen zu Cäsarius von Arles*. Münster, Westphalia, 1917.

Head, Constance. *Justinian II of Byzantium*. Madison, Wis. 1972.

Heer, Joseph M. *Ein karolingischer Missions-Katechismus*. Biblische und Patristische Forschungen, vol. 1. Freiburg, Breisgau, 1911.

Hellinger, W. "Die Pfarrvisitation nach Regino vom Prüm. Der Rechtsinhalt des I. Buches seiner 'Libri duo de synodalibus causis et disciplinis ecclesiastics.'" *Zeitschrift der Savigny-Stiftung für Rechtsgeschichte*, Kanonistische Abteilung, 48 (1962):1–116; 49 (1963):76–137.

Henninger, Eugen. *Sitte und Gebräuche bei der Taufe und Namengebung in der altfranzösischen Dictung*. Halle, 1891.

Höfer, A. "Zwei unbekannte Sermones des Caesarius von Arles." *Revue bénédictine* 74 (1964):44–53.

Holzherr, Georg. *Regula Ferioli. Ein Beitrag zur Entstehungsgeschichte und zur Sinndeutung der Benediktinerregel*. Zurich and Cologne, 1961.

How, George E. P. *English and Scottish Silver Spoons*, 3 vols. London, 1952–57.

Ingham, John M. "The Asymmetrical Implications of Godparenthood in Tlayacapan, Morelos." *Man*, 2nd series, 5 (1970):281–289.

Jeremias, Joachim. *Die Kindertaufe in den ersten vier Jahrhunderten*, 2nd ed. Göttingen, 1958. Tr. David Cairns. *Infant Baptism in the First Four Centuries*. Philadelphia, 1962.

Joachim, Johannes F. *Commentatio historico-iuridica de donis baptismalibus sive pecunia lustrica, vulgo von Pathen-gelde*. Halle, 1736.

Jombart, Emile, and Marcel Viller. "Clôture." *Dictionnaire de spiritualité, d'ascétique et de mystique*, vol. 2, pp. 979–1007. Paris, 1953.

Jonas, Hans. *The Gnostic Religion*, 2nd ed. Boston, 1963.

Jones, A.H.M., Philip Grierson, and J. A. Crook. "The Authenticity of the 'Testamentum S. Remigii'." *Revue belge de philologie et d'histoire* 35 (1957):356–373.

Jones, Cheslyn, Geoffrey Wainwright, and Edward Yarnold. *The Study of Liturgy*. New York, 1978.

Jundt, Isaac. *De susceptorum baptismalium origine commentatio*. Strasbourg, 1755.

Kearney, Richard. *Sponsors at Baptism According to the Code of Canon Law*. Washington, D.C., 1925.

Keefe, Susan A. "Carolingian Baptismal Expositions: A Handlist of Tracts and Manuscripts." *Carolingian Essays*, ed. Uta-Renate Blumenthal, pp. 169–237. Washington, D.C., 1983.

Kelly, J.N.D. *Early Christian Doctrines*, 5th ed. London, 1977.

Kelly, William. *Pope Gregory II on Divorce and Remarriage*. Analecta Gregoriana, vol. 203. Rome, 1976.

Kerlouegan, François. "Essai sur la mise en nourriture et l'éducation dans les pays celtiques d'après le témoignage des textes hagiographiques latins." *Etudes celtiques* 12 (1968/69):101–146.

Klauser, Theodor. *A Short History of the Western Liturgy*, 2nd ed. Tr. J. Halliburton. Oxford, 1979.

Koeniger, Albert M. *Die Sendgerichte in Deutschland*, vol. 1. Veröffentlichungen aus dem kirchenhistorischen Seminar München, vol. 3, pt. 2. Munich, 1907.

Konda, Guillaume. *Le discernement et la malice des pratiques superstitieuses d'après les sermons de Saint Césaire d'Arles*. Rome, 1970.

Konecny, Silvia. "Eherecht und Ehepolitik unter Ludwig dem Frommen." *Mitteilungen des Instituts für österreichische Geschichtsforschung* 85 (1977):1–21.

Kottje, Raymund. "Das Aufkommen der täglichen Eucharistiefeier in der Westkirche und die Zölibatsforderung." *Zeitschrift für Kirchengeschichte* 82 (1971):218–228.

———. *Studien zum Einfluss des Alten Testamentes auf Recht und Liturgie des frühen Mittelalters (6–8 Jahrhundert)*. Bonner historische Forschungen, vol. 23. Bonn, 1964.

Krener, Eva. "An Evaluation of the Major Theories Concerning Compadrazgo in Latin America." *Folk* 14/15 (1972/73):103–118.

Kresten, Otto. "Datierungsprobleme 'isaurischer' Eherechtsnovellen I.Coll.I 26," *Forschungen zur byzantinischen Rechtsgeschichte*, vol. 7: *Fontes Minores*, vol. 4, pp. 37–106. Frankfort am Main, 1981.

Krusch, Bruno. "Reimser Remigius-Fälschungen." *Neues Archiv der Gesellschaft für ältere deutsche Geschichtskunde* 20 (1895):537–565.

Kuttner, Stephan G. *Harmony from Dissonance: An Interpretation of Medieval Canon Law.* Wimmer Lecture no. 10. Latrobe, Pa., 1960.

Labriolle, Pierre de. "Papa." *Archivum latinitatis medii aevi (Bulletin Du Cange)* 4 (1928):65–75.

Laistner, Max L. W. *Thought and Letters in Western Europe, A.D. 500 to 900,* 2nd ed. Ithaca, N.Y., 1957.

Lambot, Cyrille. "Le prototype des monastères cloîtrés des femmes, l'Abbaye Saint-Jean d'Arles au vie siècle." *Revue liturgique et monastique* 23 (1937/38):169–174.

Lancaster, Lorraine. "Kinship in Anglo-Saxon Society." *British Journal of Sociology* 9 (1958):230–250, 359–377.

Lasch, A. "Das altsächsische Taufgelöbnis." *Neuphilologische Mitteilungen* 35 (1935):92–133.

Latouche, Robert. *The Birth of Western Economy.* Tr. E. M. Wilkinson. New York, 1966.

Latte, Robert de. "Saint Augustin et le baptême. Etude liturgico-historique du rituel baptismal des adultes chez Saint Augustin." *Questions liturgiques et paroissiales* 56 (1975):177–223.

———. "Saint Augustin et le baptême. Etude liturgico-historique du rituel baptismal des enfants chez Saint Augustin." *Questions liturgiques et paroissiales* 57 (1976):41–55.

Laurent, V. "L'oeuvre canonique du concile *in Trullo* (691–692), source primaire du droit de l'Eglise orientale." *Revue des études byzantines* 23 (1965):7–41.

Laurin, Franz. "Die geistliche Verwandtschaft in ihrer geschichtlichen Entwicklung bis zum Rechte der Gegenwart." *Archiv für katholisches Kirchenrecht* 15 (1866):216–274.

Leage, Richard W. *Roman Private Law founded on the Institutes of Gaius and Justinian,* 3rd ed. A. M. Prichard. London, 1961.

Lebrun, François. "Le *Traité des superstitions* de Jean-Baptiste Thiers. Contributions à l'ethnographie de la France du xviie siècle." *Annales de Bretagne et des Pays de l'Ouest (Anjou, Maine, Touraine)* 83 (1976):443–465.

Leclercq, Henri. "Parrain et marraine." *Dictionnaire d'archéologie chrétienne et de liturgie,* vol. 13, pt. 2 (1938), pp. 2236–2240.

Legasse, S. "Baptême juif des prosélytes et baptême chrétien." *Bulletin de littérature ecclésiastique* 77 (1976):3–40.

Levison, Wilhelm. *England and the Continent in the Eighth Century.* Oxford, 1946.

Liebermann, Felix. "Über die Gesetze Ines von Wessex." *Mélanges d'histoire offerts à M. Charles Bémont,* pp. 21–42. Paris, 1913.

Lindner, Dominikus. *Der Usus Matrimonii. Eine Untersuchung über seine sittliche Bewertung in der katholischen Moraltheologie alter und neuer Zeit.* Munich, 1929.

Lohfink, G. "Der Ursprung der christliche Taufe." *Theologische Quartalschrift* 157 (1976):35–54.

Lynch, Joseph H. "Baptismal Sponsorship and Monks and Nuns, 500–1000." *American Benedictine Review* 31 (1980):108–129.

———. "Spiritual Kinship and Sexual Prohibitions in Early Medieval Europe." *Monumenta iuris canonici.* Series C: Subsidia, vol. 7, pp. 271–288. Vatican City, 1985.

Maassen, Friedrich. *Geschichte der Quellen und der Literatur des canonischen Rechts im Abendlande,* vol. 1. Graz, 1870.

McCarthy, Maria Caritas. *The Rule for Nuns of St. Caesarius of Arles: A Translation with a Critical Introduction.* Catholic University of America. Studies in Mediaeval History, new series, vol. 16. Washington, D.C., 1960.

McKitterick, Rosamond. *The Frankish Church and the Carolingian Reforms, 789–895.* London, 1977.

McNally, Robert E. "The 'tres linguae sacrae' in Early Irish Bible Exegesis." *Theological Studies* 19 (1958):395–403.

Maertens, Thierry. *Histoire et pastorale du rituel du catéchuménat et du baptême.* Paroisse et liturgie. Collection de pastorale liturgique, vol. 56. Bruges, 1962.

Magnou-Nortier, Elisabeth. *Foi et fidélité. Recherches sur l'évolution des liens personnels chez les Francs du viiᵉ au ixᵉ siècles.* Publications de l'Université de Toulouse-Le Mirail, series A, vol. 28. Toulouse, 1976.

Malnory, A. *Saint Césaire, évêque d'Arles, 503–543.* Bibliothèque de l'Ecole des hautes études, vol. 103. Paris, 1894.

Manrique, A. "El bautesimo en el judaismo contemporaneo de Jesus." *El Ciudad de Dios* 89 (1976):207–220.

Manselli, Raoul. "Vie familiale et éthique sexuelle dans les pénitentiels." *Famille et parenté dans l'Occident médiéval.* Collection de l'Ecole française de Rome, vol. 30, pp. 363–378. Rome, 1977.

Maranda, Pierre. *French Kinship: Structure and History.* Janua Linguarum. Series practica, vol. 169. The Hague and Paris, 1974.

Martène, Edmond. *De antiquis ecclesiae ritibus libri quatuor,* 4 vols. Antwerp. 1736–1738.

Mastricht, Gerhard von. *Susceptor; seu de susceptoribus infantium ex baptismo, eorum origine, usu et abusu schediasma.* Duisburg, 1670.

Mauss, Marcel. *The Gift: Forms and Functions of Exchange in Archaic Societies.* Tr. Ian Cunnison. New York, 1967.

Melnikas, Anthony. *The Corpus of the Miniatures in the Manuscripts of Decretum Gratiani,* 3 vols. Studia Gratiana, vol. 16. Rome, 1975.

Metz, René. *La consécration des vierges dans l'Eglise romaine. Etude d'histoire et de la liturgie.* Bibliothèque de l'Institut de droit canonique de l'Université de Strasbourg, vol. 4. Paris, 1954.

Meyvaert, Paul. "Bede's Text of the *Libellus Responsionum* of Gregory the Great to Augustine of Canterbury." *England Before the Conquest: Studies in Primary Sources Presented to Dorothy Whitelock,* pp. 15–33. Cambridge, 1971.

Mikat, Paul. "Die Inzestverbote des Konzils von Epaon—Ein Beitrag zur Geschichte des fränkischen Eherechts." *Rechtsbewahrung und Rechtsentwick-*

lung. Festschrift für Heinrich Lange zum 70. Geburtstag, pp. 63–84. Munich, 1970.

———. "Zu den Voraussetzungen der Begegnung von fränkischer und kirchlicher Eheauffassung in Gallien." *Diakonia et ius. Festgabe für Heinrich Flatten zum 65. Geburtstag*, pp. 1–26. Munich, 1973.

Millemann, H. "Caesarius von Arles und die frühmittelalterliche Missionspredigt." *Zeitschrift für Missionswissenschaft* 23 (1933):12–27.

Mintz, Sidney W., and Eric R. Wolf. "An Analysis of Ritual Co-Parenthood (Compadrazgo)." *Southwestern Journal of Anthropology* 6 (1950):341–368.

Mohrmann, Christine. *Etudes sur le Latin des chrétiens.* In Storia e Letteratura, 65 (1958), 87 (1961), 103 (1965), and 143 (1977).

Molle, Marie-Magdeleine van. "Les fonctions de parrainage des enfants, en Occident, de 550 à 900." Unpublished mémoire. Année de Pastorale Liturgique. Abbaye de Saint André. Bruges, 1961.

———. "Les fonctions du parrainage des enfants en occident. Leur apogée et leur dégradation (du viᵉ au xᵉ siècle)." *Paroisse et liturgie* 46 (1964):121–146.

Mordek, Hubert. *Kirchenrecht und Reform im Frankenreich.* Beiträge zur Geschichte und Quellenkunde des Mittelalters, vol. 1. Berlin, 1975.

Morrison, Karl F. *The Two Kingdoms: Ecclesiology in Carolingian Political Thought.* Princeton, N.J., 1964.

Moss, Leonard W., and Stephen C. Cappannari. "Patterns of Kinship, Comparaggio and Community in a South Italian Village." *Anthropological Quarterly* 33 (1960):24–32.

Mühlbacher, E. "Urkundenfälschung im Echternach." *Mitteilungen des Instituts für österreichische Geschichtsforschung* 21 (1900):350–354.

Müller, Michael. *Die Lehre des hl. Augustinus von der Paradiesesehe und ihre Auswirkung in der Sexualethik des 12. und 13. Jahrhunderts bis Thomas von Aquin.* Studien zur Geschichte der katholische Moraltheologie, vol. 1. Regensburg, 1954.

Munier, Charles. *L'Eglise dans l'Empire romain (iiᵉ–iiiᵉ siècles).* Histoire du droit et des institutions de l'Eglise en Occident, vol. 2, pt. 3. Paris, 1979.

Nautin, Pierre. "Divorce et remariage dans la tradition de l'église latine." *Recherches de science religieuse* 62 (1974):7–54.

Neufeld, Vernon H. *The Earliest Christian Confessions.* New Testament Tools and Studies, vol. 5. Grand Rapids, Mich., 1963.

Neunheuser, Burkhard. "Die Liturgie der Kindertaufe. Ihre Problematik in der Geschichte." *Zeichen des Glaubens. Studien zu Taufe und Firmung. Balthasar Fischer zum 60. Geburtstag*, pp. 319–334. Zurich, 1972.

Niles, Philip. "Godparents and the Naming of Children in Late Medieval England." Unpublished paper, Carleton College.

Norberg, Dag. "A quelle époque a-t-on cessé de parler Latin en Gaule?" *Annales. Economies, sociétés, civilisations* 21 (1966):346–359.

Nutini, Hugo G., and Betty Bell. *Ritual Kinship: The Structure and Historical*

Development of the Compadrazgo System in Rural Tlaxcala, 2 vols. Princeton, N.J., 1980 and 1984.

Ogris, W. "Aufnehmen des Kindes." *Handwörterbuch zur deutschen Rechtsgeschichte*, vol. 1 (1971), pp. 253–254.

O'Meara, John J. *The Young Augustine: The Growth of Augustine's Mind Up to His Conversion*. London, 1954.

Oxford Latin Dictionary. Ed. P.G.W. Glare. Oxford, 1982.

Pappenheim, Max. "Über künstliche Verwandtschaft im germanischen Rechte." *Zeitschrift der Savigny-Stiftung für Rechtsgeschichte*, Germanistische Abteilung, 29 (1908):304–333.

Patlagean, Evelyne. "Christianisation et parentés rituelles: le domaine de Byzance." *Annales. Economies, sociétés, civilisations* 33 (1978):625–636.

——. "L'histoire de la femme déguisée en moine et l'évolution de la sainteté féminine à Byzance." *Studi medievali*, 3rd series, 17 (1976):597–623.

Paul, Benjamin D. "Ritual Kinship: With Special Reference to Godparenthood in Middle America." Ph.D. diss. University of Chicago, 1942.

Pelikan, Jaroslav. *The Christian Tradition: A History of the Development of Doctrine*, vol. 1: *The Emergence of the Catholic Tradition (100–600)*. Chicago, 1971.

Perkow, Ursula. *Wasserweihe, Taufe und Patenschaft bei den Nordgermanen*. Ph.D. diss., Hamburg, 1972.

Petersen, William. *Population*, 2nd ed. New York, 1969.

Pétré, Hélène. *Ethérie. Journal de voyage*. Sources chrétiennes, vol. 21. Paris, 1948.

Petrovits, Joseph. *The New Church Law on Matrimony*. Philadelphia, 1921.

Pieske, Christa. "Über den Patenbrief." *Beiträge zur deutschen Volks- und Altertumskunde* 2/3 (1958):85–121.

Pitt-Rivers, Julian. *The Fate of Shechem or the Politics of Sex: Essays in the Anthropology of the Mediterranean*. Cambridge, 1977.

——. "The Kith and the Kin." In *The Character of Kinship*, ed. Jack Goody, pp. 89–105. Cambridge, 1973.

——. "Ritual Kinship in Spain." *Transactions of the New York Academy of Sciences*, 2nd series, 20 (1957-58):424–431.

Plumpe, Joseph C. *Mater Ecclesia: An Inquiry into the Concept of the Church as Mother in Early Christianity*. Catholic University of America. Studies in Christian Antiquity, vol. 5. Washington, D.C., 1943.

Prinz, Friedrich. *Frühes Mönchtum im Frankenreich. Kultur und Gesellschaft in Gallien, den Rheinlanden und Bayern am Beispiel der monastischen Entwicklung (4. bis 8. Jahrhundert)*. Munich and Vienna, 1965.

Rambaud-Buhot, Jacqueline. "Une collection canonique de la réforme carolingienne (ms. lat. de la Bibliothèque nationale n° 4278, ff 128–167)." *Revue historique de droit français et étranger* 34 (1956):50–73.

Ravicz, Robert. "Compadrinazgo." In *Social Anthropology*, vol. 6 of *Handbook of Middle American Indians*, ed. Manning Nash, pp. 238–252. Austin, 1967.

Richard, Jean. "La donation en filleulage dans le droit bourguignon." *Mémoires de la Société pour l'histoire du droit et des institutions des anciens pays bourguignons, comtois et romands* 16 (1954):139–142.

Richards, Jeffrey. *The Popes and the Papacy in the Early Middle Ages, 476–752.* London, 1979.

Riché, Pierre. *Daily Life in the World of Charlemagne.* Tr. Jo Ann McNamara. Philadelphia, 1978.

——. *Education and Culture in the Barbarian West.* Tr. John J. Contreni. Columbia, S.C., 1976.

Riley, Hugh M. *Christian Initiation: A Comparative Study of the Interpretation of the Baptismal Liturgy in the Mystagogical Writings of Cyril of Jerusalem, John Chrysostom, Theodore of Mopsuestia and Ambrose of Milan.* Catholic University of America. Studies in Christian Antiquity, vol. 17. Washington, D.C., 1974.

Rouche, Michel. "Les baptêmes forcés de juifs en Gaule mérovingienne et dans l'Empire d'Orient." *De l'antijudaïsme antique à l'antisémitisme contemporain,* ed. V. Nikiprowetzky, pp. 105–124. Lille, 1979.

Russell, Josiah Cox. "Recent Advances in Mediaeval Demography." *Speculum* 40 (1965):84–101.

Rutledge, Denys. *Cosmic Theology, The Ecclesiastical Hierarchy of Pseudo-Denys: An Introduction.* Staten Island, N.Y., 1965.

Sabean, David. "Aspects of Kinship Behaviour and Property in Rural Western Europe Before 1800." In *Family and Inheritance: Rural Society in Western Europe 1200–1800,* ed. J. Goody, J. Thirsk, and E. P. Thompson, pp. 96–111. Cambridge, 1976.

Santyves, P. "Les trois nuits de Tobie ou la continence durant la première nuit ou les premières nuits du mariage." *Revue anthropologique* 44 (1934):266–296.

Sauget, Joseph-Marie. "Pelagia." *Bibliotheca Sanctorum,* vol. 10, cols. 430–432. Vatican City, 1968.

Sayres, William C. "Ritual Kinship and Negative Affect." *American Sociological Review* 21 (1956):348–352.

Schauerte, Heinrich. "Volkskundliche zur Taufe." *Europäische Kulturverflechtungen im Bereich der volkstümlichen Überlieferung. Festschrift zum 65. Geburtstag Bruno Schiers,* pp. 41–61. Göttingen, 1967.

Schieffer, Theodor. *Winfrid-Bonifatius und die christliche Grundlegung Europas.* Freiburg, 1954.

Schmidt, Albert. "Zur Komposition der Mönchsregel des heiligen Aurelian von Arles" *Studia Monastica* 17 (1975):237–256; 18 (1976):17–54.

Schmidt, Andreas. "Der Traktat *Peri gamon* des Johannes Pediasmos." *Forschungen zur byzantinischen Rechtsgeschichte,* vol. 1: *Fontes Minores,* vol. 1, pp. 126–174. Frankfort am Main, 1976.

Schneider, Reinhard. *Brüdergemeine und Schwurfreundschaft.* Historische Studien, vol. 388. Lübeck and Hamburg, 1964.

Scholz, Bernhard Walter. *Carolingian Chronicles.* Ann Arbor, Mich., 1972.

Schröder, Isolde. *Die westfränkischen Synoden von 888 bis 987 und ihre Überliefe-rung.* Monumenta Germaniae historica. Hilfsmittel, vol. 3. Munich, 1980.

Schuler, Andreas. *De susceptoribus ex historia ecclesiastica.* Wittenberg, n.d. [1688]. Reprinted in *Thesaurus commentationum selectarum et antiquiorum et recentiorum illustrandis antiquitatibus christianis inservientium*, vol. 2, pp. 106–113. Ed. J. E. Volbeding. Leipzig, 1849.

Schulte, O. "Taufsitten und Bräuche in einem oberhessischen Orte vor 250 Jahren und heute." *Hessische Blätter für Volkskunde* 7 (1908):65ff.

Schumacher, W. N. "Byzantinisches in Rom." *Römische Quartalschrift für christ-liche Altertumskunde und Kirchengeschichte* 68 (1973):104–124.

Schwartz, E. *Über die pseudoapostolischen Kirchenordnung.* Schriften der wissen-schaftliche Gesellschaft in Strassburg, vol. 6. Strasbourg, 1910.

Schwarz, Helga. *Das Taufgeld. Ein Beitrag zur historischen Entwicklung der Tauf-bräuche.* Ph.D. diss. Graz, 1950.

Seckel, Emil. "Die ältesten Canones von Rouen." *Historische Aufsätze Karl Zeu-mer zum sechsigsten Geburtstag als Festgabe dargebracht von Freunden und Schülern*, pp. 611–635. Weimar, 1910.

Simon, Dieter. "Zur Ehegesetzgebung der Isaurier." *Forschungen zur byzanti-nischen Rechtsgeschichte*, vol. 1: *Fontes Minores*, vol. 1, pp. 16–43. Frankfort am Main, 1976.

Staudt, Reinhold. *Studien zum Patenbrauch in Hessen.* Ph.D. diss. Johann Wolf-gang Goethe-Universität. Frankfurt am Main, 1958.

Steidle, Basilius. "Heilige Vaterschaft." *Benediktinische Monatschrift* 14 (1932):215–226.

Stenzel, Alois. *Die Taufe. Eine genetische Erklärung der Taufliturgie.* Forschungen zur Geschichte der Theologie und des innerkirchlichen Lebens, vols. 7 and 8. Innsbruck, 1957.

Stirrat, R. L. "Compadrazgo in Catholic Sri Lanka." *Man*, new series, 10 (1975):589–606.

Tappolet, Ernst. *Die Romanischen Verwandtschaftsnamen.* Strasbourg, 1895.

Tellenbach, Gerd. "Vom Zusammenleben der abendländischen Völker im Mittelalter." *Festschrift für Gerhard Ritter zu seinem 60. Geburtstag*, pp. 1–60. Tübingen, 1950.

Theis, Laurent. "Saints sans famille? Quelques remarques sur la famille dans le monde franc à travers les sources hagiographiques." *Revue historique* 255 (1976):3–20.

Théry, Gabriel. *Etudes dionysiennes*, 2 vols. Etudes de philosophie médiévale, vols. 16 and 19. Paris, 1932 and 1937.

Thomas, Joseph A. C. *Textbook of Roman Law*, 2 vols. Amsterdam, 1976.

Tukey, Ann. "Kinship Terminology in the Romance Languages." Ph.D. diss. University of Michigan, 1962.

Tuschen, Antonie. *Die Taufe in der altfranzösischen Literatur.* Ph.D. diss. Rhei-nische Friedrich Wilhelms Universität zu Bonn, 1936.

Tylor, Edward B. *Anahuac.* London, 1861.

Tyson, Joseph B. *A Study of Early Christianity*. New York, 1973.
Ullmann, Walter. *The Growth of Papal Government in the Middle Ages*. 2nd ed. London, 1962.
Unnik, W. C. van. "Les cheveux défaits des femmes baptisées. Un rite de baptême dans l'ordre ecclésiastique d'Hippolyte." *Vigiliae christianae* 1 (1947):77–100.
Van den Eynde, Damien. "Baptême et confirmation d'après les Constitutions Apostoliques, vii, 44.3." *Revue des sciences religieuses* 27 (1937):196–212.
———. "Les rites liturgiques latins de la confirmation." *La Maison-Dieu* 54 (1958):53–78.
Van der Meer, Frederik. *Augustine the Bishop: Church and Society at the Dawn of the Middle Ages*. Tr. B. Battershaw and G. R. Lamb. London, 1961.
Van Eijk, Ton H. C. "Marriage and Virginity, Death and Immortality," *Epektasis. Mélanges patristiques offerts au Cardinal Jean Daniélou*, pp. 209–235. Paris, 1972.
Vasiliev, Alexander A. *History of the Byzantine Empire*, 2 vols., 2nd edition. Madison, Wis., 1964.
Vogel, Cyrille. *La discipline pénitentielle en Gaule des origines à la fin du viiᵉ siècle*. Paris, 1952.
———. "Les échanges liturgiques entre Rome et les pays francs jusqu'à l'époque de Charlemagne." *Le chiese nei regni dell'Europa occidentale e i loro rapporti con Roma sino all'800*, pt. 1. Settimane di studio del Centro italiano di studi sull'alto medioevo, vol. 7, pp. 185–295. Spoleto, 1960.
———. *Les 'Libri Paenitentiales.'* Typologie des sources du moyen âge occidental, vol. 27. Turnhout, 1978.
———. *Le pécheur et la pénitence au moyen-âge*. Paris, 1969.
———. *La réforme cultuelle sous Pepin le Bref et sous Charlemagne*. Graz, 1965.
———. "La réforme liturgique sous Charlemagne." *Karl der Grosse. Lebenswerk und Nachleben*, vol. 2: *Das geistige Leben*, pp. 217–232. Ed. Bernhard Bischoff. Düsseldorf, 1965.
Vogüé, Adalbert de. "La Règle de Césaire d'Arles pour les moines: un résumé de sa Règle pour les moniales." *Revue d'ascétique et de mystique* 47 (1971):369–406.
Vööbus, Arthur. *Celibacy: A Requirement for Admission to Christian Baptism in the Early Syrian Church*. Papers of the Estonian Theological Society in Exile, vol. 1. Stockholm, 1951.
Vykoukal, E. "Les examens du clergé paroissial à l'époque carolingienne." *Revue d'histoire ecclésiastique* 14 (1913):81–96.
Wagenvoort, Hendrik. " 'Rebirth' in Profane Antique Literature." *Studies in Roman Literature, Culture and Religion*, pp. 132–149. Leiden, 1956.
Wallace-Hadrill, J. M. "The Bloodfeud of the Franks." *Bulletin of the John Rylands Library* 41 (1959):459–487. Reprinted in his *The Long-Haired Kings*, pp. 121–147. New York, 1962.
———. *The Frankish Church*. Oxford, 1983.
———. "The Work of Gregory of Tours in the Light of Modern Research."

Transactions of the Royal Historical Society, fifth series, 1 (1951):25–45. Reprinted in his *The Long-Haired Kings*, pp. 49–70. New York, 1962.

Wartburg, Walther von. *Französisches etymologisches Wörterbuch*, 21 vols. Bonn, Leipzig, and Basel, 1928–1965.

Weibust, Knut. "Ritual Coparenthood in Peasant Societies." *Ethnologia Scandinavica* (1972):101–114.

Wemple, Suzanne. *Women in Frankish Society: Marriage and the Cloister, 500 to 900.* Philadelphia, 1981.

Wendel, François. *Calvin: The Origins and Development of his Religious Thought.* Tr. P. Mairet. London, 1963.

Werner, Karl F. "Liens de parenté et noms de personne. Un problème historique et méthodologique." *Famille et parenté dans l'occident médiéval.* Collection de l'Ecole française de Rome, vol. 30, pp. 13–34. Rome, 1977.

Weyl, Richard. *Die Beziehungen des Papstthums zum fränkischen Staats- und Kirchenrecht unter den Karolingern.* Untersuchungen zur deutschen Staats- und Rechtsgeschichte, vol. 40. Breslau, 1892.

Whitten, Norman W. *Class, Kinship and Power in an Ecuadorian Town: The Negroes of San Lorenzo.* Stanford, 1965.

Wiegand, Friedrich. *Die Stellung des apostolischen Symbols im kirchlichen Leben des Mittelalters*, vol. 1: *Symbol und Katechumenat.* Studien zur Geschichte der Theologie und der Kirche, vol. 4, pt. 2. Leipzig, 1899.

Wielers, Margret. *Zwischenstaatliche Beziehungsformen im frühen Mittelalter (Pax, Foedus, Amicitia, Fraternitas).* Ph.D. diss. Münster, Westphalia, 1959.

Williams, George H. *The Radical Reformation.* Philadelphia, 1962.

Wilson, Robert M. *The Gnostic Problem: A Study of the Relations Between Hellenistic Judaism and the Gnostic Heresy.* London, 1958.

Wolf, Eric R. "San José: Subcultures of a 'Traditional' Coffee Municipality." *The People of Puerto Rico*, Julian H. Steward, pp. 171–264. Urbana, Ill., 1956.

Wolff, Philippe. *Western Languages A.D. 100–1500.* Tr. F. Partridge. London, 1971.

Yarnold, Edward. *The Awe-Inspiring Rites of Initiation: Baptismal Homilies of the Fourth Century.* London, 1972.

Ysebaert, Joseph. *Greek Baptismal Terminology: Its Origin and Early Development.* Graecitas Christianorum primaeva, vol. 1. Nijmegen, 1962.

Zachariä von Lingenthal, Karl. *Geschichte des griechisch-römischen Rechts*, 3rd ed. Berlin, 1893. Reprint Aalen, 1955.

Ziegler, Josef G. *Die Ehelehre der Pönitentialsummen von 1200–1350.* Studien zur Geschichte der katholische Moraltheologie, vol. 4. Regensburg, 1956.

Zuellich, Samuel. *Jura conviviorum . . . submittit Samuel Zuellich, altenburgomisnicus . . . ad d[blank] Februarii, anno m. d.c. lxxiii.* Iena, 1673.

INDEX

abbot as spiritual father, 167, 168
Abrunculus, 183
Adam, 264–265, 273, 274
Adam's sin. *See* original sin
Adelphius, abbot of Remiremont, 182
Admonitio generalis, 306–308
Admonitio synodalis, 310–311
adoption, 215, 260; forms of, 179–181,
 183; sponsorship and, 226, 247
adoptivus pater, 215
Adso, abbot of Montier-en-Der, 200
adults, sponsorship of, 13, 36, 37, 38,
 41, 42, 83–116, 122; assimilated to
 sponsorship of infants, 30, 134–140
Agericus, bishop of Verdun, 187, 197
Aimon of Fleury, 215
Aland, Kurt, 118
Alaric II, king of the Visigoths, 214
Alcuin, 295, 297
Amalar of Metz, 300
Amatus, 182
Ambrose of Milan, 95
Amiet, Robert, 310–311
Amphilocus of Iconium, 166
Anabaptists, 20, 21, 25, 117
anadechomenos, 105–106
anadochos, 136, 138
Andelot, pact of, 174
Anderson, Gallatin, 216–217, 305–306
Andrieu, Michel, 170, 290, 294, 295, 301
Angenendt, Arnold, 74–75, 76, 150, 211,
 285n
Anglican Church and sponsorship, 24,
 39, 117
Anglo-Saxon Chronicle, 243
Anglo-Saxons, 235; and sponsorship, 77,
 78, 213, 242–249; and penance, 328–
 329
anthropologists and sponsorship, 57–74
Antioch, 37, 100, 104–105, 106
Antonina, 226–228, 234
Aper, 182–183
Apostolic Constitutions, 89
Apostolic Tradition. See Hippolytus

Apuleius of Madaura, 114, 165
Arnobius of Sicca, 101
Asterius the Sophist, 120
Atlas der deutschen Volkskunde, 50
Audovera, 278
Augustine of Canterbury, 242, 269
Augustine of Hippo, 15, 30, 40, 54, 98,
 116, 120, 122, 134, 145, 159, 287, 314,
 321; and catechumenate, 94–96, 102,
 115; *Confessions* of, 95–96; and infant
 baptism, 125, 127, 139; *Letter 98* of,
 13, 128–133; *Seven Books Concerning
 Baptism* of, 127–128; and sexuality,
 263, 264, 265, 271
Aunacherius, bishop of Auxerre, 155
Aurelian, bishop of Arles, 153–154
Auxerre, synod of, 155

Bailey, Derrick Sherwin, 39–40, 70, 113,
 126
Balthildis, 182
baptism, delay of, 95–96, 118, 135
Barraclough, Geoffrey, 235
Basil of Caesarea, 221, 250
Bede, 168, 242–243, 244, 269, 277
Beichte, 329–330
Belisarius, 226–228, 234
Bell, Betty, 59, 60, 63, 72–74, 218
Bell, Clair Hayden, 47
Benedict the Levite, 331–332
Benedict of Nursia, 154
Bennett, J.A.W., 48
Bercharius, 200
Berthefred, 196
Bertinus, 198
Bertram, bishop of Le Mans, 198
Betto, 203
Bieler, Ludwig, 248
Binchy, Daniel A., 248
Birinus, bishop of the West Saxons, 244
biscepsunu, 243
bishop as spiritual father, 166–167
Bismarck, Otto von, 35
Boniface VIII, pope, 18

371

LIBRARY OF CONGRESS
CATALOGING-IN-PUBLICATION DATA

Lynch, Joseph H., 1943–
Godparents and kinship in early medieval Europe.

Bibliography: p.
Includes index.
1. Sponsors—Europe—History. 2. Kinship—Europe—
History. I. Title.

BV1478.L96 1986 234'.161 85–43297
ISBN 0–691–05466–5 (alk. paper)

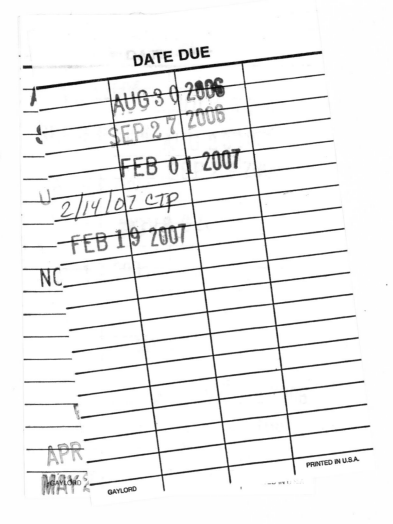

DATE DUE

AUG 3 0 2006		
SEP 2 7 2006		
FEB 0 1 2007		
2/14/07 CTP		
FEB 19 2007		
NC		
APR		PRINTED IN U.S.A.
MAY	GAYLORD	